THE LOWELLS

And Their Seven Worlds

by FERRIS GREENSLET

LOWLE

THE LOWELLS
And Their Seven Worlds

Occasionem Cognosce

With Illustrations

19 46

HOUGHTON MIFFLIN COMPANY BOSTON

The Riverside Press

The Riverside Press
CAMBRIDGE · MASSACHUSETTS
PRINTED IN THE U.S.A.

Preface

Many years ago, while writing a short life of James Russell Lowell, I came across some faded family letters that stirred an interest in his three soldier nephews as well as in his cousins and his aunts, his father, his uncles, his grandfather, his great-grandfather, and so on back to his seven times great-grandfather, Old Percival, who first brought the name across the sea in 1639. Later in the course of conversations, or perhaps interlocutions would be the juster word, with Amy Lowell, I heard more about an ancestry of which she was proud, and filed away in the back of my head the idea of sometime looking further into it for my own account.

Three years ago, after this had become possible, I communicated the germinating idea of a book on the Lowells and the worlds they lived in to a friend, one of the most learned and acute of younger American historians. It could be, he wrote back, 'a history of the heart, mind, imagination, animal spirits, and pocketbook of New England.' This is what I have tried to make it, not so much the success story of a family as a chronicle play of New England history for three centuries, seen through the family's eyes and dramatized in its actions.

I have not burdened the book with an elaborate Bibliography. *The Dictionary of American Biography* contains eighteen double column pages about a dozen different Lowells. To each article is appended a full list of sources. All of this source material I have read, together with some hundreds of other volumes of history, biography, and autobiography; old newspapers, court records, and letters and diaries of contemporaries, both published and unpublished. Special obligations to some of these will be noted in text or footnote. The most important source has been a beautifully ample and revealing mass of correspondence, diaries, financial accounts, unpublished poems, and miscellaneous memoranda, still in the possession of members of the family, and by them placed in my hands for this work. For these I must acknowledge a deep indebtedness to Ralph Lowell and Mrs. James H. Ropes (Alice Lowell). Eventually, no doubt, this rich body of documents will be added to the collections of the Massachusetts Historical Society or the Houghton Library at Harvard. It will supply the biographers and historians of the future with material for better books than this *mémoire pour servir*.

To the staffs of the above mentioned libraries, as well as to those of the Boston Athenaeum and of the Manuscript Division of the Library of Congress, I am grateful for many civilities.

F. G.

Contents

Illustrations

Between pages 196 and 197

Between pages 228 and 229

Between pages 260 and 261

ANNA CABOT JACKSON LOWELL
From a photograph
Courtesy of Miss Elizabeth Putnam

JOHN LOWELL, 'JUDGE JOHN'
From a portrait by William M. Hunt

AUGUSTUS LOWELL
From an engraving made from a photograph

Between pages 388 and 389

PERCIVAL LOWELL AT WORK
From a photograph
Courtesy of Mrs. Percival Lowell and the Adler Planetarium

GUY LOWELL
From a drawing by John Sargent
Courtesy of Boston Museum of Fine Arts

AMY LOWELL
From a photograph by Florence Ayscough McNair
Courtesy of Harley Farnsworth McNair

LAWRENCE LOWELL
From a photograph by Sherry
Courtesy of the Harvard Alumni Bulletin

BOOK I

The New World

CHAPTER 1

Old Percival

IN THE MONTH OF AUGUST, 1638, just three troubled centuries
before Neville Chamberlain flew to Munich to pluck the flower
safety from the nettle danger and secure peace for our time,
Percival Lowle, a solid citizen of Bristol, 'the Venice of the
West,' found himself in great disturbance of mind.

Sixty-seven years of his life had, it would seem from what little
we know of its external features, passed pleasantly. The station
in life to which it had pleased God to call him, with which
his Prayer Book advised him to be content, was not unsatisfac-
tory. He had been born in 1571 somewhere in North Somerset,
most probably at Kingston-Seymour, and well born, too. Half
a century ago one of his American descendants from Kansas visited England and with the aid of a corps of heralds and genealo-
gists explored the roots and branches of the family tree. The
names of Lowell, and of Percival, were found in the Battle Abbey

3

Roll of authentic early Normans who came to England with the Conqueror.[1] After a blank of a century and a half, the name was found again attached, in 1220, to William Lowle of Yardley in Worcestershire. Thence down, the line is clear to Percival in the tenth generation. Some of the men made marriages with the daughters of county families, culminating in the espousal by Richard Lowle in the ninth generation of a Percival directly descended from a cousin of the Conqueror. At some point in the fifteenth century the Lowles became armigers, and our Percival Lowle was born with the well-authenticated right to bear and exhibit a coat of arms, doubtless bestowed on an ancestor, as the custom was, for some long-forgotten gallantry in battle. In the bastard French of the Heralds' College the Lowle escutcheon was described as:

'Sable, a dexter hand couped at the wrist grasping three pointless darts, one in pale and two in saltire argent.'

James Russell Lowell, who in his later life took a deepened interest in the family genealogy, believed that the salient feature of the coat of arms was not three pointless darts, but three crossbow bolts, quite a different matter. He brought back from Germany three such objects 'with very formidable points to them, as I trust those of the family will always have.'

Of the education of little armigerous Percival no details are known, but the *Elegy* of nearly a hundred lines he was to write at the age of seventy-eight on the death of Governor Winthrop discloses a considerable fluency in English verse, a working knowledge of classical mythology and enough Latin to warrant lapses into that language, of some originality. He may have had at the local grammar school a formal education equal to that of Shakespeare.

[1] *The Historic Genealogy of the Lowells of America from 1639 to 1899,* by Delmar Lowell, a work of eight hundred pages which occupied its compiler and his father before him for twenty-five years, is invaluable for the study of the family. Its arrangement is somewhat complicated and occasional accidental departures from it, confusing. Not all of the *errata* were caught before binding. Used with a certain caution, it is a mine of genealogical and biographical information and genetic suggestiveness.

When and where Percival took his wife Rebecca, and what her surname was, has not been ascertained. He reappears in the recoverable record in 1597, when at the early age of twenty-six he was appointed to the responsible office of 'Assessor' of Kingston-Seymour which his father had held before him. This is all that is known of his first thirty years, except that always before his eyes from the North Somerset shore was the noble prospect across the ten miles of the Severn Sea to the bold Welsh coast at Cardiff, and behind it on rare clear days the distant peaks of Glamorganshire.

Sometime after the turn of the century, perhaps after his father's death and a helpful inheritance, Percival in his early thirties with a growing family moved into Bristol to begin business as a 'merchant,' which meant in those days, as it did through many later generations of his family, a wholesale trader in exports and imports. As the years went by and his business grew, he took in as partners his sons John and Richard together with his future son-in-law, William Gerrish, and became the prosperous house doing business under the style of Percival Lowle & Co.

The picturesque city of Bristol was situated at the junction of the Avon and Frome Rivers, at tide-head seven miles from the sea. Its ships, heavily laden with woollen cloth, glassware, salt-cod and pickled sturgeon, went down with the tide through a deep gorge. Some weeks or months later, by the same impulsion through the gorge, they returned from France, the Baltic, or the Mediterranean with burdens of wine and woad — source of the deep blue dye for the sound woollen cloth that went out on the next voyage.

Freed by its remote and protected situation from the constant fear of pirates and the French that hampered the South coast towns, Bristol prospered early. By the middle of the fifteenth century, it had become the leading port of England. Its records show that many of its merchants owned a score of ships apiece, some of them Leviathans of three hundred tons. Direct access to the Western ocean gave it importance in Atlantic exploration and fisheries. From Bristol in 1497, Sebastian Cabot sailed to discover Newfoundland, and thither Sir Ferdinando Gorges returned from the New England coast in 1605, bringing five Indians as passengers, with news of the attractions of the country and possibilities of trade with its innocent population.

It was a thriving little city, at once cosmopolitan and pioneering. Percival, as he admired the lovely landscape *urbs in rura*, from the top of Brandon Hill, or walked to his place of business along the High or Corn Street or Wine Street, must have been glad that he was alive and a part of it. Before long a new interest opened to him.

Twenty miles north of Bristol, near one of the long curving salmon-thronged reaches of the Severn Estuary near the mouth of the Little Avon, stood the grey pile of Berkeley Castle. Since 1086, twelve Barons Berkeley and their forbears had dwelt there. There in 1327, that profligate monarch, Edward II, had been shaved in ditchwater, tortured, and liquidated quite in the modern manner. For generations the Berkeleys had contested with the burghers of Bristol the right to overlordship of the town. By the time of Elizabeth, the dispute had been settled to the advantage of the town. Dying at a great age in 1613, the twelfth Baron, outliving his son, had been succeeded by his grandson, George Berkeley, a little boy of twelve. Sometime during his minority, his grandmother, the Lady Elizabeth Berkeley, selected Percival Lowle, successful and gentlemanly merchant of Bristol, to be the estate's bailiff for the outlying manor of Portbury in the county of Somerset, six miles from Bristol and two miles from the shore of the Channel which had been in the family's possession from very early times. He became landlord of the Berkeley Arms Inn, and had the usufruct of a small farm.

Part of his work there was to convene the manorial court and act as permanent foreman of the jury — a quasi-judicial function that was to flower in his descendants into four Federal judgeships.

The contact between the families was to have strange recurrences. Two centuries later, John Lowell, the 'Boston Rebel,' with as we shall see some risk to himself, was to approve and applaud the orders of Admiral George Cranfield Berkeley in command at Halifax, which led to the history-making affair of the *Leopard* and the *Chesapeake*. In 1924, when Mary Emelen Lowell of Brookline married Randal Thomas Mowbray Rawdon Berkeley, twentieth Baron and eighth Earl, an eminent scientist and a Fellow of the Royal Society, she was to her surprise welcomed at the castle by the librarian, Captain Gerald O'Flynn,[1] as the descendant of a man who looked after some of the family's business in the difficult times of King Charles the First.

That George Berkeley, who came of age in 1622, while still a student at Christ Church, was an active-minded man. His lordship was a traveller and a linguist. He was interested in the New World, and owned land in the Carolinas. He was the friend and patron of Robert Burton, anatomist of melancholy, through whose darkly humorous stream of consciousness flowed all the curious learning of the Renaissance. To him when only twenty Burton's great book, perhaps with a lively sense of favors to come, had been dedicated. In 1630, he presented Burton, already the incumbent of a living in the gift of Christ Church College, with that of Seagrave in Leicestershire. The agent for the outlying manor in Somerset was a reader, we know, and may have taken a special interest in the work of his co-protégé.

In the same year that saw the beginning of Robert Burton's fiscal ease through a second living, clouds began to gather around the pleasant busy life of Percival Lowle. The year before Charles Stuart had prorogued Parliament, and the bureaucratic government of Archbishop Laud and Thomas Wentworth, Earl of Strafford, had begun. Taxes, tonnage, and poundage soared; inquisitorial supervision of business became universal. In 1635, the final straw was laid on the burdened British back. In place of the single ship each port was expected to furnish annually for the Royal Navy, it was ordered that each pay an equivalent, or much more than an equivalent, sum in cash, as

[1] To whose research I am greatly indebted.

the Earl of Clarendon wrote in his *True Historical Narrative of the Rebellion and Civil Wars in England*, 'For a Spring and Magazine that should have no Bottom, Ship Money, a Word of lasting Sound in the Memory of this Kingdom.'

In its first year the intake was more than two hundred thousand pounds, equal in purchasing power to many million dollars today. What this did to the little city of Bristol is strongly stated by two local historians.

'From September to December the city was never free from commissioners and pursuivants, who examined on oath merchants what commodities they had sent to sea, what entries were made at the Customhouse, what foreign goods imported, etc., for years past? Agreeable to these informations they examined, whereby some were compelled to accuse one another, and were sent for up to London. Shopkeepers also were examined, and had great imposts laid on them. Soap-makers paid four pounds custom per ton for soap, the brewers forty marks per annum for a commission, which were such grievances that it soured the nation much against the king and government.' [1]

'Several opulent merchants of Bristol went to London to petition the king for redress; they were graciously received by his majesty, who expressed his regret at having granted oppressive commissions, in consequence of having received wrong information, and gave them permission to prefer a bill against the commissioners in the Star-chamber. But after considerable delay, the trial remained undetermined; yet the king advised them to continue the prosecution, promising to act as mediator. The grievances of the merchants, however, remained unredressed, and they returned to Bristol much incensed at those unjust exactions of his majesty's ministers.' [2]

It was in the summer of 1638 that the opulent merchants came home over the great West Road through Oxford and Bath to Bristol, soured and incensed after having been treated to what we

[1] *The History and Antiquities of the City of Bristol*, William Barnett, 1789.
[2] *The History of Bristol*, John Corry, 1816.

should now describe as the run-around. Whether Percival Lowle was one of them has not been discovered. His connection with an important titled family would have made him a useful liaison man; but we may be sure he was in their counsels, equally sure that the next few months were given over to the business and family discussions that led to a momentous decision.

It may be that Sir Ferdinando Gorges' sales talks on New England thirty years before had put ideas into his head. In the nine years since the dissolution of Parliament, more than fifteen thousand persons had followed Governor Winthrop overseas. 'Loadstone of America,' Percival called him in his *Elegy*. It had become the thing to do. Even John Hampden and Oliver Cromwell made plans to go. Had they not been stopped, we might have had the American Revolution a century earlier, and the whole course of modern history changed.

The Bay colonists did not, like the Plymouth Pilgrims, chiefly thirst for religious freedom. They wanted liberty of thought and action, economic and political. Theocracy came later, and that was, one feels, a product of the intellect rather than of the spirit. As Amy Lowell once roundly stated to this reporter, it was taxes and more taxes, the power to destroy, that drove her family to these shores. The Lowells have always been church-goers and pillars of churches; but even in the persons of three divines, more for Good Works than Saving Grace; more concerned with doing a sound job on earth here and now than in occupying a prominent pew in heaven hereafter. Old Percival was no exception.

Sixty-seven is not an age for quick decisions on hazards of new fortunes, but Percival must have made up his mind before the end of the year to leave Old England forever and sail beyond the sunset. It would have taken months to prepare and assemble the equipment that well-to-do families brought with them to establish their lives in the New World. He sailed by the ship *Jonathan* from London, though he may have boarded her at Southampton or Plymouth, on April 12, 1639.

The *Jonathan,* like the other transports of the Bay colonists, would have been a ship of two hundred tons or so with an over-all length of one hundred feet, the size of a cup defender or Erie canal boat, but chunkier. There would be two or three very small cabins for important passengers, sardine-like accommodations in the hold for a hundred more, and deck room for cows and other domestic animals. The voyage could be hopefully expected to last not more than five or six weeks.

The Lowell party consisted of Percival himself and Rebecca, his wife, his sons, John and Richard, with their wives and four children, his daughter, Joan, and her husband, John Oliver, his partner, William Gerrish, his clerk, Anthony Somerby, with his brother Henry, and Richard Dole, apprenticed to John Lowle, sixteen in all, plus two not in the passenger list, who first opened their eyes in the New World soon after arrival. At the going rate of five pounds per person, they paid in all the substantial sum of eighty pounds. Other recorded passengers were a slightly less numerous family of Blanchards from Penton in Hampshire. They took the ship at London after waiting a month for her to sail. The great tide of Western travel had begun to subside. It may be that the two groups had the ship to themselves or had chartered her for their special use. The only other known passenger was a Nicholas Noyes, who was returning to the colony after a year at home.

They reached Boston on June 23, after a voyage of nine weeks. Of its incidents we know nothing except an item to be found in the files of the Quarterly Sessions Court of Essex County for 1652. Here it is recorded that Anthony Somerby and Nicholas Noyes testified in a civil suit concerning some troubles of their fellow passengers as follows:

'The testimonie of us Inhabitants now of Newburie whose names are here under written, who about thirteen yeares past came over in a ship called the Jonathan of London with Thomas Blanchard now of Charlestown, at what time his wife dyed in the ship hee was conceived to be very poore and in great necessity, by reason of his wives and his childrens sicknesse that the passengers made a gathering for him in the shippe to helpe to put his child to nurse his wives mother also being sicke all the while wee were at sea and wee knew no other man that looked to her but Thomas Blanchard, but there was a maide which was her neece tended her.

'Further I Anthony Somerby testifyes that about the time the ship came to Anchor in Boston Harbor the woman his mother in law dyed. And Thomas Blanchard procured to carry her to shore to be buryed, I know no other man that was about it but hee.'

It could not have been a very jolly crossing.

There is some indication that Old Percival may have been already acquainted with Governor Winthrop, and it was per-haps at his advice that the Lowles, instead of settling in Boston, or in Charlestown as the Blanchards did, decided to go north of Cape Ann, to the stretch of pleasant country between the Mer-rimack and Quascacunquen Rivers, where the younger Win-throp had already done some pioneering to forestall the French. There four years before, the Reverend Thomas Parker, a gradu-ate of Magdalen College at Oxford, who had preached at New-bury on the Kennet in Wiltshire, and his young coadjutor, James Noyes, brother of the Lowles' shipmate, Nicholas, had established the little village of Newbury.

How the Lowle party got there is not wholly certain. Just possibly they may have gone the forty miles by land. But when Governor Winthrop visited his son John in Ipswich in 1634, he had to walk the whole thirty-one miles, sixty-two for the round trip. The continuous coast road from Hingham to Newbury was not begun till 1639, and several of the rivers between Boston and Newbury had not yet been bridged. The old Indian trails were not wide enough for wheeled conveyances, and although the General Court of 1637 had ordered that the men of Saugus, Ipswich, and Newbury 'mend' the roads between them, the transportation of a party of sixteen, with their furniture, warming pans, feather beds, muskets, fowling pieces, bandoliers, pikes, swords, fishing gear, cooking utensils, garden tools, books, clothes, and perhaps animals, would have been a difficult business.

Almost certainly they went, as the Parker party before them had from Ipswich, by water. Their boat would have been a shallop or ketch similar to the *Sparrow Hawk* wrecked on Cape Cod in 1626, and dug up out of the sand in 1862. This measured $40 \times 14 \times 8$ feet, and under the old rule [1] would have been of nearly forty tons burden, ample for the party and its impedimenta. With a southerly wind, its single large lug sail if a shallop, or mainsail, jib, and mizzen if a ketch, would have carried them out past Nahant, up along the coast by Swampscott, Marblehead, Beverly, Gloucester, where their eyes would have been gladdened by the sight of a few fishermen's huts dotting the rocky pine-dark shore; thence around the coast of Cape Ann into Ipswich Bay, all in a couple of days. There they had only to wait for the tide to float them up the sandy shallow reaches of Plum Island Sound to the Quascacunquen River. Two miles up that on the north bank a scattered cluster of small houses around a stockaded fort, how different from Berkeley Castle yet similar in purpose, marked their long-awaited destination.

As they cast anchor off a pebbly beach, they saw to the right, beyond the margin of salt marsh browning in the summer sun, a green and pleasantly rolling hill almost as high as Brandon. Along the south bank of the river ran a high ledge of dark grey rock. Beneath it surged a deep tidal pool that to eyes familiar with similar stretches of the lower Avon must have been strongly suggestive of large fish. If that generation of the family possessed the capacity for joyous excitement found in the six generations of which we have a fuller knowledge, they must have gone ashore in the highest possible spirits.

Where the party of sixteen, ranging in age from six months or

---

[1] $\dfrac{(L - 3/5B) \times B \times D}{95}$ = tons burden.

less to sixty-eight years, spent the first few days and nights one can only guess. The rude forefathers of the hamlet had passed the hard winter of 1635–36 in dugouts on the southerly slope of Great Hill, but by 1639, all were housed, and three, Plumer, Knight, and Greenleaf, had been licensed to keep ordinaries. These had been found so inadequate, 'upon occasion of great assemblies and the arrival of ships with passengers,' that three months after the Lowles were confronted by the problem of accommodation it was made legal for any householder to entertain temporary paying guests. Possibly the Reverends Parker and Noyes, who were housemates, took in a good number of Lowles along with Noyes' brother Nicholas, and the others were distributed.[1]

Certainly on landing, Percival would have been welcomed by, or paid an early call on, his spiritual commanders. Whichever way it was, he met in Thomas Parker a man of forty-four with 'a most delicate sweet voice' in which issued very definite instructions in matters material as well as spiritual. In later years he was to develop illusions of theocratic grandeur and narrowly escape being unfrocked for aiming to 'set up a Prelacy and exercise more Power than the Pope.' Towards the end of his life, totally blind, he still used his seductive voice to prepare the brighter boys of Newbury in Latin, Greek, and Hebrew for the entrance examinations at Harvard College. Cotton Mather tells us that in his last year his tongue became palsied, 'having only this help left him, that he could pronounce letters but not syllables or words. He signified his mind by spelling his words,

---

[1] No town in New England has been better served by its local historians than Newburyport. Beginning with Caleb Cushing's rather slender but correct history of the town, written just after he came home from college, we have useful works of research and reminiscence by Joshua Coffin and Mrs. E. Vale Smith. The chief authority, however, is John J. Currier, of the old shipbuilding family, who, availing himself of the researches of his predecessors, carried them further in four admirable volumes: *Ould Newbury: Historical and Biographical Sketches, History of Newbury*, and *History of Newburyport*, 2 vols. All are models of untiring investigation, logical presentation and full documentation. For the background of this and the next two chapters I owe them much.

which was indeed a tedious way, but yet a mercy so far to him and others.'

Like Old Percival himself, Parker and Noyes seem not to have gone to Puritan extremes in religious practices. They still fasted, papistically, some said, one day out of every month. Both were to denounce the execution of Charles Stuart and hold hopeful expectations for the restoration of his son. Perhaps Parker would have liked to call the Quascacunquen the Kennet from old memories of that weedy, slow-sliding stream, but it retained its tongue-twisting Indian name to the end of the century. Twenty years after his death, it became the River Parker.

At the north end of the old green was the meeting house, completed only the year before, in which the ecclesiastical team of Parker and Noyes preached twice each Sunday to a congregation whose gathering of itself together was in the highest degree obligatory. Even small children were hauled along to the church, to be terrified, no doubt, by the heads of wolves killed for a bounty of ten shillings each, later raised to forty, and nailed up along its front. The edifice was approximately $36 \times 20 \times 12$ feet, and was filled not with pews but with backless benches. It was the social, political, even the military centre of the town. Throughout the three-hour services men with muskets stood guard outside. On the top of Great Hill overlooking it, for the further protection of the congregation, was a sentry walk sixteen feet broad running east and west.

As persons of means the Lowles were not granted free land. 'Percival Lowle, Gent.,' as he is styled in the records, contributed fifty pounds to the common stock and received in return a hundred acres of marsh and meadow, bought more later, and set about the business of living.

As Benjamin Franklin was a century later to observe, 'The first drudgery of settling new colonies confines the attention of the people to mere necessaries.' Of these, shelter must have been the most difficult to arrange. Some clapboards came over in ships from England, and before long sawmills were set up to produce them here, but timber had to be cut and hewed by hand, and the building lime for chimneys and foundations made from oyster and clam shells was none too adhesive. Labor was scarce, how scarce is shown by the fact that the General Court had been forced to put a ceiling on wages at the high figure of two shillings a day. John and Richard Lowle, Anthony and Henry Somerby, William Gerrish, perhaps even Old Percival himself, must have put their own backs into the building of two or three small houses.

Food was easier to come by. Plum Island Sound and the River Parker were stiff with fish — striped bass, white perch, mackerel, cod, and sturgeon. Of the last, one diarist reported some eighteen feet long, which would have been two feet between the bulging eyes. Best of all, each spring the river came alive with leaping salmon. The first caught went to the table of the Reverends Thomas Parker and James Noyes. There were toothsome shellfish too — oysters, very different in flavor from those of Old England, clams, and lobsters sometimes weighing as much as twenty-five pounds.

Nor were the pioneers limited to a diet of fish. They brought over seeds and raised turnips, carrots, cucumbers, onions, and strawberries. Indian corn was already growing there. For meat they had venison, bear, wild turkeys, pigeon, geese, woodcock, ducks, snipe, quail, grouse, and before long, beef, mutton, and pork. On the table these were managed with fingers in place of forks, but filled in with cornmeal products, washed down with cider and home-brewed beer, with wine for occasions, and spirits in case of chill or snakebite, they provided sustaining meals that made monthly fast days decidedly beneficial.

Shelter and food assured, the little group from the Venice of the West began to fit itself into the social fabric of the New World. William Gerrish, who married Joan Lowle after the death of John Oliver, was a captain of both horse and foot in the early Indian wars and the founder of an eminent and useful family. Anthony Somerby, the clerk, became Newbury's first schoolmaster, taught the rudiments of learning to her children for nearly half a century. He was her town clerk and recorder for most of the period.

As for the Lowles, Percival in his seventieth year seems to have taken it easy, signing petitions, writing an occasional poem, and in general playing the honorable and unlaborious rôle of elder statesman. Richard was not of a very vigorous constitution. In 1650, after he had become the father of four, fanning out to as many thousands in our time, an effort was made to relieve him as overseer of an estate on the ground that he was 'sickly, and unable to look after their interests.' Thence onward he disappears from the record until the filing of his will in 1682, after his death at the age of eighty. His estate was inventoried at £671.15.0. It included housing, barn, and orchard valued at £100, sixty-two acres of 'Arable and Pasture, Salt Marsh and Meadow' at £184, and a long list of oddments, among them linen, pewter, brass, and 'a booke called Mr. Hooker's politie,' queer reading for a Puritan, which went to Anthony Somerby.

The duty of justifying publicly those points of the darts on the family coat of arms fell upon John, the elder son, then in his forty-fifth year. In the short term of life left to him he did his possible.

John's first wife, Mary, died at the birth of her fifth child, Joseph, on November 28, 1639. Before the end of the year, if the dates in the family genealogy can be trusted, he remarried, Elizabeth Goodale of Newbury, by whom he had three more children, eight in all. In 1641, he was made a constable; in 1644, he was deputy to the General Court. In 1645, he was elected town clerk and appointed one of three court commissioners for Newbury 'to end small Causes,' a sort of justice of the peace, with authority to settle civil disputes not involving more than twenty shillings. His largest public responsibility was as a member of a commission of eight, which for four years, from 1642 to 1646, considered the desirability of moving the village, meeting house and all, to a new location and in the end carried it through.

Precisely what was wrong with the original site is not fully stated. Obviously the great preponderance of salt marsh in the land on both banks of the River Parker was not in its favor. Perhaps the inhabitants had begun to feel that the Merrimack, with its more abundant water power, and even bigger fish, was a better stream to dwell beside. It was not until sometime after 1646 that Aquila Chase, a shipmaster of Hampton, first took a vessel safely over the shifting bar at the Merrimack's mouth, but John Lowle, with his memory of the magnificent sheltered harbor of Bristol, may have envisioned a Venice still farther west, with a port for larger ships than those of fifty tons which was as much as the River Parker could float. Late in 1642, at a full gathering in the meeting house, the decision to move was made. Four years later, around a new green two miles farther north, a new meeting house and habitations for the old proprietors were ready on building sites of four acres each, overlooking or stretching down to the very margin of the Merrimack.

That swift strong river, draining the massive mountains and large lakes of central New Hampshire, was to be a major source of the family fortunes in commerce and industry. Let us see how it looked to a contemporary of the first Lowles, to a sensitive poet, delicate Ann Bradstreet. As Ann Dudley she had been brought up in the household of the Earl of Lincoln, where her father was steward, and enjoyed the services of no less than eight tutors in languages, music, and dancing. After her remove from Ipswich to North Andover, she lived within a few miles of the Merrimack and found its shady banks a pleasant resort, perhaps a peaceful refuge from eight growing children:

'Under the cooling shadow of a stately Elm,
  Close sat I by a goodly river's side,
  Where gliding streams the rocks did overwhelm;
  A lonely place, with pleasures dignified.
  I once that lov'd the shady woods so well
  Now thought the rivers did the trees excell,
  And if the sun would ever shine, there would I dwell.

'While on the stealing stream I fix'd mine eye,
Which to the long'd for ocean held its course,
I mark'd nor crooks nor rubs that there did lie
Could hinder aught, but still augment its force:
O happy Flood, quoth I, that holds thy race
Till thou arrive at thy beloved place,
Nor is it rocks or shoals that can obstruct thy pace.'

The new green near the river was larger than the old one. It lacked, apparently, the stockaded fort, but otherwise it was complete, with meeting house, training ground, and frog pond. Surrounded by golden-brown houses of weathering pine trimmed with red, it had the ordered simplicity, the perfect fitness to the lay of the land, that give New England village greens their singular and touching charm.

The building site allotted to John Lowle in 1642, as the active head of the family, was Number 28 on the westerly side of the High Street. Old Percival didn't get his until later, and then it was in 'the little field' just off the main street. There he built a somewhat more commodious house than the first by the River Parker. Rebecca, his wife, had died in 1645, and the new home seems to have sheltered, at least at first, the family of Richard as well as himself. Undoubtedly, for the type was standard, it was similar to the well-known Whipple house in Ipswich of which one room and an attic were built in 1640 and additions made during the following decade. With its floor plan almost the golden section, its massive central chimney and long sloping back roof, it is a house of distinction. In his house Percival would have slept in the best bed in the parlor to the left of the entrance. He sat by day, reading his Bible or Richard Hooker's *The Lawes of Ecclesiastical Politie*, or the *Anatomy of Melancholy*, the only book that ever got Doctor Johnson out of bed two hours before he was ready to leave it, or just thinking his long, long thoughts, in the larger kitchen-cum-living-room to the right. On its walls were hung muskets, fowling pieces, warming pans, and powder horns; on shelves stood pewter, brass, and a few cherished pieces of silver. When, carrying a stout staff, he walked out to take the air and hear the news, he wore a green or blue doublet, baggy lead-colored woollen breeches, and wide-brimmed hat to protect him from sun or shower, and if the weather were cool a great cloak over all.

Of news there was plenty. From the old country as the years went by came word, a month or two late, of Marston Moor, Naseby; Regicide; Drogheda, Worcester, the Dutch War, the death of Old Noll; and at long last, the Restoration. But to ears by the Merrimack these world-shaking events must have seemed faint and far away. The talk was more of local growth and progress.

In 1650, the River Parker was arched by Thorley's Bridge, a mile or two below the falls at tide-head, and the ferry at the Old Town became so busy that as many as twenty horsemen or foot travellers and thirty head of cattle would cross it in a single winter's day. The north ferry, across the Merrimack by Carr's Island to Salisbury, was even busier with travel to Hampton, Portsmouth, York, and points east to Falmouth and the Kennebec. After the bar at the river's mouth was mastered, a fine harbor was developed by the shore of the new town. Down to it from higher upstream were floated gundalows of hay and other produce, and masts for the Royal Navy, sometimes as much as twenty-eight inches in diameter.

Overseas commerce had begun. Shipping, fishing, and the fur trade were to put useful sums of money in New England pockets, but during the later seventeenth century the Lowle family was not in a position to take advantage of the opportunity for which they had been so well prepared. Percival was too old, Richard was not strong, and John, perhaps worn out by the drudgery of necessaries, died in 1647.

After the death of wife and elder son, Percival at seventy-six, surrounded by infant grandchildren, must have felt the loneliness of old age. Little is known of his later life except that in 1649 his signature appears with that of Thomas Parker and James

Noyes on a petition to the General Court begging that Plum Island might be used as a common and exclusive pasturage for all Newbury. In the event that town only got the use of half the island, smaller portions being allotted to Rowley and Ipswich. As described by Whittier:

> 'Long and low with dwarf trees crowned,
> Plum Island lies like a whale aground.'

We shall visit it again.

In the same year Percival wrote the *Elegy* on the death of Governor Winthrop that was printed some years later as a broadside by the Harvard College Press. There was less of the true poetic fire in it than in the single eloquent phrase of another contemporary, 'Not sparing but as the burning torch spending,' yet it is sincerely felt, and quaintly phrased, with a faint flavor of the conceits that were the specialty of seventeenth-century verse from Donne to Herbert:

> 'He was (surely we may say this)
> *Rara avis in terris.* . . .

> 'He was *New England's* Pelican,
> *New England's* Gubernator,
> He was *New England's* Solomon
> *New England's* Conservator. . . .

> 'Let's shew our Love for him by weeping,
> That car'd for us when we lay sleeping. . . .

> 'Here you have Lowle's loyalty
> Pen'd with his slender Skill,
> And with it no good Poetry
> But certainly good Will.
> Read these few verses willingly,
> And view them not with Momus' eye.
> Friendly correct what is amiss.
> Accept his Love that did write this.'

The modesty of the writer is disarming, his amiability attractive. These, his only recorded accents, are the voice of *a good man*, a phrase that has no exact equivalent in any other language.

The remaining fifteen years of his life coincided with a warfare between theological creeds that found a bitter battlefield in his own Newbury. It is hard to picture him as an ardent partisan. One feels instinctively that he had simple faith as well as Norman blood, but shouted arguments, counter-arguments, and recriminations must have been dinned in his ears and disturbed his thoughts.

Two heresies were rearing their heads in the Congregational fold, the ancient Arian and the more recent Socinian. Arius in the fourth century had taught that God was alone and unknowable, that Christ, the Logos or son of God, was a created being, so not God in the fullest sense. Men had been burned at the stake for believing this. Faustus Socinius, an Italian, who had died only during Percival's early manhood, went further on the road of modernism. He denied the Trinity, the divinity of Christ, the personality of the Devil, the total depravity of man, and the eternity of future punishment. He believed that salvation was a state to be achieved by the imitation of Christ's virtue, and, most shocking of all, that the Bible was to be interpreted by, and as being in accord with, human reason. Some of these doctrines were to be embodied in the Quaker creed. Thomas Parker and James Noyes had little mercy for such views. Their preaching was as uncompromising with any softness of doctrine as the most orthodox fundamentalist could desire.

It was the Socinians with their denial of a personal devil, their reasoned interpretation of the Good Book, and their firm conviction of the native innocence of men, women, and infants, that fell into the worst trouble. Old Miss Sara Emery, whose own memory went back well into the eighteenth century, and hearsay knowledge to the middle of the seventeenth, relates in her *Reminiscences of a Nonogenarian* how two Socinian ladies from Haverhill stopped overnight in Newbury en route to Boston. Unwisely they embarked with their hosts upon a theological discussion:

'And in the time of their discourse, the wind striving in Mary Tompkin's stomach, making some noise, she having received no sustenance for the space of near forty-eight hours, one Joseph Pike, after they were departed the town said "she had a devil in her." '

They were pursued, overtaken, and it was ordered they should be '. . . stripped naked from the middle upwards, and make them fast to the cart's tail, and drawing the cart through the several towns, to whip them upon their naked backs not exceeding ten stripes apiece on each of them in each town.'[1]

This was in 1663. If Old Percival, then in his ninety-third year, was able to attend divine worship on a certain Sunday morning in March, he took part in an even more dramatic scene. On that morning, it is chronicled:

'Lydia Wardwell [née Perkins] in response to repeated demands to appear and state why she stayed away from church came naked into Newbury Meeting House.'

The effect of the cataclysmic appearance of this Susanna among the Puritan Elders is material for psycho-analysts.

And why? George Bishop, in his bitter tract, *New England Judged*, says she was 'a young, tender and chaste woman' who withdrew from the church because of the treatment its priests and rulers had meted to her husband. She went naked, he says, 'as a sign,' one supposes, of the native innocency of man. The Socinian heresy!

She was arrested, taken to Ipswich, and tried at a Quarterly Sessions Court for Essex County held in the White Horse Tavern on High Street, which had lately been reopened under a new management after a period of closure because its proprietor, Corporal John Andrews, kept open after nine o'clock and encouraged young men to drink and play unlawful games. That was the setting in which poor Lydia Perkins Wardwell, forcibly reclothed, was fined ten shillings and costs, and sentenced to be tied to the horse rail in front of the tavern, stripped again, and receive thirty lashes.

[1] Flogged through the fleet!

Perhaps Percival, as he died on the eighth of the next January, felt in his tired old heart that he had had enough of the toilsome, contentious, superstitious, brave new world he had lived in for ninety-three years. He would not have regretted missing the amphisbaena, or two-headed snake that Christopher Toppan and other citizens of Newbury were soon to observe slithering backward and forward with equal facility through their meadows. Cotton Mather, who may have read of such in Felltham [1] or Milton, posted down from Cambridge to examine it, but missed it too. For a century the townsfolk saw its reincarnation in quarrelsome couples, 'one in body and two in will.'

Old Percival's enduring bones rest with Anthony Somerby's in a little burying ground to the west of Route 1A, just north of the Old Town Green. The stone has been renewed, but the dates on it are very old and very far apart. They embrace a great period of world history, 1571–1664.

In New England an epoch of history ended in January, 1697, when Samuel Sewall, one of those brighter boys of Newbury where his father held land on the borders of Byfield, but later hanging judge of Salem witches, arose in the Old Cedar, now the Old South, Church in Boston and stood with bowed head while the Reverend Samuel Williard read his confession of pride of opinion and judicial error, and his humble plea for the forgiveness of God and man. A new century, a new spirit, a new feeling about this world and the next were foreshadowed when he wrote that same year in his *Apocalyptica*, or *The New Heaven as it makes to Those upon the New Earth:*

'As long as Plum Island shall faithfully keep the Commanded Post; Notwithstanding the hectoring words and hard Blows of the proud and boisterous Ocean; As long as any Salmon, or Sturgeon shall swim in the streams of the Merrimack; or any Perch or Pickeril in Crane Pond; As long as the Sea Fowl shall know the Time of their Coming, and not neglect seasonally to

---

[1] 'A corrupt book is an amphisbaena, a serpent headed at either end; one bites him that reads, the other stings him that writes.' Owen Felltham, *Resolves*, 1628.

visit the Places of their Acquaintance; As long as any Cattel shall be fed with the Grass growing in the meadows, which do humbly bow themselves before Turkie Hill; As long as any Sheep shall walk upon Old Town Hills, and shall from thence pleasantly look down upon the River Parker, and the fruitful Marishes lying beneath; As long as any free and harmless Doves shall find a White Oak or other Tree within the Township to perch, or feed, or build a careless Nest upon; and shall voluntarily present themselves to perform the office of Gleaners after Barley-Harvest; As long as Nature shall not grow old and dote; but shall constantly remember to give the rows of Indian Corn their education by Pairs; So long shall Christians be born there; and being first made meet, shall from thence be Translated to be made partakers of the Inheritance of the Saints in Light.'

Forty years after his death, in the fourth year of the new century of enlightenment, the Age of Reason, a Lowell was born who was to be one of the earliest voices of its spirit and feeling.

2
CHAPTER

Portrait of a Divine

Over the mantel in James Russell Lowell's sitting-room at Elmwood was mounted a diptych quaintly designed and executed. The left half depicts a bare Italian landscape rather like the rocks among which the Mona Lisa sits. In the foreground is a river bearing three boats and six swans, perhaps the Merrimack idealized. On the right we see seven eighteenth-century divines around a table, each with his long churchwarden pipe. In front of each is a smear where something that must have looked very like a pewter of ale has been painted out. At its head sits an alert, serene, square-faced gentleman in gown and bands — the Reverend John Lowell [1] presiding over a meeting of the 'Association' of all the ministers of Newbury, painted, it is said, to

[1] Percival and his sons had spelled their surname in divers ways: Lowle, Louell, Lowel, and once or twice, Lowell. Early in the eighteenth century the final spelling became fixed.

order by one Shattuck, a blacksmith of his congregation. Over the picture on a scroll, supported by a Corinthian column, are inscribed words which are an epitome of his character and creed. *In necessariis unitas; in non necessariis libertas; in utrisque charitas —* In essentials unity; in non-essentials liberty; in both charity.

This John Lowell, the first of six of that Christian name that we shall be intimately concerned with, was the great-grandson of the John that had supervised the moving of the village of Newbury in 1646, yet he was born only forty years after the death of Old Percival. For reasons already set forth, the Lowells had not prospered in the New World as they had expected, and after the division of Percival's property between two sons and again between twelve grandchildren, the individual share of each of the latter was inconspicuous. The descendants of Richard, displaying, like their father, some lack of driving energy, accepted a reduced standard of living in Newbury, or moved a little way up or down the coast or inland. They were a numerous race that provided thousands of worthy citizens and scores of good soldiers in seven wars, but the vocal Lowells that had a visible hand in making New England history were all from the loins of the more vigorous John. Two of his sons, another John and Joseph, left home early and went to the city. In Boston, a growing town of some fifteen thousand inhabitants, both followed the thriving trade of cooper, making barrels and casks for the export trade in salt fish and rum. John, the elder, had three wives and nineteen children. Ebenezer, his son by his third wife, Naomi Sylvester of Scituate, and his fifteenth child, was born in 1675. With him the family fortunes took an upward turn.

Ebenezer Lowell became a cordwainer; that is to say, a dealer and worker in cordovan leather, not a cobbler or mere journeyman shoemaker, but a manufacturer of shoes in an age when soleleather was worn out fast, a pioneer in one of New England's important industries. As we know by a renewal license granted to his widow, he had a side line, selling drink as a retailer, perhaps as an aid to the fitting and sale of shoes; and he was a member of the Ancient and Honorable Artillery Company. He died in 1711, at the early age of thirty-six, but the family tradition that he was a man of energy and character is sustained by the size of his estate which was valued at a total, substantial for those days, of £809.16.3. In the inventory prepared by Jonathan Loring, of a family that still deals with testamentary matters for the Lowells, are such interesting items as:

House and Lands.. £597.1. 9
Household furniture, viz. Beds, bedding, brass, pewter, iron,
shoemakers ware, ship goods, firing and arms, lumber, etc. . £ 97.3.10
Cash, plate, Indian boy apprentice, etc................... £120.8.10

After his death, another Ebenezer, his eldest surviving son by his second wife, Elizabeth Shailer, became the head of the family and carried on the business. He was listed as a 'merchant' on King Street (now State) and remembered as 'a stately, refined, commanding looking person,' never without his badge of position, a gold-headed cane. His younger brother, John, first of the family to be given a college education, was the fountain and origin of the family's intellectual attainment and prestige.

In the summer of 1717, six years after the death of his father, little John Lowell, aged thirteen, entered Harvard College as a member of the class of '21. It was the largest class the college in its seventy-one years of existence had yet received — thirty-one boys of the average age of fifteen. President Ezra Stiles of Yale late in the century is quoted as saying that it was famous as 'the learned class.'

Much has been made of the printed 'order of seniority' of Harvard classes as indicating the social rank of its members. It has been assumed that freshmen were graded in precise relation to the incomes and social standing of their parents until 1769, when, following a difference of opinion between two of the parents as to whose commission as justice of the peace was of prior date, the list became alphabetical. Samuel Eliot Morison, in his *Tercentennial History of Harvard*,[1] is inclined to think that the ranking until the middle of the eighteenth century was based on 'intellectual merit,' and that beginning about 1750, following, perhaps, the bad example of Yale, it became a matter of social position. This theory fits most of the known facts, but not all of them, and Clifford K. Shipton, who is ably carrying on Sibley's *Harvard Graduates*, is content, in the sixth volume in a note preceding his account of this very class of 1721, to call the whole business a 'mystery.'

Whatever the solution of the mystery may be, there was little in the zoning of the class of 1721 to inflate the vanity of young John Lowell. In the first grading, prepared by the steward at entrance, he stood at the very bottom of the list of thirty-one. In the second list, prepared four months later by the faculty, he had risen to the position of sixth above it. At the top of both lists stood the names of Foster Hutchinson and John Davenport, scions of already distinguished and well-to-do families. High in both we find the well-known names of Sewall, Wolcott, Hancock, and Winslow. Near the bottom in both, not far from Lowell, appears the name of John Adams, the so-called 'poet,' not a direct ancestor of the royal family of that name.

It was a good time to be entering Harvard. John Leverett, 'the great Leverett,' the first layman to be president of the college, had been in office for ten years. His wise and liberal administration had shaken off the incubus of the fierce orthodoxy of the Mathers. In his régime began that liberal tradition, *nil admirari*, miscalled 'Harvard indifference,' the indisposition to get really excited without just cause, which has been a balance wheel to many a powerful mental engine.

Crossing the Charles by ferry to Cambridge, young John took up his residence in Old Stoughton Hall, at that time the college's only dormitory. He shared with two or three other boys a chamber eighteen or twenty feet square, off which, to en-

---

[1] Most of the details of early student life that follow are taken from that learned and definitive work.

courage intenser application, were three small four by six studies.
Some time between four and five each morning, varying with
the season, he would arise at the clang of the college bell, knuckle
the sleep out of his eyes, and descend to the college pump to
fetch a pail of cold water for his ablutions. Then came prayers
and 'morning bever,' or breakfast of bread and beer, to be followed at eleven-thirty by a square meal of beef, bread, and beer,
afternoon bever or quick snack at five, and another square meal
with beer at seven-thirty. At nine the bell rang again, and all
students must be in their chambers. If they chose, they could
study till midnight, but after sixteen hours of books and beer,
little thirteen-year-old John should have been ready for bed.

Mentally he had gone through a stiff day. At nine he would
have been in the chamber of his tutor in Harvard Hall, looking,
with its six dormers and steepled lantern, not unlike the Old
State House in Boston, but a little less stately. There in his first
year he reviewed his Greek and Latin classics and Hebrew
grammar, and embarked upon the study of Logic which was to
continue through all the four years. In the second year Natural
Philosophy and Divinity were added to his curriculum, and he
had to 'dispute' on logical questions. In the third year he went
on to Physics, Ethics, Geography, and Metaphysics, and his
disputes were Physical, Metaphysical, and Ethical. In the
fourth, in addition to continuing instruction in Logic, Latin,
Greek, and Hebrew, he dealt with advanced Mathematics and
Astronomy and disputed on philosophical and astronomical
theses. After the successful completion of four years of this, he
received his A.B. degree in 1721 at a total cost to his mother and
generous brother, Ebenezer, of about one hundred and fifty
pounds. In the same year he was inoculated for smallpox, a progressive proceeding for that time.

After graduation it was the custom for those preparing themselves for the Congregational ministry to stay on at college for
three years or more to achieve the 'second degree,' that of
Master of Arts. The following is what John Lowell, then at the
riper age of seventeen, confronted:

'What Bachelours soever shall present unto the President a written Synopsis, or Compendium of Logicke, Naturall Philosophy, morall philosophy, Arithmeticke, Geometry or Astronomy within a weeke of the Summer Solstace in his third yeare after his first degree (which Synopsis shall be kept in the Colledge Library) and shall bee ready to defend his positions, and be Skilfull in the Originall Tongues as aforesayd, having Staid three yeares after his first degree, and herein thrice problemed, twice declaymed, and once made a Common place or else some answerable exercise in the Studyes that he is most Conversant in and remayning of a blameless Conversation, at any publique Act having the approbation of the Overseers and the President of the Colledge, shall bee Capable of his Second degree, viz to be Master of Arts.'

At the beginning of what we should now call his post-graduate course, John Lowell was appointed a 'Scholar of the House,' which, in return for certain proctorial duties, brought him some modest financial grants, four pounds a year with supplements for special services, and the honor of being described as 'Sir.' During the next three years, along with the required exercises and inhibitions, he assisted in the founding of a student society for the promotion of literature and piety. Before this body he lectured on Transubstantiation, Predestination, The Errors of Quakers, and Prejudice, and preached at least one sermon. At Commencement in June, 1724, he took his second degree by defending the negative position on the *Quaestio*, '*An Status Praeminorum, Ratione naturali, investigari possit*,' which can be freely translated: Can the spiritual state of small or unborn infants be investigated by the natural reason.[1]

He can hardly be said to have been educated. It took forty more years of living to do that; but he must have emerged from seven years of service for the academic Rachel of the M.A. degree with a toughened character and a well-trained mind.

By the end of the first quarter of the eighteenth century, the

[1] Shipton-Sibley, *op. cit.*

two parish churches of Newbury had become inadequate for the accommodation of those wishing to attend them, and their location was inconvenient for persons living along the farther end of the High Street where it marches most closely with the Merrimack. In 1725, a group of the Northenders erected a handsome church, which was approved by the General Court, for a new Third Parish.

It stood at the upper end of what is now Market Square, 'by the water side.' An old drawing shows the masts and yards of ships and the ribs of a vessel on the stocks in close juxtaposition. Compared with the first thatched meeting house on the Old Green it was a cathedral — eighty by sixty feet after an addition a decade later, and high enough for an elevated pulpit and galleries. It was surmounted by a slender spire. It had no heating arrangements, and the colorful congregation, clothed in bright greens, reds, and blues, tricked out with fancy hoods and hats, that sat out two sermons must have shivered in its box pews. But it was considered a very commodious and notable edifice.

The church was dedicated in June, 1725, and its builders looked about for a pastor. Before the end of the month, perhaps because his name was well and favorably known in Newbury, they issued a call to that learned young Master of Arts, the Reverend John Lowell, still in his twenty-second year. Although he had previously declined a call to the church in Wells, fifty miles to the north on the Indian frontier, he seems to have accepted without delay the invitation back to the old family terrain. In December he was married to Sarah Champney, cousin of a classmate. She was eighteen, but destined to show in the siege perilous of a pastor's wife 'tact, quick perception, and decision of character, united to great skill and notabilitie in domestic affairs,' qualities that were to appear in six later generations of Lowell wives. On January 19, 1726, he was formally ordained pastor of the church of the new Third Parish. The preacher of the ordination sermon, Thomas Foxcroft of Boston, pointed out, at considerable length and wealth of illustration,

that youth was no handicap to a shepherd of the flock if joined
to true learning and piety.

From the beginning his ministry was successful. He seems to
have been particularly active in the department of pastoral care
and became the intimate confidant of his people's sins and sorrows. His congregation grew so rapidly that in 1636 the church
had to be enlarged. He had an ear for music and there is a
tradition that congregational singing improved greatly under
his direction.

His sermons were not too doctrinal (one diarist noted that his
'scholarship was not deep'), but they were interesting, timely,
and delivered with a certain restrained but earnest eloquence
that must have gratified his more judicious hearers. His first
fifteen years in Newbury were busy, fruitful, and uneventful.
His congregation voted him the sum of two hundred pounds to
assist him in the building of a house in Greenleaf Lane near the
church. His first son, John was born in it in 1735, ten years
after his marriage, but died in infancy. His second and only
surviving son, another John, the future 'Old Judge,' the effective
founder of the branches of the family we are following, came
eight years later.

But this peaceful period was to prove a weather-breeder. In 1740
was to occur the first of a series of storms in the ecclesiastical and
political worlds that were to bring trouble and drama into his life.

In September, 1740, George Whitefield, the great revivalist,
then a young man of twenty-six, five years out of Oxford, of
middle stature, slender body, and fair complexion, an attractive
countenance marred only by a slight squint, preached to a congregation that overflowed the Third Parish Church into the
surrounding square and streets. If we may judge by its effect,
few masters of pulpit eloquence have ever surpassed him. 'I
would give one hundred guineas,' said David Garrick, 'if I could
say "Oh!" like Mr. Whitefield.'

The next day Whitefield noted in his diary: 'Lay at the house
of Mr. Lowell the minister of the place. Preached in the morn-

ing to a thronged congregation and saw the outgoing of God in the Sanctuary. Collection, £80.9.3. One hundred and forty-three souls were added to the parish here.'

The taking in cash which, it will be noted, precedes that in souls, could not have given unbounded pleasure to John Lowell. His annual salary at the time was but one hundred and fifty pounds. Thirty years later, Whitefield was to make his last great effort in Newbury. In 1770, very ill but holding aloft his bed light, he discoursed with his old unction from the stair of the house of another clerical host 'until his candle burned out.' Then he ascended to his bed and died in it next day. It is but fair to say that he was as charitable as eloquent. Nearly four thousand pounds of the sums received from collections was spent on Bethesda, the orphanage he had established in Georgia.

That first sermon had set the torch to the Newbury tinder for the flame of emotional religion that was sweeping the colonies from Georgia to the Kennebec. For a year or two John Lowell tried to go along with its crackling progress, but soon the 'disorderly assemblies' became too much for him. His change of heart was sympathetically described a century later by his grandson, the Reverend Charles Lowell, father of James Russell Lowell, in *Annals of the American Pulpit*:

'But, though a friend to religious fervour, and glad to see the general mind aroused to the importance of eternal interests, Mr. Lowell was, by no means, prepared for such a movement as was then beginning to agitate the entire community. Seeing the foundations of the great deep beginning to be broken up, and the sea and the waves roaring as if a coming storm was near, instead of a distilling shower, the heart of the mild and order-loving pastor began to fail him for fear. As the work went on, and the excitement grew more and more intense and pervading, his cautious and conservative spirit began to get the better of his zeal. Deplorable irregularities unquestionably discovered themselves; the rights of pastors, of which he had a high esteem, were disregarded by zealous itinerants and inexperienced youths; proprieties of all sorts were neglected by many, and in some cases, grossly outraged; and finding it impossible for him to run fast enough to keep ahead of the fierce velocity that was hurrying the church forward, he suddenly halted in his course as one out of breath, and turned aside to walk more quietly in a different path.'

Soon he took definite steps to combat this menace to true religion. He discontinued evening meetings as 'tending to disorder,' and closed his pulpit to itinerant exhorters. When, in his absence and without his consent, it was opened to one of these, a public feud flared up between two parties of his parishioners. Those opposed to him asserted that he was 'drawing away from the assemblies' rule and towards the Church of England.' The dispute became a *cause célèbre* discussed in the Boston press and debated in the General Court. His old college was with him. There the eloquent words and theatrical gestures of Whitefield had failed of their customary effect. 'Godless Harvard,' he called it — a tag that stuck. The Massachusetts Archives contain the correspondence between the contending parties. It concludes with a long letter of admirable reason and temper subscribed 'Your aggrieved Pastor, J. Lowell.' This seems to recognize that, despite his patient effort towards a reconciliation, none was possible. In 1745, thirty-eight male members of his congregation with their families, over a hundred in all, withdrew, and with the authorization of the General Court established the First Presbyterian Church of Newburyport.

This was undoubtedly a heavy blow to John Lowell. Perhaps he remembered with a certain irony the text of the sermon Thomas Foxcroft had preached at his ordination twenty years before: 'And I will very gladly spend and be spent for you; though the more abundantly I love you, the less I be loved.'

In the course of the controversy his creed like his character became fixed and clear. He was not quite a Socinian, but hell and a personal devil were never mentioned from his pulpit. Some time later, at a council of ministers to discuss the giving of a recommendation to the Reverend Mr. Barnard of West Newbury, who was leaving for another parish, the question was raised, 'Is he a believer in the doctrine of the Trinity?'

'If that question is put,' said John Lowell, 'I shall retire from the room and take no further part in this council.' The question was not put.

He was, in short, very early a Unitarian, as his descendants were to be after him.

In 1754, in the unusual month of February, by what must have seemed to the members of the First Presbyterian Church a convincing example of an 'emergent' Providence, the meeting house in Market Square was struck by lightning. Houses in the square were damaged, but the church lost only its tall white steeple. Benjamin Franklin journeyed over from Philadelphia to examine the premises, and found that the main structure had been saved by a small wire which conducted the discharge down from the bell tower through the clock and pendulum to the ground. This interesting and important discovery was communicated to the Royal Society in London. It should have furnished a strong talking-point to the thousands of lightning-rod agents that covered this country in the next century.

The following year brought the colonies their first real experience of World War. Power politics in Europe and boundary disputes in America started the Seven Years' War, carried on by land in America and Germany, and by sea in all parts of the navigable globe. New England with its exposed position was at once a threatened outpost and a spearhead for attack. Massachusetts rose nobly to the occasion. Forty-five hundred of her men, one in every eight, volunteered for service, and the taxes in Boston rose to thirteen shillings and sixpence in the pound, sixty-seven and a half per cent on all income from real or personal property. It was a heavy load for the patriotic, but less than enough for the merchants and farmers who feathered their nests by trading with the enemy.

In the north the strategy of the higher command, Governor

Shirley in Massachusetts and the Duke of Newcastle's ministry in London, called for the capture of Crown Point, a bold promontory projecting into Lake Champlain from the west shore. It controlled the water-level invasion route from Quebec and Montreal through that lake to Ticonderoga, and thence, either by Woods Creek or Lake George and the fourteen miles of the Great Carrying Place, to Fort Lyman on the Hudson, Albany, and New York. Under Shirley's energetic direction an expedition was organized and placed under the command of William Johnson from the Mohawk Valley; a personable and appealing Irishman, friend of the Five Nations and a squawman. Newbury did even more than her allotted bit. Nearly two hundred of her young men enlisted for the campaign, and the command of the Essex regiment went to one of her leading citizens who had served with distinction at the capture of Louisburg, Colonel Moses Titcomb.

On May 22, 1755, John Lowell preached a farewell sermon to the Newbury contingent sitting before and below him in miscellaneous habiliments of homespun, with their colonel and his officers in uniforms of blue with facings of red. It was printed and widely distributed under the title:

*The Advantages of God's Presence with
his People in an Expedition against
their Enemies.*

Taking as his text, Deuteronomy XX, 4, 'For the Lord your God is he that goeth with you, to fight for you against your enemies, to save you,' he announced the comfortable doctrine, 'God is never neutral, he always helps one side or the other in every war.' He urged his hearers to shed no more blood than was absolutely necessary, and to avoid sin in general and profane swearing and cursing in particular. Judging from the letters of chaplains printed in Parkman's *Montcalm and Wolfe*, the last admonition was more honored in the breach. Most interesting today are his remarks on the French character, habits, and diet.

The Reverend John Lowell (1704–1767) of Newbury, first of the Lowells to graduate from Harvard, was one of the most liberal and broad-minded divines of his day. Though a reader of French literature, he feared the deism, despotic government, and imperialistic designs of the French. He added the motto, *Occasionem cognosce*, to the Lowell arms.

In this half of a diptych, painted by a blacksmith of his congregation, the Reverend John Lowell at the head of the table smokes the pipe of peace with the other clergymen of Newbury — Baptist and Presbyterian as well as Congregationalist. The Latin inscription would read in English:

'In essentials unity, in non-essentials liberty, in both charity.'

John Lowell (1743–1802), the 'Old Judge,' son of the Reverend John, founded the triple line that shaped New England history for two centuries. As a member of the Continental Congress he widened the family horizon. Harrison Gray Otis called him 'the very mirror of benevolence.'

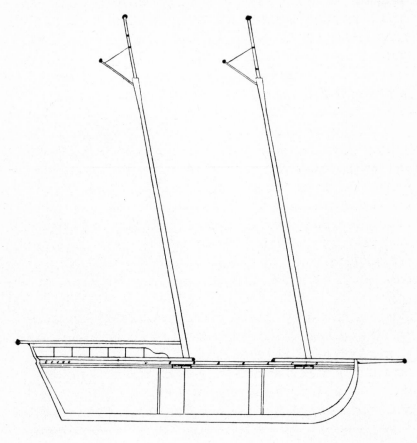

Lugsail-Schooner

42 ft Keel   17 ft Beam   9 ft Transum   8 ft Hold   10 ft St post   6 ft M. waist
6 ft Quart waist   18 ft Quart. d. Rails   8 ft Rake forward   4 ft Rake abaft

The 'Old Judge' was the leading maritime lawyer of his day in Boston and filed more than seven hundred libels against British vessels captured by American privateers. The above plan found among his papers is of that rare rig, a lug sail schooner, a museum piece for the nautically-minded. Whether privateer or prize does not appear.

At Cambridge he had been grounded in Logic from the writings of Descartes, and he is known from the books in his library to have been a reader of the French authors of his day, Montesquieu, Diderot, even Voltaire, but he reveals a deep-seated allergy towards that nation as a whole that was to be felt and expressed even more vigorously, though for quite contrary political reasons, by both his son and his grandson:

'Would you be under a despotick Prince? Would you wear wooden shoes? Would you be condemned to live upon Roots and Herbs, without much Variety, Garlick and Onions (Egyptian Fare), as the lower People among them generally are? Would you have your Country and Nation in such a State as that they could call nothing their own, their Wives and Children, any more than their Houses and Lands? Would you be dragooned, and perpetually pillaged? Would you see an End to Law, and everything depend upon the Will of him that had the Power over you?'

He had no doubt of the outcome. The French cannot stand up to the English, 'as the glorious Duke of Marlborough showed.'

Enheartened by this discourse the Essex regiment set out. After long marches across the rivers and over the mountains, they reached Albany in the valley of the Hudson. After longer delays in ascending that noble stream, they arrived late in August at the southern end of Lac Saint-Sacrement, the most beautiful lake in America, promptly rechristened by the astute Johnson in honor of his sovereign, Lake George. There they went into camp and with eyes turned northward down the green and silver lake, prepared, very much at their leisure, for the final advance on their objective.

Within a week they were to know the sharp taste of battle, most of them for the first time. Baron Dieskau in command of the French was not a man to sit quietly waiting for his enemy to come to him. A German mercenary, ready to sell his sword to the highest bidder, he was nevertheless an officer and gentleman of high ability. With a mixed force of French grenadiers,

Canadians, and Indians he rowed down Lake Champlain to South Bay at its southwestern corner, left his boats and made a forced semicircular march of a day and a night around French Mountain, some thirty miles all told, with the design of taking Johnson by surprise from the south, and in his rear.[1]

The result was one of the bravest and bloodiest small battles in our history. On the morning of September 8, Dieskau disposed of Colonel Ephraim Williams and his regiment which, warned by an Indian scout, Johnson had sent out to investigate, and advanced along the road winding down through the pine woods to the lake. From the sound of firing coming nearer and nearer, Johnson's men at last perceived what was under way and made feverish efforts for defense. They improvised a barricade before the camp from overturned wagons, bateaux, and felled trees; but it was still unfinished when stragglers from Williams' force began to come in. Close behind them the head of the French column appeared on the road and the bloodcurdling war-whoop of Indians was heard from the thick woods to right and left. Moses Titcomb in command of the English right ordered his regiment out in front of the barricade to protect its flank, but before they were fully disposed the enemy was upon them. As Lieutenant Colonel Seth Pomeroy, gunmaker from Northampton, wrote his wife, 'hailstones from heaven were never much thicker than their bullets came.'

For an hour the attack on the centre gained no ground and Dieskau turned the weight of his force against the right flank. Titcomb, who had fought Indians before, was a rod in front of the barricade armed with a musket, firing from behind well-selected trees. It was not long, however, before a wily Indian, taking advantage of a fallen primeval pine, stepped behind it, worked around to his right rear and shot him dead. Almost at the same moment, not many rods away, Dieskau, leading the attack in person, was wounded and captured. The French fled,

[1] These and following details from Parkman's *Montcalm and Wolfe*, and an early squirrel-shooting acquaintance with the terrain.

hotly pursued by the colonials with their own Indians. They had, as Dieskau handsomely said, 'fought like good boys in the morning, about noon like men, and in the afternoon like devils.'

Many bodies of white-coated Frenchmen and naked Indians were thrown into a small stagnant pool that is still known as Bloody Pond. The mortal remains of Moses Titcomb could not be taken back to Newbury, but were buried under the pines by the shore of the lake. A week later John Lowell preached to a crowded church from Joshua I, 2, 'Moses, my servant is dead,' with a note of deep personal feeling for his friend the colonel and for a score of others that were unreturning. He concluded:

'Their dust shall not be lost, not a particle of it shall be annihilated. God will keep His eye upon it that at last He may rebuild the fabric, more glorious at the resurrection of the just.'

He was not at all points a modernist.

The remaining twelve years of his life passed more serenely. Sarah Champney Lowell died in June, 1756. Two years later, he married Elizabeth Cutts Whipple, widow of a clerical colleague at Hampton Falls. In the same year his son John entered Harvard, to come back to Newbury seven years later, practise law, and make the beginnings of a fortune. The father was frugal and shrewd too. He made purchases of real estate that turned out well. The tenor of his later life is indicated in old Miss Emery's statement, 'He was a lover of all good men, though of different denominations, and given to hospitality.' From the top of the bookcases in his study looked down the busts of Plato, Pythagoras, Socrates, Cicero, and Seneca. They descended later to his clerical grandson, Charles Lowell, but he skyed them to the Elmwood attic, where his son, the poet, did some of his best early work.

It was in character that the Reverend John was an inveterate consumer of tobacco. It is recorded that one of his parishioners made with another, a small wager, half a crown, perhaps, that at any hour of day or night he would be found smoking his pipe.

They went together to his house at three A.M. and knocked on his door. After an interval their pastor appeared in his night-shirt, holding aloft a candle, and with his pipe in his mouth drawing well. As his grandson, also a smoker and father of a greater one, explains it, 'He arose, took his half-smoked pipe from his bedside table, went into the kitchen, opened the ashes, lighted his pipe, and opened the door to see what was wanted.'

He died, sincerely lamented by all who knew him, on May 15, 1767. Perhaps his greatest contribution to the family, apart from his blood, which as Bronson Alcott oracularly observed is destiny, was his addition to its coat of arms, which he carried in a ring on his finger, of an inspiring motto to which it was not slow to respond: *Occasionem cognosce*, which he freely translated, Seize your opportunity!

BOOK II

Revolution

1
CHAPTER

Youth of the Old Judge

I N VIEW OF THE NUMBER of both John Lowells and federal judges that will come prominently into this narrative, it will be convenient to follow the family's custom of designating the John Lowell that was born in 1743, and went up from Newburyport to Harvard like his father at the age of thirteen, as the 'Old Judge.' In him we meet a very notable seizer of opportunities, including that greatest of occasions offered by Clio to her subjects, a war of revolution.

By 1756, the practice of ranking freshmen in accordance with their families' wealth and/or position had been fully established. The rise of the Lowells in the estimation of college stewards is shown by the fact that, while his father of the class of '21 was placed thirty-first in a class of thirty-one, young John of the class of '60 was put seventh in a class of twenty-seven. The college, too, had developed, and the Harvard of President Edward

43

Holyoke was a very different place from Leverett's. Beef, bread, and beer, served on wood and out of pewter, had given way to a more varied ration, on tables set with china and a sprinkling of glass and silver. Life was markedly less monastic. After a dormitory fire in 1764, students claimed the loss of feather beds, mirrors, pictures, English magazines, books of plays and other light literature, pipes, tobacco, wines, rum, gin, corkscrews, glasses, punch-bowls, chafing-dishes, wigs and curling irons, and, as Morison notes in *Three Centuries of Harvard*, one Bible.

In the curriculum steps of parallel progress had been made. Hebrew was now an elective, taken chiefly by intending clergy-men. Young John, though a true man of good will, seems, like the traditional minister's son, to have been disinterested in religious matters. We may feel sure he did not elect Hebrew. This gave him more time for the politer aspects of classical learn-ing, and for the study and practice of forensic composition and delivery which were becoming an important feature in the four years of the course. There, like so many of the leaders of the Revolution, the lawyers and judges, even some of the rabble-rousers, he cut his oratorical teeth.

Of his daily life at college we know little. He applied himself creditably to his studies. All his life a good mixer, and a judge of points of Madeira as well as of law, he undoubtedly figured in the social life that centred around those punch-bowls. Exer-cise in the open air was in his time confined to walking, skating on the frozen Charles, fishing it in summer, and fowling along its reedy margins in the autumn. There is no evidence of any Lowell taking an interest in field sports before the middle of the next century, but they were all great walkers, many of them good runners. We may safely visualize the young Old Judge taking the air in tramps — surely not solitary — to Waverly Oaks and around Fresh Pond, or doing the round trip of six miles to the Charlestown Ferry to pay his respects to the young ladies of Boston's fashionable North End. They were the age of sub-debs today.

His bosom friend was young Jonathan Jackson of the class of '61, also from Newburyport. So devoted were they that they took a mutual vow of perpetual celibacy. Some years later in one evening in Salem they broke it together in a double wedding — a *partie carrée*. Jove must have laughed when Jonathan married twice and John thrice, each becoming the father of nine children. But the male twain could have laughed last when John's son by his second wife, Francis Cabot Lowell, was married to Jonathan's daughter, Hannah, by his first.

In July, 1760, after a Commencement made colorful by gold-laced hats and coats, some of them His Majesty's scarlet, the gleam of thousands of polished silver shoe and knee buckles, and soft cheeks rosier than usual for the excitement and the potent punch that was ladled out under a score of private tents, our judge *in posse*, the second scholar in his class, entered the office of the celebrated Oxenbridge Thacher in Boston, for three years of reading law. The most distinguished lawyer of his day, Thacher was the leader of a group that deplored the growing strain in relations between the colonies and the mother country. He was one of those in the mind of the lively and observant Lieutenant Thomas Anbury when he wrote in his journal [1] after being captured by the ragged Continentals at Saratoga:

'But had certain persons, who were actuated by no other motives than a welfare and prosperity to both countries, directed their resolves, they would have advised a peaceable submission to the Mother Country, and easily prevented all the horrors of a civil war. . . . I am fully persuaded in my own mind, had they but reserved their ideas of independency for half a century longer, from their increase of population and wealth, they would have fixed it without much difficulty, or even the assistance of any other power, and thus become the first nation in the world.

[1] It has recently been discovered that Anbury's *Travels through the Interior Parts of America* contains numerous passages quoted or paraphrased without credit from other works. These, however, make it hardly less valuable, certainly not less readable and interesting. See *A Note on Eighteenth Century Plagiarism* by Whitfield J. Bell, Papers of the Bibliographical Society of America.

In the present day, if they attain their boasted end, it must be by the arm of some nation, to whom, for want of resources to defray the expenses of their alliance, she will be in continual broils and disputes, which may perhaps finally terminate in a total subjection, and that abject slavery they so ridiculously pretend to dread from us. Should this be the case, she will regret the loss of that protection from the Mother Country she is now treating with so much ingratitude. Leaving you to your own remarks, for no doubt you will say, "a soldier and a Politician!" I shall divert your attention from the cabals of mankind, to the wonderful productions of nature, in describing to you a little animal that was brought me lately, called a flying-squirrel.'

This passage, with its good short-range, bad long-range prophecy, its foreshadowing of the Federalist fear of danger from France, bears a striking similarity to the ideas expressed in Oxenbridge Thacher's *Sentiments of a British American* which perhaps the Lieutenant had been reading.

Early in 1764, Thacher drafted an address to King George presenting an itemized account of the cost of the recent war to the people of the Bay Colony with a convincing argument against the increase of their taxes without their representation or consent. Later in the same year he printed it for home consumption in pamphlet form, somewhat abbreviated but with 'Sentiments' added that expressed the feeling of perhaps a majority of the professional men — lawyers, ministers, and doctors. He points out that 'Trade is a nice and delicate lady; she must be courted and won by soft and fair addresses. She will not bear the rude hand of a ravisher.' He pictures the global possibilities of imperial trade, and concludes with the ardent hope 'that the English Empire, united by the strongest bonds of love and interest, formidable to Tyrants and Oppressors of the Earth, may retain its own virtues and happily possess Immortality.'

There is evidence that John Lowell's close association with Thacher at the impressionable age of seventeen to twenty influenced his thought and made him slow to accept the necessity of revolution, and quick to set to work to heal the wounds of war when it was over.

Less than six months after he settled down to the reading of his Coke's *Institutes* came an opportunity to be seized. George II, that not very distinguished Hanoverian king, died on October 28, 1760, and was succeeded by his grandson as George III. The news reached Boston late in December. On January 1, 1761, the Reverend Doctor Henry Caner, rector of the Episcopalian King's Chapel, preached a memorial sermon from Ecclesiastes VII, 14: 'In the day of prosperity be joyful, but in the day of adversity consider: God also hath set the one aim against the other, to the end that man shall find nothing after him.'

Before him sat Governor Bernard, His Majesty's Council, the House of Representatives, and almost certainly John Lowell. The preacher was eloquent in praise of the departed monarch, and in expressions of loyalty to his successor, though, as he regretfully admitted, 'Every government will have some discontented spirits and every prince subjects of less loyalty and attachment than may be wished.'

The young law student was impressed and inspired. He went home and, having had practice in composing very fugitive poems of the school of Queen Anne, put the sentiments of the sermon into a hundred lines of verse in the couplet of Pope, to be printed in a volume of *Pietas et Gratulatio* by the Harvard Press. It begins:

> 'While through the British world great George's name,
> With mournful accents fills the voice of fame,
> Remotest nations catch the doleful sound,
> And groans re-echo at the deep-felt wound.'

Remembering that the Seven Years' War was reaching its triumphant end, the concluding lines for George III have some truth as well as poetry.

> 'While at his feet her conq'ring armies bend,
> And his command his thundering fleets attend.

Long may he reign, his rightful sceptre bear,
And Britain's crown in peace distinguished wear.
While all her free-born sons in chorus sing —
Happy and glorious ever live the King.'

This is fluent, correct, and in the mode. It lacks the touching sincerity of Old Percival on Governor Winthrop. It is not on the same poetic plane as the Lincoln strophe in a very famous if perhaps overrated 'Commemoration Ode' by one of his descendants, but it does show a ready and clever rhyming talent for a youth of seventeen. One doubts if many seventeen-year-olds of today could match it.

In the summer of 1763, having completed his legal studies and been admitted to practice at the bar, he recognized another occasion and returned to Newburyport, where Jonathan Jackson, who was soon to inherit a fortune of twenty thousand pounds and marry the daughter of Patrick Tracy, the town's richest citizen, was already established as a shipowner and importer of English merchandise. The compact waterside town with its three thousand inhabitants, separately incorporated in the following year, to which he came back to live under his father's roof, was very different from the sprawling Newbury so engagingly described by Samuel Sewall a century earlier.

In his *Travels through New England*, dictated one by one to the entire student body, President Timothy Dwight of Yale pictures it as he saw it not many years after John Lowell hung out his shingle:

'The houses, taken collectively, make a better appearance than those of any other town in New England. Many of them are particularly handsome. Their appendages also unusually neat. Indeed, an air of wealth, taste and elegance, is spread over this beautiful spot, to which I know no rival. . . . From the tower of the church belonging to the fifth Congregation, a noble prospect is presented to the spectator. On the west and south, spreads an extensive champaign country, ornamented with good farmers' houses, orchards, and cultivated fields, and varied by a number of beautiful hills. Behind them rise, remotely, two mountains, finely connecting the landscape with the sky. On the north flows the Merrimack, visible about four miles; exhibiting two islands in its bosom, near the point, where it first appears; and joining the ocean between two sand banks, on which are erected two movable Light houses. On the North shore stand the towns of Salisbury and Amesbury. Behind this the country rises gradually, parted into a variety of eminences; one of them, which from its appropriation by the savages, is called Powow Hill, particularly handsome. Over all these ascends at the distance of twenty-five miles, the round summit of Agamenticus. North eastward, the Isles of Shoals appear at the distance of eight leagues, like a cloud in the horizon. Eastward the ocean spreads illimitably. At a small distance from the shore, Plum Island, a wild and fantastical sand beach, is thrown up by the joint power of winds and waves into the thousand wanton figures of a snowdrift. Immediately beneath is the town itself, which with its churches and beautiful houses, its harbor and shipping, appears as the proper centre of this circle of scenery, and leaves on the mind a cheerfulness and brilliancy, strongly resembling that which accompanies a delightful morning in May.'

The cheerfulness of a May morning was in the business air, too. After the Peace of Paris, concluding the French War, trade everywhere was booming, and Newburyport, with her three shipyards, numerous ropewalks, and ten distilleries, was getting her share. Almost at once, perhaps by the good offices of Jonathan Jackson, John secured the legal business of the town's two leading merchants, Patrick Tracy and Tristram Dalton, with an inside opportunity for an occasional trading venture of his own. His fiscal rise was rapid. In January, 1767, he married Sarah Higginson, the daughter of Stephen Higginson and Elizabeth Cabot Higginson of Salem. This was the first of three marriages, not for money, but all contracted where, as the phrase is, 'money was'; also in each case, the profitable legal business of a large and well-to-do family.

He was making a reputation in criminal cases, too. In his decade in Newburyport, before moving to Boston, he was counsel for the defense in fifteen murder cases. Two of these noted by his son fifty years later are of special interest.

'Dom. Rex vs Ames & al — against a mother-in-law for poisoning her son's wife. A very distinguished case — one of as great excitement as that of Fairbanks in 1802 for murdering the lady to whom he was engaged which I had the misfortune to argue. I have this case of Ames *in extenso* — J. Adams was with my father — in 1769 I presume, as my father's argument is partly written on a recognizence of that year's date. He was then twenty-six years of age.'

'Dom. Rex vs Wilkins, Hillsborough, N. H. for murder, a most touching case which called out all my father's peculiar power of moving the tenderest feelings — A son for the murder of his father — The whole *witnesses of the family*. The father declared before his death the son did not kill him, or rather inflict the blow. The others swore he did — It was a noble case for an able and eloquent man.'

But it was the case of Dom. Rex vs Ames & al that was of the greater historical interest, involving as it did the last recorded instance in Massachusetts of the ancient 'Ordeal of Touch.'

In December, 1768, Jonathan Ames of Boxford married Ruth, the oldest daughter of the widow, Ruth Perley. Unwisely, as it turned out, he took his bride home to live with his own parents. Relations between the elder and younger Mrs. Ames were not sympathetic. In May a child was born and a few days later the young mother died and was expeditiously buried. The neighbors, none of whom had been invited to the funeral, became suspicious, accusations of murder were made, and a coroner's inquest was held in the meeting house which stood in the pasture beside the cemetery. The church was packed. The court was opened with prayer, the coroner gave the jury their solemn charge, and the entire company proceeded to the burying ground and the body of the bride was exhumed. After the entire 'promiscuous multitude' had inspected the remains, they were carried to the meeting house, where an autopsy was performed and the jury brought in their verdict that Ruth Ames 'came to her death by a felony, that is to say by a poison given to her by a person or persons to them unknown, which murder is against the Peace of our said Lord, the King, his Crown and Dignity.'

When it was found that evidence was insufficient to hold either the husband of the murdered girl or his mother, demands were made for the then almost extinct English institution of the Ordeal of Touch. The body was laid upon the table with a sheet over it, and Jonathan and his mother were invited to establish their innocence. The suspected party was required to touch the neck of the deceased with the index finger of the left hand. If he were guilty, it was believed that blood would immediately incarnadine the whiteness of the sheet. Mother and son steadfastly refused to undergo the ordeal. From this it was concluded that they were guilty. They were arrested and confined in the Old Jail in Salem, which had held the poor bodies accused of witchcraft nearly a century before. Jonathan Ames turned King's evidence against his mother. It was midnight before the counsel began their arguments. In giving the case to the jury two of the three judges in summing up the evidence stated that there was 'a violent presumption of guilt,' but at nine the next morning the jury came in with a verdict of not guilty. The first and very notable example of the ability and eloquence of John Lowell in the courtroom!

In May, 1767, his father, the minister of the Third Parish, died, and his stepmother, Elizabeth Whipple, moved to Portsmouth. The young couple of twenty-four and twenty-two took over the neat white house in Greenleaf Lane, and there his son, the so-called 'Rebel' was born. Sarah died in 1772. After her death, having sold his father's house for nine hundred and twenty pounds, John, in preparation for the reception of a new bride, joined with Jonathan Jackson in the building of the twin mansion houses which, as numbers 201 and 203, are still among the chief

ornaments of Newburyport's handsome High Street. John
Adams, always a little jealous of the financial success of other
men, wrote to his Abigail: 'He has built himself a palace like a
nobleman's, and lives in great splendor.' To it he took his
second wife, Susanna Cabot of Salem, the mother of two more of
his children, one of whom, Francis Cabot Lowell, was to found
the widespread fortunes of the family.

It was an impressive residence for a young man of thirty, and
it is perhaps the only house ever built or bought by any Lowell
with the idea of impressing, or other desire than that of space
and comfort for a large family.

Four-square, three-storied, rather like Elmwood but larger,
standing well back of the south side of High Street, it is bisected
by a stately hall eleven by forty feet, from which ascends one of
the noble staircases of the place and period, with three different
balusters to each broad step, repeating themselves upward in
pleasing *terza rima*. On either side are large square rooms each
with its capacious fireplace and ornate overmantel. Although
it fronts on a busy street, the view from the back is over a mile or
more of sloping meadow to a distant wood.

Soon after John Lowell had sold this house in 1778 to Patrick
Tracy for ten thousand pounds (depreciated currency) and
moved to Boston, the Marquis de Chastellux of the French
Academy, with MM. de Montesquieu, de Talleyrand, and de
Vaudreuil, relatives of more famous bearers of those names,
stopping at the Wolfe Tavern, were invited to dine by John
Tracy, who was then occupying it. Even they were impressed.

'The house,' wrote de Chastellux in the narrative of his travels,
'is very handsome and well furnished, and everything breathes
that air of magnificence accompanied by simplicity which is only
to be found among merchants.' His account of the evening's
entertainment colors the picture:

'Towards midnight the ladies withdrew, but we continued
drinking Madeira and Xery. M. Tracy according to the customs
of the country offered us pipes which were accepted by M. de

Talleyrand and M. de Montesquieu, the consequence of which was that they became intoxicated and were led home where they were happy to get to bed. As to myself I remained perfectly cool and continued to converse on trade and politics.' [1]

Who was it that led MM. de Talleyrand and de Montesquieu home to the tavern and put them to bed? It should have been the colored slave remembered in Patrick Tracy's will, with the usufruct of a small cabin on the place and six pounds per year for life, under the simple and fitting name of Apropos.

Apropos, so paternally dealt with, was, owing in some measure to John Lowell, the last Negro slave in the town. In 1773, he took the case of one Caesar Hendrick, a 'mulatto man,' against Richard Greenleaf, for 'holding him in bondage,' and secured a verdict releasing him with damages to the pleasant tune of eighteen pounds. A year later Jonathan Jackson gave his own black servingman, Pomp, a bill of sale of himself for a token payment of five shillings. Pomp proved a good soldier in the Continental Army.

These abolitionist activities, which were widely bruited through the Bay Colony, doubtless gave rise to the legend that John Lowell, as a member of the State Constitutional Convention in 1779, was responsible for the insertion of the clause which was later held by the Supreme Judicial Court to make slavery unconstitutional in the Commonwealth: 'All men are born free and equal and have certain inalienable rights, among which may be reckoned the right of enjoying and defending their lives and their liberties.' But substantially the same language had been used much earlier in the constitutions of Pennsylvania, and even of Virginia. It seems unlikely that the useful clause could have escaped the attention of John Adams, who drafted the Massachusetts document. The phrases that were the tonic

---

[1] Chastellux had a neat wit and must have given the ladies, before they discreetly retired at midnight, a thoroughly good time. At the age of eighty-three, Voltaire, in a fiery speech before the Academy on the need of a revision of the French Dictionary, concluded, 'I thank you, gentlemen, in the name of the alphabet.' 'And we, Sir,' replied Chastellux, who was in the chair, 'thank you in the name of letters.'

chords of the sentence, 'free and equal' and 'inalienable rights,' came echoing down from John Locke and Rousseau through the Declaration of Independence.

While John Lowell was acquiring ease, affluence, and position in his so delightful town, he was, as has been foreshadowed, beginning to exercise a native leadership in local and colonial politics.

The oppressive and obnoxious Stamp Act, passed in 1765, one of the last of George Grenville's government, to make the colonies pay their share of the cost of the Old French War and generally put them in their place, was repealed in '66; but in '67, Parliament, in demonstration of its right to levy and collect taxes, imposed in the Townshend Act a heavy duty on paper, glass, tea, and other necessary articles imported into the Province of Massachusetts Bay, while the necessities of the Southern colonies were spared. The powerful and belligerent merchants of Boston immediately put through an agreement to import no more goods from Great Britain, and sent out, through their selectmen, a circular letter asking the merchants of the other towns to take a similar step, and stop the sale of all goods on which the objectionable duties had already been paid.

This presented to Newburyport a more serious problem than to the other towns. Its chief industry was building ships; the principal purchasers of the ships were the seagoing traders of England; payment for the ships was in articles of British manufacture. Non-importation of such would therefore ruin the shipyards, and perhaps the town itself. Consternation swept through the stores of Fish Street and the mansions of the High. At a meeting of the townspeople, December 17, 1767, a committee of seven was appointed to prepare an answer to the Boston selectmen. John Lowell, though only twenty-four, was named first, perhaps as chairman; other members included Patrick Tracy, Tristram Dalton, and Jonathan Jackson.

A report written by John Lowell was accepted at a town meeting three months later. After forcibly setting forth the peculiar difficulties of the situation for Newburyport, and the hardship of forcing a population to 'suddenly strike into a new Channel and carry on a business to which they have always been strangers,' it went on:

'Hence tho' we highly respect the Town of Boston for its zealous attachment to the Liberties of the Country and are ready to assist them in all measures to which Prudence may direct, we cannot think it can consist with their particular Resolutions relating to the importations and purchase of the enumerated articles of British Manufactures, and not only from this Principle but from one less selfish we cannot wish that the frequent and mutual Intercourse which has hitherto subsisted between Great Britain and us should abate. Tis but of late Date that we regarded Great Britain with all the respectful affection of a Child to its Parent, and tho by some late measures which we conceive to be highly misjudged there seems to have arisen a cloud which obscures the true Interests of the Nation from the eyes of those at the Helm we cannot but expect as well as impatiently desire that it will be soon removed and a Mutual Confidence be established on the firmest Foundation.

'In the mean Time as Jealousy in a Constitution like the British is the great preserving Principle, we think it necessary to be watchfull against any Encroachments on our Rights as Englishmen or Freemen and to be uniformly and resolutely determined that these shall not be infringed while our Fortunes or even our Lives continue.'

Here speaks the able advocate of the interest of his town, the ex-student in the office of conciliatory Oxenbridge Thacher, and a lifelong exemplar of Franklin's policy of seizing the stick by the soft end, and making diplomatic concessions to contrary schools of thought.

There can be no doubt that at this time John Lowell felt, with a million or more of the three million inhabitants of the colonies, that war with the mother country would be the greatest of calamities. The sentiment of the town was with him. For six years he had the support of his fellow citizens and was three times elected a selectman. In 1774, however, he found himself out of tune with the martial music of the hour. On May 24 of that year he appears as one of twenty-two barristers and attorneys-at-law who signed a farewell address to Governor Thomas Hutchinson on his recall to London 'for consultation.' The address praised Hutchinson's 'wise, zealous, and faithful administration,' its 'amicable character,' a 'fresh instance of the paternal goodness of our most gracious Sovereign.' It suggested that the returning governor would employ his interest at court 'for the relief of the town of Boston from its present distresses.'

A month later he was one of a group of twenty-eight of slightly different composition to sign a similar address of welcome to the arriving governor, General Gage. Of the signers of these conciliatory documents, many were to betake themselves to Halifax in March, 1776, but the majority remained with the patriotic cause. Their attitude was identical with that of John Dickinson of Pennsylvania, a signer of the Declaration of Independence, who, up to the last desperate minute, had pinned his hopes on the powerful championship of Edmund Burke and worked for conciliation.

As for John Lowell, he found that he had unleashed a whirlwind. There was a storm of protest, cries of 'King-lover' and 'Tory.' The trouble grew throughout the summer and fall, and he must have given deep consideration to his future course. Temperamentally and by inheritance and early training, he was of the conservative type from which Tories were made. As far back as 1666, two Lowells from Old Newbury had signed a petition to the General Court to follow 'the advice of the wise man to keep the King's commandment.' In 1690, a Samuel Lowell had gone back to Bristol, preferring monarchy to theocracy. For forty years his own father from the high pulpit of the church in Market Square had petitioned the Almighty to preserve the health of the reigning monarch, and the cases he had pleaded so eloquently in court were under the jurisdiction of

Dominus Rex. Of three hundred Tories formally banished from the Commonwealth in 1778, sixty were graduates of Harvard College. John Lowell might easily have been one of them had not his alert mind and intuitive insight into popular movements given him a vision of the great new things that might be in store for the people of America. Perhaps he was not unaware of fresh opportunities that would be offered for seizure by able young men.

On the day after Christmas, 1774, he sent to the *Essex Journal and Merrimack Packet* the following unconventional, manly, yet rather pathetic letter which was printed in the next weekly issue:

'To the Inhabitants of Newburyport.

'As I find cut on your minds an ill impression of me on account of my having signed an address to Governor Hutchinson, which I am desirous of removing, I can truly say, that when I did this, I flattered myself, I was serving the interest of my country, and that it would have a tendency to your relief; I never wished to have any of your liberties abridged, or any unconstitutional power submitted to, but on the contrary, am ever ready to join in preventing such mischief; I was far from being aware that this step would have given the uneasiness I am sensible it has, or could be made use of to injure the country —; if I had I never should have taken it, and am heartily sorry I ever did.

'John Lowell.'

The letter was well received; before the next year was out, he was re-elected selectman as well as to more important offices, and on Wednesday, April 19, the muskets of Concord were heard around the world announcing the decision between peace and war.

Two days later, Newburyport had its own war-scare. On Friday afternoon, just as the Reverend Thomas Cary was opening with a prayer a meeting of citizens at the town house to consider the great news, a dusty messenger, one Ebenezer Todd, rushed in, shouting, 'For God's sake turn out! Turn out! Turn out! Or you will all be killed. The regulars are at Ipswich and will soon be here, cutting and slashing all before them.'

The news spread like wildfire, and there was a general and very hasty exodus to the north. One young woman, after running four or five miles, stopped on the steps of a meeting house to suckle the child in her arms and found to her horror that she had brought the cat instead. Yet the hour was not without its heroes. According to recorded local tradition, Mr. J—— L——, no surname mentioned, seeing Mr. C—— H——, a very corpulent man, standing at his door loading a musket, inquired if he were not going. 'Going? No,' said he; 'I am going to stop and shoot the devils!'

In the early evening the panic was quelled by the arrival of a messenger from Ipswich, riding the twelve miles in the excellent time of fifty minutes, with authoritative news that no redcoats were in evidence anywhere north of Boston.

Nothing could have been more effective in stimulating enlistment and other preparations for war. Two companies were raised immediately, and later increased to a regiment of four companies under the command of Colonel Jonathan Titcomb. John Lowell was for a time major and adjutant. Military drill began under the guidance of the basic soldiers' handbook of the Revolution, *An Easy Plan for the Discipline of Militia*, by Timothy Pickering, future chief of the Essex Junto and John Adams's Secretary of State. On September 19 he saw Colonel Benedict Arnold set sail down the Merrimack on the expedition against Quebec, with thirteen hundred men in eleven sloops and schooners. As Joseph Ware of Needham wrote in his diary: 'Early this morning weighed anchor with a pleasant gale, our colours flying, drums and fifes playing, and the hills all around covered with pretty girls weeping for their departed swains.'

John Lowell, however, was to prove more useful to his town and commonwealth as a lawmaker than as a man of war. As a selectman he was *ex officio* a member of the Committee of Safety, of which Jonathan Jackson was chairman. In April, 1776, he was chosen delegate to a county convention at Ipswich to prepare a more equitable plan for the representation of the towns in the General Court. He drafted a memorial which a month later he presented in person, having in the meantime been elected to that potent body. His plan provided for the election of three representatives from towns of two hundred and twenty freeholders, and an additional representative for each additional one hundred freeholders. The act was passed and seems to have worked well. He also put through a bill for the fortification of Newburyport's harbor, soon to become of importance as the home and hideout of a hundred privateers. This was to be his final service to his ancestral town. At the end of the year he removed to action on a broader stage in Boston.

On his departure the only Lowells left by the Merrimack were Captain Abner Lowell's family of the Richard Lowell line from Old Percival. After distinguished service as a commander of an armed sloop employed as a naval scout vessel, involving at least one report in person to the commander-in-chief, Captain Abner was appointed by President Washington keeper of Plum Island Light. For half a century he, his son, Lewis, remembered for many gallant rescues, and his grandson, Joseph, walked the long beach on bitter winter nights, and faithfully tended the light that guided and welcomed Newbury sailors home from all the Seven Seas.

2
CHAPTER

Swelling Pocketbooks

W HAT THE TOWN OF BOSTON had come to look like by the historic year of 1776 can be seen today by a walk through the older streets of Newburyport or Portsmouth. The high-gabled houses of weathering pine that Old Percival had known, and Ebenezer had lived and traded in, were beginning to give place to rows of red brick. On the prominent corners stood Georgian mansion houses of stone, or of clapboards of weathered golden-brown or painted red or white, grey or yellow, as the owner fancied. With its many green squares and gardens Boston offered to the eye nearly all the colors of the rainbow.

It occupied a quarter of an almost-island of eleven hundred acres, shaped menacingly like a closed fist with a very slender wrist. In Blackstone's pre-colony time the likeness was enhanced by five knuckle-like hills, but before the Revolution these had been pared down to three. The highest, Beacon Hill, 'Mount

Whoredom' its western shoulder was called, dominated the scene, though to a soldier's eye it was commanded on the north by Bunker Hill, and on the south by the heights of South Boston and Dorchester. To travel west, one started north by ferry to Charlestown and thence by road to Cambridge, or, alternatively, south over a mile by cart track, if not submerged by high autumnal tides, across the neck to Roxbury and so to Brookline. To the east one still went most easily by boat. Along the line of the present Charles Street curved the marshy beach of the Back Bay, where the British troops embarked for Cambridge en route to Lexington and Concord, and Boston's leading sportsman, Colonel Thomas Handasyd Perkins, enjoyed excellent snipe shooting for a generation. Paul Revere's [1] well-known print of Boston shows twelve spires, others have sixteen; not shown are the thirty establishments where superior New England rum was distilled from hogsheads of Cuban molasses to retail at four pence the quart. All prints show the long wharves and sail-flecked harbor of a thriving seaport.

On the seventeenth of March in that wonderful year, General Howe, having had a good look at the heights to the south frowning with the cannon the fat brave Boston bookseller, Knox, John Lowell's friend and client, had dragged down through the snow from Ticonderoga, left with his troops for Halifax. He carried many distinguished passengers, and large well-placed houses stood empty on the best corner lots. Exactly when John Lowell came down from Newburyport to occupy one of these is uncertain. His son, John, the 'Rebel,' in a newspaper communication half a century later, written to vindicate his father's memory from an injurious and silly charge of having been an *émigré*, says it was within ten days after Lord Howe evacuated the town. He came, he says, 'in consequence of the number of lawyers who

---

[1] Any reader who would like the experience of living in Revolutionary Boston, with its agitations and pleasures, sights and sounds and smells, may do so by spending his evenings for a week or two with Esther Forbes's *Paul Revere and the World He Lived In*.

became refugees or went into public life.' An obvious opportunity.[1]

It is evident from the several offices the Old Judge held in and for Newburyport through the balance of the year that he kept a residence there at least till the end of 1776, but he may very well have opened a law office in Boston before the end of March. In December his family was living with his wife's people, the Cabots, in Salem. His fifth child, Susanna, was born there on the twenty-eighth, and there its mother died in the following March. William Pynchon noted in his diary that her funeral cortège was headed by a distinguished group of bearers that included 'H. Derby, J. Derby, and Mr. Pickman.'

The following day John Lowell wrote to his brother-in-law, William Cabot, of his sister's 'great and long continued pain,' and concluded rather philosophically: 'That lively hope with which she expected Death and realized future Happiness make it selfish to wish her to stay in this scene of Perplexity, Sorrow, and Despair.'

Soon after this, a widower of thirty-four with five children, he moved into one of the most attractive houses in Boston. The former home of John Amory, it stood on the northwest corner of Tremont and Beacon Streets directly opposite King's Chapel, designed and built by Peter Harrison a generation before; dour and dignified without, harmonious and reposeful within. Its rector, the Reverend Doctor Caner, had left for Halifax with Lord Howe, taking with him the sacramental silver, which has not been heard of since. As some of it was the special gift of George III in return for that memorial sermon, perhaps he thought he was within his rights. The Amory house, for which John Lowell paid the state the reasonable rent of forty pounds a year, was an oblong of three stories set well back from both streets in a lot that measured 68 by 170 feet. The long frontage faced the easy

---

[1] He was already known in Boston as a sound man of business. In 1774, in the will of Josiah Quincy the elder he was named as an executor along with Francis Dana, Jonathan Jackson, William Phillips, and John Adams.

ascent of Beacon Street. To the north behind the Amory peach orchard, also vacant, stood the residence of Doctor John Jeffries, who was to fly the English Channel in a balloon in 1785. For a time the house seems to have served John Lowell for his office as well. Much of his public business was carried on with the Committee of Correspondence, the actual political headquarters of the Revolution, in Lieutenant Governor Oliver's former elegant mansion at the farther end of Tory Row in Cambridge. Under the name of Elmwood it was to become the most publicized of Lowell homes.

According to the text of the Reverend Delmar Lowell's *Genealogy*, John Lowell married his third wife, Rebecca, the thirty-year-old widow of James Tyng of Dunstable, and daughter of the Honorable Judge James Russell of Charlestown, on Christmas Day, 1778. In a late *erratum* he suggests that owing to the confusion of calendars perhaps the date of the marriage should have been June 27 instead of December 25. Made at thirty-five it was the happiest of his alliances. Rebecca was charming, wise, and sympathetic. She gave the Old Judge four more children, and, surviving him by fourteen years, was deeply loved and cherished by all branches of the growing Lowell-Higginson-Cabot-Jackson clan. John Lowell, the 'Rebel,' the only son of Sarah Higginson Lowell, wrote in his diary when at the age of nine, a sensitive, and despite a little brother and three sisters, a lonely child, he was brought from the schoolroom to be presented to his new mother:

'If ever an angel has appeared upon Earth, one has come down now!'

Meanwhile, the elder John Lowell, the old Judge, prospered at the Bar. From the beginning he acted as legal adviser to the commission that was handling the confiscated Tory estates, and its accounts are sprinkled with payments to him of thirty shillings for drawing deeds for the sale of their houses. Some of the sales were at auction, where a standard item of cost was 'Liquor £15.' But real-estate law was small beer compared with the prize cases brought in by privateer owners, most of whom were his friends or in-laws. Privateering in two wars with Old England, though by no means always profitable, was the source of some New England fortunes. The Marquis de Chastellux says that Patrick Tracy told him in 1782 that in 1776 and '77 he lost forty-one ships, including the brig *Yankee Hero* of twenty guns, commanded by his son, James, which went down somewhere at sea with one hundred and seventy men — fifty of them sons of Newbury's best families, and that he was deeply in the red. He admitted, however, that his final profit from preying on the enemy's commerce came near to the useful sum of £120,000. The younger John Lowell, who was later his father's law partner, is authority for the statement that out of eleven hundred libels against prize vessels in the Boston court, the Old Judge filed seven hundred and was concerned as assistant counsel in nearly half the rest. A typical fee was that charged and received for his services in the case of the prize brig *Juno*, £72.18.6. Multiplied by seven hundred, the total sum would be not inconsiderable. Unfortunately he made later, what his son John calls 'a most disadvantageous arrangement with the enterprising adventurers of Essex,' that he would carry through their libels for fifty silver dollars in each case. From these he accumulated during the war no less than two hundred thousand dollars. This he generally accepted in paper instead of the agreed hard money and 'it stood about in cords on his table.' Still, as time went on the accretive power of a successful law office brought him in many important executorships and appointments as administrator of plump estates. Profitable, too, after the war, was his agency for numerous rich Tory *émigrés*. He was attorney and business adviser for the Hutchinsons, Coffins, Lorings, Lechmeres, Vassals, and many others living in London, or, as those from Salem preferred as more homelike, Bristol.

But it was his success as counsel for the defense in another sensational murder case that brought him his greatest repute. On the eleventh of April, 1779, Rebecca Whitney of Townsend, seemingly in perfect health, died suddenly under suspicious circumstances. Levi, her husband, was popularly suspected of poisoning her. The war was now going better, but news from the front was a fortnight in reaching Boston, and for months the Whitney case seems to have been the chief topic of conversation both in parlors and taprooms, sometimes leading in the latter to blows between those who thought he did and those who thought he didn't. After considerable delay he was arrested, indicted by the grand jury, and in November brought to trial before the Superior Court of Middlesex County sitting in Cambridge. Pleading poverty, although described as 'gentleman,' the prisoner asked that counsel be appointed to defend him. As the kindly custom then was, to make sure that justice was done, the court designated three unquestioned leaders of the Massachusetts Bar, John Lowell, John Sprague, and Theophilus Parsons. Squeezed in the crowded courtroom, an eager listener was a thirteen-year-old freshman from Harvard, young Harrison Gray Otis.

The case and its conclusion is reported in the records of the court in the following masterpiece of legal concision:

'Levi Whitney of Townsend in the County of Middlesex, Gentleman, not having the fear of God before his Eyes, on the Eleventh Day of April in the Year of our Lord Seventeen Hundred and Seventy Nine, at Townsend in the County of Middlesex aforesaid, contriving with Poison to Kill and murder Rebecah Whitney his Wife, then at said Townsend did with force and arms, feloniously, Wilfully and of his malice aforethought, mix and mingle a Great Quantity of White arsenick, being a Deadly Poison in a certain Quantity of Egg and Wine, and said Levi Whitney, knowing said White arsenick to be a Deadly poison and that the said Levi Whitney there afterwards, Viz, on the same Day the poison aforesaid so mixed, and mingled as aforesaid, with force and arms, feloniously, Wilfully, and of his malice

aforethought did offer and Give to her the said Rebecah Whitney, to take, Drink and Swallow Down, and that the said
Rebecah Whitney, not knowing the poison aforesaid to have
been mixed and mingled as aforesaid in the Egg and Wine
aforesaid, there afterward, Viz, on the same Day by the procure-
ment and perswasion of the said Livi Whitney Did take Drink,
and Swallow Down the poison so as aforesaid, taken Drank and
Swallow'd Down, then and there became Sick, and Distempered
in her Body, and that the said Rebecah Whitney of the Poison
aforesaid, and of the Distemper and Sickness thereby occasioned,
did Languish, and Languishing did Live from the morning of
the same Eleventh Day of April until the evening of the same
day on which same Eleventh Day of April in the Evening thereof
at Townsend aforesaid, in the County of Middlesex aforesaid, the
said Rebecah Whitney died of the poison aforesaid, and of the
Sickness and Distemper thereby Occasioned as aforesaid, and so
the Jurors aforesaid upon their Oath aforesaid, do say, that the
said Levi Whitney, the said Rebecah Whitney in manner and
form aforesaid, feloniously, Wilfully, and of his Malice aforethought did poison kill and murder, against the Peace and Dignity of the Government and People aforesaid: And now here
cometh the said Levi Whitney in his own proper person, under
the Custody of the Sheriff of the County of Middlesex and being
arraigned upon this Indictment, is Demanded how he will acquit
himself thereof he saith that thereof he is not Guilty, and thereof
for trial puts himself upon God and the Country, and the
Prisoner Signifying his Desire for Council, John Lowell, John
Sprague, and Theop. Parsons Esqrs. are assigned for said Purpose; And now a Jury is Impannelled and sworn to try the issue,
Viz, Noah Bowman, Foreman, and fellows namely, Edwd.
Gardner, Joseph Lynd, Elisha Livermore, John Trowbridge,
Wm. Munroe, Jonas Prescott Junr., Zebediah Rogers, John
Cutter, David Wheeler, Jonathan Foster, and Jonas Minot, who
being sworn to speak the Truth of and concerning the Premises,
who after having fully heard the evidence as well in the behalf

of the Government, as well as the Prisoner, and the Cause being fully argued by Council, upon their Oath returned the following Verdict and upon their Oath do say, that the said Levi Whitney is not Guilty, Whereupon the Prisoners Council moves that the said Levi Whitney be Discharged. It is therefore consider'd by the Court that the said Levi Whitney go Without Day.'

All this, as aforesaid, was accomplished in a single day. What evidence was offered by the defense we don't know. Young Otis thought that the favorable verdict was due to the persuasive tongue of John Lowell. Perhaps, as he wrote later of his then late senior partner's almost invariable success in court, 'He soon warmed and moved on with impassioned eloquence and vehement gesture, taking up the jury in his balloon and landing them where he pleased.'

In the same characterization Otis tries his hand at a pen portrait:

'He was about five feet ten inches in height, and inclined to corpulence. His gait was rapid and hurried, his conversation rapid and ardent. He was the very mirror of benevolence, which beamed in and made attractive a countenance not remarkable for symmetry of feature or beauty; and his companionable talents, though never displayed at the expense of dignity, made him the delight of the society in which he moved, and which he always put at ease.'

This corroborates and complements the likeness of his portraits, even to its suggestion that the subject was not ill *content de lui-même*.

On September 6, 1777, William Pynchon had written in his diary, 'Mr. Lowell in Town. Says 1400 prisoners en route from Bennington to Boston.' And three weeks later, 'Mr. Lowell says Gates writes that he has the greatest encouragement to think he shall soon rout the whole army and dispose of them.' Clearly he was *au courant* with the progress of the war as seen from headquarters, and he was soon to take part in wartime legislation.

As Burke pointed out, the American Union was governed by lawyers in the legislative and judicial branches. John Lowell was one of them. In 1778, he represented Boston in the General Court; in 1779–80, in the State Constitutional Convention, and in 1782, in the Continental Congress.

The part he took in the deliberations of the General Court seems not to have been important. In the State Constitutional Convention he ably supported his double brother-in-law by his second marriage, George Cabot, who had also married a Higginson. As chairman of the committee that examined and reported on the returns from the popular vote, Cabot seems to have so reclassified them — the Republicans said 'juggled' — that every clause received the necessary majority. The result was the first great triumph of the Federalist Party as embodied in the Essex Junto. The new constitution in effect set up Congregationalism as the state religion, doubled the property qualification for the ballot, and increased the dominance of the mercantile seaport towns. For this the Old Judge for many years was subjected to virulent attack in the Republican press. It was to him the *Independent Chronicle* was referring when it said:

'An old Tory (an addresser to Hutchinson) openly said the aristocratic party could never gain an interest in America till they enlisted the clergy on their side. They have too far succeeded.'

Forty years later, John Adams told Josiah Quincy that he regretted 'the want of an absolute negative in the Executive' in all our constitutions. He had 'sought it in Massachusetts, but Theophilus Parsons, Jackson, Lowell, and other Essex gentlemen would not injure their popularity. For what is the Constitution of the United States but that of Massachusetts, New York, and Maryland? There is not a feature in it which cannot be found in one or the other.'

The deathless phrases, 'created equal' and 'inalienable rights,' were still to be implemented by Thomas Jefferson who wrote them.

From 1779 on to the end of the war, both public and private business was taking John Lowell very frequently to Philadelphia, the political, social, and artistic capital of the embattled colonies. To this separation from his Rebecca we owe a series of love letters warmer and more revealing than were commonly composed at that period by the rather inhibited colonials. On October 18, 1779, while in Philadelphia on legal business concerning some Cabot-owned ships, he writes:

'My best beloved Girl:

'I had determined as I have written twice within the last three Days, and intend writing by a private Opportunity tomorrow, which Letter I expect will reach you before the Post, to have let none pass without one; but the Possibility that the others may fail, and this reach you, induced me to take my Pen in hand; and at that Moment the arrival of the Eastern Post being announced I flew to the Office, and there received the dear testimonial of your returning health. . . .'

(At this point two lines have been heavily inked out by some modest hand.)

'Its glowing warmth, would have been sufficient to have convinced the most sceptical Infidel; such a soulful feast I would not part with for every enjoyment of any other Kind that the Wealth of Croesus could furnish. Indeed, my dearest Love I am happy beyond Expression — and even beyond the Understanding of any but those who have themselves the endearing Connection of exalted Friendship softened and made highly delicate by a union of the nuptial kind, by which are ineffably blended every personal and relative interest. I have such ardent Desire to remove the painfull Sensations you experience from my Absence, as well as to gratify my supreme wishes of pouring my whole soul into your bosom, that I leave no Means untried to bring an end to my present Engagement here to fly to a *Home* that contains all I have and all I *wish*. But tho we have now begun the trial of our causes, yet the engagements of the judges

who hear us only from seven in the evening till ten I am sensible
will protract my Stay much longer than I intended or at first
hoped.　By the Post of next week I hope to be able to form a
probable Conjecture when I shall make as rapid a Progress as
the Season and Roads will permit, and I can't help flattering
myself that four Weeks may place me at my own fireside.

'The Post Hour is come.　May every Blessing attend the Beloved of my Heart.　My sincere Love and let the Children know
I never forget them or the Testimony I have of their good Behavior.

　　　　　　　　　　　　　　　　　'Your very affec.

　　　　　　　　　　　　　　　　　　　　　　　'J. Lowell.'

Again in 1782, when a member of the Continental Congress,
he writes from Philadelphia to his 'Dearest Girl':

'. . . Like most other Theatres when you are once behind the
Scene the Movements appear so little extraordinary that the Eye
of Curiosity once abated everything appears common — there
appears to me to be but few great and not many little People
among us — they are generally of the middle size. . . .

'I am now looking out with eager Impatience for W. Jackson.
I have for so great a Part of my Life been used to an unbounded
Communication of Thought to a faithfull Bosom that when I
cannot have that near me which from every concurrent cause
furnishes the best repose for the Mind after Fatique or Enjoyment I feel too great a Vacuity to be supplied even tolerably by
any other substitute than its next best Counterpart — a tried
and valuable Friend. . . .

'I send two Pincushions for Nancy and Salley.　They are not
very valuable but they will receive them as the Tokens of an
absent and affectionate Father who promises himself much
Enjoyment from their Virtues, Providence having given them the
Power of being good and in Consequence Happy, but more of
being agreeable and rendering others happy — My Love to the
other Children.'

In Philadelphia he lived in the same house with James Madison and they became warm friends. Politics that makes strange bedfellows also puts strange swords in friendly beds. John, the Rebel, his son, was to make Madison the object of his bitterest attacks, but when the passions of war were over, Madison bore no grudge against the family. In a letter written much later, John tells how his brother, Charles, always a seeker-out of eminent men, went to call on the ex-President in his retirement at Montpelier on the eastern slope of the Blue Ridge. 'When he left him Mr. Madison accompanied him some miles out of respect probably to his professional character and perhaps struck with his deportment. When my brother left him, Charles said to him, "I believe you knew my father." Who was he? "He was the late Judge Lowell." Madison's eyes filled with tears, he chid him for concealing the fact while at his home, and insisted on his going back and spending some days with him, which my brother was obliged to decline. Madison said that he lived in the same house with my father in Phila. and spoke in terms of the highest respect and regard for his virtues and talents.'

Like all Lowells the Old Judge was an ardent lover of his own fireside, but also like many of them he was not averse to moving it about. In December, 1780, the commissioners for Tory estates were simplifying their business and raising money for the prosecution of the war, by disposing of many desirable houses under an odd arrangement by which the tenant made a payment against future rent, and apparently took title, but agreed to 'surrender quietly' when the payment had been entirely worked out by the income. On this basis John Lowell, for a payment of £270 and a continued annual rent of £40, took title to the Amory house. Two years later, Samuel Eliot, Amory's agent, who was to marry as his second wife Catherine Atkinson and become the grandfather of Harvard's second most effective president, took it over for his residence. The Old Judge, however, did not leave the neighborhood. Just across Tremont Street on the north side of King's Chapel burying ground stood the rough-cast half-timbered residence of Doctor Caner, the former rector. Under the 1780 plan this had been taken by one Samuel Henley for a payment of £235 against a rent of £30. In April, 1782, Henley bought it again, this time outright for £750, and resold it a few months later for a sum unspecified to John Lowell. From its three tiers of sunny southern windows John and Rebecca and the eight children could still admire the architecture of King's Chapel, seen now in profile like a lion *couchant*, across the tombs and monuments of Boston's early soldiers, ministers, and governors.

His first year at the new address, 41 Tremont Street, the last year of the war, was a busy and prosperous one, in which at the age of forty he finally ascended the bench. Congress appointed him one of three judges of appeals in admiralty cases, a post for which his experience in maritime law peculiarly fitted him. He heard arguments in the Bunch of Grapes Tavern on State Street, arrayed as William Pynchon notes in a silken robe of scarlet, adding, rather wickedly, *forma saepe dat esse*.

In the same year he achieved settlement in a case he had been conducting with that gallant soldier and wise administrator, Sir Guy Carleton, who had succeeded Sir Henry Clinton as British governor of New York. The citizens of Martha's Vineyard had put in a claim for £7923 in payment of money due them for cattle, sheep, and hay supplied in September, 1778, to General Grey for the British fleet. In July, 1782, Judge Lowell finally secured from Sir Guy a cash payment of three thousand pounds, which proved satisfactory. He found time also to order Paul Revere to design and cut a seal for the New Phillips Academy at Andover where his son, John, was preparing for Harvard College.

In the fall of 1783, as the treaty of peace between England and the newly United States was being signed at Paris, he went to New York and Philadelphia accompanied by his legal acolyte, young Harrison Gray Otis, as secretary and companion. 'The whole journey was a continued scene of pleasant and instructive

conversation, sparkling anecdotes and poetical quotations.'
In New York he was entertained by Sir Guy Carleton at a dinner, 'as brilliant,' says Otis, 'as Alexander's feast.' In his companion's opinion the Old Judge was the life of the party.

After the conclusion of peace with the mother country, the
former colonial children, newly on their own, a little intoxicated
with independence, set out upon new adventures. In the late
autumn of 1783, John Lowell, having purchased in Philadelphia
a pair of prancing carriage horses from John Paul Jones, then of
Bethlehem, Pennsylvania, and perhaps assisted him in the collection of 181,000 livres of prize money from Louis XVI, associated himself with William Phillips, Jonathan Mason, his
in-laws, Thomas Russell and Stephen Higginson, and others to
found the Massachusetts Bank, later to become the First National Bank of Boston. Until the end of the Revolution the
banking needs of the colony had been met by wealthy merchants
who accepted deposits, made loans, and issued drafts on overseas
correspondents. For this private business the Bank of England
acted as a central clearing house. It seemed now that the time
had come for achieving financial as well as political independence. The Old Judge as the lawyer and ready writer of the
group probably drafted the preliminary circular:
'Taught by the Experience of many Nations that well regulated Banks are highly useful to Society, as they promote Punc-
tuality in the Performance of Contracts, increase the medium of
Trade, facilitate the Payment of Taxes, prevent the exportation
of, and furnish a safe deposit for Cash, and in the way of Discount,
render easy and expeditious the anticipation of Funds at the
expence only of Common Interest.'
None of the gentlemen signing the circular had enjoyed any
banking experience and John Lowell was one of a committee of
three appointed to write to Thomas Willing, president of the
new Bank of Philadelphia, for advice and instruction. This was
received in considerable volume. 'The world,' Willing wrote,

'is apt to suppose a Greater Mystery in this sort of Business than there really is,' and explained it very fully. A charter was obtained in February, 1784, and the capital stock was set at three hundred thousand dollars. John Lowell, with two shares of five hundred dollars each, was one of twelve directors who elected as first president the scientist, philosopher, and future governor, James Bowdoin. On the well-chosen date of July 5, the bank opened for business in the handsome brick Manufactury House that stood on Tremont Street across the way from the Old Granary Burying Ground. The first teller, at a salary of seven hundred dollars per year, was another John Lowell, first cousin of the Old Judge, who, before his death in 1793, was to rise to the important post of cashier.[1]

Indeed, 1784 was perhaps the Judge's busiest year, for during it he was chairman of the boundary commission that finally settled the vexed question of the line between Massachusetts and New York, involving, says his son, eleven million acres of land that were sold for a mess of pottage.

For a time the Old Judge became more, as the phrase is, 'in the money.' Like most of his well-to-do contemporaries he dealt in the depreciated currency and securities of the new country — eventually at a profit. These operations were cleverly interlocked with various insurance projects, as the following memorandum among his papers reveals:

'Subscribed to the Tontine.......................... £100,000
Cost of £50,000 3 per cent, Consolidates & 75 per cent is . 37500
Do. of 600,000 Dollars & 6/8 in the £ is.............. 45000   82500
                        Remains for the Scheemers   . £17500

to pay agents Commission paying the Annuities and the remainder for themselves — and if the United States preserve their

---

[1] This John Lowell, who lived in Charlestown, was the son of Michael, one of the three brothers of the Reverend John Lowell of Newbury. His sister, Elizabeth, married John Hancock's brother, Ebenezer. He assisted Paul Revere in the hasty removal of John Hancock's famous trunk from Lexington to Woburn on the historic morning of April 19, and during the British occupation of Boston did what he could to protect the contents of the Hancock mansion from damage and theft.

faith — £50,000 — 3 per cent. Cons. — to be divided amongst them after 14 years. If per Contra the United States pay neither principal nor Interest the Scheemers have sold their Certificates at 6/8 in the £ and the subscribers to the Tontine have an Increasing annuity to the survivors and at the extinction of each class that classes share of the 600,000 Dollars Continental Certificates deposited — and if the United States do not pay either principal or Interest the subscribers have only an Increasing annuity beginning at better than 6 per cent for their purchase to continue 14 years — the Expense of paying the Annuities may be done for £100 per Ann—'

It would seem that the subscribers could not lose and the 'scheemers' were sure to win.

In the years after the war his legal and financial business for the *émigrés* in England steadily increased. He was constantly sending substantial remittances to Hutchinsons, Lorings, and Lechmeres. As evidence of his personal international relations, we find that, on the day he wrote Thomas Hutchinson the younger in regard to the sale of land on the town dock in Boston, he wrote also to Peter Coffin of Nantucket ordering five barrels of the best white sperm oil, two to be sent to George Washington, two to Robert Morris, and one to himself.

His Alma Mater was not slow to avail herself of the talents of her increasingly distinguished alumnus. In the last years of the Revolution, President Joseph Willard and Treasurer Ebenezer Storey were having a hard time making the two ends of outgo and income meet. In 1779, they departed from the ancient custom of selecting the Corporation, the board of five with which the President and Treasurer *ex officiis* conducted the practical affairs of the college, exclusively from those who were already fellows clerical or pedagogical. They secured the election of one of the solidest citizens of Boston, James Bowdoin. This was followed in 1784 by the election of another 'solid' man, John Lowell, whose 'judgment and integrity' Morison says brought the college through the hard times after the war, and by 1789 doubled its investment in public securities from fifteen thousand pounds to thirty thousand pounds. To one aware of the sporting spirit which inspired many of the Old Judge's financial adventures, it is not surprising that the successful lotteries conducted in 1788 and 1793, which rebuilt Stoughton Hall and helped the college in its progress along Easy Street, were due to his advocacy of that French idea. At the meeting of the President and Fellows on February 17, 1786, he had been appointed chairman of a sub-committee to revive the lottery 'granted by the General Court before the late war,' and continued to be in special oversight of the dealings with the Goddess Fortuna. He gave financial and legal advice as a member of the Corporation as long as he lived. For eighteen years the records show him present at almost every fortnightly meeting.

From 1784 until the death of Lawrence Lowell in 1943, a stretch of one hundred and fifty-nine years, there was only one decade in which some member of the family was not a member of the Corporation, of the Board of Overseers, or of the faculty — five Fellows, five Overseers, two professors, one president, contributing altogether to the work of carrying on the college two hundred and ten man-years. On a secret memorandum of possibilities for the corporation, passed around among the overseers in the eighteen-forties, Colonel Henry Lee wrote against the name of one Lowell, 'Very eligible, if an orphan.'

In 1785, John Lowell, at forty-two, retired from the more active practice of the law and purchased a house and thirty acres of land in the country — at Roxbury, three miles out. It was then rolling country with a resemblance to a healthy suburb south of London that led John Lowell, 'the Rebel,' returning in 1806 from three years abroad, to christen it Bromley Vale.[1] The site, just north of Centre Street, covered now with breweries, factories, and jerry-built houses, still boasts a small square named Bromley Park.

[1] The Rebel himself and some of his more meticulous descendants always spelled it 'Broomley.'

In the Old Judge's time and that of his son, it must have been retired and lovely. To the north, across the short-pitched valley of Stony Brook, the steep acclivity of Parker Hill hid the spires and wood and soft-coal smoke of Boston. Not far to the south rose Great Blue Hill and the Chickataubut Range. Towards the sunset stretched the shaded hills and bowery hollows of Brookline. Eastward, before the hill was pared down, the Old Judge taking his hundred steps on a sunny morning could see the bright waters of Boston and Dorchester Bays studded with the white sails of ships and brigs taking the mercantile ventures of his clients and his family to Bristol or Bordeaux, and returning laden with English goods and potables from Bordeaux, Lisbon, or Madeira.

The house itself, which sheltered John and Rebecca, and after a year, nine children, closely resembled Charles Eliot Norton's Shady Hill, which still stands on the eastern frontier of Cambridge. Within, as we know from the inventory of his estate, were two parlors with fireplaces and expensive mirrors over them, six bedrooms, three of them described as 'small,' and a dining-room which contained *inter aliis* three punch-bowls, twenty-one decanters, four dozen wineglasses, and forty-one for that rather unattractive ladies' drink, syllabub — the Federalist anticipation of a milk-shake with a stick in it. There was a library of nine hundred volumes, and in a small bedroom on the ground floor, perhaps in later years the Old Judge's own, in addition to a narrow bed were a camera obscura, an air pump, an electrical machine, and a solar reflecting microscope. Back of the house was a dairy with three cows, a greenhouse which was to become famous in the next generation, and a barn complete with three horses, two for the carriage and one for saddle or chaise.

Indoor service was supplied by two colored women. They may have been freed slaves, for when young John went to college he had difficulty in refusing the offer of their hoarded gold pieces, and to his brother, Charles, while at Harvard, the younger, Phillida, sent each week a cake accompanied by a rhymed chronicle of the family doings for the preceding seven days.

As the years went by, John Lowell became more and more reluctant to absent himself from the felicity of this charming and exceedingly comfortable abode. Otis says: 'His consultations with clients were principally at his own house in Roxbury, and in short interviews. He generally amused himself in his garden until it was time to hurry into court, where he never arrived too early, and then plunged *in medias res* in causes with the points and merits of which he had been superficially informed.' Yet he seldom failed to grasp the essential and taking the jury up in his balloon (as aforesaid), to land them where he liked.

Nevertheless, those horses of Paul Jones's and their successors must have whirled him very frequently across the narrow neck to town. There were the meetings of the Harvard Corporation and the bench of his Admiralty Court to be warmed, and soon that of the Federal District Court to which he was appointed by George Washington. Then, too, he was a great joiner of societies learned and otherwise. In 1780, he was associated with John Adams, Samuel Adams, John Hancock, Timothy Pickering, Jonathan Jackson, and James Bowdoin in founding the American Academy of Arts and Sciences, in patriotic emulation of Franklin's Philosophical Society in Philadelphia. He attended its meetings to hear papers like James Winthrop's 'account of the Transit of Mercury observed at Cambridge, November 12, 1787,' or Edward Wigglesworth's 'Observations on the Longevity of the Inhabitants of Ipswich and Hingham.' In 1791, he himself pronounced a stately eulogy on James Bowdoin, its first president. He was likewise an early member of the Humane Society, president of the Massachusetts Society for the Promotion of Agriculture, and vice president of the Society for the Advice and Information of Immigrants. This last organization seems to have occupied itself in smoothing the paths of the 'factors' British manufacturers sent out to the States to promote trade. For this he was attacked by the press of the Republicans.

After the election of James Bowdoin in 1785, as the first Federalist Governor of Massachusetts, that party had become at last integrated and organized around the able and powerful group of the Essex Junto. Although classed by the Opposition as one of its chief devils, the Old Judge never had much time for practical politics. He shared the political views of his friends who were at its centre, but he had also close friends in the other camp, notably James Sullivan, a fellow member of the Continental Congress and many committees and commissions, a future Republican Governor with whom both he and his family lived in amity for many years. We find him giving legal advice to Timothy Pickering, revering and all but worshipping George Cabot, by both of whom he was frequently consulted. Perhaps now and again he made a clever suggestion for some political *démarche*. But the truth is that he was a man of good will with an intuitive gift for seeing both sides of a question. Despite his successful eloquence in court, he was not the stuff of which aggressive political partisans are made. But that age-old irrepressible conflict between the haves and have nots was taking shape in Massachusetts as in all the states, perhaps a sharper shape than in any other. John Lowell and his friends, merchants and lawyers all, definitely had it. As Goethe said, 'You cannot escape the air you breathe.'

Shays's abortive rebellion in 1786 revealed the violent passions of the people. The Old Judge, who had gone to New York with Rebecca to transact legal business and enjoy the society of Manhattan, wrote to Thomas Dwight of Hartford to inquire if it was safe for them to drive home across Connecticut. 'I cannot conceive,' Dwight replied, 'there will be the least danger in your returning to Boston by this road. You need but see the tameness of the poor storm-beaten lads that are returning to be convinced that they have lost their intentions of offering injury to anybody.'

The 'poor storm-beaten lads' were largely of the debtor class and it was hoped that the inflation of the currency would ease their troubles, but the 'Tender Act,' making even a cow legal tender in payment of taxes, failed to please. As the *American Herald* said in 1787, 'Human nature revolts at one-sixth of a year's earnings being wrested from the individual.'

On the evening of February 6, 1788, all the bells in Boston rang. The new Constitution of the United States had been ratified in Massachusetts by a vote of 187 to 168. To the constituents of the 168 who voted against ratification it seemed that it would 'increase the power, wealth, and influence of those who already have them.' Even the father of his country was denounced as 'The Old King.' A member of the state convention wrote, 'Debtors generally are on the other side and this comprehends more than one half the people; persons guilty of crimes or wishing to commit crimes, Rhode Island Immigrants, and almost all of the denomination of Baptists, and boys.'

For three decades the pendulum of popular feeling swung back and forth. The Fall of the Bastille,

> 'Bliss was it in that dawn to be alive,
> But to be young was very Heaven,'

gave the Republicans inspiration and a wider influence. Jacobin societies sprang up everywhere; but four years later the execution of Louis XVI and the Terror, plus the outrageous conduct in this country of Citizen Genet, gave aid and comfort to the Federalists. Burke's *Letters on a Regicide Peace* became their political bible, and the two committee rooms of the Senate Chamber in Philadelphia were adorned with full-length presentation portraits of Louis Seize and Marie Antoinette. With a few exceptions like the Reverend William Bentley of Salem the Congregational clergy preached against French infidelity, one even going so far as to assert that the American Revolution itself had 'opened the flood gates of iniquity.'

The Old Judge, never so much a rugged moulder of contemporary opinion like John Adams as its brilliant reflector, was less passionately disturbed about all this than his son, John, then just beginning his public career, but still he was worried when he had time to think about it. Perhaps he was a little reassured when in October, 1795, he received the following lively letter from his second son, Francis Cabot Lowell, a clear-eyed youth of twenty who had sailed as supercargo on one of the Russell ships, and after being twice stopped by British cruisers had arrived safely in France:

'Bordeaux, August 28, 1795

'. . . The ideas you have of France in America are quite erroneous. There is full as much safety here as in America. We walk about the streets without being troubled and a pickpocket or thief has not been heard of this long time. It is true no man here regards his life at all and other peoples very little. A duel yesterday was fought at 'change time between two Gentlemen by the Riverside. After trying with the sword for some time they took their pistols. One of them shot and killed his adversary. Left him and went immediately on Exchange again. The conduct of six of the national convention tryed for the insurrection of the 20th of May you have probably heard. When found guilty one of them took a knife and stabbed himself and passed it to the next. He did the same and so did the whole six. Three had life enough left to be dragged to the Guilotine as they went along one of them laft and said if there should be a revolution in the world they were going to he should take care and keep out of the scrape. People here have as much religion as ever. None but the public officers mind the new style and the churches on Sunday are well filled. The beggars ask Alms for the love of the virgin. . . .'

The Old Judge, however, was more interested in growing Boston than in Paris or Bordeaux. He took shares in the bridges that were being built and canals that were being dug in the surrounding territory, and had a hand in the law that the judges were making in its courts. In 1801, President John Adams, on the eve of giving place to Thomas Jefferson, appointed him Chief Justice of the First Circuit Court at a salary of $666 per quarter. This honor and emolument, however, was of brief duration. The following year the court was abolished by President Jefferson's first Congress. The circumstances cannot be better stated than they were put by another Judge John Lowell at a dinner given him by the Bar Association of Boston on his own retirement from the Federal Bench in 1884:

'My great-grandfather was judge of the district Court appointed by Washington. Then he was made circuit judge by Adams. Well, Adams made a good many circuit judges and they were all Federalists, and when the Democrats came in, — they called themselves Republicans all the same, you know, — when the Republicans came in they abolished the court to get rid of the judges.'

In August, 1800, the Old Judge had received a letter from John Rutledge of South Carolina, appointed Chief Justice of the Supreme Court by Washington, but not confirmed by the Senate. It was subscribed, 'accept the homage of sentiments of high respect and veneration,' and asked him to suggest steps that could be taken to defeat Thomas Jefferson for the presidency at the coming election. Eight months later, when he lost his seat, he must have wished he could have thought of something. His serenity, however, seems to have been undisturbed. Eliza Southgate, a bright girl seventeen years old, proceeding that summer by boat from Wiscasset to Bath, found the Lowells and two of their six daughters on board. She wrote home:

'Judge Lowell appears to be one of the mildest most amiable men I ever saw, Mrs. Lowell is a fine lady-like woman, yet her manners are such as would have been admired thirty years ago. There is too much appearance of whalebone and buckram to please the depraved taste of the present age. Nancy, the oldest daughter, is very easy and pleasing, Eliza, fat short artless but a sweet charming creature.'

It was not to be the Old Judge's fortune to enjoy much longer his delightful garden, hospitable home, and affectionate family on the Roxbury hilltop. For several years he had been 'tortured by gout,' and was thinking of taking a trip to England. On

May 6, 1802, at the age of fifty-nine, he died suddenly. The courtrooms, the banking and board-rooms, the halls of the learned societies of Boston, the meeting-room of the Senior Fellows in Cambridge were to know his brisk and smiling presence no more; or 'the pleasure in every countenance when he spoke.'

Like so many lawyers, able drawers-up of last wills and testaments, he died intestate. Three leading citizens, George Cabot, Martin Brimmer, Sr., and Joseph Williams, were appointed to appraise his estate. As is not uncommon in the case of professional men who have lived well and reared large families, it was less than expected, a net total, including the mansion house and seventeen acres of land at Bromley Vale valued at $10,500, of some $80,000, the equivalent of perhaps a quarter of a million today. This was not large in comparison with the million-dollar estates of the great Salem and Boston merchants, but it was the first long upward step in the fortunes of the Lowell family. The largest single item of his investments was the sum of $30,500 under the heading 'Adventures at Sea' on eight ships — *Perseverance*, *Regular*, *Thomas Russell*, *Horace*, *John*, *Ocean*, *Indies*, and *Hannah*, all shipped by Francis Cabot Lowell, who, according to his brother, the future 'Rebel,' had 'accomplished the restoration of my father's dilapidated fortunes.'

In the character of the Old Judge already quoted, Harrison Gray Otis says that, although inclined to be a *malade imaginaire*, his health was good. Certainly he was a notable example of prepotence in the male line. Each of his three sons, one by each of his three wives, were to found branches of the family that drew diverse qualities, temperaments, and capacities from the distaff side, yet the basic traits of character and countenance transmitted by the Old Judge were perdurable. This indeed is true of three families that have played important rôles in the drama of New England history.

From George Cabot of the Junto down, the Cabots have been tall spare men, high of brow, long of nose and jaw, marked by a determination approaching grimness.

The Adamses have been shorter, with classically oval faces, finely arched eyebrows, slightly aquiline in profile. With a tendency to baldness they have resembled the late portraits of William Wordsworth and the busts of Julius Caesar. As for character, their surname has entered the language as an adjective which needs no definition.

The Lowells have normally been middle-sized men, sensitive yet vigorous. They have had plenty of hair, usually a deep reddish-brown. Their faces have been, like the Old Judge's, of a typically square configuration, lighted by lively eyes of brown or hazel, more rarely a china blue, expressing their animal spirits and readiness for instant action in any good or profitable cause — sharp eyes *occasionem cognoscere.*

BOOK III

The Turbid Time

CHAPTER

1

End of a Century

In the last decade of the eighteenth century, the beginning of
that turbid and contentious time that lasted from the presidency of John Adams through that of his son, the three sons that
appeared among the nine children of the Old Judge grew to
manhood. John Lowell, son of Sarah Higginson, was born in
1769; Francis Cabot Lowell, son of Susanna Cabot, in 1775;
Charles Lowell, son of Rebecca Russell Tyng, in 1782. All
three were high-strung delicate men, prone to overwork and
periods of nervous exhaustion. Perhaps each, like his father,
had a streak of the *malade imaginaire* in him, or it may have been
merely lack of outdoor exercise and an exciting sport, or a vita-
min deficiency which develops similar symptoms and responds
to the same therapy. Yet each started a branch of the family
tree that was to bear noble fruit, John's in law, politics, and good
works; Francis's in commerce, industry, and good works;

Charles's in the church, good works, poetry, and war. As new generations came on and intermarried with their cousins, Cabots, Amorys, Jacksons, and other Lowells, their achievements became less specialized. Each line made a mark in all, and the family pocketbook, now in the form of large strong-boxes, continued to swell.

John Lowell, short, slender, frail, and fiery, self-styled 'Rebel,' with something the look of the young Shelley, was best in Latin and Greek of any boy of his time at Andover. A classmate there describes him as 'frank, ardent, generous, and pure.' His father wrote him letters addressing him as 'My dearest friend.' At Harvard, where he graduated in 1786, he was ranked high in the classics and public speaking. When the following year at the age of eighteen he delivered an oration before the Phi Beta Kappa Society, young John Quincy Adams, always slightly allergic to Lowells (and vice versa), wrote in his *Diary*, 'Lowell '86 gave us an encomium on history which contained a number of very good observations, but his delivery was not without a share of that affectation which, if I may so express myself, is natural to him.'

After graduation he studied law in the offices of his father, Harrison Gray Otis, and Rufus Amory, was admitted to the bar in 1790, and opened an office of his own in a new stone house on School Street, back of King's Chapel and in front of the present City Hall. Three years later he married Rebecca Amory, daughter of John Amory, whose house the Old Judge had occupied in '76,[1] and set up their home beside and over the office.

At the bar, John Lowell immediately prospered. Eventually he took over his father's Tory agencies and estate business, but his greatest successes were in the courtroom as an advocate in difficult cases, in which, it is said, his ardor often exceeded that

---

[1] Strictly speaking, the Amorys were not *émigrés*. John Amory had gone to England on business in 1774, and not being wholly in sympathy with the Revolution, had at its outbreak stayed there. He was never formally banished. Towards the end of the war, he came back to New York and at its conclusion, home to Boston.

of his clients. It was a short step from law to politics. He was involved more deeply in the plans and policies of the Federalist Party through the years of its rise and decline than his father had been in its inception. Soon by tongue and pen he became known as one of its ablest propagandists. Forty years later, John Quincy Adams made a break-down of the Federalist frame of mind that it would be hard to better. It was, he says, 'compounded of the following prejudices':

'1. An utter detestation of the French Revolution and of France, and a corresponding excess of attachment to Great Britain, as the only barrier against the universal, dreaded empire of France.

'2. A strong aversion to republics and republican government, with a profound impression that our experiment of a confederated republic had failed for want of virtue in the people.

'3. A deep jealousy of the Southern and Western States, and a strong distrust of the effect of the slave representation in the Constitution of the United States.

'4. A belief that Mr. Jefferson and Mr. Madison were servilely devoted to France, and under French influence.'

It was the first of these prejudices that filled and fired the mind of young John Lowell during the presidencies of Washington and Adams. *Egalité* and *fraternité* in practice had never meant much to a race of shipmasters and seagoing owners accustomed to exact instant obedience from their crews, and damn their eyes. If pushed to it they would have admitted that their political philosophy was that of an aristocracy. Well-educated men who, or whose fathers, had shown competence in practical affairs by amassing fortunes should do the ruling. The clergy left no doubt in their minds that the French were a race of infidels and atheists. John Lowell was not speaking for himself as an individual, or as the mouthpiece of a minority, but for a majority in New England, when he proclaimed that Napoleon Bonaparte, the giant of the middle class with his 'continental system' and abolition of religion, subverter of monopoly and destroyer of privilege, was, quite simply, Anti-Christ.

After two or three minor forays in the newspaper press, he printed in 1797, over the pseudonym 'A Citizen of New England,' his first important political pamphlet: *Anti-Gallican, Or the Lover of his Own Country, wherein French Influence and false Patriotism are fully and fairly displayed*. In this with copious but not always convincing eloquence he displays 'the false patriotism' of Jefferson, Monroe, and Gallatin, while disclaiming the odious epithets, 'British Satellites, Aristocrats and Monarchists,' with which his own party, the true friends to government, had been branded.

This tract for the times was printed in Philadelphia, the seat of the government, and had a considerable circulation. It seems to have given general satisfaction within the Federalist fold. But a greater opportunity was soon to present itself and be eagerly seized.

By the summer of 1798, French naval interference with our seaborne commerce and the intransigence of the Directoire reached such a point that an American fleet was sent to the West Indies. On February 9, 1799, the American frigate *Constellation*, under the command of Thomas Truxton, thirty-six guns and three hundred and sixteen men, encountered the French frigate *Insurgente*, forty guns and four hundred and ten men, off St. Christopher — St. Kit to sailors — in the Leeward Islands. They had words leading to broadsides. Those of the *Constellation* were heavier and better aimed. On the *Insurgente* twenty-nine men were killed and forty-one wounded before she struck her colors. The *Constellation* had one killed and three wounded. In June she was at Charlestown reoutfitting, and the frigate *Boston*, built by local subscription, had just been launched. A bottle of champagne had been broken on her bow and hogsheads of rum drunk to her death-dealing honor. At this psychologic moment, John Lowell, now approaching his thirtieth birthday, was invited to make the Fourth-of-July Oration in the historic South Church where Josiah Quincy at twenty-six had made it the year before. The Federalists led by the Essex Junto were all out for war with France. Even some of the Republicans were beginning to see red. 'Millions for defense but not one cent for tribute!' John Lowell decided to abandon the conventional twisting of the British lion's tail and instead pull out the tail feathers of Napoleon's eagles. He let himself go. Our own eagle screamed.

The character of the speech, which he was told gave great pleasure to President John Adams, is sufficiently evident in its peroration and poetic conclusion:

'Then shall our Navy ride triumphant in every clime and future TRUXTONS be victors of the Nile. Discard a mean, parsimonious policy, a disgraceful calculation of pecuniary interests — Then we should not want able and courageous defenders — Then, should Gallic lightning assail us, "Our WASHINGTON, unmoved, would conduct, with his sword, every flash to the deep." — Then these sacred Altars of the Most High should be secured from profanation; your wives from defilement, and your children from slaughter — Then should United America join in one choral gratulation of

' "ADAMS, LAW, AND LIBERTY.

' "Then —
Ne'er should COLUMBIA stoop to the Gallic sway,
Trust to their arts, or their proud laws obey;
One Cent for tribute, nor one homage yield,
While yet *one Son* his trusty sword could wield.

' "Then should our Eagle wing his rapid way
To the bright regions of unclouded day —
Upheld by Justice — arm'd in Virtue's cause —
Nerv'd to protect our Government and Laws;
With vengeful ire should hurl the bolts of Fate,
And pierce proud *Gallia's* tyrants in their haughtiest state.[1] " '

The following year an American commission, headed by Patrick Henry, who resigned and was replaced by William H. Davis, came to terms with Talleyrand, a convention was signed

[1] The quotation was the penultimate stanza of a poem by Robert Treat Paine, son of the signer. He was at the time nationally celebrated as a poet, and locally as a serious drinker and friend and patron of ladies of the stage. The first draft ended with the piercing of proud Gallia's Tyrants, but when he appeared to read it at a dinner of the Charitable Fire Society he was told that he wouldn't be allowed a

and war averted. Alexander Hamilton, John Lowell, and the Junto were disappointed, and felt that the President had let them down. With the end of the eighteenth century, the age of enlightenment and reaction, the peak of Federalist power, though not of their ambition, was passed. In the second year of the nineteenth, Thomas Jefferson was to take command of the Ship of State and ease her off before the rising gale of Democracy.

The two years either side of the turn of the century were busy ones for John Lowell. His legal work was prospering and for three sessions he was a very active member of the state legislature, writing five of the contentious replies of that branch to the semiannual messages of the governor. Elected in 1797 a director of the Massachusetts Bank, following his father, he seldom missed a meeting of the board and was a member of nearly all important committees.

The population of the house on School Street was increasing. His first child, named for her mother, Rebecca Amory Lowell, was born in 1794. Known in the family as Amory, she lived on unmarried until 1873, and was the intimate favorite cousin of James Russell Lowell. In 1798 was born the first and only son, John Amory Lowell, whose busy and useful life covered more than four fifths of the next century.

The house on School Street, supplemented by the Roxbury hilltop, was becoming a hospitable centre for distinguished

drink until he had added a stanza about George Washington. Seizing a pen and a bottle of ink he retired to a side room, produced the following, and received his reward:

> 'Should the tempest of war overshadow our land,
> Its hosts could ne'er rend Freedom's temple asunder;
> For unmoved at its portal would Washington stand,
> And repulse with his breast the assaults of the thunder.

> 'His sword from the sleep
> Of its scabbard would leap,
> And conduct with its point every flash to the deep;
> For ne'er shall the sons of Columbia be slaves,
> While the earth bears a plant, or the sea rolls its waves.'

travellers of the Federalist persuasion from all over the country. Some of them seem to have been particularly impressed by the charm and talents of the Old Judge's unmarried eldest daughter, Anna Cabot Lowell. 'Col. Burr dined at our house last night with his daughter, and all he said about Nancy!' Alexander Hamilton also had an opportunity to sample and approve the Lowell Madeira.

In the second year of the new century, John Lowell the Federalist became head of the family at the death of the Old Judge — 'A father most excellent in that tender relation.'

Meanwhile, Francis Cabot Lowell, with a bland unconcern with political excitements, was pursuing his career as an international merchant in the face of the difficulties presented by search parties from both British and French cruisers. A member of the Harvard class of 1793, he had been rusticated in his senior year for lighting a bonfire in the Yard, an ebullition of the animal spirits that were to get other members of the family into academic trouble. He graduated, nevertheless, with the highest honors in mathematics. The Reverend Zedekiah Sawyer of Bridgewater, with whom at the age of eighteen he spent the period of his exile, wrote to the Old Judge: 'He has a happy genius for mathematics. I presume few if any of his class equal him in mathematics and astronomical attainments. He is very accurate in calculating and projecting eclipses.'

After his graduation and several voyages as supercargo to get the feel of the sea and foreign trade, he set up in premises on Long Wharf as a merchant for his own account. In 1798, he married Hannah, daughter of his father's lifelong friend, Jonathan Jackson. His first son, John, always, to make it harder, known as John Junior, was born May 11, 1799. A six-months child, a sickly youth, a dominating industrialist, a world traveller, he was to die before forty — next to Lawrence Lowell of our own time, the family's most generous educational philanthropist.

His younger brother, Charles, the amiable Charles, graduated from Harvard with the class of 1800, first of the new century. For a year he read law in the busy office of his brother, John. Coke and Blackstone, however, failed to engage his deeper interest. After family conclaves and discussions, it was decided that both by character and cast of mind he was best suited for the profession of his grandfather, the Reverend John Lowell, and that he must spend three years in Scotland studying philosophy under the great Dugald Stewart.

The nineteenth century opened with the three branches of the Lowells well entrenched, or starting under the most favorable auspices, in the professions and pursuits of the three ruling classes of New England, the law, commerce, and the Congregational ministry.

2
CHAPTER

Love and Death in Dedham

In the summer of 1801, John Lowell the 'Rebel' was of counsel for the defense in the trial in Dedham Court of a crime of passion that became a *cause célèbre* of pity and terror throughout the country. It was a crisis and turning-point in his own life.

On a gentle grassy slope, a few hundred yards from a small brook that slips through the Dedham meadows to merge with the circuitous Charles, stood and still stands the Fairbanks house, built in 1636, and claimed locally to be, in part at least, the oldest frame house now standing on the American Continent. In three low sections, staggered along an axis of some sixty or seventy feet, it faces the sun with its easterly wing abutting on the highway that carried lumbering coaches and whirling chaises from Boston to Wrentham and Providence. On both sides of the great chimney of the earliest and central section, the ridgepole sags in symmetrical curves with the weight of three centuries. From the tiny entrance hall five doors lead to a labyrinth of sitting-rooms and bedrooms, some on the ground floor, others reached by independent stairways ascending to the low-studded, high-roofed second stories of the two outer sections. From the large living-room one steps down to the kitchen by an ancient log, worn concave and thin by the feet of twelve generations of Fairbanks'.

Many an old New England house has lurid tales to tell, but few so poignant as this, a story of star-crossed lovers, and

'The fearful passage of their death marked love,'

as piteous, could a great poet have told it, as that enacted in the palace of the Capulets in Verona.[1]

In one of the ground-floor bedrooms in 1781 was born Jason Fairbanks, nearly twenty years after the preceding child. Owing to the age of his mother, he was nourished at the breasts of his sister-in-law and married sister. Freudian analysts may make what they will of this. He looked up to the elder offspring of his own generation as a son rather than as a brother. 'Never,' writes his brother, Ebenezer, 'was a child so caressed, so beloved, or who appeared to have so many claims upon the attachment of his surrounding family.' He was seldom punished, as he was always 'submissive to the kind injunction of conciliating authority.'

At the age of twelve, an active and good-looking boy, he was inoculated for smallpox. Leaving the hospital too soon, to help

---

[1] The principal sources for this chapter are the following pamphlets:

Report of the Trial of Jason Fairbanks for the murder of Elizabeth Fales. Boston, 1801.

The Solemn Declaration of the late Unfortunate Jason Fairbanks, to which is added some account of his life and character. (By his brother, Ebenezer Fairbanks.) Dedham, 1801.

A Discourse, the Lord's Day After the Execution of Jason Fairbanks, by Thomas Thacher, A.M. Dedham, 1802.

A Sermon on the Death of John Lowell, LL.D., by F. W. P. Greenwood, D.D. Boston, 1840.

The Life of James Sullivan, by Thomas Amory, Boston, 1859, also contains a full rather *parti-pris* account of the case from the point of view of the prosecuting Attorney-General of the Commonwealth.

with the farm work, he fell sick with an attack of the dread disease in its most virulent form, and his life was despaired of. It was saved, but the 'mercurial remedies' administered by the medical science of the time affected his limbs and joints. He was restored to half-health with the loss of several bones of his right arm. It withered and was useless from shoulder to wrist.

The damage of this disaster to the mind and character of an adolescent boy would be well understood today. Even in 1793, his brother had an inkling of it. When Jason struggled with a rake to assist in getting in the hay, with efforts beyond his strength that brought on bleeding at the lungs and fever, Ebenezer tried to convince him, tactfully on business grounds, that 'his labor would not indemnify the costs of his recovery.' The family reached the wise decision that Jason's good mind and his sensibility qualified him for a liberal education. 'The idea caught and we may say enchanted him.' He was entered at Wrentham Academy. Soon hard study brought on severe nervous headaches and he was taken out of school, but not before he had learned to find delight in books, an appetite that grew by what it fed on. At his earnest wish his brother-in-law, the registrar of deeds at Dedham, gave him employment as a copyist, but this, too, proved too arduous and confining.

After a period of rest and partial recovery, he was sent back to the Academy, but the headaches came on again accompanied by the old symptoms of hemmorhage and 'hectic fever,' tuberculosis, in short. He became so weakened that he could no longer take off or put on his clothes without help. For a second time he was taken out of school and came back for better or worse to the old house by the brook.

Reading now became a serious occupation and his chief comfort. He devoted his hours to an endless variety of politics, novels, history, and philosophy. His brother indignantly denies 'the unblushing falsehood that Paine's *Age of Reason* was dearer to him than his *Bible*. That accursed book never spread its pollution within the blameless habitation of my honored parents.' One wonders!

Another solace was music. The family was 'musical,' and the ancient rafters echoed with the tones of voice and flute. Jason was their star performer. 'The labours of the longest days were lightened by the melody of his song.'

This was the boy, sick, sensitive, eager of mind, well-read, musical, imaginative, who at the age of sixteen discovered that Betsey Fales, his neighbor just fourteen, the age of Juliet, had a voice that blent itself uniquely well with his in a harmony of sweet sounds. They became alternately preceptor and pupil, and began to read books together. Her choice was 'usually confined to works of Fiction in which the Passion of Love was generally transcendent.'

Thomas Amory, writing in 1859 and presenting the official view of their affair, says, 'A strong magnetic influence not to be controlled by her better judgment drew her towards him.' The simple fact is that they fell passionately, purely, madly in love. What Betsey was like, and what they were like together, is told by Ebenezer:

'Though not strikingly beautiful, her person and manner were infinitely engaging; her natural understanding of the first class; her conversation and attainments beyond her age, her station and her instruction. Self-taught and original, the passion she felt, was like that she inspired, enthusiastic and extraordinary. Yet some features of their characters were marked by the most distinguishing contrast. She was healthy, active, animated, and of opinions the most decided, energetic and undeviating — he, weakly, sedentary, conciliating and pacific. — Yet as the most melting sensibility was the reigning principle of both their minds, there was, when brought to the test, a reciprocal and delightful unison of disposition. — Wherefore, sometimes, assuming each other's qualities, you would find him gay, sportive and independent — her pensive, submissive and contemplative: while in the dearest sentiment of their hearts, they were equally united and invariable.'

For a year Jason was received at the Fales home as a favored lover. Later, however, as the result of 'the most trifling events imaginable,' he was forbidden the house — Montague and Capulet! He tells the story in his *Solemn Declaration*.

'Being one evening at their house in a very merry mood, and hearing her sister *Clarissa* tell their brother to go out and purchase a pint of brandy, I jocosely observed that it were easy to discover when *Benjamin Wait* was expected, as *Clarissa* never failed sending for a bottle of brandy — at which she appeared greatly affronted; though I certainly intended no offence, and the expression was but a jest: yet, from that evening, *Clarissa* was my inveterate enemy, and induced by her influence, the parents — one, if not both of them — became my inveterate enemies also.

'A Short time after this slight occurrence, there appeared some poetic lines which had been composed in ridicule of *Mrs. Fales*, and this daughter *Clarissa*. After they were written, a young man brought them to me and asked me what I would give to see them published? I replied, not more than four and six pence. Soon after which, the verses were published; and I do confess that I was, at the time, much pleased with them: but it is equally true, that I did not assist in any way whatever, to the composition of them; yet this *Clarissa* and her mother, always imputed them to me: and from that period to the present unhappy moment of my existence, they have continued my bitter and reproachful enemies.'

After this, the lovers took to meeting at the houses of friends or at a little glade near the brook in a corner of the pasture of a neighbor named Mason, equidistant from both their houses. At the trial, Reuben Farrington, Jason's best friend, was asked by his counsel if he had ever seen them together outdoors.

'Yes,' he answered 'Myself, Jason, and Betsey, and a number of others, were together one evening. I lay down on some chips, and Jason and Betsey went away at some distance, under a tree, and lay down on a blanket. I went to sleep; when I awoke, I found Jason and Eliza on the blanket under the tree.'

In the last year of their lives, Jason became too ill to walk far, and their meetings, longer and more tender, took place in one of the ground-floor chambers of the ancient Fairbanks abode. Sukey Davis, Jason's favorite niece, nearly his own age, testified:

'Friday evening, May 8, 1801, between nine and ten o'clock, *Polly and Betsey Fales* came to our house. *Betsey* went to *Jason's* bed-room window and thumped. *Jason* came out and let them in. They sat half an hour; I then asked *Betsey*, if she would go into the other room? She said yes, if Grandma is in bed. *Polly*, *Betsey*, *Jason* and myself then went into the room, Polly and I went immediately outdoors, and staid about an hour. When we came in, the light was out. Polly and I went up chamber and staid till 12 o'clock. Then we went down, and they went home — when *Betsey* went out, she took *Jason's* hand, and kissed it

'The Wednesday before *Betsey Fales* died, she went with me to Mr. Mason's on a visit to Miss Hoskins. When we came home, it was 10 o'clock — *Jason* was up. Mr. Sprague wished to wait on *Betsey* home. She told him, she was going to stay all night. He asked her again — she gave him the same answer. When she got into the house, she took off her shawl and bonnet and sat a little while; then she said, "I believe I must go home." Mr. Guild said, if she wished to go home, he would go with her. She made no answer. I went into another room and staid till 12 o'clock. When I came back, the light was out. I got a candle and was going to light it, but they objected, and said so much, I did not; but went to bed, and left *Jason* and *Betsey* alone, and it was between day and sun-rise when she came to bed to me. She said, she was sorry Polly was with me, because she wanted to tell me something. I told her, Polly was asleep — she said, she would not risk it. I began to talk to her. She desired me not to talk, for she was afraid it would wake Grandma and then she would know what time she came to bed. She got up about sunrise, and said she must go home. I urged her to stay to breakfast — she said no; for she must get home before her mother was up, for she would kill her if she knew where she staid. She asked me to go out with her — I went as far as the gate, and asked when she would come again? She said she would come and stay with *Jason* much oftener, if it were not for Mr. Farrington's folks; for she could not come without their knowing it, and then they would tell her mother.'

The stage was set for the terrific third act. Jason, beside himself with love and the conviction that his illness was fatal, that he would 'die before election,' was talking too much. He was overheard to say that he would 'settle with the Fales family.' He told his two closest friends that he would stop at nothing to seal Betsey his forever, and particularized unpleasantly.

On Sunday, the seventeenth of May, eleven days after the meeting reported by Sukey, Betsey sang in church as lustily as usual. Next morning she did her usual housework and the Monday wash. At half-past twelve she stopped in at the house of another neighbor, and asked Eliza Guild if she might see a book belonging to her sister, a book called *The History of Lady Julia Mandeville*, by the translator of Lady Catesby's *Letters*. It was given her and she sat down and read it for half an hour.

This tale by an Irish lady named Frances Moore, published in Dublin in 1765, had been for a generation a popular best-seller. It overflowed with the very voluptuousness of sorrow. The story, told in letters, chiefly those of Lady Anne Wilmot, a lively widow whose character develops as she becomes the author's mouthpiece, is of very high society. Julia is the ward of Lord and Lady Belmont of Belmont House, and the beloved of Henry Mandeville, her impoverished cousin. Many obstacles are erected in the course of true love. In the end all are removed. Henry is discovered to be the true heir to the earldom. Plans for the wedding are well under way. But alas! Through a misunderstanding Henry is led to think Julia has been unfaithful to him, fights his fancied rival, and is killed. Julia, after a day's illness, dies of a broken heart:

'She felt her approaching dissolution, of which she had been warned, at her own earnest request, by Dr. Evelin; she summoned us all to her apartment; she embraced us with the most affecting tenderness; she called me to her, and giving me her picture for Col. Mandeville, begged me to tell him, she who murdered his son, died for him.'

Like the lovers of Verona they were buried in the same tomb.

With this tale of woe filling her mind, yet apparently cheerful as usual, Betsey picked up a little child by the door, played with it for a few minutes, and about one-thirty o'clock set off for Mason's pasture and the glade by the brook, to meet Jason.

He, that morning, wishing to mend a pen, had borrowed a penknife from one Ephraim Hardy, who worked for his father. It had cost ten cents and had a blade two and one half inches long. At one o'clock with this in his pocket, and though it was August his greatcoat thrown over his shoulders — he could not by himself put it on properly — he too set out for the brookside.

At three o'clock the Farrington sisters, who lived near-by, thought they heard the voice of Betsey calling out from the woods, 'O Dear! O Dear.' One sister thought she was in distress, the other that she was laughing and on her way to them. They did nothing about it.

A few minutes later, Mrs. Fales, looking from her front door, saw Jason Fairbanks approaching the house for the first time in two years, wild-eyed and staggering, the ten-cent knife in his hand, blood flowing from fourteen wounds. 'Betsey,' he gasped, 'has killed herself.'

At her scream Samuel Fales, Betsey's uncle, came running, and Jason, froth bubbling from a long gash across his throat, repeated, 'Betsey has killed herself,' adding, 'And I have killed myself, too.'

(*Well, Juliet, I will lie with thee tonight!*)

'Where?' shouted Samuel Fales.

'Mason's pasture,' said Jason.

Fales held him by the hand, 'lest he do some mischief, for he seemed like a person insane,' until his son came, and then committing Jason to his keeping ran for the fatal glade.

There he found Betsey.

Clad in a short calico 'loose gown' and a green skirt, she lay on the ground, her head on a rough stone. Her throat was cut. There were stab wounds in her breast, her arms, and one in her back. She was still conscious, but unable to speak. Her father came and said, 'O Betsey.' He asked her if she wanted some water. She signed that she did, and died.

After a medical examination by Doctor Nathaniel Ames, her body was carried home. A further survey and measurement of her wounds was made and her clothes examined for another weapon. In her pocket were some lemon peel, two thimbles, a pincushion, and a towel.

Next day the coroner's jury viewed the body, and held the formal inquest. In another room in the house lay Jason. Doctor Charles Kitteridge, who attended him, found, in addition to the wide gash across his throat, three in his breast around and over his heart, three in his right side, three in his thigh, one in his right arm, and three, one of them three inches deep, in his belly. He thought them dangerous. They were. The deep wound in the abdomen mortified and a lockjaw set in that lasted for eight days. It was not till nearly a fortnight after the event, and Betsey had been borne out from the floor below him to the burying ground, that it was possible to move him from the hostile house of the Fales' and commit him to Dedham jail under indictment for the murder of his beloved girl.

Never before in the one hundred and sixty-five years of its existence had that peaceful village known a capital crime. Now here was one that involved two of its best-known young people, lurid to the last degree in circumstance of passion, blood, and horror. Feeling against Jason ran high, and soon took both a political and a religious turn. The orthodox Federalists of Dedham thought him a 'Liberty Pole Boy' and an infidel reader of Tom Paine. He was brought before the Supreme Judicial Court sitting at Dedham Court House on Wednesday, August 5, 1801. On the long bench in flowing black robes were four dis-

tinguished jurists, Francis Dana, Robert Treat Paine, Simeon
Strong, and Thomas Dawes. Attorney-General James Sullivan
for the prosecution was a Republican. Jason showed a shrewd
sense of political values when he begged the court that two outstanding Federalist lawyers, Harrison Gray Otis and John
Lowell, should be appointed to defend him. They undertook his
case and handled it with such vigor that Otis, in his final plea,
took occasion to protest against the public complaint that
prisoner's counsel had shown undue enthusiasm for his cause.
With eloquence he set forth the duties of an officer of the court,
and affirmed with convincing sincerity that 'his private sentiments coincided with his client's interest.' After several chal-
lenges by prisoner's counsel, a jury was impanelled and the court
adjourned to convene the following day in the more capacious
meeting house of the First Parish.

All of Thursday and the forenoon of Friday were given to the
examination of witnesses for both sides. The issue, said the
Attorney-General, was reduced to the dilemma that the prisoner
murdered the deceased or that she murdered herself with his
knife. Step by step the lawyers developed the tragic story: the
finding of the body; the exact location and depth of the wounds;
were there or were there not teeth marks on her left thumb; the
course of the intimacy between Betsey and Jason; the precise
chronology of the events of May 18; rather hearsay evidence of
Jason's threatening remarks on the Fales family; the direction
of the wounds in relation to Jason's right arm; the limits of his
physical weakness; what was the meaning of torn fragments of
a certificate of the issuance of marriage banns that Sukey had
playfully written for them the day before; how much could have
been seen or heard, the wind being as it was, at various distances
and directions from the spot where the body was found.

No pertinent factual point was overlooked by either side.
Modern criminal lawyers for the defense would have introduced
more psychology, and perhaps have read to the jury passages
from *Julia Mandeville*, or pleaded their client's insanity, a clear

begging of the basic question. Lowell and Otis had a serious setback at the very beginning of the trial when the court refused to admit as evidence Jason's own confession made after the first discovery of a murder, since it had not previously been presented by the prosecution to prove him guilty. Otis and Lowell did not press the point. Perhaps they were urged not to by Jason for reasons which will appear in his own *Solemn Declaration* that do him credit.

On Friday afternoon, six hours were occupied by the final pleas and arguments of the counsel for the defense, and two by the prosecution

First for the defense Otis reviewed the case with an appealing humanity, and analyzed the presumptive evidence in a way to leave a very definite reasonable doubt in the mind of a reader today. He concluded with a strong statement of the doctrine of Lord Chief Justice Hale, that it is better five guilty persons should escape than that one innocent man should suffer. John Lowell's final argument has not been preserved, but knowing his gift of copious and flaming eloquence it is not hard to imagine. We do know that he narrowly escaped cutting himself in a demonstration to the jury of how Betsey stabbed herself in the back, which the medical witnesses had declared to be entirely possible. His third child had been born in his house the night before, and his muscular control may not have been of the best.

For the prosecution, Sullivan, the future governor, made what his biographer thought one of the great speeches of his life. After deploring at length the current slackness in the moral training of youth, he tore the character of Jason to shreds, and reviewed the evidence of his guilt of murder in the first degree with malice prepense with a richness of color, and no doubt, of voice, that in the inflamed state of public opinion could have had but one result.

After the careful charge of the learned judges, 'delivered in a minute and solemn manner,' the jury retired at 10 P.M. An hour later they sent in word that they had been unable to agree up to that time. At eight Saturday morning, August 8, they came in with a verdict of Guilty, and Chief Justice Dana pronounced the sentence of death by hanging, 'and may God Almighty have mercy on your soul.'

The execution was set for early September, and Jason lay in Dedham jail awaiting the end.

On the morning of August 18, Dedham quaked with consternation. Jason Fairbanks had broken jail, and in company with one Henry Dukeham, was Heaven knew where. The Federalists said the delivery was the work of the Liberty Pole Boys. Republicans thought it had been done by Negroes. James Sullivan's biographer fifty years later reports a tradition still persisting in Dedham that it was planned by 'a lady of great beauty and much literary reputation, the wife of one already eminent at the bar, who subsequently rose to its highest office.' [1]

Whoever it was that believed so steadfastly in Jason's innocence, that he or she was ready to incur the risk of aiding him to escape, had provided both money and excellent mounts, and Jason in the saddle, despite his barely healed wounds and chronic weaknesses, displayed his basic stamina. The hurried riders took the road to Worcester, slept at Spencer, and on the second evening trotted through Amherst and crossed the Connecticut at Hadley. Well over a hundred miles in thirty-six hours. Good going for men and beasts!

Next morning they proceeded at a more leisurely pace, through Chesterfield, Cummington, where the future author of *Thanatopsis* may have paused in his play to watch the two men on horseback, and over Hoosac Mountain down to the river valley at Adams. Thence they rode north to Bennington and past the battlefield to Arlington on the Battenkill, where Dukeham made the mistake of asking change for a ten-dollar bill and of saying

[1] At that time the presidency was considered the bar's highest office. But Mrs. John Quincy Adams was in Baltimore, not Braintree, in August and 'subsequently,' unless put in as a red herring, lets out Abigail. No wife of a Chief Justice of Massachusetts or of the United States seems quite to fit. Thomas Amory evidently knew to whom the tradition referred, but didn't like to say.

they came from Dorchester. At a still more comfortable gait they went on through Manchester in the shadow of Mount Equinox, and so by way of Granville to Skenesborough, now Whitehall, at the head of Lake Champlain. There for fifteen dollars they engaged a boat to convey Jason down the lake to St. Johns across the border, provisioned it, and returned to the tavern for a restful night.

In the morning as they sat at breakfast hoofbeats were heard. Before they had time to more than rise from the table, Captain Henry Tisdale of Dover and Seth Wheelock of Medfield burst into the room and put them under arrest. They made no resistance, Jason calmly remarking that if he had known they were in pursuit, they would have had to ride a hundred miles farther. Brought back by easy stages home they were committed for better safekeeping to the central jail in Boston. Jason shared a cell with John Rowe, who was being held upon a charge of enticing a soldier to desert.

To Rowe he dictated his *Solemn Declaration*, to be delivered after his death to his brother, Ebenezer. Here is his own story of the fatal interview:

'I hear that it has been generally reported, through the country, that there was a previous agreement to take each other's lives: — I do affirm, that there never passed a word relative to such a thing, our only object being then to meet for the purpose of private conversation. When I had remained at the fatal place of assignation for a few minutes only, she arrived; and after the usual compliments of health, etc., had passed, she remarked, *"that something always happened to disappoint us; for she now could not stay long, as Mrs. Marsh had sent for her to come to her house that very afternoon."*

'In the course of a long conversation upon the subject of our marriage, it occurred to my mind that I had a certificate in my pocket-book, which had been written the day before that last ill-fated meeting, by *Susan Davis*, one of my young nieces, and was occasioned by the following circumstance: — *Sukey* being at my father's house on Sunday, and standing at my writing desk, I requested her to write something: she accordingly wrote a certificate of marriage; but when the name of the parties was to be inserted, she asked me "what name she should add?" I told her that I did not care — she might put in any one of the pretty *Dedham* girls that pleased herself — she then wrote *Elizabeth Fales*, saying "she believed that would suit me better than any other through the whole town."

'After she had written, she brought the certificate and gave it to me; I putting it in my pocket-book, and after going to the place of appointment, as we were talking, I took out my pocket-book and finding the certificate, I read it to BETSEY — at the same time observing, that I believed this brought us as near the marriage state as would ever be our lot together. — Then we read the certificate: after which, I took it myself and tore it to pieces — yet at the same time assuring her that I was instantly ready to marry her; but that she must, of necessity, return, and continue to live at her father's house, as I had no means, nor any place of my own to carry her to.

'Upon hearing this, she began to weep bitterly — saying, *"that was impossible; for her mother would never speak to her, but would turn her out and shut the doors upon her immediately."* She then went on to exclaim that *"I could not love her,"* and to tell me *"how often Mrs. Whiting and her own sisters had told that I did not love her,* etc., etc."

'And now with all sorrow, and blame to myself, do I pursue the remainder of this melancholy history; for I replied angrily and roughly, that if she were capable, and willing to believe all that her sisters and Mrs. *Whiting* said upon the subject, she might go to the devil with them, since she so well knew that I had already *possessed her person, and received the pledge of her most tender attachment!*

'She then, with great quickness, demanded of me — *"if I had ever told any one of our connection?"* I rashly, but sincerely, answered, that I had indeed entrusted our secret to my intimate friends, *Reuben Farrington* and *Isaac Whiting*. — Upon which she violently exclaimed, "Oh! you are a monster!" — and looking on me, as I sat whittling a small piece of wood with a pen-knife, she cried out "*give me that knife, I will put an end to my existence, you false hearted man! — for I had rather die than live!*"

'At the same time, stretching out her hand, she took the knife, and began, as if in a state of distraction, to stab her breast and body — screaming out, and walking violently from me to the distance of two or three rods; while I, struck with astonishment, remained without power, and in a cold state of insensibility; but was too — too soon awakened from this dreadful stupefaction, by her coming, and either falling or sitting down by me. — Her throat was cut — which seeing, I immediately seized that cruel knife which had robbed me of all my fond heart held dear! And while it yet remained wet with her blood, stabbed myself in many and repeated places; only leaving off when I had finished cutting my own throat, and when I believed all was over with me! . . .

'JASON FAIRBANKS

'N.B. These are, and shall remain, the last words which I ever utter, or convey to any person whatever, by pen, ink and paper. — Be pleased to impart them to my loved RELATIONS, and let them be comforted under the consideration, that this world having now passed from before me, a merciful GOD has, in all hope, pardoned the repented errors of my youth, and to HIM have I made the expiation of what I have committed: for HE knows the veracity of all that I have here acknowledged, and that THIS is the only cause of my condemnation.

'J. F.'

To this was appended the following attestation by his counsel: 'We the Subscribers, having been of Counsel for Jason Fairbanks, at the importunate request of his relations, do attest that the foregoing narrative was declared by him in our presence, to contain a true statement of facts; and that the same having been written by him in the foregoing form, without our advice or assistance, we promised him to attest the same, when requested by his friends.

'Harrison G. Otis,
'John Lowell, Jun.'

His story, written in the expectation of certain and immediate death, was undoubtedly the same in all essential points as that told them in privileged communication before his trial. Honorable gentlemen both, of wide experience and high intelligence, they believed it true.

On the morning of September 10, guarded by a troop of cavalry, he was driven out through the hills and meadows of Roxbury to Dedham. There, the military escort augmented by a volunteer guard of two hundred and fifty citizens, he was led to the scaffold. With him walked the Reverend Thomas Thacher, who had been constantly with him in the last days and ridden out by his side from Boston. In the presence of an immense crowd he was blindfolded, the rope was put round his neck, and he was given a handkerchief to hold in his hand. The sheriff told him to drop it when he was ready. He dropped it instantly.

From his pulpit in the Third Parish Church in Dedham three days later, Thomas Thacher said:

'He hath been condemned by the laws of his country, and if guilty, hath expiated them by his punishment. But this we scruple not to say — that had the same measure of fortitude been possessed by a truly virtuous man, it might have made him a martyr for religion; a patriot bleeding on the scaffold for vindicating the rights of his country; or a hero crowned with glory expiring on the bed of honor.'

His pitiful case had strange sequels. A year to a day on the exact spot, at the precise hour of three, Mason, the owner of the pasture, murdered his own brother. A year or two later, the French author, Renaud, made the case the theme of a romantic and popular novel. In our own day a distinguished novelist both learned and fanciful, meditating a story of love and death, and musing where Jason and Betsey used to meet, saw two orioles making their nest — and wondered.

The effect on John Lowell of the execution of his client was catastrophic. He had thrown himself into the case heart and soul, and made heavy overdrafts on an energy that was always more nervous than constitutional. For months, as the Reverend Doctor Greenwood, his minister at King's Chapel, tells us, he suffered from a complete exhaustion.[1]

He recovered sufficiently to have some verbal encounters with John Quincy Adams in the State Senate, and as the latter set down in his *Diary*, to try to oppose his nomination for the United States Senate. 'At the caucus Mr. Otis and Mr. Lowell were warm partisans for Mr. Pickering. Of the latter I could have expected no less.'

But his hurt was deeper and more definite than mere nervous exhaustion or the 'melancholy state of mind' which he says persisted for years after his father's death. Profoundly convinced of Jason's innocence of the crime he was charged with, he felt, as millions the world over were to feel a century and a quarter later of another trial in Dedham Court, that the verdict, sentence, and execution was, quite simply, judicial murder. The practice of law at which he was making nine thousand dollars a year, became distasteful to him and his health further deteriorated. When in the spring of 1803, his physicians ordered him to take a long rest, he retired from the bar forever, leaving ninety-three cases on his docket marked for trial.

---

[1] As a child of five Doctor Greenwood, visiting in Dedham, had heard the 'solemn, even awful sound of the bell which tolled for the death of the poor victim.' It spoke to his 'heart in tones that were never forgotten.'

111   Love and Death in Medium

3

CHAPTER

Wanderjahre of a Clan

THE LOWELLS, HIGGINSONS, AND JACKSONS,' wrote ironic Colonel Henry Lee, 'came up from Newburyport to Boston social and kindly people, inclined to make acquaintances and mingle with the world pleasantly. But they got some Cabot women that shut them up.' His statement is confirmed from the inside but with a different slant in a letter written to a friend in Scotland by Hannah Jackson, wife of Francis Cabot Lowell.

'I began the year very badly for a domestic woman.· I was at two private balls last week, besides another evening in company, and have to struggle hard not to be in company all this week. I have begun it by refusing invitations. The fact is that for several years past our *Clan*, as we denominated ourselves, have agreed among ourselves that we have kept too much secluded from general society, but the pleasure of our easy intercourse is daily felt, and the advantages of an enlarged acquaintance it required some reasoning to be persuaded of. As is usual, feeling prevails over reason, and the Clan remains *in statu quo.* The most incorrigible members of the Clan are of my side of the house. Mr. Lowell's family have too much vivacity and good taste to confine themselves exclusively to it.'

In point of fact for three generations the Lowell men seldom sought relaxation in feminine society outside the tribal boundaries. In the generations that came on the stage between 1770 and 1830, there was an excess of the fair sex of more than fifty percent. The clan was rich in delightful maiden aunts and attractive girl-cousins. The weekly reunions at Bromley Vale, Colonnade Row, and Pemberton Square, or on Bedford, Park, and Beacon Streets, gave the young men both their social and their sentimental education. Numerous marriages were arranged and the ties that held the clan together tightened as they stretched. Not the least satisfactory result of this procedure was like that of the entail in England. Property was not dissipated in alien hands.

Writing home from abroad, John Lowell, the Rebel, sends his remembrances to his Uncle Cabot and his Uncle Jackson and adds: 'I find I love them more than I ever believed I did. I am fully persuaded that the society Heaven has been pleased to place me in in America embraces as much virtue, intelligence and information as can be met with in any domestic circle in any country.'

When a Lowell was 'run down' from too ardent application to his chosen work, he went abroad for a couple of years to rest and recuperate, taking with him not only his wife and children, if he had them, but also his wife's sister or his own, and perhaps a nephew or niece. Once on the other side he usually joined forces with travelling uncles, cousins, and aunts. Between 1801 and 1930, nine leading Lowells spent in the aggregate more than fifty years abroad. If we add to this the number of the other members of their family parties multiplied by the years of their stays, the total sum is in centuries. They were a seagoing, well-travelled, and cosmopolitan family. But before any of the men went abroad, it was thought to be the thing for him to see America first and travel for some months through the Eastern and Middle States.

John, having settled the Old Judge's estate, disposed of his law practice, and saw Ballston Spa, Niagara Falls, and the scenic valleys of the Connecticut, Mohawk, and St. Lawrence Rivers. On October 4, 1803, having been told by Thomas Amory that he could live abroad with his family like a gentleman for twelve hundred pounds per annum, he entrusted his real estate and other investments to the care of his brother, Francis, and his brother-in-law, Samuel Gardner, and sailed for England on the ship *John Adams*. With him went his wife, her sister, Mary Amory, and his daughter, Rebecca Amory Lowell. His boy of five, John Amory Lowell, 'that little rogue' as his Aunt Nancy called him, was left at home with her to join them two years later.

John Lowell was not so much annoyed as thrilled when four days out they were stopped and searched for British seamen in the crew by the frigate *Leander* of fifty guns, famous for her fight at the Battle of the Nile as she broke through the French fleet to carry dispatches home. Thereafter the voyage was tempestuous, and it was not until November 12 that the *John Adams* hove to and anchored off the Mersey bar.

For six months, with London as his headquarters, he led a life that slowly restored his nervous poise and healed the psychic lesions left from those two terrific days in the Dedham Court. Letters given him by Timothy Pickering, ex-Secretary of State, and courtesies shown him by his own important Tory clients, opened many difficult doors. He attended the opening of the Academy and was impressed by the entrance of the royal family. He spent many hours in the distinguished strangers' gallery of the House of Commons at the time England was threatened with invasion by the great army in barges Napoleon Bonaparte had on the beach of Boulogne. He heard William Pitt tell the Commons that England had a standing army of 260,000 men and 300,000 well-equipped volunteers. 'His grace, dignity, beauty of gesture, deep-toned voice, smooth and sometimes thundering eloquence rivet the attention, and command respect and astonishment.'

London life, however, was expensive and he began to take the low view of his financial position which persisted intermittently through his life, even when least necessary. At the end of the first month he wrote Francis to tell Thomas Amory that he was only half right as to what it took to live like a gentleman with a family in England. He had already spent two hundred pounds, and for the first time in his life had known what it was to deny himself 'any real gratification.' Nevertheless, he contrived to begin sending home by every Boston-bound ship the articles of use and beauty that attracted him. In the course of his three years abroad these included music, spirits, seeds, trees, books, marble mantel-pieces, statues, bas-reliefs, iron guards for railings, merino sheep, and a piano.

In the spring at Edinburgh he joined his young brother, Charles, who had spent only one hundred and twenty pounds in a year, and was introduced by him to the circle of Scotch philosophers and reviewers which made that acropolitan town consider itself mentally as well as topographically the true Athens of the British Isles. Best of all for the family welfare, as it turned out, he met Charles's landlady, Mrs. Anne Grant of Laggan.

As a child Anne had accompanied her father, an officer in Amherst's army, to America. While the army was engaged in moving the Marquis de Montcalm out of Ticonderoga, she was taken into her house by Madame Philip Schuyler of Albany. After the war the family settled at Greenbush across the river from the Schuylers and she remained Madame's cherished protégée. In the Revolution her father lost his property and returned to England. There Anne wrote a charming life of her benefactress under the title, *Memoirs of an American Lady*. It had a great success and won its author a position in literary society.

Sir Walter Scott thought her 'a most excellent person.' For two decades she took in members of the clan as paying guests, was foster-mother to their children, and their constant correspondent. When Charles came home he brought a copy of her second book, *Letters from the Mountains*, and an American edition of eight hundred copies was financed by 'two ladies of Boston,' Louisa Storrow and her sister Laura, the wife of Stephen Higginson, Jr., 'a name,' wrote Nancy to Mrs. Grant, enclosing a check for royalties of one hundred pounds, 'which serves all the purposes of eulogium.'

Early in January, 1804, it became clear to Napoleon that he was not going to get across the 'ditch,' and the Peace of Amiens was arranged, though it left him, as he said, 'in a pickle.' His reflections on his failure communicated to Las Cases in St. Helena, are of both historical and timely interest:

'I frightened them pretty well with my invasion of England, didn't I? Well, you may have joked about it in Paris, but Pitt wasn't laughing in London. Never was the English oligarchy in greater peril!

'I had made a landing possible; I had the finest army that ever existed, that of Austerlitz; what more can be said? In four days I could have reached London; I would not have entered as a conqueror, but as a liberator; I would have acted the part of William III again, but with greater generosity. The discipline of my army would have been perfect; and it would have behaved in London as it might in Paris. From there I would have operated from south to north, under the colours of the Republic, the European regeneration which later I was on the point of effecting from north to south, under monarchical forms. The obstacles before which I failed did not proceed from men, but from the elements; in the south it was the sea destroyed me; and in the north it was the fire of Moscow and the ice of winter; so there it is, water, air, fire, all nature and nothing but nature; these were the opponents of a universal regeneration commanded by Nature herself! The problems of Nature are insoluble!'

Now that there was no longer danger of having to make his way to Paris *au rebours* some thousands of invasion barges, John Lowell was able to proceed to the Continent. After a tour of Scotland and Wales with Charles, the entire family, augmented by Charles and his friend, Edward Dwight, Yale '99, moved over by way of Rotterdam to Paris, to see what that infidel country was really like, and perhaps even get a look at Anti-Christ himself.

On July 5, 1804, soon after his arrival in Paris, where Napoleon Bonaparte, recently elected a corresponding member of the New York Academy of Art, had been, on May 18, proclaimed l'Empereur, he wrote his brother Francis a letter which, along with some excellent advice, gives a picture of the confused opinions and passions of that turbid time:

'I was yesterday gratified by receiving your favour of the 16th of May, but unhappy at hearing of your indisposition. Your constitution, even more than mine, requires indulgence but never receives it. Believe me, for I speak the words *of sober experience*, no pecuniary reward can compensate the loss of health. Be indulgent to yourself if not for your own sake at least for your family. Recollect that to a young and growing race, your life and your health are invaluable, and even if you undervalue your own comforts, think of their *worth*. No man is so heedless of this first of blessings as you are, and very few require more constant attention to preserve it. Let the Distillery and the Wharf perish, rather than hazard that, without which the profits of both, will be of no avail to you. I have suffered by the errors of which I now warn you to beware, and I am now profiting by the example which I recommend you to follow. Many an active, vigorous young man has sacrificed his health to the attainment of property, and because he had not the resolution to quit his golden pursuits has fallen a victim to his thirst of acquisition. . . .

'Yesterday was the 4th of July. The American Minister celebrated it by a sumptuous dinner given the Americans here. If we had felt disposed we could not have refused his invitation. I expected insult and mortification though my young friends Dwight and Charles thought they would not be so indecent. I dare say, that the minister and his friends thought themselves moderate and tender to our feelings but you shall judge the extent of democratic delicacy. After dinner, the toasts were:

'1. The day — May we always have occasion to celebrate it.

'2. The President of the U.S.

'*3. The Emperor of the French.*

'4. The Govt. and People of the United States — May the *former* never enact laws which the latter may not be *disposed* to obey.

'The exact reverse of what it should be. A *perfect* picture of democracy. *Head* down. *Heels* up.

'5. The Memory of Washington and the Heroes Who fought and bled for our liberties.

'6. James Monroe Esqr.: May the success of his mission equal his virtues and his talents.

'A pleasing specimen of sincerity. It is asserted that a great coolness has subsisted between these great men about the *merits* of the Louisiana treaty which had no *merit* in it whatsoever.

'7. C. Pinckney Esq. our Minister in Spain. May he succeed in adding another link to our chain by adding *East to West* Florida.

'When we do not protect the *latter* — Pinckney is indeed a very worthy subject of democratic Prayer. His virtues are so radiant — his morals so pure — and his Modesty so unaffected.

'A French Gentleman, I believe a subsecretary to Mr. Livingston, favored us with *French* songs which we did not understand but which he told us were the history of the American War. If you know the French character, you will easily believe that he was not sparing of gross compliments to us and as gross abuse of our Enemies. But "Le Comble de cet jeu" was a verse addressed to Monsieur Livingston at which the Songster rose and addressing himself to the Minister, who is so deaf that he could not hear, and if he heard (it is said) could not understand him, sung the praises of the diplomatic hero, who had put a seal to the American Revolution by the purchase of Louisiana. At this gross compliment it was insisted that the verse should be repeated and that we should all rise during its performance "cum multis laudibus magnoque strepitu."

'When the Minister retired, Citizen Swan favored us with a voluntary in which the Minister was puffed in a style that *even Hancock* could not have swallowed and at this *toast* and this *alone*, we gave three cheers.

'Young Livingston, the Nephew, entertained my next neighbor with an account of the excellent footing Mr. L. was upon with the Emperor, that his answer to Talleyrand had offended the British because it was too free, but that it pleased his Imperial Majesty who deigned to express himself to this effect — "that Mr. Livingston was the *only* man who had delivered his sentiments *independently* and worthy of a *great people*."

'Or in other words neither the German or Dutch Ministers crushed under the power of France, nor any of the agents of the little States dependent upon her will, had expressed themselves in terms of so much devotion and submission to the feelings of the Emperor.'

That the Louisiana Purchase Treaty had no merit in it and would ruin the country by its extension of the power of the slave-holding agricultural South was the view of all the Federalists whose firm yet limited minds lacked unfortunately that last gift of the gods without which the people perish. Even John Quincy Adams, still a nominal member of the party, had his doubts about its constitutionality. His grandson, Henry, the final though not the friendliest authority on the administrations of Jefferson and Madison, thought the deal put through by Monroe and Livingston 'the greatest diplomatic success recorded in American history.' Even the blindest can see now that it made possible the great migration across the Mississippi and unfolded the Empire of the West.

In 1803, the year that John Lowell sailed for the Old World, the Reverends John S. J. Gardiner, rector of Trinity, and William Emerson, father of Ralph Waldo, brought together a group of gentlemen to start a new magazine, *The Monthly Anthology, and Boston Review containing sketches and reports of Philosophy, Religion, History, Arts, and Manners.* In the first number the editors state their hopes and aims for their 'Infant.'

'Though we shall have constantly in view his literary and scientific attainments we purpose that he shall not be destitute of the manners of a gentleman nor be a stranger to genteel amusements. He shall attend Theatres, Museums, Assemblies, Balls etc. and whatever diversions the town may furnish, so that whilst he is familiar with the lore of books, and the wisdom of the sages, his dress and conversation shall borrow the mode and graces of the most polished circles of society.'

This ambitious enterprise came only a year after the founding of the *Edinburgh Review* and preceded the *Quarterly* by six. In variety and tone, though not perhaps in weight, it was inferior to neither. Josiah Quincy was not wholly wrong when he hailed it as marking the revival of polite learning in America. But in Philadelphia Mathew Carey's *American Museum* and Joseph Dennie's *Portfolio*, with contributions by Thomas Paine, Nicholas Biddle, and Philip Freneau, were equally learned and polite.

The editors of the *Anthology* had seen some of the highly informative letters John Lowell was writing home to his family that seemed exactly to fill their bill. They printed as leading articles a long series of them under diverse pseudonyms, as by 'a gentleman who has all the qualities which taste, talents, fortune and liberality can give to make him a pleasant traveller.' They had a trick of ante-dating or post-dating them to suit their convenience. This, with the variety of *noms de plume*, makes attribution dangerous, but there is both internal and collateral evidence that Smelfungus, who gives in an early number an account of the pictures in the Louvre, was using the 'fervid genius and rapid pen' of our pleasant traveller in a family letter.

'Here,' he says near the end, 'is a female head by Leonardo

da Vinci. Were it alive it would set all the men crazy. I never saw anything so fascinating, and it smiled so bewitchingly that had I been alone I should certainly have kissed it.'

In September the wandering clan, after a visit to some Boston Lees in Bordeaux, journeyed to Genoa. Here they fell in with an interesting circle, Washington Irving, who notes the acquaintance in his diary, the fifth Lord Shaftesbury and his lady, a Mrs. Bird with her covey of many daughters, and Andrew Wilson, the talented young Scotch painter. In Genoa they may even have confronted Anti-Christ, for it was at an exhibition there that same October that Napoleon, standing in admiration before one of Wilson's serene landscapes, was told that the artist was a native of *Albion la perfide* and epigrammed, '*Le talent n'a pas de pays.*'

From Genoa the Lowells proceeded by easy stages to Milan, Florence, Rome, Naples, made the Sicilian *giro*, and then back to Rome for the winter. Thence he sent home news of his improving health, the low state of the Italian people, the treatment of Americans abroad, and the eternal charm of Italy.

'Rome Nov. 27th, 1804

'... I have in a very considerable degree restored the tone of my nervous system tho' you know by experience how difficult it is to shake off the remnants of these complaints. The least deviation, the least anxiety, disturbs my nerves and makes me dread a relapse — I hope however that time will fortify me against this most terrible of all maladies — As to general health, I have as much as I have enjoyed for several years — They even say, that I have gained flesh, so as to be materially altered — This however I think, *badinage*. . . .'

'Rome Dec. 9th, 1804

'Paris, London, Amsterdam, Marseilles, Bordeaux united cannot shew so many objects of real distress as meet you in every direction at Rome. It is, my friend, the most distressing most heart breaking sight I ever beheld — you are pursued at *every* corner by beggars and if you give to one, you are instantly thronged with others; While at the same moment you see *Dapper Priests* in stockings of bright purple, with hats girt with the same bright colour, tripping it lightly along from the shop of the Frisseur, unspoiled by these poor wretches who perhaps have solicited them too often in vain or who think that the language of nature will plead more powerfully with strangers unaccustomed to such scenes of horror — The Rich and Proud Cardinal too, wrapped in his double folds of purple, arrayed with proud magnificence, and accompanied with his princely train of liveried domestics rolls along unheeding these objects of horror which meet him on every side — You see the Poor at this bleak season almost without clothes, and you are told that death often sets them free from these complicated miseries produced by famine and Nakedness ——'

'Naples, Dec. 18, 1804

'I derived a high degree of satisfaction on my arrival here to see the *Streamers* of a Ship of War of the United States fluttering in the Gale — An American who has not been in Europe can form no idea of the contemptuous opinion which Europeans in General have of America — Though he soon finds that this proceeds from profound ignorance, an ignorance which pervades *even the literary* part of the Community, yet, he cannot avoid the sensation of vexation — The Europeans confound all America, Southern and Northern, and the Islands of the Gulf of Mexico under one common name — They think they are the same. A Swiss Governor of a city proposed to me to take a letter for *Jamaica*, and even at *Naples*, where we have commercial connections, they subjected a vessell from Salem which left it when there were two feet of snow on the ground to a quarantine of forty days, because they have heard that some parts of the United States are afflicted with Epidemics — Upon the arrival of Commr. Preble, and a remonstrance from him, she was released and a promise made, that regulations less vexatious should be decreed. Wherever our Frigates have made their appearance, the American character has instantly risen, its citizens treated with more respect, and more correct ideas are entertained in relation to our consequence.

'Next to the English, the Americans are now favored in all places, where the dread of France does not control their secret wishes. Those who stay in their own country, and hear only the ridiculous puffings of ourselves in Presidential Addresses, and in our bombastic newspaper paragraphs may believe that we are dreaded abroad as much as we are puffed at home, but those who encounter the thousand mortifications that American travellers experience, will think a Barbary was of great utility, if it only serves to make us known and respected by other nations.'

In Rome and Naples he began to take an interest in music and the Opera Buffa. 'The person that can hear without pleasure the delightful airs of Cimarosa and Paisiello is fit for treason, stratagems, and murder.' Had he known that their flowing and graceful melodies made these musicians personal favorites of Anti-Christ, he might have been disquieted. Perhaps he was reassured by the knowledge that both were also protégés of the Empress Catherine. Cimarosa, indeed, was her official *compositeur de chambre*, a tricky assignment. One letter of twenty thousand words was a translation of the Duca del Torre's minute account of the last eruption of Vesuvius, which ran serially through three numbers of the *Monthly Anthology*.

In the early summer of 1805, he was back in Paris and sent Francis a concise statement of the Emperor's plan for the new totalitarian order in Continental Europe.

'Napoleon plans to make Bavaria as strong as Austria and Prussia, Poland a new kingdom, and unite Holland, Germany, France, Spain, Turkey, and Italy under one emperor to defend

Europe against the Scythians. . . . My respect for the government whose temporary protection I enjoy would prevent my
giving you any decided opinions if I had formed any.'

In the spring of 1806, he was again in England and made a
tour to the north, to visit the literary shrines of Cowper, Burns,
and Scott. The Lake poets admired by Charles were not included and he had doubts about Scott. His poetic taste and
feeling for nature never outgrew the eighteenth century: 'Buxton
to Birmingham sixty-one miles in a day. Charming country.
Ceres and Flora laid their heads together to lay it out. Thom-
son's Summer is a perpetual commentary on the country I have
been travelling.'

His chief interest, however, was in the scenes of Doctor Johnson's life. He scoured London for memorials, spent some days
in Litchfield and drove the ten miles out to Bromley where in
the parish churchyard lay Samuel's Letty idealized under the
epitaph, *Formosa, Culta, Ingeniosa, Pia.* The long ridges overlooking the smoky valley of the Thames and the distant spires,
towers, and domes of London recalled the Roxbury hilltop he
had inherited from the Old Judge. We can hardly doubt that
it was then and there that in his mind he christened it Bromley
Vale, and made the sketch of the stone castellated tower of
which he was to erect a replica on his own ground.

Throughout his years abroad he had been flooding Francis
with letters about the additions and repairs that were being
made to his stone winter house in School Street. Francis must
have had to do some quick thinking, for John changed his mind
about the architecture after each of his letters — it took more
than two months to receive a reply — and in the next sent a
rough pen drawing showing how his last could be improved.
In the autumn of 1806, the house was ready and he came home
to occupy it with his wife, two daughters, and son, little John
Amory, who had been in school for a year in London and Paris.

Meanwhile, Francis had been overworking himself at the

characteristic Lowell pace. Besides his assiduities in connection with the doing over of John's house, he was deep in house property on his own account. From Paris in November, 1805, John wrote him: 'Thirty days before you write me that you can not afford to keep your Somerset St. house, which I suppose cost $7000, and in five weeks you buy a house at $20,000. So we preach, so we practice.' The new house was on the recently developed Park Street, which was to be for two generations inhabited by Lowells, Lawrences, Ticknors, Amorys, Gores, Cabots, Gardners, Masons, Warrens, Dexters, Ameses, Paynes, Motleys, and Quincys — the geographical centre of the Brahmin world.

In the decade beginning in 1802, the Registry of Deeds in Boston shows the transfer to Francis Cabot Lowell of more than a score of properties on India Wharf, Long Wharf, and in the North and West Ends. He also acquired lands in Maine. His commercial ventures were equally multifarious, ranging from the purchase of cotton and foreign exchange and the discounting of innumerable notes for all and sundry to the shipment of a cargo of juniper berries to Madeira. He was doing even better for himself in commerce than John had at the bar, but the fears for his health were proving only too well founded. He was approaching a breakdown, and despite her Jackson verve, Hannah, his wife, worn out with household cares, was in nearly as bad a case. They decided to try John's therapeutic measures and go abroad for three years. Before doing so, Hannah made a trip to New York, where she wrote a letter to her 'Dear Mother,' as nearly all the members of the clan called the Old Judge's 'best-beloved' girl, his third wife Rebecca:

'Protected by a flannel waistcoat, drawers, a greatcoat and a shawl [it was the last week in June], I rode very comfortably to Providence where we arrived at half past ten on Friday morning. You will perhaps think it extraordinary that we found the ride tolerably pleasant when I tell you that most of the stages were very crowded; but I assure you I found it so notwithstanding a neighbour of mine, a fat gentleman (who went upon the plan of equalization) put upon me a large portion of two hundred and fifty — which he informed us was his weight — if he would have made it a permanent gift, and I had possessed the power of distributing it over my frame of bones nothing could have been more acceptable — but I could not see the advantage to myself of supporting it so partially — and after the day became warm I don't know that I should have preserved my good humor — had I not recollected the text "bear ye one another's burthens." '

The stage-coaches of the day were built with three transverse seats supposed to accommodate nine adult passengers. Heavy baggage was put on behind, but hand baggage and children occupied the floor, causing, as Edward Everett noted in his diary, discomfort to long legs.

In the autumn of 1810, Francis and Hannah sailed for Glasgow. With them went 'John Lowell, Jr.,' aged twelve, Francis Cabot Lowell, Jr., aged eight, who was to be Emerson's classmate and lifelong friend; Edward Jackson Lowell, seven; and little Augustus Thorndike, whose twice great-grandson was to marry a Lowell. They carried substantial funds in the form of Spanish gold doubloons, pieces of eight, which could be exchanged in England at the rate of £4.7.6 per doubloon.

At first they took a furnished house in Edinburgh, but later for the sake of Hannah's health left the small boys in the custody of Mrs. Grant and toured England in leisurely fashion. Like John, Francis had letters of introduction from Timothy Pickering, 'a true old Roman with an old-fashioned integrity of patriotism little known in modern days.' One was to George Henry Rose, who had been the special emissary of the Crown in Washington to try to settle the unfortunate affair of the *Chesapeake* and the *Leopard*. With him, the old Roman, at that time a senator, had carried on a correspondence concerning the possibility of New England's withdrawal from the Union, that, under his own Logan Act, put through when he was Secretary of State, made him liable for a fine of five thousand dollars and three years in jail. Sir George, as he had now become, introduced Francis to governmental and parliamentary society, where he found the speaking in the House of Commons 'superior to ours at home. Slow and distinct, not loud, or ranting.'

While the children were with the admirable Mrs. Grant, who brought them safely through serious attacks of scarlet fever, Francis and Hannah journeyed to Bristol to make the acquaintance of their kinsmen, descended from the Samuel Lowell who had left Newbury to return to the old home in 1691. They found them agreeable people in easy circumstances, the current head of the house a clergyman of the Church of England.

'With our cousins Lowell,' wrote Hannah, 'we are quite charmed. Mr. Lowell in manner and looks retains the animation and vivacity of youth. In person and face he is quite a Lowell. A likeness of him taken some years since strongly resembles brother Lowell.'

For Francis, however, the high point of the Bristol visit was a meeting with old Mr. Richard Lechmere, nephew of Lord Lechmere of Evesham, Privy Councillor and Chancellor of the Duchy of Lancaster in the government of Sir Robert Walpole. Born in 1727, he had emigrated as a boy to the New World, risen by his early thirties to be collector of the port of Boston, but left the Bay Colony forever on that melancholy seventeenth of March in '76. In a letter to Sam Gardner, Francis tells of the encounter in a paragraph that, with Mr. Madison's War, detested and opposed by the Federalists, just around the corner, is of significance in the history of the family.

'Old Mr. Lechmere is a wonderful man for his years, eighty-four. Seeing an American always puts him in fine spirits. He says he has never regretted leaving Boston but once, *and that is ever since*. The example of the refugees should be a warning to our friends if trouble comes to stay by and fight it out.'

On his journeys back and forth between Edinburgh, Bristol, and London he spent several weeks in Lancashire, standing for hours completely absorbed before the machines in the cotton mills, and asking a thousand questions of owners and operatives.

A few months later he wrote to his sister-in-law of the degeneration of the London stage.

'Your two letters were not the less acceptable for being unexpected. We have now been in London more than three weeks and yet we have seen or done nothing it takes so long a time to get used to London. I suppose we shall soon begin to do something. We have seen Mrs. Siddons twice. I think she has fallen off very much since I saw her before. Either I have grown old and lost the little fondness I had for the stage or else the acting has greatly degenerated. I cannot but think this last is the case. Too much time is concerned in the parade of the play. Processions and horses are introduced on every occasion and they so interrupt the story that you lose all interest in it. They will on some trifling occasion bring ten or twenty live horses on the Stage. These horses have been taught all the tricks of the Circus. Indeed I am told they are the same horses that perform in the Circus. So these horses are taught to rear up on their hind legs and act like gay and unruly horses. But the poor beasts have no spirit in them. They appear to be affecting it, like the soldiers (in one of Hogarth's pictures) who being worn out by a long siege and looking like skeletons are taking off their hats and affecting to Huzza at the command of their Captain, but you imagine the sound to die on their lips and perceive the rejoicing is all affected. Mr. Kimball is a very indifferent performer, the other actors imitate him, and the actress is Mrs. Siddons.'

From London they went to Cheltenham, where Hannah wrote her mother:

'We have been here upwards of a fortnight and as the water seems to agree with Mr. Lowell we shall stay some time longer. When we quit this we shall go directly to Bristol unless we conclude to take an excursion into Wales first. We live here at a boarding house which contains about fifteen or sixteen boarders who are constantly changing so that we see a considerable variety of company. From those who are here and who have been at other houses we learn that ours is one of the most sociable as well as the smallest in the place. But still we are very far from the sociability you would expect in such a place. The English character is very reserved, and very different from the Scotch or ours. The English seem to like to confine themselves very much to their own circles and not to dislike solitude. This proceeds partly from the habits which all the Nobility and Gentry have of spending several months in every year at their country seats which makes them very unsocial. They only come to town to get clothed and go to the public amusements, and give one Great Rout in the season.

'The Gentlemen in general here are Idlers and do not discover as much talent as you would expect. I think they are much inferior in intellect to the Company you meet at Ballston, and they you know are not a fine specimen of the Country. The place is thinner than usual this season, said to be owing to the general embarrassment of trade.'

A week later she wrote, after news that the little house in which her stepmother-in-law and her daughter had been established was satisfactory:

'I am glad Sally finds the new house so pleasant; and hope you like it as well as you did the other. They tell me you have got a rather steep pair of stairs but that you intend to remedy that inconvenience by putting a bed below — I think you should do that and everything else to make yourself comfortable — you have always kept such strict watch over yourself upon this point that I do not think you will get before the rest of the world if you indulge from this time to the end of your life — but before you will practice as I would have you I am afraid you must take a trip across the Atlantic and see how the nice comfortable ladies here grow fat by a little salutory self attention.'

In November, 1811, they went to Paris for the winter. In the spring they came back to London, but it soon became evident that the war with England the 'Rebel' at home was using his gifts of pen to avert was inevitable. Just before hostilities were declared, they took an American ship for home. Halfway over they were captured by a British frigate and taken into Halifax. After some delay, as Hannah wrote back to Mrs. Grant, they 'hired a small dirty boat at a great price to take us to Boston. It took ten days. I decided on entering Boston Harbor it was more beautiful than anything I had seen in my absence.'

The British had twice searched their baggage, but it was in his brilliant and tenacious brain, toughened by the calculations of eclipses, that Francis Cabot Lowell brought back the plans of the most advanced machines for the spinning of cotton into yarn and power looms for weaving it into cloth. Exportation of either machines or plans was forbidden under British law and punished by heavy pains and penalties, but this piece of purely mental exportation never became an international incident.

It was these secrets of manufacture intangibly hidden in his brain that were to create the huge factories of Lowell and Lawrence.

4
CHAPTER

Mr. Madison's War [1]

W HEN, SIX YEARS EARLIER, John Lowell and family after three years abroad landed back in Boston, they found many changes in that thriving town that Alexander Hamilton had called the 'Headquarters of Good Principles.' The population had reached the round figure of 25,000, but was fast falling farther behind New York with 60,000 and Philadelphia with 70,000. The North and West Ends were being built up. John Quincy Adams, back from Washington during the Senate's recess in 1806 to give his lectures on Rhetoric and Oratory at Harvard,

[1] For the War of 1812, its causes, course, and results, the indispensable text is to be found in the nine volumes of Henry Adams's *History of the United States in the Administrations of Jefferson and Madison.* The breadth and liveliness of the narrative displays an historical imagination of the first order, and the research must have been colossal. The preliminary study, Henry Adams's first book, *Documents relating to New England Federalism* covers this portion of the field with even greater detail. *The Maritime History of Massachusetts* by that best of seagoing historians, S. E. Morison, is also valuable.

noted in his *Diary*: 'Walk in the evening with George over Beacon Hill. Saw the numerous new houses on the north side of the hill which have quite metamorphosed the appearance of that part of the town.' If he went by way of Summer, soon to be renamed Mount Vernon Street, he saw an even greater change. A year before the Mount Vernon Proprietors, Stephen Higginson, Harrison Gray Otis, Jonathan Mason, Mrs. Hepsibah Swann, widow of General James Swann, and Charles Bulfinch, had begun the erection of the stately Federalist houses that still stand, their trim a little shabby, fighting for a forlorn hope against small apartments and boarding-houses. At the foot of its facile descent, Charles Street had been constructed and protected with piles against the high tides of the Back Bay. Colonel Perkins had shot his last snipe in that terrain. Along the borders of the Common, Tremont, Park, and Beacon Streets were being lined with commodious residences of red brick, grey stone, or both together. Their dates can be distinguished by progress from the Doric to the Ionic to the Corinthian column. Over all, no longer in an airy isolation, presided the admirable Bulfinch State House. A century later a 'Restless Analyst' from Rye or the Cinque Ports, revisiting the American scene, found its gilded dome still 'fresh as a Christmas toy seen across the floor of a large salubrious nursery.'

On Cambridge Street in 1806, a new West Church, a spacious brick edifice, replacing a decayed wooden place of worship, was dedicated and Charles Lowell was ordained as its minister. In Edinburgh his education had been social and practical as well as theological. The eloquent and attractive personality of Dugald Stewart, a liberal Whig and an intuitional philosopher, had deeply impressed him. His lectures were 'like the opening of the heavens' and made a young hearer 'feel that he had a soul.' Charles, like his grandfather in Newburyport, was never deeply concerned about dogmas. He preached Grace and Good Works, and formed friendships with those who achieved them. In Edinburgh and London he met many eminent and

John Lowell (1769–1840), 'The Rebel,' the Old Judge's eldest son by his first wife Sarah Higginson, Federalist pamphleteer, bitter opponent of Jefferson and Madison, was considered by future generations of the family its most brilliant member. After the shock of his failure to save the life of Jason Fairbanks, he abandoned the law and devoted his life to travel, agriculture, and good works. He was active in national and civic affairs from the days of George Washington to those of Andrew Jackson.

Edward Malbone, the boy miniaturist from Newport, painted on ivory the features of the Rebel's sister Anna Cabot Lowell, 'Nancy' (1768–1810), and his wife Rebecca Amory (1771–1842). Nancy, eldest of the Old Judge's nine children, had her hands full at Bromley Vale with younger brothers and sisters and small nephews and nieces, to say nothing of the distinguished guests who sampled the Lowell Madeira.

Rebecca Amory Lowell came back from three years abroad in time to take over the duties of hostess at the Vale after the death of Nancy. With wifely discretion she moderated the Rebel's excitements and cheered him in his depressions. She survived him by two years.

Mrs F. C. Lowell.

Francis Cabot Lowell I (1775–1817), for whom the city of Lowell was named, son of the Old Judge's second wife Susanna Cabot, was too busy with his distilleries, real estate, and cotton mills to be bothered to sit for his portrait in oils; but he and his wife Hannah Jackson did not escape the maker of silhouettes who cut the profiles of his clan.

He brought back from England in his head plans of the power loom for weaving cotton cloth, and applied a paternalistic philosophy of labor to the first mass production in New England.

F. C. Lowell.

Richard Staigg's miniature of the Reverend Charles Lowell (1782–1861), the Old Judge's youngest son, fruit of his third marriage to the widow Rebecca Russell Tyng, reveals his refined and gentle nature. He married Harriet Traill Spence, purchased the historic residence of Elmwood, and was the father of James Russell Lowell. He, too, like his older brothers, had the benefit of foreign travel as part of his education. For half a century he was pastor of West Church in Boston.

worthy characters, the Earl of Buchan and Wilberforce among them, and made pilgrimages to the homes of Southey and Wordsworth. But despite lectures, country excursions, dinners, and tea parties, he always had time to do errands for the clan, sending home books to his sister Nancy, and to Francis complete plans of one of the best Scotch distilleries. He brought to the West Church a humanity and lifted horizon, for which he was admired and loved by his people. He was practical, too, as well as kindly. It was he, as the Reverend Doctor William Bentley records in his invaluable diary, that first broke away from the old Puritan custom of baptizing infants only after the sermon. Charles baptized them before it, 'that they might not be so long separated from their parents and those that fed them.'

After his installation he married, outside of the clan, Harriet Traill Spence of Portsmouth, whose family came from the Orkney Islands. They were Tories in sympathy and Episcopalian in religion. From their foggy northern home they brought a certain mystical dreaminess that sometimes obscured the need for immediate action in the small imperative affairs of daily living. In the clan this was known as 'the Spence negligence.' Harriet, however, was cordially welcomed. They felt that she was practically a cousin, as she was the grand-niece of the Reverend John Lowell's second wife, who was accepted by the clan as a grandmother by brevet. She and Charles had played together as children in Portsmouth. On her engagement John Lowell wrote her: 'I embrace you my sweet girl with pleasure. My youngest brother from his age, his sentiments, his manners, and his virtues, has the strongest claim upon my love, my protection and my ardent friendship.'

It was 'this protection' and an inheritance from his mother that in 1818 enabled Charles to buy from the estate of Elbridge Gerry the delightful house of Elmwood, where he was to live for the rest of his long life. Several times a week he left its bird-haunted gardens to drive the four miles into the North End of Boston, to do along with another Cantabrigian, Andrews Norton, what he could to brighten the lives of the scantily privileged black and white dwellers in that section. Those *in extremis* found comfort and support in his gentle presence and simple faith. Even the Republican Governor, James Sullivan, the Old Judge's friend, but his brother the Rebel's old legal antagonist and political foe, on his deathbed at sixty-four sent for Charles, less than half his age, and made an edifying end.

Meanwhile, John himself, back from abroad in better health, was finding plenty of occupation. After a short winter in the newly enlarged house on School Street, complete now with greenhouse, he moved out to Bromley Vale in the spring of 1807, and applied himself to improving the estate. He built a small stone castle to give it atmosphere, and remind him of the England that he loved, a little pond to bathe in, a windmill for irrigation, and five greenhouses full of rare flowers, including some of the earliest orchids grown under glass in America. His first consignment of Madeira wine after his return arrived that summer. It consisted of a pipe and a third. A pipe was a double hogshead of one hundred and twenty-six gallons. He received, therefore, six hundred and seventy-two full quarts for the very reasonable price of sixty pounds. This, no doubt, was shared and appreciated by the circle of 'Federalist talkers' as they were called by the Opposition, of which he was by no means the least fluent. As Doctor Johnson said of Burke, he was never unwilling to talk or in haste to leave off. Mrs. Mary Lee, the youngest daughter of Jonathan Jackson, sister of Francis' wife, Hannah, wrote of 'Brother Lowell,' 'you know he can talk himself into a belief of anything. . . . I was such a good listener that I detained him for nearly two hours.'

And in 1807, the Federalist drawing-rooms of Boston, where, as an old lady said, you would as soon expect to see a cow as a Jacobin, had something to talk about. Thomas Jefferson, 'that man' in the White House, was their flaming topic. Even John Adams, the Sage of Quincy, who for the last twenty years of his life was to correspond intimately, even affectionately, with the Sage of Monticello, was talking *lèse majesté*. John Lowell writing to Caleb Cushing recorded: 'Just before Mr. Adams wore ship to follow his son who had just gone in stays, he said in my presence with great emotion: "Jefferson is the deepest dissembler and most artful hypocrite I ever knew." '

In his first inaugural on March 4, 1801, the philosopher-President, lover of family and fireside, of mountain and meadow, of music, of French letters and Greek poetry in the original; architect, agriculturalist, botanist, bird-lover, fisherman; connoisseur of claret, distruster of oratory, that civilized man of whom Emerson said the glow of one warm thought was worth more to him than money, had extended the olive branch:

'Difference of opinion is not difference of principle. We have called by different names brethren of the same principle. . . . We are all Republicans — we are all Federalists. If there be any among us who would wish to dissolve this Union or to change its Republican form, let them stand as monuments of the safety with which error of opinion may be tolerated when reason is left free to combat it.'

Unfortunately, the principal monuments, Timothy Pickering, George Cabot, and Fisher Ames, would not stand quietly. The Louisiana Purchase, and what seagoing New England thought supine acceptance of both French and British interference with American commerce, exacerbated them to the limit of exacerbation. By the end of his first term, a substantial working majority in the five northeastern states was convinced that Thomas Jefferson was no better than Tom Paine, that he believed in Voltaire as much as he did in Christ, and put *The Age of Reason* before the Bible. The Federalist press and the party's representatives in Congress expressed this view with a virulence unsurpassed in political warfare. In 1803, Timothy Pickering was in correspondence with like-minded men in other states concerning a plan to elect Aaron Burr governor of New York and use that as a stepping-stone to the presidency of a new inde-

pendent confederation of Northern States. Fortunately John
Lowell was safely abroad while this was going on.

Despite the President's broad and humorous mind, 'The unbounded calumnies of the Federal Party' seem at last to have got
under his skin. In his second inaugural, March 4, 1805, he
struck a different note. He delicately compares the Essex Junto
to the medicine men of the Indians; 'interested and crafty individuals who feel themselves something in the present order of
things and fear to become nothing in any other.'

The gage was publicly thrown and the battle renewed with
even greater violence.

The month of June, 1807, was nearly as momentous and exciting to the newly United States as April, 1775, had been for
the colonies. On the twenty-second of that month the new
American frigate, *Chesapeake*, forty-four guns, sailing out of
Hampton Roads on a shake-down cruise, Commodore James
Barron in command, with a green crew, and her decks a litter of
spars and supplies, was accompanied, and just outside the three-
mile limit accosted, by the British frigate *Leopard*, fifty guns,
asking permission to send over an officer with dispatches. On
his arrival the 'dispatches' turned out to be an order from the
admiral commanding at Halifax, George Cranfield Berkeley,
second son of the fourth Earl and twelfth Baron Berkeley, the
great-great-grandson of Old Percival's employer, to Captain
Humphries of the *Leopard*. He was to search the *Chesapeake* for
certain deserters from the British frigate *Halifax*. Barron de-
murred at mustering his men at the order of an officer of another navy. The *Leopard's* boat returned to her, and before the
American ship could be made ready for action she received
three raking broadsides at point-blank range, killing three men
and wounding eighteen, the Commodore among them. Defense was hopeless, and to avoid further slaughter, the Stars and
Stripes was struck. As the flag came slowly, ignominiously
down, a solitary gun was fired from a live coal carried from the
cook's galley by one of the lieutenants in his bare hand.

From the British point of view there was some modest measure of justification, at least for the search. England was involved in what seemed, and probably was, a life-and-death struggle. Her sea-power was her one dominant weapon against the conqueror of Continental Europe and his New Order. Her victory at Trafalgar eighteen months before had made her mistress of the seas, and little disposed to permit anyone to jeopardize that position. From the time of our own naval wars with France and the Tripolitan pirates, there had been a rising tide of deserters from the British Navy to seek employment on American ships both public and private, where the pay was better and the cat-o'-nine tails less active. It is estimated that at the time of the incident from thirty thousand to forty thousand English seamen were sailing under the American flag.

The summer before, a French squadron of ships of the line had taken refuge in Chesapeake Bay and had been allowed to refit, claim deserters, and receive other aid and comfort. It was still there. International law required that the British fleet, watching and waiting for them outside the capes, should not be in any way hampered. The five English seamen thought to be on the *Chesapeake* were not only deserters but mutineers. On March 7, while the frigate *Halifax*, Lord James Townsend commanding, was weighing anchor, they had risen against their officer, threatened to murder him, made off in a boat, and enlisted the same day in the American Navy. Efforts to secure them through diplomatic channels brought promises and referrals from one authority to another, but no men back. In short, the well-known and always annoying run-around. All five men were on board the *Chesapeake*. Four deserted from her just before she sailed. The fifth, Jenkin Ratford, a native of London, was found hiding in a coal hole, taken, tried in a British naval court, and executed as a mutineer. With him they took three other deserters from the *Melampus*, one a citizen of Buenos Aires and two colored men born slaves in Maryland, natives of the United States but not citizens; a nice point of international law. Twelve other British seamen found on the *Chesapeake* were not deserters and were not taken.

These palliative facts did little or nothing to obscure for the majority of patriotic Americans the high-handed attack on a 'public' vessel flying our flag. They were, however, given full consideration by the Massachusetts Federalists, and particularly by the logical legal mind of John Lowell, who 'could talk himself into a belief of anything.'

On July 9, 1807, John Quincy Adams noted in his *Diary*, 'A debate somewhat warm with Mr. John Lowell at the Suffolk Insurance Office,' and on the eleventh, 'J. Phillips told me I should have my head taken off for apostacy by the Federalists.'

In connection with an *ex post facto* dispute concerning the aims and results of the Hartford Convention, he amplifies the story of the 'debate' in a document first printed by his grandson in 1877:

'In relating this transaction at the distance of two and twenty years since it happened, will my countrymen forgive the emotion which, upon the recital of it, I cannot suppress! It was the last step in a gradation of outrages which it was painful enough to an American to see his country endure from foreign insolence and oppression. Judge then, now — judge upon this cold narrative, twenty-two years after the event — of my feelings when I heard this transaction of the British admiral, Berkeley, openly justified at noonday by one of my now confederate correspondents, in a public insurance office upon the exchange at Boston.

'This then, was the cause, and not (as the inventive Mr. Giles would make you believe) the embargo, or *his* political pandarism, which alienated me from that day and forever from the councils of the Federal party. I contested warmly, in the insurance office, the position of this gentleman — that British naval officers had a *right* to seize and carry away from an American ship-of-war any deserter from the British navy. The discussion between us assembled became so painfully animated that, from that day, there has been little personal intercourse between that citizen and me.'

In the late summer of 1807, John Lowell printed his own and the Federalist view of the incident in one of the ablest of his many political pamphlets, *Peace without Dishonour — War without Hope. Being a calm and Dispassionate Enquiry into the Question of the Chesapeake and the necessity and Expediency of War. By a Yankee Farmer.* The *nomme de guerre* was shrewdly chosen, since 'that man' was supposed always to stand for the ideals and interests of the agricultural South against the designs of the commercial North.

Reviewing the facts as above set forth with accuracy and amplitude and 'despising the threats of prosecution for treason,' John Lowell said he would use his right of free speech to save his country from an unjustifiable and hopeless war. What did the *Chesapeake* affair or anything else amount to in the face of the tremendous fact of England's struggle with France? All thoughtful men knew that only her armies and her fleet stood between us and the slavery that would be our portion should France prevail. The piece was well-reasoned and vigorously written, but through the clarifying perspective of history it is seen to be lacking in the vision and feeling that led to John Quincy Adams's highly honorable apostasy from the party. War in 1807 might have been more glorious than it was in 1812. 'That' man in the White House, however, also had a passion for peace. In December he put through his least successful *démarche* in philosophical government. He sought to avoid war and make both Engand and France listen to reason by touching *their* pockets and their daily lives through the Embargo, an 'experiment noble in purpose,' which, spelled backwards, as Federalist wits were not slow to point out, is O grab me!

The effect, immediately on the ship-owning North, and presently on the land-owning South, was calamitous. All foreign and much coastwise commerce, other than smuggling, ceased and determined. Dismantled ships rotted at mouldy wharves, merchants closed their doors, and artisans dropped their tools. The value of inventories of American commodities for export —

timber, salt-fish, cotton, tobacco — sank close to zero. There
was no ceiling on the price of smuggled imports. The debtor
class all but unanimously went bankrupt. Tens of thousands of
sailors were idle and their families hungry. The supply of rum
was greatly reduced. The Federalists had again a fighting cause,
and talked more openly of secession. The Newburyport Sea
Fencibles, a military organization of sailors out of work, of-
ficered by their former captains and owners, raised an only five-
star-spangled banner over the old fort on Plum Island.

The sequel in industrial England was equally violent. There
were few mill-owners like Robert Owen, who closed his cotton
mill for four months and paid his operatives full wages, seven
thousand pounds, out of his own personal pocket.

It was, of course, the Essex Junto that led the fight against
the administration. Timothy Pickering and George Cabot were
its policy-makers with advice from James Hillhouse of Connecticut and Gouverneur Morris of New York. After the death
of Fisher Ames in 1808, a year before Jefferson in his last days
of office was forced to sign the bill repealing the Embargo, John
Lowell became their chief propagandist in press and pamphlet.
It may be as his son, John Amory Lowell, says, that he was
against all disunion, that to accuse the Federalists of enmity to
the Union was to 'accuse them of murdering the child of their
bosoms,' but, as one reads his pamphlets today, it seems clear
that he did not look at secession as the worst of possible evils.[1]

---

[1] Between the Embargo and the close of the War of 1812, John Lowell wrote and
published fourteen pamphlets under various pseudonyms or anonymously: *Peace
without Dishonor — War without Hope, being a calm and dispassionate inquiry into the
question of the Chesapeake and the necessity for war*, by a Yankee Farmer, 1807; *Analysis
of the late Correspondence between our Administration and Great Britain and France*, 1808;
Supplements to the same, 1808; *Thoughts upon the conduct of our Administration in relation
both to Great Britain and France, more especially in reference to the late negotiation concerning
the attack on the Chesapeake*, by a Friend to Peace, 1808; *Remarks on the Hon. J. Q.
Adams's Review of Mr. Ames's Works*, 1809; *The Diplomatic Policy of Mr. Madison un-
veiled, by a Bostonian*, 1810; *The New England Patriot — being a candid comparison of the
principles and conduct of the Washington and Jefferson Administrations*, 1810; *The Impartial
Inquirer — (on the Nonintercourse and Florida questions,)* by a citizen of Massachusetts,
1811; *Mr. Madison's War*, by a New England Farmer, 1812; *Perpetual War the policy*

After the repeal of the Embargo in 1809, business looked up, despite the Non-Intercourse Act forbidding trade with France or England during the continuance of the British Orders in Council and Napoleon's Berlin and Milan Decrees. But war clouds still obscured the eastern horizon and the New England States still talked secession. John Lowell, however, in the three years before 1812, produced only four pamphlets and those not of a very inflammatory nature. Unlike some of his fellow Federalists he seems to have had no intimate relations with John Henry, the British *agent provocateur* from Nova Scotia, or George Rose, the special envoy to Washington for the settlement of the *Chesapeake* affair. He took more time for his greenhouses and public service in other fields.

In 1810, he was elected a member of the Harvard Corporation, further strengthening its Federalist and Unitarian position. He became the prime mover in the activities of the Massachusetts Society for the Promotion of Agriculture, of which the Old Judge had been president. He was elected a member of the Anthology Society. He declined the honor, however, in a letter of sound self-criticism.

'While I could not on the one hand suffer it to be believed, that I was indifferent to the good opinion which you have been pleased to express of me, on the other I could not in justice to myself permit for a moment, that any literary man in our Country should believe, that I considered myself as entitled to be ranked among that small phalanx of intrepid men, who have

of *Mr. Madison*, by a New England Farmer, 1812; *The Road to Peace, Commerce, Wealth and Happiness*, by an Old Farmer, 1813; *Examination of Mr. Dexter's Address to the Electors of Massachusetts*, 1814; *Review of a Treatise on Expatriation by George Hay, Esq.*, by a Massachusetts Lawyer, 1814; *Gov. Strong's Calumniator Reproved*, by Nobel-esprit, 1814.

He was also a frequent and important contributor to the Federalist Boston *Advertiser*, and in 1810 helped to finance and found the *Weekly Messenger*, an organ for the expression of the views of young Federalists, edited by James Cutler, Nathan Hale, and H. D. Sedgwick. Its aims as stated in the prospectus were 'to diffuse such information as may be useful to citizens of every condition, to soften the asperity of party spirit, to vindicate the truth, and to maintain the interests of our country.'

undertaken the arduous and almost hopeless task of rescuing the literary character of our Country from the state of merited disgrace into which it had fallen. . . . I have no right to be placed among the correctors and dictators of the publick taste.

'I am aware, that those who do not know me may attribute these remarks to an affected modesty, and may think them little consistent with the practice of a man who is filling the publick ear with half-digested political essays — but you will excuse me for defending myself against this charge by saying, that political discussions must be adapted to the depraved taste of the Country, and that they are ill calculated from their objects and the temper in which they are written, to advance the cause of literature.'

The episode seems to have caused him to reflect further on the progress of intellectual achievement in America. A little later he wrote to Francis in Edinburgh:

'As to the mechanick arts, and even the fine arts it may be truly said that we have a great natural turn for them, and that we excel in them as much as could be expected considering the degree of encouragement they receive or could receive in a new country.

'We have invented more usefull machines within twenty years than have been invented in all Europe, and we need but mention our Wests, Copleys, Stewarts, Trumbulls, Alstons, etc., to convince any liberal foreigner that the Fine Arts do not refuse us their aid, and that we only want the European Capital to give them encouragement.

'As to our literature, while it ought to be admitted that it is yet in its infancy yet it ought to be strenuously contended not only that it is daily improving but that we can show individuals in every profession who would be honored in any city of Europe.

'No Law reports published in England are superior to Tyng's and no legal opinions more sound or more elegantly expressed than those of Parsons. Ames's works which you ought to have may be safely put in competition with any work of any English or Scotch writer now living.

'Kirkland's biography of Ames is as fine a model of that species of writing as has been produced these twenty years in the English language, and I wish you would get Dr. Brown to read it and give his opinion of it.

'Tell him the author is now the President of our University, and that we have a host of young men who are treading fast on his steps.'

On August 5, 1811, he wrote a long letter which reveals the tightening of the political situation and his growing influence in it, as well as one of his 'poor fits,' as the clan called them.

'Your letter of the 16th of June was yesterday received — I acknowledge that I have been negligent in not writing to you since the arrival of the gardner. The Publick papers must be my apology. I have written more than sixty pages of a large Octavo within twenty days in answer to the most violent Philippick which Gerry has made against the town of Boston for adopting certain resolutions which I, without consulting any one on my own responsibility proposed, and which were passed by nearly five thousand people unanimously and with applause.

'I was therefore bound in honour to defend the Town — how I have done it you may judge by one circumstance. The subject was local, *affecting only our own town and state* — Yet without the smallest influence, or exertion my pieces (signed a "Boston Rebel" in ridicule of Gerry who declared us in a state of Insurrection) were reprinted in twenty-seven papers in Massachusetts, and in *eight other states* of the Union including Charleston, South Carolina — on the 4th of July the *Boston Rebel* was given as a toast in Boston — Salem — Sterling in Worcester County — in Northampton — in New Bedford — in Hallowell and in Charleston, South Carolina. . . .

'. . . Gerry's speech breathes nothing but defiance and oppression. It proposes civil war — and threatens massacre and exile. It has a thin covering of moderation but such is its spirit and so was it received. The democratic majority did more towards an open civil war in three weeks session of the legislature than was done in ten years before the revolution. But the Federalists are neither dispirited or divided. They will avoid collision as long as possible but when Attacked and compelled to defend themselves they will do it, I hope, and believe, *like men*. So much for Egotism and politicks. Now for an answer to your letter. The gardener has arrived and I am much obliged to you for him — he is civil — sober — steady, not much of a gardner, but a good underworkman — he fulfills my expectations and wishes except that I fear he will never make a first Gardner — Time may however improve him. . . .

'. . . I cannot answer you what you can or cannot bring home — as the case stands I do not see that you can have a *second* shirt and as you are a Federalist I presume they would strip you even of your first if made in England.

'. . . You ask about the sale of my house — I have not sold it because I had three applications for it, and to sell it because I could not keep it consistently with the *interests of four dependent children* — This is all the secret — in the full hope and expectation of selling it I bought another house below S. Cabot's, a corner house of a new unfinished block — I paid him 7500 dolls. I intended to sell my own for 20,000 — but I have failed. I shall now put up offices round my yard and live in my own, and let or sell Quincy's.'

This is the first report of the self-chosen epithet 'Rebel' which has clung to him ever since. Unlike other rebels, he was not against the established order, but against those with rising power to destroy it. The resolutions were not for out-and-out secession, but for nullification of the Non-Intercourse Act, and a complete disassociation of New England from the hostilities that the Western 'War Hawks' were fomenting.

By the end of 1811, it was obvious that war was inevitable. The War Hawks were convinced that England was inciting the Indians to resist our expansion to the northwest; and Harrison's victory over Tecumseh at Tippecanoe in November inspired a clamor for the invasion, conquest, and annexation of Canada.

In the East it was proving, as Harrison Gray Otis observed, that 'John Bull, though a good sailor, soldier and on the whole a good fellow, is a bad negotiator and politician.' Captain Mahan believed that adequate naval preparation on our side would have averted war. But the multiplication of unseaworthy gunboats for harbor defense threatened the mistress of the seas with nothing more serious than a slap on her muscular wrist. She persisted in her rude indifference. On the eighth of June, 1812, war was declared on England, on the grounds of impressment, violation of the three-mile limit, paper blockade, and orders in council — not very impressive camouflage for the aims of the War Hawks.

Actual war was closely followed by civil tumult. In Baltimore, breeding-place of riots and the national anthem, where Federalists were in a minority, an armed mob broke into the jail in which a group of prominent men of that persuasion were being held in protective custody, and killed nine including the Revolutionary general, Lingham. They crippled Light Horse Harry Lee for life. Even in Federalist Boston, John Lowell at Bromley Vale received threats of arson and murder. Friends in Boston and neighbors in Roxbury offered to organize for defense. He declined the offer and unsheathed his pen. In the course of the summer he produced two of his most substantial tracts, *Mr. Madison's War*, of sixty-three closely printed pages, and *Perpetual War*, of one hundred and nineteen. Could he have understood that Michelangelo's maxim, 'The more the marble wastes the more the statue grows,' is as pertinent for the pen as for the chisel, they would have been masterpieces in their polemic kind. But those were leisurely times and perhaps the effort necessary to follow and absorb his full and close reasoning may have left a more abiding impression than the concise editorial or radio comment of today. He argued that 'From the moment war was declared those who had conscientiously opposed its declaration have the right, and to preserve consistancy are bound, to endeavor to bring about a peace by showing the folly, the wickedness and the evils of the war.' He was eloquent against 'Conscript militia and the establishment of an immense standing army of guards and spies under the name of a local volunteer force.'

Despite the war that was being waged, his 'poor fit' was over. He built himself a new house, Belle Vue, Number 19 of the new Colonnade Row on Tremont Street, facing the Common from West to Mason Streets. It was of stone with Ionic columns on the first floor, ironwork and brick above. Its like may be seen in many squares in the West End of London. The followers of Governor Gerry called it Codfish Row, sometimes Rotten Row.

The spirit of the clan in that wartime is revealed in a series of letters from Hannah Jackson Lowell to Mrs. Grant. Mr. Madison's War was so far from total that correspondence between friends in Massachusetts and the British Isles seems to have freely carried on, and without censorship at either end:

'Roxbury, Aug. 17, 1812

'From the nature of our government our men of first rate talents are almost exclusively devoted to politics. They give all the time not absolutely necessary for individual occupation to politics. At any interesting crisis their thoughts are entirely engrossed, their feelings are engaged, their passions are influenced, and they speak with an animation you can have no idea of, for it is not felt in England. If Mr. Hayward can take them I think I will send you some political pamphlets. If you were to see all our daily prints you would find that the government of Great Britain had some more zealous supporters in America than almost any in her own dominions. By other papers (I believe for I never read them) you would conclude that we are devoted to Bonaparte. I cannot give you any notion how high parties run here. This declaration of war with England by our government has inflamed them to the highest pitch, but I am enlarging upon a subject of which I know nothing.'

'Roxbury, Oct. 1, 1812

'Be not alarmed for us, my dear madam, I do not think our situation will ever be worse than it is at present, and we hope for some change which will increase our income. In any event we feel safe. Mr. Lowell's oldest brother too, has more than a competency and Mr. C. Lowell is secure from being a clergyman. My oldest brother, the age of my husband, is at the head of his profession, the law, and his pecuniary circumstances are not much injured by the present events. You will perhaps think it is vanity or partiality when I tell you that my second brother holds a high place in his profession of physician and probably in a few years will be as wealthy as he will wish. My youngest brother you may recollect Mr. Lowell had some fears about when Mr. Lee sailed. I felt a good degree of confidence myself respecting him, he is quite secure but has not increased his property as he hoped to have done. If Mr. Lee is not captured his voyage will prove a very profitable one — we can hardly hope that he will not be — but even in that event I shall not regret his going as it served to keep his mind in a proper state for future exertions.'

'Boston, Jan. 6, 1813

'The war is a subject on which I feel half inclined to think with you, that I will say nothing about it. Never, I do believe, was a country in the situation that our country is in, we rejoice over the victories of our enemies and mourn over those of our countrymen. I do not mean but what any instance of valour and intrepidity in an American is gratifying — but the pleasure that we feel at the success of an individual is clouded by regrets, and the consideration that any success on our side but serves to prolong the war. Our gentlemen scold very hard at England for not taking more decisive measures to put us down — for they will never be deterred from their present measures till she lays a strong paw upon us — anything which serves to make the war popular among the people, serves, as you may suppose, to strengthen their hands exceedingly.'

The rejoicing in Federalist Boston at the victories of the Allies over Napoleon was annoying to John Quincy Adams, who wrote his father from Paris in 1814 that no man hated the Yankees like the Duke of Wellington.

Friendly visitors went to and fro between the embattled countries almost as easily as letters. In 1812, S. F. B. Morse won first prize for sculpture at the Royal Academy in London, and in 1813 a guest at Bromley Vale was Francis, later Judge and Lord, Jeffrey, editor of the *Edinburgh Review*. Jeffrey, a widower of forty, had landed in New York in August in pursuit of a certain charming Charlotte Wilkes, and had come to Boston to visit a brother already established there. Hannah found him 'the very first of entertaining companions.' Young George Ticknor, a good judge of men, was equally fascinated:

'He enters a room with a countenance so satisfied, and a step so light and almost fantastic, that all your previous impressions of the dignity and severity of the *Edinburgh Review* are immediately put to flight and, passing at once to the opposite extreme, you might, perhaps, imagine him to be frivolous, vain, and supercilious. He accosts you, too, with a freedom and familiarity which may, perhaps put you at your ease and render conversation unceremonious; but which, as I observed in several instances, were not very tolerable to those who had always been accustomed to the delicacy and decorum of refined society. . . .

'It is not until you become interested in the mere discussion, until you forget his earnestness, his volubility, and his skill, that you begin to feel something of the full extent of his powers. You do not, till then, see with how strong and steady a hand he seizes the subject, and with what ease, as well as dexterity, he turns and examines it on every side. You are not, until then, convinced that he but plays with what is the labor of ordinary minds, and that half his faculties are not called into exercise by what you at first supposed would tax his whole strength.'

John Lowell was less profoundly impressed: 'Very clever,' but 'supercilious,' 'argumentative,' 'despotic.' 'I do not place him in the first class of minds.' Is it possible that in their interviews he himself could not get in a word even edgewise? As his own taste in poetry never progressed beyond Pope and Cowper, he would have agreed with Jeffrey's devastating review of Wordsworth's *Excursion*, beginning, 'This will never do.' Yet, since it did do, world opinion now shares John's opinion that Jeffrey's mind was not first class.

At the end of the year the Scotch reviewer married Miss Wilkes and returned with her to Edinburgh, a warm advocate of conciliation.

Throughout the war the instances of American valor and intrepidity that gratified even Boston Federalists were chiefly on the water, fresh for Perry and McDonough, salt for Lawrence and Hull. Not approving the war, New England shipowners let the bulk of the huge privateering profits go to Baltimore and New York. The Republican Crowninshields of Salem, with their ships *Diomede* and *America*, and armed yacht *Jefferson*, did well. The rakish brig *Harpy*, of three hundred and fifty tons, fourteen heavy guns, and one hundred men, Baltimore-built but Newburyport-owned, under the command of Captain William Nichols, did very well. Among her prizes were two enemy transports en route to Halifax with the major general commanding and numerous other officers. Despite a fanatical and rather fearsome countenance, but not devoid of humor, Captain Nichols's treatment of his prisoners was such that he received handsomely engrossed testimonials and invitations to visit in England after the war. His total take in goods and specie was well over a million dollars. Attractive as these opportunities were, no member of the Lowell family seized them. Francis, the most likely to have done so, was, as we shall see, very much otherwise occupied.

In December, 1814, while the Peace Conference, sitting at Ghent, with John Quincy Adams the brains of the American delegation, was completing its work, the Hartford Convention assembled to voice New England's opposition to the war. Gouverneur Morris had hoped to bring in New York. He wrote Pickering: 'A coy but willing damsel may for Form and Fashion's sake require what the French call *une douce violence*, but her embrace will not be the less ardent.' New York, however, was not to be seduced even by that great lover with the wooden leg.[1]

In November, John Lowell in the *Advertiser* had stated his view of what the Convention ought to do: To declare New England neutral for the remainder of the war, and to recommend the Northern States to suspend the Constitution, in which case they could not be treated as traitors or rebels, 'if a wrecked and abandoned and desperate policy should induce the National rulers to declare war against such a state.' But on December 8, he wrote to Timothy Pickering:

'I was opposed sincerely and most zealously to the Convention because I found no one man among its advocates prepared to *act*. When you ask any of them what the Convention will do, you will find it is expected they will talk: talk of amendments, talk of militia, talk of defense, talk of being paid out of the national taxes what we advance, but nothing more. I was not anxious for any decisive measures at present. I deprecate, as one of the greatest of evils, a separation of the States. I thought, and think now, that the people *en masse* will act in six or twelve months more. I think the remedy *then* will be more effectual, and will produce more *lasting* good effects.

'But I was wholly opposed to a premature and feeble effort. Nothing sinks the character of a people, or diminishes the force and influence of a party, so much as suppressed efforts, vain and futile exertions.'

---

[1] If Morris also wrote John Lowell, his letters have not been preserved. Some years before Lowell while on a visit to New York wrote to his wife: 'Yesterday I dined with Gouverneur Morris, one of the most extraordinary men of our country — Few men of this nation exceed him in genius, and no one equals him in good breeding. He is a perfect courtier, *bred* in the court of France prior to the Revolution, or at least improved by it, having been an Ambassador there in the most eventful period of its history. His house, furniture, and style of living are all after the model and not inferior to that of the French nobility.'

His instinct was correct. Under the sagacious chairmanship of George Cabot, who had mellowed and perhaps become a little sceptical with age, the Convention did precisely what he had feared. The debates of the twenty-six delegates, college graduates and lawyers for the most part, fizzed off in talk.

Harrison Gray Otis, Thomas Handasyd Perkins, and William Sullivan, *en route* to Washington with the Convention's temperate and toothless report, were between New York and Philadelphia constantly preceded by three black crows, 'waddling and looking wise,' as Otis wrote to his 'dearest friend,' his wife. 'These,' he added, 'are ill-omened birds, sad precursors of the three ambassadors.' They were indeed. In Baltimore on the twelfth of February, the ambassadors had the news of Jackson's decisive victory at New Orleans, and at Washington on Saint Valentine's Day, of the signing of the treaty of peace, restoring the *status quo*, though avoiding the more controversial points, and leaving the question of the Canadian boundary to be settled by a commission. Seldom has so much wind in such swelling sails been so suddenly and completely deflated. After 1815 the Federalist Party, though it continued to furnish good government to Massachusetts for another decade, was dead as a national force.

In Boston official celebration of the peace was deferred till Washington's Birthday. On the twenty-second, all the Lowell clan, with the Quincy girls as guests, sat well wrapped up on the iron balcony across the second story of Number 19 Colonnade Row and saw a quaint parade slide by on runners over the frozen snow. At the head rode Josiah Quincy, president of the Washington Society, then, after a band blaring patriotism with chilly lips, came a long procession of sleighs. On each was a group of workmen symbolizing and practising their trade. Masons built a little house, carpenters erected a six-by-four temple of Janus, hatters fabricated imposing headpieces of castor, printers produced pamphlets and threw them to the crowd literally hot from the press. The piping times of peace were there again!

In Europe after the world peace of 1815, a new balance of power replaced the Continental system. Of Napoleon, now at St. Helena under the repugnant custody of Sir Hudson Lowe, Thomas Jefferson, his supposed admirer, said to George Ticknor: 'The penance he is now doing for all his atrocities must be soothing to any virtuous heart. We cannot but wish to the inhuman wretch a long life that time as well as eternity may fill up his sufferings to the measure of his enormities.'

Half a century later, in his bitter poem *L'Expiation*, Victor Hugo developed the idea further:

> 'Alors, géant broyé sous le talon des rois,
> Il cria: Le mesure est comblé cette fois!
> Seigneur! C'est maintenant fini! Dieu que j'implore
> Vous m'avez châtié! — La voix dit: — Pas encore!' [1]

Mr. Madison's War had been neither necessary nor glorious, yet out of four million contentious individualists, divided by class and sectional interests into hostile groups, it fused a united nation. John Lowell had written his last political pamphlet, but it was a comfort to him that his *Review of a Treatise on Expatriation* by George Hay, Esq., printed in 1814 and found by Chief Justice John Marshall to possess 'a solidity of argument and array of authority which in my judgment is absolutely conclusive,' had saved the lives of three British officers. They were confined in the low brick jail that still stands on the bank of the Ipswich River, as hostages for the lives of three British sailors who had absconded and were found fighting against their country on the *Chesapeake* in her last battle.

---

[1] Twice before in the poem Napoleon had expressed the opinion that his expiation of his aggressions was already sufficient, once after Moscow, again after Waterloo. Each time a voice from the shadows had answered monosyllabically, '*Non!*' In a free English version the final lines of the piece read as follows:

> The Giant ground to dust by claws of kings
> Cried out in agony, 'Lord, O Lord, at last
> The cup of dark chastisement has been filled.
> God, I implore, my anguish must be past.
> Now I shall sleep, now, now I shall forget!'
> And then the great voice answered: AH, NOT YET!

Hay, an ardent Republican, had been appointed by Jefferson Attorney-General of Virginia, and in that capacity had conducted, unsuccessfully, the trial of Aaron Burr for treason. In his *Treatise* he had argued that the three Englishmen on the *Chesapeake* had expatriated themselves by free choice and were not therefore traitors. John Lowell's learned and powerful argument to the contrary seems to have carried conviction even to Mr. Madison's government.

The British sailors in Halifax were executed, but not the British officers in Ipswich — in the language of Mr. Justice Marshall, 'unfortunate, honorable and innocent men.'

5
CHAPTER

Whirling Spindles, Clicking Looms [1]

W HILE JOHN LOWELL was hurling hot verbal shot at Jefferson and his Embargo, the realistic mind of Francis had been casting about for opportune enterprises to take up the slack of the slump in commerce and distilling.   He could hardly overlook the acute shortage and soaring price of cotton cloth after the source of supply from the mills of Lancashire was shut off, nor the feverish but ineffective efforts that were being made to produce material for sheets and sails and shirts and skirts and petticoats here at home.   Thomas Jefferson himself had a hundred spindles spin-

---

[1] The classic if somewhat slender source for the story of the mechanization of the cloth-making industry in the United States is in the thirty-six-page pamphlet, *Introduction of the Power Loom and Origin of Lowell*, by Nathan Appleton.   For its subsequent development see *The Early New England Cotton Manufacture*, by Caroline F. Ware, *Mill and Mansion*, A Study of Architecture and Society in Lowell, Massachusetts, 1820–1865, by John Coolidge, and for pleasure as well as business, *A New England Girlhood*, by Lucy Larcom.

ning yarn on his estate of Monticello, and the spinning mills of Cabot cousins at Beverly, and of Almy and Brown and Samuel Slater at Pawtucket, were running overtime. Weaving was the constricted neck of the cotton bottle. It was still being done by hand or foot power, at home, or in small unorganized groups. When Francis went abroad for his and Hannah's health in 1810, it was in the back of his busy head to take a look at the power looms that had revolutionized the cloth-making industry of England, and established the factory system for better and worse.

This had been accomplished in less than forty years through the inventions of four oddly assorted characters, James Hargreaves, Richard Arkwright, Samuel Crompton, and Edmund Cartwright. Hargreaves, a shiftless Jack-of-all-trades, startled Jenny, his wife, one day, perhaps by coming home from his pub earlier and soberer than usual, and caused her to upset her spinning wheel, making it revolve horizontally with the spindle vertical. He noted with surprise that it seemed to work better in that position. He patented his happy observation in 1770, and named the device, by which a single operative turning a crank could whirl forty or more spindles, the spinning jenny. Arkwright, born a barber, invented the roller spinner and frame driven by water power and died a baronet. Crompton, an underpaid cotton worker with a passion for music, tried to achieve leisure for the study of it by devising the spinning mule, so called as the fruit of the union of the jenny with the frame. As the result of these efforts, yarn piled up beyond the capacity of all the hand looms in England to weave it. In 1785, Edmund Cartwright, a clergyman of the Church of England, who knew little of mechanics and had never seen a loom at work, invented the power loom, motivated by water power, and before long by steam. In 1809, Parliament voted him ten thousand pounds. He retired from the pulpit, bought himself an estate, and applied his talents to improvements in farming tools. Francis Cabot Lowell was the first educated man, with mathematical and mechanical interests, commercial experience, and personal command of capital, to expend his whole energy in organizing and improving the industry, both for profit, and, as it seemed at the time, for social and moral gains.

During two years abroad, his constant correspondent was his brother-in-law, Patrick Tracy Jackson, who was making a fortune in trade and acting as agent for Francis' affairs during his absence. At first, the letters deal with real-estate transactions, India ventures, the course of foreign exchange, and the price of cotton for export; but in 1811, we begin to read comments on the making of cotton cloth. In that year he was joined in Edinburgh by Nathan Appleton, the father of Longfellow's second wife and of Boston's most celebrated wit, a successful merchant, and of course, a cousin, though a remote one, through Joan, the daughter of Old Percival. The two put their heads together, and it was decided that Francis should make more than a casual observation of the processes employed in Manchester and Birmingham. For many weeks he walked the long aisles of cotton factories, asking questions and making mental notes. Safely home with these in 1812, despite, as we have seen, capture and search, he proceeded with plans to turn the making of cotton cloth from a household avocation into big business. The clan as a whole, Colonel Henry Lee says, considered the plan 'a visionary and dangerous scheme, and thought him mad.' Francis Lowell and Patrick Jackson, the brothers-in-law, undeterred, secured a charter for 'The Boston Manufacturing Company' with an authorized capital of four hundred thousand dollars, and themselves put up most of an initial subscription of one hundred thousand dollars 'until the experiment should be fairly tried.' They purchased the property of an unsuccessful paper-cum-spinning mill at Waltham, where for a mile or two the smooth-sliding Charles quickens its pace to provide water power, and set about the 're-invention' of machinery to perform for the first time anywhere under a single roof, all the processes of carding, spinning, and weaving — converting pounds of cotton into yards of cloth.

Francis' mathematical abilities came to the aid of his visual memory and the new machines had many improvements over those he had studied in England. Nathaniel Bowditch, the Practical Navigator who had subscribed for four shares of stock, said that the calculations that gave accuracy to the complicated movements of the new 'double speeder' required the greatest mathematical power of any piece of mechanism with which he had become acquainted. In transmuting these calculations into the actual machines, he had the aid of the unique mechanical talent of Paul Moody of Amesbury. Their second most brilliant joint achievement was thought to be a device for spinning directly on the 'cops,' conical masses of thread on spindles, without the preliminary process of winding. Nathan Appleton tells a pleasant anecdote which shows at once the Moody mechanical genius and the characteristic Lowell gift of instant decision.

'Mr. Shepherd, of Taunton, had a patent for a winding machine, which was considered the best extant. Mr. Lowell was chaffering with him about purchasing the right of using them on a large scale, at some reduction from the price named. Mr. Shepherd refused, saying, "you must have them, you cannot do without them, as you know, Mr. Moody." Mr. Moody replied — "I am just thinking that I can spin the cops direct upon the bobbin." "You be hanged," said Mr. Shepherd. "Well, I accept your offer." "No," said Mr. Lowell, "it is too late." '

By the autumn of 1814, they were ready to begin. Mr. Appleton had been invited to put ten thousand dollars into the enterprise, but was a little sceptical of its immediate success and settled for five thousand dollars. Nevertheless, he was made a director and took a deep interest in the preparations. He tells of the great moment when he first saw everything work:

'Mr. Lowell said to me that he did not wish me to see it until it was complete, of which he would give me notice. At length the time arrived. He invited me to go out with him and see the loom operate. I well recollect the state of admiration and satisfaction with which we sat by the hour, watching the beautiful movement of this new and wonderful machine, destined as it evidently was, to change the character of all textile industry.'

They were off! Within a few years the small Waltham mill was producing thirty miles of cotton cloth per day and paying dividends of ten per cent or better. For 1817 they paid twenty per cent. The rapidly ramifying clan, Lowells, Jacksons, Amorys, Higginsons, Russells, Gorhams, Tyngs, Duttons, and Lees, who had been dubious two years before, were soon buying the shares at an advance of forty and fifty per cent over the subscription price. In 1815, immediately after the close of the war, the British manufacturers launched a counter-offensive in the form of a flood of cheap cotton goods priced to sell well under the average current price of the new American product, which was twenty-five cents a yard. As a defensive measure Francis conceived the idea of a reasonable protective tariff. Loud and conflicting voices rose. The Rhode Island manufacturers, who were not doing so well, wanted an import duty of one hundred per cent. The merchants and shipowners, who were doing better again, were content with free trade. They prophesied, if a tariff were put through, another era of ruined wharves, decaying warehouses, and rotting ships. The Southern planters didn't know what they wanted, only that they wanted nothing that anyone from Boston did.

It was in this confused and unfavorable climate that Francis arrived in Washington. By what must have been a masterpiece of difficult and delicate negotiation he convinced young William Lowndes of South Carolina, chairman of the Ways and Means Committee, and powerful John C. Calhoun, from the same state, that the interests of the growers and processors of cotton were identical, and that while a duty was needed, the superiority of the American product was so evident that a moderate one would serve. A bill was forced through the House recognizing and establishing the protective principle for 'infant industries' and setting the duty on foreign cotton goods at six and a quarter cents per yard or twenty-five per cent of a fixed minimum invoiced price of twenty-five cents. It proved sufficient, as it amounted to a duty of more than eighty per cent on the coarse India cotton which competed with ours for sheeting. Within a decade the price of the cloth in this country had fallen to thirteen cents a yard, and in another to six and a half cents.

Whether Francis had visited Robert Owen's industrial Utopia at Lanark on the Clyde, described in his *A New View of Society*, based on the thesis that as character is made by circumstance all anger is out of place, or even read that pamphlet, is not known, but he was, we do know, concerned about the character and health of his people from humanitarian as well as business motives. It was part of his larger plan to build in Massachusetts a great inland industrial city near its seaport of Boston, so to begin a close co-operation of commerce with industry like that he had seen between Liverpool and Manchester. Nathan Appleton says:

'The introduction of the cotton manufacture in this country, on a large scale, was a new idea. What would be its effect on the character of our population was a matter of deep interest. The operatives in the manufacturing cities of Europe were notoriously of the lowest character, for intelligence and morals. The question therefore arose, and was deeply considered, whether this degradation was the result of the peculiar occupation, or of other and distinct causes. We could not perceive why this peculiar description of labor should vary in its effects upon character from all other occupation.'

Francis, whom he called 'the soul' of the enterprise, planned a system of community housing which included a number of detached houses, a long block of boarding-houses which he filled with able and ambitious girls from country farms in search of hard money and urban adventure, two schools, and a church. This was the beginning of the paternalistic system, which in the future cities of Lowell and Manchester reached its peak in the days of his sons, John Lowell 2d so called Junior and Francis Cabot Lowell, Jr., and his nephew, John Amory Lowell, and passed it in the time of his grand-nephew, Augustus.

For Francis Lowell the two busy years following the war were brilliant with outward success, but sombre in his personal life. In May, 1815, his high-spirited Hannah died. Thereafter he followed less than ever John's advice to be indulgent to himself, not to jeopardize his health, 'this first of blessings.' He became definitely an invalid. He tried the waters of Ballston Spa, which seems to suggest one of those malignant maladies by which Nature revenges herself upon delicate and high-strung men who work too hard. One of his sisters wrote to another, 'He came back from his stay there sicker than when he went.' He died on August 10, 1817, at the age of forty-two. In his short life he had done more than any other member of his effective family, more perhaps than any other man, to swell the pocketbook of New England and shape its economic future.

BOOK IV

Periclean Age

1

CHAPTER

Public Services of a Rebel

W<small>ITH THE INCREASE</small> of industrial wealth in New England, strangely coinciding with its flowering in literature, began its Periclean Age. In it the Rebel, his political passions muted by age and disappointment, was to play a notable part.

When in 1820, Samuel Eliot, Boston's most successful merchant, died in his sunny house on the corner of Beacon and Tremont Streets, it was found that he had left a truly remarkable will. This instrument, a holograph document of some twenty closely written pages, disposed of an estate of well over one million dollars in trusts and public and private bequests, with such justice, precision, and lucidity that it was considered a model of its kind. After it was probated, there were numerous requests from members of the bar for copies to be used as patterns in their own will-drawing for prosperous clients. Not its

163

least remarkable feature was the paragraph it contained furnishing a brief biography of John Lowell, the Rebel:

'I give to my dear friend John Lowell Esquire of Roxbury Eight thousand dollars, in case of his decease before me, which God forbid, I give the same sum to his son John Amory Lowell. With Mr. Lowell I have had a long Friendship and I thank God for the great Blessing. This Gentleman has been the eminent friend of his country and of every good man. Witness his labours for the public as evinced by several able Judicious and luminous Pamphlets and many other Publick Writings. Consider him in the Corporation of Harvard University, in the Agricultural society, in the Establishment of the General Hospital and that Excellent institution the Savings Bank, and in one word wherever good is to be performed there you will Constantly find Mr. Lowell exerting his strong mind and not sparing the most Laborious Services.'

This is a fair but far from complete outline of the last quarter of a century of John Lowell's life, which coincided with that happy age in the history of Boston, the tight little American Athens, for which the adjective 'Periclean' fits better than the 'Augustan' of Imperial Rome. His ill health continued and with the years increased, but while his son and two of his nephews, sons of Francis, were sowing the seeds of still greater prosperity for New England, and another, son of Charles, was one of the first buds of its poetic flowering, his own active mind, restless nervous energy, and abundant good will drove him to good works for which his city still owes him much.

In 1805, the Anthology Club voted to start a library of periodical publications for its own use and that of associates willing to subscribe to its support. By 1807, George Ticknor and Andrews Norton had come in and were advising the purchase of basic books of scholarship and those which should be in every gentleman's library. John Quincy Adams, leaving for Russia to be our minister at the court of the Emperor Alexander the First, left his books on loan to the newly named Athenaeum. The Reverend Joseph Buckminster, young pulpit orator and eloquent prophet of a great literary age just around the corner, brought back from London and Paris three thousand well-selected volumes for the shelves of the rooms in the Scollay Building that stood in the centre of the present square. John Lowell, also just back from abroad, was elected treasurer. Doctor Caner's rectory, which the Old Judge had moved out of in 1786, was leased in 1809 and soon became the reading base for Boston's Best. But it was felt that 'Athenaeum Shaw,' the librarian, one of the original anthologists, was disposed to give too much time and money, often some of its own, to the acquisition and arrangement of old coins and rare pamphlets, not enough to the books people really wanted to read or consult.

In 1816, at the annual meeting of the Proprietors, John Lowell was elected president. The next year he was abroad and there was no stated meeting. In January, 1818, he called a special meeting at which he was re-elected president, with Josiah Quincy as vice president and Nathan Appleton, treasurer. This was the beginning of a vigorous administration. Finances were regulated, records cleaned up, more and better books acquired, a new assistant librarian found, and the actual library service greatly improved. He resigned as president in 1820, but continued as a trustee, and was chairman of the committee to discover a more convenient and commodious location. He secured by gift from James Perkins, perhaps over the Madeira, his mansion on Pearl Street, where the library was suitably housed for thirty years.

For a century he and his descendants were the moving spirits on the board of trustees that built the Athenaeum into the nostalgic temple of literature and art that it is today.

In 1841, a year after his death, his son, John Amory Lowell, executor of his estate, presented to the Athenaeum, as a monument to his memory, Horatio Greenough's bas-relief, The Judgment of Paris, and his statue in the round of Venus Victrix, who received the award. She still stands at the far end of the third floor, white and callipygous, an agreeable counter-irritant to the chastening view through the window of the Old Granary Burying Ground. The recrudescent Puritans that keep watch and ward over Boston's *élan vital* have never fallen afoul of her. Not a few young couples have found the Athenaeum a port of embarkation for Cythere — sailings that for a century were duly announced in the *Boston Evening Transcript*.[1]

John Lowell was interested in the public's health and solvency, as well as in its acquaintance with literature and art. He was one of fifty-six gentlemen who raised funds for the Massachusetts General Hospital, and engaged Bulfinch to plan the erection of its first building, which still stands on the downslanting axis of Anderson Street and affords Boston one of its most charming architectural vistas. No hospital in this country has done more to alleviate the ills our flesh is heir to, or for the progress of the science and art of medicine.

A year after the signing of the Treaty of Ghent, one of his friends, James Savage, a young man of thirty-two, a literary lawyer, a member of the Anthology Club, a founder of the Athenaeum, and librarian of the Historical Society, conceived

---

[1] It was there in the middle eighties that John Jay Chapman read *The Divine Comedy* with Italian-born Minna Timmins, in her mother's tongue:

'There was a large airy room at the top of the old Athenaeum Library in Boston whose windows looked out on the churchyard. It was a bare and quiet place: no one ever came there. And during the winter we read Dante there together, and in the course of this she told me of her early life in Milan. There were five children, three of them boys, and there were tempestuous quarrels between the parents. I saw that it was from her mother that she had inherited her leonine temperament. The mother had been a fury. I could see this, though she did not say it. . . . The Dante readings moved gradually like a cloud between me and the law, between me and the rest of life. It was done with few words. I had come to see that she was in love with someone. It never occurred to me that she might be in love with me.'

One feels the warmth of memory in his incomparably successful translation of the fifth canto of the *Inferno* in *terza rima*:

'Alone we were, unconscious, innocent.
And oft the story, when our glances met,
Kindled the blush that with a tear is blent;
But what o'erthrew us wholly, was not yet.'

the idea of a savings bank in Boston. It was the second to be established in this country and the first to be incorporated. The time was very ripe for it. During the post-war depression before the protective tariff had begun to take effect, the monetary condition of the United States was as bad as it well could be. Wildcat banks issued bank notes and shinplasters down to a minimum denomination of two and a half cents. Much of this spate of paper carried no provision for redemption. There was a general suppression of specie payments everywhere save in Massachusetts.

Bookish but financially shrewd James Savage saw the need of a Provident Institution for the savings of the people, similar to the voluntary association for that purpose he had read of in London. His fellow lawyer and book-lover, John Lowell, helped him to present the plan to the solid men of Boston — Phillips, Parkman, Perkins, Sturgis, Quincy, Amory, Coolidge, Ticknor, Channing, Dorr, Tuckerman, Putnam, Prince, Motley, *et al.* They saw the point for the public good if not direct benefit for their own pockets. Jean Lefebvre Cheverus, classical scholar and man of sensibility, the first Roman Catholic Bishop of Boston, was an ardent advocate of a place for his parishioners to deposit their savings instead of squandering on rum and rebellion. Nine years before, John Lowell and Cheverus had a sharp encounter in print concerning some opinions of the evil economic effects of Catholicism in Italy which the former had published in the *Anthology*. During the founding of the bank they discovered a mutual respect which grew into friendship.

The Provident Institution for Savings was duly chartered in December, 1816, with William Phillips as president and James Savage, secretary. The records of the early meetings of the trustees, of whom John Lowell was one, show him taking a leading part in the actual organization of the bank, and carrying his associates through days of doubt and discouragement. In 1840, the year of his death, deposits had increased more than tenfold, from less than two hundred thousand dollars to more than two million dollars. For some years the Institution occupied rooms in the Scollay Building, formerly used by the Athenaeum. In 1830, still pursuing the Athenaeum, the trustees purchased the site of the Caner rectory when the library moved to Pearl Street, erected a three-story building of Quincy granite, and by actual deed sold one half of the second story with all of the third to the Massachusetts Historical Society. James Savage, through most of his life an officer of both institutions, had but a flight of stairs between his jobs, an interlocking of learning and lucre not common, even in Boston.

As the War of 1812 came to its inconclusive end, the thirty years' war between the Orthodox Congregationalists and the Arian, Arminian, or Socinian Unitarians entered its most violent stage. It brought strange changes of front. The ruling powers of Harvard were both Federalist and Unitarian, but men split on different lines in religion and politics. Thomas Jefferson, Federalism's arch foe, wrote to Doctor Benjamin Waterhouse, of the Harvard Medical School, 'I trust there is not a young man now living in the United States who will not die a Unitarian.' Many an old Federalist found himself in inky fratricidal strife with another over the doctrine of the Trinity, infant damnation, and a physical hell. None was more bitter than that between John Lowell and the Reverend Doctor Jedediah Morse, pastor of the First Church in Charlestown, founder of an Orthodox organ, *The Panoplist*, 'father of American Geography' and of that eminent American painter and all-around Leonardo da Vinci, S. F. B. Morse. In the heat of it the Rebel wrote to Timothy Pickering of the arrogance of the Orthodox clergy, and questioned, 'Does the arrogance spring from the orthodoxy or the orthodoxy from the arrogance.'

The duello reached its decisive bout in the publication, in 1815, of John Lowell's pamphlet, *Are you a Christian or a Calvinist? Do you prefer the authority of Christ to that of the Genevan Reformer?* written in reply to the rude question of his antagonist's tract, *Are you of the Christian or the Boston Religion?*

There are few topics less fascinating for modern readers than old theological controversies. This pamphlet and four others on similar themes urged on him, John Lowell says, after great resistance, by President Kirkland of Harvard, Doctor Channing, Samuel Thacher, Andrews Norton, Edward Everett, 'and several other *such* men,' are not exceptions, but they are of importance in the religious history of New England. All have the close reasoning and copious expression found in his political writings. They were the earliest significant contribution to the war of words by any layman, and they helped to bring the real issue to light. At the time they were written, John Lowell's own King's Chapel, the first Episcopal church in New England, was the only church in Massachusetts openly and avowedly Unitarian. Many ministers, like John Lowell's own Newburyport grandfather, his brother, Charles, his friend, William Ellery Channing, had in the language of Charles Eliot's inscription on the Channing monument 'breathed into Theology a humane spirit.' Yet, they were still within the influence and jurisdiction of the Massachusetts Established Church. The Reverend Doctor Edward Dorr Griffin, of the new Park Street Church, that John Lowell could see out of the corner of his eye as he looked from his front windows in Colonnade Row, 'the most interesting mass of brick and mortar in America' Henry James was to call it, was well within his ecclesiastical rights when he denounced Channing and Norton and Kirkland as heretics and apostates. John Lowell's pamphleteering accelerated the separatist movement which gave his friends their doctrinal independence. Yet in the end he was not quite happy about it. A dozen years later, he wrote to a young clergyman searching his heart to reconcile his belief with his career: 'It probably stimulated the laity to read and think for themselves, and then relieved their pastors from the charge of heresy by assuming it themselves. But I regret the course I have taken. I think I exasperated rather than subdued the spirit of religious intolerance.'

However that may be, the slings and arrows of his attacks on the battlements of orthodoxy had been of incalculable service to his beloved 'seminary,' as he liked to call it.

'We can never measure,' says Morison, its historian, 'the relief, the stimulus, the exuberant joy felt in the dark century by thousands of young men who, after a stern upbringing in expectation of a hard struggle to escape eternal damnation, entered a college where hot-gospelling was poor form, hell was not mentioned, and venerable preachers treated the students, not as limbs of Satan, but as younger brothers of their Lord and Saviour.'

By the time John Lowell had reached his grand climacteric, he was as eager in the pursuit of charity to all as his grandfather had been before him, but never tolerant of intolerance. During the roaring Democratic régime of Andrew Jackson, when a wave of hysterical fear and hatred of Catholicism swept the country and bitter attacks were made upon Bishop Cheverus, who had gone home to France and become a cardinal, he wrote to a friend:

'The Catholic priesthood near *us* certainly and so far as I have *heard*, in the United States, have been truly honorable, and excellent men. Those I have *known* have been pious, charitable, prudent, modest, and have had as large a portion of personal respect among protestants as any other class of clergymen. Bishop Cheverus was beloved and admired for his excellent virtues, his enlarged views, and his liberal feelings. He was a blessing to *this Country* for the judicious control he possessed, and exercised, over an ignorant population.

'I never knew an act of a Catholic Clergyman in this country to justify Dr. Beecher and others in their illiberal conduct towards them. I believe that these attacks are wanton, and I *know* they are most pernicious to the State, and hurtful to Christianity.'

After the publication of that sensational best-seller, *Six Months in a Convent* and other 'awful disclosures,' and the burning of the Ursuline Convent in Charlestown by a mob of 'truckmen' while firemen stood by and played their hoses on the surrounding dwellings, he wrote:

'We may chase, by blood and fire, the Catholics from our land if we can reconcile ourselves to such an horrible principle, still our institutions might exist — But the events of this short summer shew with the force not of a sunbeam only but of *lightning*, that there is at work in our great cities, a principle, far more dreadful, of which the commotion at Charlestown is only a feeble example. The attack on the *anti-slavery* Society of New York, and upon the Blacks of Philadelphia prove, that the first principles of *social order* are, in jeopardy, in our nation.'

His own personal religion, and what it meant to him, is simply stated in his first letter to his son, John Amory Lowell, who at the age of twenty-one had sailed for England to make a tour of the British Isles:

'I have reproached myself bitterly for letting you part from me, possibly forever, without giving you my ideas on the subject of religion. If I have never said any thing on that topick before, it has rather arisen from *mauvaise honte*, and a feeling that religion is a thing of a private nature and belongs to every man's own conscience.

'But a man who has no sense of religion in my opinion is utterly unworthy of confidence and trust. . . . It is impossible for any sensible man who surveys his own frame and moral and intellectual character to doubt the existence of an infinitely wise, intelligent cause, who made and governs the world in infinite goodness — nor can a man of logical mind refuse his assent to the truth of the Christian dispensation. The external evidences, its astonishing propagation against the will of the ruling powers, its continuation to this day, its excellent effects on that part of the world that has embraced it, the dispersion of the Jews — Its internal evidence arising from the simplicity of its narration, and the incomparable wisdom of its moral rules, must convince every clear and unprejudiced mind — and if doubts should arise, which I can hardly conceive, how much safer to believe than to reject! My son, I hope and trust you have principles of religion as well as of morality — I know not what your practice has been but I recommend to you private prayer. It wonderfully calms the mind and fortifies our good resolutions.

'In danger and distress it produces a serenity which nothing else can give.'

The name of John Lowell, the Rebel, first appears in the records of the meetings of the President and Fellows of Harvard College in the spring of 1804, in a vote of thanks for a communication on galvanism, together with two galvanic batteries for the Philosophical Department. A supplementary vote authorizes the loan of one of them for two days in every year to Doctor Benjamin Waterhouse for his use in demonstrating to his medical classes the effects of the electric current on human beings and frogs. It next appears when at the meeting of March 29, 1810, in the lull between Embargo and War, he was elected a fellow of that self-perpetuating body and duly approved by the Overseers, whose relation to the Corporation is roughly that of a board of directors to its executive committee, and its proper attitude, as President Eliot was to point out in his inaugural sixty years later, 'suspicious vigilance.'

He attended his first meeting on April 17, 1810, at the house of Chief Justice Parsons on Pearl Street in Boston. It opened with prayer and concluded, after formal adjournment, with Madeira. As he looked around the table, he saw President Samuel Webber, soon to be removed by death from an office that was proving too big for him, Treasurer Jonathan Jackson, his father's best friend, Theophilus Parsons, Mr. Justice Oliver Wendell, maternal grandfather of the Autocrat of the Breakfast Table, and two clerical Fellows, the Reverend Doctors Eliot and Lathrop. The first assignment to John Lowell was to act with the treasurer in the final cash settlement with the managers of the lotteries that his father had initiated a quarter of a century before.

Just three months after he became a Fellow, President Webber died suddenly. The Corporation met next day at the house of Judge Wendell in Cambridge, voted suitable resolutions and arranged the *pompes funèbres*. Three weeks later, at Mr. Justice Parsons' house [1] in Boston, they elected as his successor the Reverend John Thornton Kirkland, Federalist, Unitarian, and genial rosy-faced bachelor, who immediately inaugurated a new system in the management of college boys. 'A complete gentleman in his manners,' wrote one of them, 'Mr. Kirkland aimed to treat the students as gentlemen in the hope that, if possible, he might make them so.' In the eighteen years of his tenure of office, Harvard became a national, not merely a New England college. Soft Southern voices were heard in the Yard on warm spring nights, and ice from Fresh Pond melted in mixtures strange to Puritan palates. The curriculum was overhauled and modernized, and the medical and law schools were put on their feet. It was a period of expansion and reform. When John Kirkland finally married Elizabeth, mature and well-endowed daughter of George Cabot, and resigned in 1828, the small college that he had taken over from Samuel Webber had become a university. An important street was named after him. Today, after a hundred years, if you wish to communicate by telephone with Harvard, you must first say '*Kirkland*.'

From the first meeting of Kirkland's incumbency, John Lowell became the Fellows' man-of-all-work. To him was assigned all the small odd jobs, from supervising painting and repairing students' rooms in the dormitories, or building a bathhouse at the end of the long wharf, to defending the rights of the college against the encroachments of the General Court. Many committees consisted of only Lowell and Kirkland, the former doing the work and the latter supplying the weight of authority to support and implement it. Perhaps assistant to the president would best describe his position.

The first dozen years of Kirkland's administration, coinciding

---

[1] At the same meeting, August 7, 1810, John Lowell's fellow clansman, James Jackson, was appointed Professor of Clinical Medicine.

with the term of John Lowell's service on the Corporation, saw the faculty strengthened and liberalized by a new group of eminent, in some cases great, teachers. All were men closely connected with him by family or personal and political ties, and his correspondence shows that he took an important part in the suggestions and preliminary conversations that led to their appointments.

In 1814, four years after the appointment of James Jackson as clinical professor, Samuel Eliot gave twenty thousand dollars to found a chair of the Greek Language and Literature. To fill it the Corporation chose a young man of twenty-one whom Emerson described as of 'radiant beauty' and 'precise and perfect eloquence,' Edward Everett, no less. He was instructed to spend two years, later extended to four, in Germany on full pay, twelve hundred dollars per annum, to prepare himself for the place. With him went a greater, more single-minded scholar, George Ticknor, the future historian of Spanish literature. In 1816, while still at Göttingen with Everett, he too received word from the Corporation of his appointment to the new Smith Professorship of the French and Spanish Languages and Belles Lettres.

In the fall of 1819, after meeting, and in Ticknor's case making lifelong friends, with the most distinguished scholars and writers of England and the Continent, both were back in Cambridge spreading in their classrooms new ideals of scholarship and an enlarged horizon in the fields of humane learning. In the same term, Edward Tyrrell Channing began his work as Boylston Professor of Rhetoric and Oratory. By him were exercised and trained in English composition Emerson, Holmes, Charles Sumner, James Russell Lowell, and Henry Thoreau. By his fruits quite a tree!

Finally in 1822, the last year of John Lowell's service on the Corporation, Thomas Nuttall, emigrant printer from Yorkshire, was called from Philadelphia to be the second curator of the Botanical Garden, a Lowell family enterprise, suggested by the

Old Judge, largely financed from funds raised by Francis Cabot Lowell in 1805, and seen through the Corporation by John. Nuttall, as competent in ornithology and paleontology as in botany, was the first important Harvard scientist. He resigned after ten years to explore the littoral of the Columbia River.

In 1814, by resolution of the President and Fellows, John Lowell not voting, he had been admitted *honoris causa* along with his friend and learned legal brother, Harrison Gray Otis, to the degree of LL.D. This so preyed on his worrying mind that a few years later, when a new Quinquennial Catalogue was in preparation, he wrote to Kirkland:

'I wish that the degree which the College was pleased to confer upon me may be omitted. It is true, that I assented fearfully. In an evil hour, my vanity got the mastery of my judgment, but I have been severely punished for it — *C'est entre nous, cela.* Many persons could not comprehend such feelings — but with me, distinctions ill-merited are like the parti-coloured clothes of the Convict — they proclaim one's shame. As it has never appeared in the Catalogue it will be happily for the College and myself soon forgotten.'

He felt, too, that his uncertain health stood in the way of his full usefulness as a Fellow. At the meeting of June 16, 1818, he formally resigned. At the same meeting his brother, Charles, was elected to succeed the Reverend Samuel Thacher, deceased. Charles, however, declined, and at the meeting of July 15, John was elected to succeed Thacher, and the body continued as before with the useful addition of William Ellery Channing succeeding John Lowell.

In the autumn of 1822, he resigned again, and at the meeting of November 23, his resignation was regretfully accepted. Resolutions were passed that have a clearer ring of sincerity than is always to be heard on such occasions. He was described as 'ardent friend of literature and of every elevated and generous design,' and a deep indebtedness was recorded to his 'ability, exertions, and zeal.'

After his retirement from the Corporation he was elected to the Board of Overseers where he was active in dealing with the Great Rebellion of 1823, the revision of the curriculum to conform to some of the modern ideas of George Ticknor, and the abortive attempt of the faculty to take over the business as well as the scholarly administration of the college. He was chairman of a committee that prepared an exhaustive report, but he was less effective in the larger group of the Overseers and more hampered by ill health. On November 13, 1826, he wrote to President Kirkland:

'The only reason of my not attending the last examination was indisposition — indisposition of a sort, for which, no man has any sympathy, and which as perfectly incapacitates the subjects of it, from the performance of their duties as a paralytick shock.

'There is an apparent physical vigour and health, but such a morbid state of the nervous system, as deprives the patient of all power over his own faculties, and volition —

'I have too long permitted myself to continue an idle incumbent in places, for which I am not qualified, in consequence of these constantly increasing infirmities. Before I received your note, I had resolved to resign my seat at the Board of Overseers.

'I now send you my formal resignation which I request you to present to the board at their first meeting.'

The resignation was accepted and for the remaining years of his life his relation to the 'seminary' was only that of a loyal and generous alumnus.

The Massachusetts Society for the Promotion of Agriculture was founded in 1792. John Adams was its first president, the Old Judge, from 1796 to 1802, its second. Soon after his return from Europe in 1806, the Rebel became its secretary and later its president. It is estimated that from 1816 to 1832 at least one half of the articles that appeared in its bulletin, *The Massachusetts Agricultural Repository and Journal*, were from his pen. He was acclaimed the 'Columella of the Northern States,' as Thomas

Jefferson was of the Southern. New York, New Jersey, and Pennsylvania had their Columellas too, in Bryant, Cooper, and Crèvecoeur. But none of them had the time, energy, and money to acquire and disseminate the knowledge *De Re Rustica* that John Lowell had. Both as an officer of the society and as a private farmer his correspondence was tremendous. From Europe he received seeds of rare flowers, cuttings of shrubs, merino sheep, 'scions of fruit from pomologists' and vines from the best vineyards of France and Italy. All did well at Bromley Vale. At one of the society's shows in rural Brighton, he took a first prize with a bunch of grapes weighing three pounds.

He corresponded with Timothy Pickering, no longer about the designs of the Junto, but in great detail concerning the fine points of Alderney bulls. He used the common interest in farming to heal old wounds. For twenty years John Adams had not seen Pickering, whom he had dismissed from the office of Secretary of State, until the Rebel took him to Quincy one day to an agricultural lunch party *chez* Adams. It passed off pleasantly and the old foes parted with regret.

To see him and hear him converse in his garden, where he could be found daily from spring to autumn, would, it is said, make one suppose that his only occupation was farming and gardening. He would discuss the qualities of a fruit tree or exotic plant with the same earnestness and the same copiousness, the same ready and various learning, he would have brought to a question of politics, a point of law, or a case of divinity.

His irritable energy had found the best and the sanest of outlets.

Three times in his later years the comparative peace of John Lowell's life, pruning and discoursing in his Roxbury garden or admiring the sunset across the Common from Colonnade Row, was sharply invaded.

In the spring of 1817, Nicholas Ward Boylston, a leading Boston merchant, came to him with an urgent piece of legal business. A substantial sum of money had been owing to him in London since before the war, but the affair had been so complicated with contra-accounts, so tangled up by the lawyers, that he had despaired of ever collecting. As a last resort he besought his friend John to undertake the hardship of the voyage, look into affairs personally on the ground, and see what he could do. John declined to do anything, but in the end friendship, and perhaps the call of battle to an old legal warhorse, prevailed. On June 9, reluctantly and fearfully, he set sail upon, as he says, 'the sick-making sea.'

In London he was stupendously busy, and it appears constantly homesick. Hardly a day went by without a letter or a transcript from his journal going off to his wife or one of his daughters at Roxbury. But in five weeks, including ten days in Paris, the job was done. A letter to his son, John Amory Lowell, recited the details of the transaction. It is an illuminating revelation of the speed with which the wounds of war had healed in the personal and business relations between citizens of the two countries. Perhaps its touch of pride is pardonable to a lonely parent in an alien land:

'My dear Son, 'London, Aug. 11, 1817

'I hope this, and a duplicate I shall write immediately after will be the last letters which I shall write you from London, and I write these not in the expectation or hope that you will receive them before I reach home, but only in the event of my never arriving, or having a long passage it may be some consolation to have had the latest possible intelligence from me.

'This day at twelve I have no doubt I shall touch £7500. Tomorrow I am promised also £3000 but of that I do not feel so sure because *three lawyers* have some hand in it, and while a thing is under *their* management a man may *well have* his fears. I met on Saturday Mr. Geo. Lee, the first of the Assignees, a Great banker, a prompt, able intelligent man, whom I *exactly suited*. Had this man been in London when I arrived on the 6th of July

I should have got the money on the *tenth of that month*. I read a very short statement which I had made, to prove the security with which he could pay the money; he kept constantly exclaiming "right, right, exactly right, very clear," and when I closed, "Sir, he said, you must give me a copy of that paper, it is every thing in a nutshell."

'In effect it was so — it was irresistible and silencing because it was principally *figures* which will not deceive — When he got this, Lee said, "Mr. Lowell, I thank you, you have behaved like a man of honor and of talents, you are just what I was taught to expect you would be. Egad, I do not know how we should ever have got through without you." — You must understand that he is a man of £250,000 who lives in the country on a great landed estate but who is so looked up to in this business, that nothing is done without him. He had been perfectly acquainted with me by character not only twenty years ago in their counsel in America, but from all my letters since I have been here which had been transmitted to him. As soon as we had dined he went to his iron chest, took out £14,000 in Exchecquer bills, counted them into my hands or rather before me asking me to look after him, sent them off to be sold, and then turned round to me and said how much money shall you want on Monday or Tuesday? I told him £10,000 for myself, and £5000 for Weston, the Lawyer (who is to have 1700 more next winter) — Well, said he, £16,000 will cover it? "Yes." "I shall give orders to have it paid" and gave them instantly. Now here is a true British banker; Frank, intelligent, prompt, confiding in others as he expects others to confide in him —

'As soon as it was finished I told Mr. Latham I would dine with him the next day (yesterday, Sunday) as he had often wished me to do. He asked all the other parties to meet me. This is the English fashion. All great affairs are *eaten off*. They spoke with great admiration of Genl. Lyman the former Atty. of the Town of Boston in this cause, on acct as they avowed of the fine dinner he gave at the Crown and Anchor.

'Weston, the solicitor, with whom I had had the most un-
pleasant discussion and who had been the cause of so much pain,
instantly told me "You don't know how much my mouth waters,
said he, to be with you tomorrow at Latham's but I have asked
company at home. I will however get off if I can" and he did
and dined with us. He added taking my hand, "I do not mean
to say anything in *praise* or *dispraise* of you but I have *my thoughts*.
You have stuck to me like a burr" and intimated I was the
cleverest fellow he ever saw. At dinner when Mrs. Latham
asked him to take something he had declined, he said before the
company, "Madam you are as authoritative and despotick as
Mr. Lowell. He says a thing must and shall be done and it is
done." He has some reason for this, for I have made him shake
almost as much as Balshazzar (which occurs to me as a simile
because I have lately visited West's pictures of which that is one)
— Mr. Lane, Mrs. Lane, Latham and Mrs. Lee, rolled up their
eyes when they heard I had got *Weston's bill and settled it*. They
said they thought *it impossible to do the one or the other*. They have
been at him for ten years to get it but without the least success.
You may tell Mr. Boylston I could have got off £2000 more I
have no doubt by frightening Weston more but not without
hazarding the whole which I was bound not to do. I did say, the
sharpest things possible *almost*, as it was, but if we had once
parted Mr. Boylston would never have seen the money or any
part of it. I dare say he will hear from a thousand quarters what
effort I have made but neither he or any of you can ever conceive the anxiety, chagrin and sleepless hours I have had. . . .

'Oh! my son if you knew the agonizing sensations which the
doubt of my finding you all as I left you produces, you would
pity me.

'I am truly wretched at the thought.

'Adieu, yr father

'J. Lowell

'At ½ past 2 o'clock I have received and have now in my
pocket £7572.8.11 — This is past all accident. I am tomorrow
to receive £3000 —'

He had, in short, after the necessary out payments, collected a net amount well over ten thousand pounds, from which as his account shows he was to deduct a commission of sixteen hundred pounds. His passage home was less boisterous and sick-making than the voyage out. With the comfortable feeling that follows a difficult and dreaded job well done, he spent his days on the deck writing marginally annotated verses of joyful reunion to the younger ladies of the clan. One of these for his niece, Frances Amory, with pungent side notes, is a poetic expression of the Federalist taste in poetry.

Oft as we glide the sea along
I try the power of *limping** song   modest poets would say '*magic song*'
Kill time, and cheat my *yawning* leisure,*
     Pierpont in his Hebrew melodies is my authority for dbl rhymes and American authority is always good — our Muses are all born near Helicon
With verse which boasts nor rhyme, nor measure;
But, Francis, should it give you *pleasure*,
I'll prize it more than golden treasure.
(For neither Pope, the bard of yore,
Or Scott or Byron could do *more*.) . . .

Heav'ns! How I hate the Stilting crew,*
     Coleridge and all the race of Modern poets are but little better than the Della Cruscan Insects, Gifford crushed under his thumbnail — see the Baviad.
All Fustian, Froth, and nonsense too:
The spawn of Della Cruscan school,
The praise of ev'ry half read fool.
The age is mad: Good taste is fled,
Bold Folly triumphs in its stead:
Jeffry,* the Despot of the day,   See Edinburgh Review of Swift.
Has Laugh'd at Pope, and Swift, and Gay:
Says Cato, Milton are forgot,
And all must yield to Walter Scott! ! !
That Caledonians, poor and proud,
In Scotia's praises ever loud,
Should raise their Laureat to the skies,

His ambling, skipping verse shouid
    prize,
Is fit: by fiction we are told
Each Scottish Thief's* a Baron bold: Scott's Heroes are all Robbers or
And not a wench at fair, or wake   assassins.
But struts a 'Lady of the Lake'
Yet, dearest niece, *we* still, I hope,
Will ramble with the Muse of Pope,
Will range with her, thro' grove, and
    field,
'See what the open, what the covert
    yield.'
Still sneer with Swift, still laugh with
    Prior,
Still weep at Cato's strains, and Thom-
    son's song admire.
              Yr Affectionate Uncle
                 J. Lowell

In 1823, the thin ice of his serenity was again broken when one
Jarvis, editor of *The Independent Chronicle and Boston Patriot*, in a
snappish paragraph attacked the memory of his father as a Tory
and a refugee, and his own record as that of a 'factious' rebel.
He replied to 'the beardless slanderer' in a fiery letter to the
Advertiser, and proposed to young Caleb Cushing, M.A., of
Newburyport, just out of Harvard and of a fine old crusted High
Street Federalist family, that he should undertake a definitive
biography of the Old Judge to 'vindicate' his memory. 'I accept
you,' he wrote, 'as my champion and that of my race.'

For nearly six months beginning in October, 1823, aided by
his favorite nephew, Edward Jackson Lowell, he examined old
family papers and searched court records for material that he
sent down to Newburyport with covering letters of personal reminiscence running all told to more than a hundred closely written
folio pages.[1] 'They are,' he wrote, 'but food for your mind to be

[1] These will be found among the Cushing Papers in the Library of Congress.
They are of considerable interest and importance for the history of the Federalist
period.

digested by unknown processes (for we know but little of mind, Dugald Stewart notes) and reproduced under new and more beautiful forms, as we see the odious caterpillar reproduced with the most gorgeous and delightful color and proportions.' He gave him, nevertheless, shrewd advice about the importance of significant detail and warned him, 'An artificial warmth of expression feels like ice to every one but the writer.'

In January, 1824, Cushing sent him the rough draft of a chapter on the matter of the Old Judge's signature to the farewell address to Governor Hutchinson that had started all the trouble. On the twenty-fourth of that month he wrote: 'I am entirely satisfied, and gratified with the substance and the form, the matter and the style. I could not wish to change.' He makes, however, some sound suggestions for filling out the characterization of Hutchinson and the account of the effects of the Old French War on the life of New England. After a lapse of six weeks he wrote that he had undergone an operation on his eye and was for the present forbidden to use it in further research, though he hoped to finish his part of the undertaking at some future time. He never did. One or the other, or both, lost interest, and the Old Judge, the Rebel, and his race had to await another champion.

A decade later, one of the smouldering volcanoes of the Turbid Time erupted with great violence. He tells the story in a letter dated January 10, 1836.

'I have never had an opportunity till this moment, to explain to you the very mortifying affray, in which I was involved without the slightest fault, or the remotest want of due *self command* on my part. A severe illness, followed so rapidly on the cruel and assassin like attack on my *life*, that I have not been able to do myself justice.

'I can, now most solemnly assure you, that without the slightest provocation, without even the suspicion, that any human being felt towards me a feeling leading to personal outrage, I found myself suddenly assaulted with menaces, with foul language, with threats of personal injury, and followed by severe and death dealing blows.   I felt the danger and disgrace, but I abstained from any defence — I submitted, like a Christian, to every outrage, till I was assailed by the assasin from behind, with a blow which deprived me of any consciousness, and then like the worm when trodden upon, I turned upon my assailant and caused him to repent his attack upon a peaceable man.   I have lived to sixty seven years, and never either as man or boy, even in the hasty passions of childhood, or the still stronger excitements of immature and headstrong youth, did I *ever give*, or *receive one single blow* in anger.   I have the most thorough contempt, the most piercing sense of the degradation of a rational being in resorting to brute force as a vent for his passions.

'I know you will give me full credit for my assertions and it will give you pleasure to hear that there are three disinterested witnesses who confirm my testimony.   They had never *seen me*, and yet they confirm my whole account with a minuteness which truth alone can give.

'Still it must remain a mystery to you, why an old man, so inoffensive, so disposed to be kind to all men should be the object of so virulent and ferocious an attack.   This can only be explained by details, which a letter cannot give.   Suffice it to say, that the fidelity to my duties, and the ardour of friendship and affection to my relatives has enkindled a mortal hatred to me in the breast of an unprincipled and passionate man who has chosen to identify me with them — Such are the sacrifices we are compelled to make to our duty.

'NB.   I never had the slightest intercourse with Mr. Vans, the assailant nor had I seen him for thirty years.'

The assailant was himself in his seventy-third year.   The spectacle of the two old men exchanging fisticuffs, regardless of the rules laid down by the Marquis of Queensberry, must have been of the most macabre.

The cause of the attack appears in the extensive reading matter on the title-page of a pamphlet Vans had caused to be printed three years earlier:

Life of William Vans,

A Native of Massachusetts,

Who lent and placed with John and Richard Codman, merchants and Copartners, at Paris, in the kingdom of France, 45,513 francs Rents, per year, of the Public Debt of France, that amounted in 1832 to upwards of $500,000, they were condemned to pay him. — THIS NARRATIVE also contains the Report made by Leveret Saltonstall, Chairman of a Committee of the Senate, who refused to concur with the House of Representatives, and grant a trial by Jury to William Vans. This Report is reviewed by Vans, and shown not to be correct.

The text begins:

'Being absent many years from Boston, some persons asked who William Vans was, that lost so much money by the Codmans. This question has been answered by them, with John Lowell, Esq. and the Amory's, all brothers to Mrs. Catharine Codman, nee Amory that Vans was an old French Democrat, Gambler, Drunkard, and very little known in Boston. For this reason Vans gives a short history of his life, that the public may know this Democrat — how he got his money, and lost it — who his family and connections are.'

Born in Salem in 1763, Vans had been in his early twenties a supercargo on the Derbys' ship *Grand Turk*. During that period, and later as United States Consul at Bordeaux, he had amassed useful sums of money that he had invested through Messrs. John and Richard Codman of Paris, merchants and representatives in France of many American traders and shipowners, though John Codman had retired from the firm before any business had been done with Vans and died in 1803. Vans put in a claim to a sum that the representatives of his estate held to be 'fraudulent and based on forgery,' asserting that anyway the money, whatever the correct amount might be, came from the profits of pandering and prostitution. The case was tried in the French courts and Vans secured a judgment which the Codman heirs in America declined to pay. When John Lowell was in Paris in 1804, Vans had called on him, and tried to enlist his interest and sympathy. John was prepared to go no further than to suggest an 'adjustment.' Thereafter for thirty years Vans besieged the legislature of Massachusetts for the passage of an act granting him a jury trial in Boston. A committee of the lower House at one time reported favorably, but the Senate took the contrary view. Finally in 1833, a new committee of the Representatives, under the chairmanship of Theron Metcalf, re-examined the records and the evidence, and brought in a summary report, concluding, 'Vans has no claim in Law or Justice against the estate of John Codman.' This decision was reaffirmed again for the fourth time in 1835 by a committee headed by Robert Rantoul.

In the light of this and of his attack on John Lowell, who, according to a pencilled note by his son on one of his letters of that period, weighed only one hundred pounds, it seems clear that William Vans was a bad actor.

In his last years John Lowell's bodily ailments multiplied and he made no secret of them in his correspondence. He was afflicted by *tic douloureux*, by heavy colds every winter, and by a chronic nervous indigestion. After the death of his niece, Frances Amory, he writes, 'I am threatened very seriously by the malady which has proved fatal to her, to my father, my brother Francis, and which was so alarming to Charles. I can take no food even of the simplest kind without distress.'

Yet he was always busy, in his garden, in his correspondence by which he ran a kind of travel bureau for members of the clan going abroad, in free legal advice to strange widows and orphans as well as to friends and kinsmen, while Chief Justice Parsons never sent an article to the press without its passing through his hands. He contributed to many diversified charities. Doctor Greenwood, who acted as his almoner, tells us that each autumn he was given a substantial sum to dispense in firewood for the poor, and quotes from his letter of instruction, 'There is no variety of physical distress for which my heart suffers more than that produced by cold.'

In the winters of 1839 and 1840, he fled from it himself to the West Indies, with only a male companion. As usual, when he was separated from his home and his family, his letters are mournful, yet in his descriptions of the blue seas, sunlit peaks, and luxurious plant life of the tropics, animated by his old unquenchable ardor. He came home noticeably improved in flesh and apparent health. On the morning of March 12, 1840, he sat by his fire in Colonnade Row reading the *Advertiser*, with what memories of wordy newspaper battles long ago!

There was provocative reading in it that morning — a speech in Congress by Daniel Webster in reply to Calhoun on the protective tariff, concluding, 'Well employed and prosperous communities can buy and consume, ill employed communities cannot buy and consume. This is the solution of the whole matter.' There was an editorial also flavored with Cotton Whiggery, criticising resolutions passed by the legislators of the State House, censuring those of the Capitol for their vote forbidding the consideration of Abolition petitions put forward by John Quincy Adams. Before John Lowell had finished the reading, the paper dropped from his hands and the Rebel was no more.

Of the seven worlds that the New England Lowells lived in, the Rebel had known three and been himself close to the centres of their activation. He remembered the Revolution; he was a principal actor in the Turbid Time; and he lived well into the dawn of the Periclean Age. In politics he saw the courtly tidewater Federalism of George Washington give place to the rowdy frontier Egalitarianism of Andrew Jackson — and the great panic of 1837. As a result of the enterprise of his brother,

Francis, he had seen Massachusetts change from a commercial community, dealing in commodities carried by white sails over blue water, to an industrial state of whirling spindles and clicking looms.

Within his time there were greater changes in the conditions of daily living than in that of any other member of his family save those who flourished at the turn of the twentieth century. He lived long enough to see the invention of the balloon, the airship, the steamboat built of iron, the steam locomotive with the railroad for it to travel on, the electric telegraph, the gas light, the paper-making machine, the type-setting machine, the cylinder press, and lest we should arrive at the millenium prematurely, the percussion cap, the shell gun for artillery, and Colt's revolver — long strides towards the Tommy-gun and the bazooka.

In literature Emerson had delivered his epoch-making address, *The American Scholar.* 'We have listened too long to the courtly muses of Europe. . . . We will walk on our own feet; we will work with our own hands; we will speak our own minds.' Hawthorne had published the first series of *Twice-Told Tales*; Prescott his *Ferdinand and Isabella*; Holmes had written 'Old Ironsides' and 'The Last Leaf'; Whittier his *Legends of New England*; and his own nephew of Elmwood, weary of the law he was studying in the office of the Lorings in Boston, crossed in love, and not seeing how he could arrange his life to devote it to the writing of poetry, put a cocked pistol to his forehead, but fortunately was afraid to pull the trigger.

The career of the Rebel was pivotal in the history of the family. He revered his father and his grandfather and liked to talk of them, and his own descendants revered and liked to talk of him. As he said in the *Memoir* of Dudley Atkins Tyng that he wrote for the Historical Society: 'Even though virtue and not descent is important, it is surely a strong motive to good conduct that your predecessors have done worthy service to the state.'

As you enter the Athenaeum to search the records of his

family, the bust of John Lowell, made in 1834 by John Frazee, stares at you with sightless eyes from the left rear corner of the hall. It lacks the grace of the bust by J. C. King that adorns the wall of King's Chapel beside the family pew. Yet, carefully observed, it impresses you more memorably than the out-size George Washington that overshadows it, or its vis-à-vis Daniel Webster. You feel that as portraiture it has the physical fidelity of a death mask. The furrowed brow, the hollows under the eyes, the tension of anxiety in the lines of cheek and jaw are not perhaps those of a man you would choose for a companion in your hours of ease. But they are the features of one good to have beside you in a fight for a worthy cause when informed by his soul.

> *Animula, vagula, blandula,*
> *Hospes, comesque corporis!*
> *Quae nunc abibis in loca?* [1]

[1] Pope, Prior, Byron, all had a try at turning Hadrian's lines into English, but Elinor Wylie came nearest to the mood of the moribund Emperor:
> 'Little soul, like a cloud, like a feather,
> My body's small guest and companion,
> Where now do you rest, in what places —'

2
CHAPTER

Grandsons of the Old Judge
The Cabot-Jackson Line

In the third generation, counting the Old Judge as the first, the predominance of girls in his issue declined. John Lowell, son of a Higginson, who married an Amory, had only one son out of five children, but Francis, son of a Cabot, who married a Jackson, had three out of four. Charles, son of the Widow Tyng, born Russell, and husband of a Spence, had four out of six. For the generation as a whole there were eight sons to seven daughters. All the boys looked out from behind the square countenance of their grandfather and exhibited traits of his character, but the diverse temperaments of the families on the distaff side conditioned their divergent careers.

Of the three sons of Francis Cabot Lowell and Hannah Jackson, two, like their frail and devoted parents, died in early life, but not before making their mark, in the case of one of them,

'John Junior' a deep and permanent mark, on the life of the community. After 1836 the Cabot-Jackson line had fewer leading characters on the stage of New England than the senior Higginson-Amory line. There is chronological propriety in considering the Cabot grandsons first.

'It is not enough,' wrote Emerson in his *Journal* that he called his 'savings bank,' 'that people should be intelligent and interested in themselves. They must also make one feel that they have a controlling happy future opening before them, and inevitably brightening their present hour. Edward Lowell and Charles Emerson [his own brother] suggested their future in their salutation, or in the least transaction.'

This was written in 1843. Edward had died in 1830, Charles Emerson in 1834.

Edward Jackson Lowell, born in 1805, was taken abroad by his parents along with his elder brothers, John and Francis Cabot Lowell, Jr., in 1810. In the following winter, while staying with Mrs. Grant of Laggan, he suffered a severe attack of scarlet fever, followed by *sequellae* from which he never fully recovered.

In 1818, a year after his father's death, he entered Harvard, graduated in 1822. He completed the law course, dug out of old court records a vast amount of material for the definitive biography of the Old Judge that Caleb Cushing was planning to write, and was admitted to the degree of Master of Arts three years later. Throughout the period of his education his mentor was his Uncle John, who a member of the Corporation took a special interest in the Harvard phase of a young Lowell's life. Always a worrier about the actions of the younger generation, he seems to have had particular anxieties in Edward's case. In 1822 he wrote to his sister:

'... All the trouble I had in the education of J. A. Lowell cannot be compared to that, which I suffered from the *difficulties*, in which Edward was involved. Yet I always saw in him a noble spirit, which would *finally amply* compensate me for the temporary anxiety — It *might* have proved *otherwise*, but as it *is*, how rich my reward in his *gratitude* and *affection!*'

The difficulties in which Edward was involved arose chiefly from overspending his allowance for the purchase of books. But his gratitude and affection were very real. The record of his short life is found almost wholly in his correspondence with his Uncle John. The letters from both were passed around as required reading in subsequent generations. This first report of the law lectures of the celebrated Chancellor Kent, under whom he sat for a few months in the autumn after leaving Harvard, gives its flavor:

'We receive five lectures a week. They are partly written and partly extemporaneous; and the day after the conclusion of each written Lecture he gives us an examination — not merely on the Lecture itself, but on the subjects which were discussed in it — a mode which his very great readiness at putting cases renders extremely useful and agreeable. He will finish with the Law of Nations next week, and immediately after take up the Constitutional and Federal Law of the United States — which subjects will probably occupy us till I see you in winter. I am sorry to add that the Chancellor is not very well attended, there being only eleven pupils — a circumstance however which does not seem to affect or surprise him at all. I told him you desired your best respects — upon which he exclaimed in his peculiar quick manner — "Did he? He's a clever fellow, Sir, a very clever fellow, that U. Lowell of yours," . . .

'Writing is so easy to you and so troublesome to me that as far as time and effort go 3 pp. from me are equal to 30 pp. of yours — the value on the other hand unhappily being in infinitely more than the inverse proportion.'

During the early winter months in New York it became evident to his friends that his health was too insecure for the confining practice of the law. He was given the customary family prescription of two years abroad. In the preceding summer he had made the obligatory American tour: to Philadelphia, over the mountains to Pittsburgh, down the Ohio by steamboat to Cincinnati, back overland to Buffalo across 'a wilderness of stumps,' with a few luxuriantly fertile farms, 'like the taps boys cut in watermelons to see if they are worth stealing,' by Erie Canal, 'the Big Ditch,' to Rochester, across Lake Ontario and down the St. Lawrence by boat to Montreal, and so home. This accomplished, with a letter of instructions and advice of nearly thirty pages from his uncle, he set sail for the Old World shortly after his twenty-first birthday.

His *Wanderjahre*, though not as studious as those of Ticknor and Everett, covered much the same ground and always with a quick ear and a seeing eye. During some weeks with his Uncle and Aunt Dutton in Paris, he met, with his never-to-be-realized future brightening his salutation, Cuvier, La Place, Sismondi, and dined with the Duchesse de Borghese, Benjamin Constant, and Lafayette. Thence he journeyed up the Rhine to Switzerland, climbed a few minor peaks, turned back into Germany, made a study of the bookshops and beer gardens of Berlin and Dresden, turned south again to winter in Florence and Rome.

In Italy he first realized the existence of a world of art of which copies and replicas in the Athenaeum were but pale promises. He poured out his enthusiasms in his letters to his Aunt Amory Lowell. Like all travelling New Englanders of the period other than those who were themselves artists, he found a deeper satisfaction in the firm intellectual forms of sculpture than in the voluptuous color and sentiment of painting.

'If I was somewhat disappointed — as I confess — in the great masterpieces of painting — I was still more so — but in the opposite sense — in those of sculpture — Having seen a dead man and woman of M. Angelo and some sleeping children of what's his name? oh Chantry — you fancy that you know what fine statuary is — I am sorry to undeceive you, but really you are greatly — marvellously — wretchedly mistaken — Out of Rome where will you look for a statue that — after having seen those in it — deserves the name? For even the Venus herself — though still the head of her sex — sinks before the marvels of the Vatican — out of Rome where can you see an Apollo — a Laoccoon — a gladiator — or the only statue of modern times that can be named in the same sentence with them — the Moses of Michel Angelo.'

The winter of 1827 and '28 he spent in Paris sitting part of every day in the law courts, reading international law and European history, attending the sessions of the French *Chambre des Députés*, dining in select society and going to the Opéra or Théâtre Française in the evenings. What he heard made him reflect on the pleniloquence of Americans. He wrote to his friend Tom Bradford:

'If you want to do your country service, my dear Tom, translate Tacitus, render Montesquieu word for word, and teach our contemporaries that eloquence does not depend upon abundance, but selection and position. Just at the moment when all the world should be labouring to become sententious, everybody on the other hand seems to have the *manie* of diffuseness and amplification. In England Southey and Scott, in France Chateaubriand, in America Irving, and in all these the legislative assemblies. But it is in the United States apparently that this evil has reached its summit — the French language and style by nature and by criticism are neat and clear — the English are by temper a brief-spoken nation — but the Americans (our worthy and well beloved fellow-citizens) unite the natural loquacity of the French people to the natural looseness, licentiousness of the English language, and from this union these terrible *longueurs!* Rather all the iron despotism of French verbal hypercriticism (which like good discipline in an army often supplies the place of the more generous qualities which it has perhaps a tendency to repress) rather an Academy and a *Dictionary of Authority* than this endless inundation of superfluous verbiage, forever overflowing and burying under its mud the unhappy ideas — Voilà doctrine and example!'

In England in the spring he divided his days between the law courts in the morning and Parliament in the afternoon. He heard Lord Brougham give a 'good sparring exhibition,' and thought the Duke of Wellington a 'very indifferent orator.' In weekly letters he sent Uncle John minute information of city governments, the prices of everything, and reflections on national characteristics. In the autumn of 1828, he was home seemingly in sound health and began at twenty-three the practice of law.

On a business trip to Philadelphia he had a glimpse of the future.

'I went with Seybert on Saturday to see a steam-carriage which they are building here — on the model I understood of the English "Novelty." It is a tremendous clumsy looking affair and will certainly frighten all the horses in the country to death. It is to weigh about 6000 lb. I think they said the engine to have a 15 horse power. It will be ready for experiment they say next week — Success very doubtfull, tho' I certainly expect to travel in some such machine before long.'

For two years he made headway in his profession, and was a figure of outstanding brilliance and charm at the gatherings of the clan. But before the second year was out, his health broke again. In the summer of 1830, hoping that fresh air and exercise would restore it, he took a solitary horseback trip through the White Mountains. The result was disastrous. He came home to be bedridden in his brother Frank's house at Waltham. His medical uncle, James Jackson, fought hard for his life, but he died in September. One of his cousins who was with him at the end wrote to another in the style of the time:

'Had you beheld his noble countenance with the cold marble hue of death upon him, his eyes, those expressive symbols of his mind and heart, closed, mildly, softly closed to all earthly objects, his manly brow, still covered with the rich dark locks, which seemed to relieve the deadly paleness of this forehead, but above all his lips still expressing in death all the gentle and kind affections of his affectionate heart, with that most beautiful smile still seeming to hover around them, with which in life, he used to warm our hearts, and enliven his social intercourse, I know not what feeling would have preponderated — you might have gazed and gazed on, loth to leave so dear and beautiful an object.' (*Tam cari capitis!*)

Surely it was such as he and his cousin, Frances Amory who too had died young, of whom Emily Dickinson wrote:

> 'This quiet dust was Gentlemen and Ladies,
> And Lads and Girls,
> And laughter and ability and sighing,
> And frocks and curls.'

John Lowell, eldest son of Francis and Hannah, born in 1799, and always for the greater confusion of his contemporaries and posterity known as John, Jr., enjoyed a span of life not many years longer than Edward's. It was crowded with action — psychological upheavals, business successes, domestic tragedy, travel on the scale of a royal progress, dangerous adventure, and far-sighted benefaction. It is recorded in a mass of letters and a set of morocco-bound diaries and journals, almost but not quite illegible, and providentially transcribed in a clerkly hand after his death. It is material for an autobiographic narrative of one of the great 'characters' of the family, in whom its typical traits were present to the *n*th degree.

'I was born,' he writes, 'in Boston the 11th of May, 1799, at an immature birth, my mother having brought me into the world three months before the completion of the usual time, the consequence of which was a feeble constitution in my earliest years.'

He was not expected to live, but his Uncle James Jackson, just home at the age of twenty-three from two years walking as an interne the best hospitals in London, announced, contrary to all local prognosis, that he would pull him through and did so, to the vast advantage of his professional reputation. Still delicate, the boy had a peripatetic preparation for college, cul-

This old house on a Roxbury hilltop in the centre of an estate of thirty acres was purchased by John Lowell, the Old Judge, just after the Revolution. There at the early age of forty-two he retired from the more active practice of the law. His son, John Lowell the Rebel, who inherited it, christened it Bromley Vale, and added three new greenhouses, a windmill, a swimming pond, and the tower of a ruined castle. Through the lives of both it was a centre of hospitality for foreign travellers and leading Federalists. Entertained there at different times were both Alexander Hamilton and Aaron Burr.

Just after the Civil War, the Vale was pierced by a railroad, and the Old Judge's great-grandson, Augustus, sold the land for development and moved to Brookline. The Rebel's two daughters, Anna and Amory, lived in a small cottage on a corner of the estate for another decade.

John Lowell (1799–1836), world traveller, was always called 'John Jr.' although he was actually the son of Francis Cabot Lowell I. After acquiring a fortune in the textile industry, the early loss of his wife and two children determined him to fulfil a boyhood plan of following the Marco Polo route to China. He made by the banks of the Nile a remarkable and beneficent will founding the Lowell Institute.

Marc Gabriel Charles Gleyre, companion of John Jr.'s travels in the Near East, painted *en route* more than two hundred pictures, including this portrait of his patron in Arab costume and of the hold of the brig chartered to convey him from Smyrna to Alexandria, with the impedimenta and amenities of his royal progress.

Francis Cabot Lowell II (1803–1874), whose grave and serene character is reflected in his face, was a classmate and friend of Emerson, who thought he 'looked like a king.' He retired early from active business, spending his summers at his country place in Waltham, his winters in a house on Beacon Street, facing the Common.

minating in two years at the high school in Edinburgh and a
few months with the Reverend Zedekiah Sawyer of Bridgewater, with whom his father had been rusticated twenty years
before. At Harvard he was lonely and unhappy, both by temperament and as a result of his wandering and solitary youth.
After two years he persuaded his father to send him to sea, 'to
qualify himself to be a captain and to come forward in the world
in that way.' He made two voyages to India. Of these we know
little except that he read the travels of Marco Polo, made his
way unaided into higher mathematics, and in the summer of
1817, being in France at the same time with his Uncle John
the Rebel showed no enthusiasm for joining him in Paris.

In his twentieth year, in better health and with a substantial
inheritance from his father in his possession, he started his business life as a merchant and a manufacturer of cotton cloth. In
the same year he began his strange introspective journal.

The first entries show him in the throes of a belated adolescent
'conviction of sin' more characteristic of a young Calvinist than
of the Boston religion. He struggles for mastery of his besetting
sin, 'nervous vanity and self-conceit,' and after smoking two
cigars while reading Low's *Serious Call to a Devout and Holy Life*
writes, 'Oh, my God! when shall I delight in the beauty of
holiness.' Lessons on the flute seem not to have helped him.
He devised a system of large black figures sprinkling the pages
of the journal 'so that I can ascertain at a glance which virtue
I have most frequently sinned against in a given space of Time,'
that is, by the sins of sloth, anger, indolence, neglect of duty,
gluttony, or unruly thoughts.

One sinful day, after trying to read Paley's *Evidences of Christianity*, he became 'listless' and took up *Tom Jones* which engrossed him:

'With respect to the book I can only say that its strain of
humour, sentiment and tenderness is generally admirable, and
its moral sentiments are frequently pure and exalted; but in some
passages it is grossly immoral, and so voluptuous as to have a

dangerous tendency. . . . At dinner I gave away a little too freely
to my appetite.'

He was always an omnivorous reader, but as he became more
deeply involved in business and politics, serving both in the
common council and the legislature, the formal diary was discontinued for a dozen years, and we hear no more of either sin-
ning or playing the flute. At twenty-five he fell in love with his
cousin by marriage, Georgina Amory. Following the protocol
of the clan, he put his proposal in writing. His letter is not preserved, but Georgina's is, endorsed on the envelope in the writing
of the Rebel, 'Georgina's note in her own handwriting answering
John Lowell Junr's offer. Given to me before I expressed my
assent. I knew neither of his designs, nor indeed of his wishes,
till after this had been sent.'

Nineteen-year-old Georgina wrote: 'I need not, I hope, assure
you that the contents of your letter were totally unexpected to
me; it was therefore, after mature deliberation, that I determined to hazard an answer. I have always felt for you the
greatest esteem, founded on the deep principles which you
possess. But I do not depend only upon myself. I am still very
young; and perhaps my Uncle may, on that account or on some
other, object to your proposal. I have always felt for him the
affection of a daughter to a father — you will, therefore, take
some *private* opportunity to make your sentiments known to
him; and it is only with his free and *entire* consent, that I will
ever subscribe myself, yours ever,

'Georgina M. Amory.'

Aware that he had not always listened to avuncular advice
with patience, or taken it with profit, John, Jr., must have gone
to his private opportunity with some misgiving. Doubtless he
underwent an experienced examination and was favored with
good counsel. In the end, however, he received the desired
'entire' consent. They were married on April 6, 1825, and took
a honeymoon trip in a chaise through Newburyport to Ports-

mouth, returning by Haverhill and the newly built city just christened Lowell after his father. They lived at first in a house on Colonnade Row next door to Uncle John, later in one in Bedford Place, the other court end of the town, with another boasting a 'beautiful library' on the bank of the Merrimack in Lowell.

Five years passed while family and fortune grew. John, Jr., read science, biography, voyages and travels, and studied public affairs. He spent the autumn of 1829 in Richmond listening to the debates in the convention called for the making of a new constitution for the mother of presidents. It was a rich and happy life, shaping in his mind, one divines, towards national office. A year later, the jealous gods prepared their *revanche*. In November, 1830, Georgina died of scarlet fever. Within the next eighteen months her two little girls of two and five years followed her with the same disease. John, Jr.'s, good life was shattered. He sold his houses, put his business affairs in the hands of his cousin, John Amory Lowell, made the required preliminary tour of the Middle West, and on November 21, 1833, sailed on the ship *Henry G.* bound from New York to Havre. He had carefully worked out a plan to proceed by leisurely stages through France — with a side trip to England — Italy, Greece, to Asia Minor, thence following the Anabasis of Xenophon's ten thousand in reverse, to Teheran, winter there learning Persian, then over the Marco Polo overland route to the fabulous lands of Cathay, 'not coming home till I see the circle of the earth.'

The first day out he resumed his journal:

'Left New York yesterday at 2½ P.M. with a N.W. wind; made about 2°. at 12 M. this day. Since 7 this morning wind adverse, weather, a little rough; and all the passengers but Mr. Appleton [1] and self qualmish.

'Have had a slight cough and cold in the head for several weeks, but on getting out of sight of land yesterday, they en-

[1] His father's friend, Nathan.

tirely disappeared. Have taken many a long breath with delight. Perhaps the land air contains carbonic acid gas which is
irritating to the aerial canal. The difference to the feeling is
like that between hard water and soft. How many good thoughts
have taken in this soft breeze. Thanks to Him to whom I owe
all; I have not felt so well for years. Good appetite, good sleep
and a quiet mind are restored to me. But what shall I do in this
world? What object have I to live for? No one depends upon
me; no one loves me as I am wont to be loved. I have lived in
vain. Monotony and listlessness remain in store if I live; and if
I die, am I prepared for the next world? Hope faints within
me; the elasticity of youth is gone.'

Old seafarer that he was, wind and wave, the creak of blocks
and scent of tarry shrouds dispelled his listlessness. On December 11, he saw Casket Light off Alderney 'from the mizzen-top,'
and three days later landed in Havre eager to see and hear and
do. His letters to his cousin, John Amory Lowell, even the
pages of his intimate journal, reflect something approaching
high spirits.

In Paris he settled for the winter in an apartment on the Rue
de Rivoli. For four months he attended an average of five
dinners, soirées, or balls per week in the 'salons of the best tone
where it is rare to see a gentleman invading the formidable circle
of sparkling eyes and brilliant complexions that adorn the walls
between the dances.' One night at dinner he 'sat next to a
French girl of sixteen who told me she understood Shakespeare.
I believed her. I have grown sensibly fatter since my arrival
here. I am satisfied my life at home had been too monotonous.'

On May 1, 1833, he journeyed to London, settled at the
Clarendon Hotel in Bond Street, and applied himself to more
serious matters. He inspected the cotton mills of Manchester
and Birmingham and the potteries of Derbyshire and reported
to John Amory Lowell on their arrangement and management.
After a month in Ireland, he spent the early autumn in Edinburgh, where, despite terrific headaches, no doubt the result of

eye-strain, he devoted eight hours a day in the study of mineralogy and the Italian language. Back in London in early November, he dined with the Right Honorable Charles Grant, later
Lord Glenelg, President of the India Board of Control, and
secured advice and letters of introduction to facilitate his progress
across that difficult terrain, and made the necessary arrangements through the Barings to finance it. On December 1, 1833,
he left for the Continent for a visit to its capitals.

Typical selections from his journal for Belgium, France, Italy,
and Greece present a panorama of the Grand Tour a century
ago seen through the eyes of an observant and reflective traveller:

Belgium

'During the forenoon of the 1st I visited the cathedral of Ghent
which is adorned with several pictures of Rubens and other
Flemish masters, and with much rich sculpture and the costly
tombs of several bishops. I never before have seen a church
whose interior was so richly ornamented. I also visited the
church of, I think, St. Michael, which is adorned in a similar
but less costly manner. Many of the paintings in these churches
paid a visit to Paris during the supremacy of the French, and one
masterpiece, now in the church of St. Michael, was concealed
and has suffered more by that than it would have done by a
dozen trips to Paris. But the Belgians did right: had I been a
Fleming, I would sooner have buried them all in damp cellars
and taken the chance of their destruction, than that the invaders
of my country should have stripped her of the embellishments
of her native genius. I remained an hour and a half in the
splendid gallery of M. Schamp and would have staid two hours
longer, had time and propriety permitted. There were three
rooms to contain his pictures. Every particle of the walls of
each was covered with them, in many cases they were folded
one over the other and besides this there were one or two dozen
on stands in the middle of the apartments. I should suppose

there might be in all 200 pieces; the greater part by well-known masters, and not one among the whole that would be called ordinary. There were the two wives of Rubens and the second was certainly a beauty, his brother and himself. An exquisite landscape of Teniers, some admirable Madonnas, one of which is in the style of Corregio; several portraits of Van Dyck, and one of Rembrandt by himself; a Cleopatra and Anthony by Carrachi, a most beautiful and innocent mother and child, which they call a Madonna; and innumerable portraits and scriptural or mythological masterpieces of the Flemish school; all of which left entirely in the shade everything that I have seen in America, excepting always the pictures of Allston. I have met with nothing in Ghent that I would rather own than his last admirable scene from the Italian. Certainly I would prefer the works of Raphael, and above all the cartoons, to what I have seen from the pencil of Allston; but there are few of the productions of the other old masters, unless it be Murillo's or Carrachi's that I like so well as his. This however, is the opinion of one who is not only not a connoisseur; but who has not visited Italy, and is entirely ignorant of the rules by which a refined taste would be guided in these matters. Still the idea has taken possession of my mind so strongly, that partly on that account, and partly because I would willingly be of some service to so meritorious an artist, I am determined to make an attempt to become the possessor of one of his pictures even if I never live to see it. I have accordingly written to Frank to engage one of him, if he should be sufficiently at leisure to undertake the thing. I have desired that the picture should be of the size of that taken from the Italian, the price of which was, I understand, $500; and that Mr. Allston should choose his own subject, with a hint merely that a pretty woman might be acceptably introduced into it.'

France

'Here are the two great nations of the world in our day;
France and England! It is here that the arts, the luxuries, the
elegancies of life and its polished society exist. Here there is
science, intellectual attainment, talent cultivated to the very limit
of human proficiency in our age, glory and reputation which
leave those of all the other tribes of men far in the rear; so far
that the gleam of a helmet among the last is not equal to the
glitter of a shoe-buckle among the French and English. Sincerely
combined, and exerting their full energies; what human power
could presume to resist them. Such a union is not to be expected; but even this long peace has been mutually most ad-
vantageous. The English are certainly less rude, and are no
longer accustomed to treat the people of all other nations with
meaningful disdain; while at the same time I do not suppose
that the solid excellencies of character that distinguish them
have been at all diminished. The French perhaps have gained
still more; not only by imitating English arts, but in some degree
as may be hoped English virtues also; so that the day may come
when we will be able to trust the word of a Frenchman, as well
as to be charmed by his polite address. America in the days of
our grand-children will be grand; and in those of our great-
great-grand-children [1] perhaps the scene of great actions, and
the mistress of nations; if she can only remain united. That
is the only point in our national existence about which I feel the
slightest anxiety. Her enlightened and above all a moral people,
which I trust we are, may suffer for a time but can never long
remain subject to a very bad government; but if we are to be
divided, the fate of Italy, of Germany, or at best of ancient
Greece will be our fate. Her aggregation of tyrannical democracies, a many headed monster without one directing soul, a
mean congregation of declamatory demagogues, an association

---

[1] This would bring us to 1950.

of all that is ignoble, caluminous, base, and weak will pollute with their incessant broils the broad valley of the Mississippi, and even profane the beautiful hills and streams and plains of the descendants of the pilgrims.' [1]

Italy

'The ex-Queen Caroline resembles Napoleon very much and has been handsome. She is still a good-looking woman of about fifty and rather corpulent. She is perfectly graceful and unassuming in her manners and bears her reverses with dignity. One morning when only her niece, Potochi, Pussin,[2] and myself were present she began to converse very freely of her former manner of life while she was Queen of Naples. She said that she had three carriages made perfectly alike, and so constructed, that it was not necessary to quit either for the sake of eating, sleeping, etc. In these she and her suite travelled, without stopping, between Naples and Paris. The usual time employed was seven days to go and return, and she made the journey seven times. On one occasion she was detained in a miserable inn among the mountains of Switzerland. She and her suite all lodged together in a single room. Her indisposition prevented her from proceeding during three days; but did not prevent her indulging, as much as possible in every amusement that could be devised in such a place. They danced, laughed, talked and probably made love, for that is the regular occupation of continental ladies. A comedy was also composed and acted by her suite. That same morning that she entertained us by her natural description of past grandeur, Pussin sang the following couplets of which I consider the last quite touching. They were written

[1] This was written in the year in which the Whig Party was formed from the survivors of the Federalists and those who shared their views of the policies of Andrew Jackson.

[2] His brother-in-law who had married an Amory and travelled with him as far as Greece.

after the fall of Napoleon; and the planters of cabbages there alluded to, were the distinguished soldiers of the emperor:

> ' "La Grèce regrette Achille,
> Corinthe Timoléon,
> Rome le grand Paule Emile,
> La France Napoléon,
>
> ' "Dieu qui protège la France,
> Ramène le parmi nous,
> Terminer les souffrances
> Des pauvre planteurs des choux."

'The Queen was so much affected with this allusion to the former condition of the family that her eyes filled with tears. Truly the fall of Napoleon, a man so full of every sort of talent and so abundant in every kind of resource, is a proverb and a prodigy in the world and a lesson given by Providence to human pride that ought not soon to be forgotten.'

Meeting in the ex-Queen's salon the beautiful and famous Princess Galitzin, John, Jr., expressed admiration of the flower-figured silk of her skirt and was pleased and touched the next morning to receive from her at his lodgings a piece of it for a waistcoat. One gathers that he was neither without interest in the ladies, nor devoid of attraction for them.

From Naples he wrote to his Cousin John, reporting an arrangement that was to give a new color to his travels:

'I have mentioned a young Swiss artist, who is with me. This requires explanation. Considering the touchy situation in which I should be, travelling over barbaric regions after the departure of Pussin, and the agreeable recollection that good designs of various interesting objects, many of them rare and unusual would excite my return home, I determined, while in Rome, to engage an artist both as a travelling companion and as a painter. I applied to the celebrated Horace Vernet, who is at the head of the French academy there, and with whom we were well acquainted. He at first recommended a captain in the French army, a Carlist and nephew of the Duke of Lauciton, who is a man of the world and a respectable artist. The captain declined because he feared his dignity or rather delicacy of feeling might be wounded by accepting such a place; but having since informed himself more fully touching my character and income has deeply regretted the loss of so fine a chance of gratifying his natural love of travel and adventure. Vernet next proposed Mr. Gabriel Gleyre, a Swiss of Lausanne 26 years of age, very plain, a little melancholy, very diffident, of gentlemanly and delicate notions, and according to Vernet a most accomplished artist. He paints in water-colors Vernet says, better than anybody he knows, is excellent in landscapes and perhaps still better at costumes and portraits. In short, he was engaged to take Mlle Vernet's portrait at that very moment. Making a good deal of allowance for French imagination, exaggeration and want of exactness, for the French have all three qualities to a great degree in common life; and the recommendation will still appear a good one. I have taken Mr. Gleyre. He has been with me a fortnight. I like the man and think his pictures good. He is intelligent and by no means a mere artist. He spent four years at Paris and five and a half at Rome. He speaks French with a pure Parisian accent. He is very attentive without being very polite; an excellent quality in a travelling companion. I hope to be equally agreeable to him as he is to me.[1]

---

[1] Marc Gabriel Charles Gleyre is the subject of a full and appreciative illustrated biography by C. Clement. Born in 1806, he was twenty-eight at the time he became the associate of John, Jr. After the unfortunate termination of that experience he returned to Paris and became an intimate of the circle that included Alfred de Musset, Flaubert, Berlioz, and Mérimmée. His canvases, numbering nearly a thousand of which two hundred are still in the possession of the Lowell family, include a succulent Venus Pandemos riding a goat, and a charming Daphnis and Chloe. He is characterized as *d'une talent très pure, souvent symbolique et plein d'élévation.* His biographer makes much of his celibate temperament and conviction. He considered marriage *une esclavage reciproque* — 'to come home in the evening and find a stranger there!' But this did not stand in the way of an *affichement* with a beautiful Nubian princess. In 1874, he dropped dead while looking at an exhibition of 'modern' French paintings at the Palais Bourbon.

Greece

'On this spot was unfolded the gorgeous web of the Odyssey; from that cliff Sappho threw herself into the sea; on my left hand lay the gardens of Alcinous, — and the olive, and the grape, and the orange, still cover the soil; before me rises the embattled citadel which Virgil describes; on my right are the infamous Acroceraunian rocks of Horace; and within that blue, mountain barrier, which bounds the horizon, were concealed the mystic grove and oracle of Dodona, — the cradle of the mythology of Greece.

'Last night we had a scene quite peculiar to Greece and to the countries near the sun. A little party of a dozen Greeks began to amuse one another by telling stories. One fellow seemed to be very humorous, at the end of each sentence he was honored with a laugh. Another had a long and very interesting story about an American who was beloved by the empress of the Morrocco. He returned home but she sent their sons in search of him, who made him drunk, and then branded him on the back with the same mark that their other slaves have. They then claimed him for a slave, on the ground that he had their mark. The justice of the American pashaw, before whom they appeared could not resist this argument.'

The companionable travellers spent five months in Sicily, Malta, and Greece, the 'bright clime of battle and song.' They visited Missolonghi, met the surviving family of Marco Bozzaris, and spent two months at Athens, 'the poor remains of whose ancient taste in the arts exceed in beauty everything I have yet seen in either Italy, Sicily, or any other portion of Greece.' There John, Jr., began to take daily readings of the thermometer, barometer, and hygrometer, and noted the results in his journal. This for some reason annoyed his sensitive fellow traveller. The first rift in the lute!

In September, 1834, they crossed to Smyrna, explored the rich valley of the Meander, which in size and fertility reminded him of the Mohawk, visited the ruins of Hieropolis and Sardis, saw the house of Croesus, proprietor of the ancient world's most swollen pocketbook, drank the golden waters of the River Pactolus, and by the help of a Toorkman girl and a Greek boy crossed the steep pass of the Sifrytus back into the smiling plain of Smyrna.

Bad news awaited them. The plague was prevalent in the hinterland. They were forced to abandon the plan of entering the Black Sea and crossing by way of Armenia and Georgia into Persia. They chartered the Greek brig *Bellerophon*, stocked its hold, as one of Gleyre's paintings discloses, with hogsheads of wine, boxes of bacon, macaroni and cheese, and an Arab horse, and set sail for Alexandria on December 9, 1834. They coasted by the islands of Mitylene and Samos and on the eighteenth day sighted the obelisk bearing the name of Cleopatra's Needle, which marked the port of Alexandria, and sailed up the Rosetta branch of the Nile to Cairo. They transshipped there to a dahabeah for Memphis, arriving in February, 1835. At Memphis the divergent interests of the travellers became more apparent. Apart from one passage on the vast historic view from the top of the great pyramids, 'the radiant valley of the Nile, the City of the Dead, the innumerable tombs, the Sphinx,' page after page of John, Jr.'s, journal is filled with mathematical calculations of the cubical contents of the pyramids which he was never able to complete and prove to his satisfaction.

The journal of Gleyre, *rêveur et penseur* his biographer calls him, takes on at this time and place the mood of Byron, his favorite poet, and the prose rhythm of Chateaubriand:

'Beau spectacle. Quelle paix! quel silence! le large fleuve coule avec tant de majesté. La lune, en effleurant ses rides légères, semble y laisser comme une trainée de perles. Les palmiers balancent avec grâce leurs têtes echeveleés. Les formes adoucies de la montagne-temple, par cette belle nuit, ont quelque chose de plus imposant; le mystérieux et vaste désert étale de toutes parts ses plaines inconnues. Oui, cela est beau. Mais pourquoi cette inquiétude? Pourquoi sentais-je se reveiller en mon coeur ces vague et mélancolique souvenirs? Oh! chères et douces illusions de ma jeunesse, hélas! trop tôt dissipées; vous êtes donc perdues! perdues à jamais. L'âme régimbe a cette dure, triste et fatale conviction.

'J'ai tout rêve, même un nom glorieux.'

As the dahabeah sailed, or was towed, up the river towards Thebes, they overtook Mohammed Ali, King of Egypt, who was proceeding by similar conveyance. Visits were exchanged and the American traveller was minutely cross-examined about the United States, very particularly as to the success of steam navigation on large rivers.

Before reaching Thebes both travellers were attacked by the endemic malady of dysentery and intermittent fever. Both had temperatures, and the allergy that had been secretly developing between them broke into open argument over the terms of their arrangement. John, Jr., had agreed to pay Gleyre five hundred dollars a year and expenses, and had written John Amory Lowell that in the event of his death he was to deal liberally with the painter. For this he considered that he was entitled to the ownership of all work produced by the painter while in his employ. Gleyre thought otherwise. He was, he insisted, only engaged to produce paintings of assigned subjects in each country, nothing more. When his '*rapace compagnon*' confiscated even his pocket sketch-book, the feverish dispute became open rebellion. Nevertheless, Gleyre stuck by his employer during their joint illness, but after partial recovery they separated '*en assez mauvais termes.*' Gleyre took on his beautiful black Stella. She left him, however, when he became temporarily blind from dysentery and the desert sun. Thereafter he went native, and it was not until 1840, five years later, that he regained his sight, returned to Paris, opened a studio on the Rue de Bac, capitalized his Egyptian experience in a series of biblical pictures and became a *cher maître.*

John, Jr., retained all of the paintings and many of the

sketches, as apparently he was within his legal rights in doing. 'Rapace' was hardly the right word, though we may perhaps without violence to the family character concede that he was imperious and demanding.

At Luxor, weakened by his disease but with a normal temperature, John, Jr., encamped, like the lion and the lizard in the poem, on top of a ruined palace, and devoted himself to assembling the largest collection of Egyptian antiquities ever up to that time collected by an American, perhaps by any individual for his own account. He wrote Cousin John, warning him to be prepared to respond to drafts up to fifty thousand dollars and authorized him to put one hundred thousand dollars into one of the cotton mills he was building in the new city of Lowell, provided he would manage it himself. It was in the ancient city of the Pharaohs that he completed the noble will by which he is long remembered, endowing the Lowell Institute.

The eighteen-twenties in Boston were the heyday of the lyceum and the improving lecture. John, Jr., interested in this new form of what we should now call adult education, had been a founding member of the Boston Society for the Diffusion of Useful Knowledge, which in 1830, with Daniel Webster as president, had begun its career with a two-hour discourse by Edward Everett on the life of Benjamin Franklin. Before sailing for France, he had drafted a provisional testament directing that in the event of his death one half of his fortune should be employed in carrying on the work in perpetuity on a more comprehensive scale. At Luxor he completed the terms of the bequest and clarified its aims in a document remarkable for its thoughtful vision.

'For the more perfect demonstration of the truth of those moral and religious precepts, by which alone, as I believe, men can be secure of happiness in this world and that to come, I wish a course of lectures to be delivered on the historical and internal evidences in favor of Christianity. I wish all disputed points of faith and ceremony to be avoided, and the attention of the lecturers to be directed to the moral doctrines of the Gospel, stating their opinions, if they will, but not engaging in con- troversy, even on the subject of the penalty for disobedience.

'As the prosperity of my native land, New England, which is sterile and unproductive, must depend hereafter, as it has here- tofore depended, first, on the moral qualities, and secondly, on the intelligence and information of its inhabitants, I am desirous of trying to contribute towards this second object also; — and I wish courses of lectures to be established on physics and chemis- try, with their application to the arts; also, on botany, zoology, geology, and mineralogy, connected with their particular utility to man.

'After the establishment of these courses of lectures, should disposable funds remain, or, in process of time, be accumulated, the trustee may appoint courses of lectures to be delivered on the literature and eloquence of our language, and even on those of foreign nations, if he see fit. He may, also, from time to time, establish lectures on any subject that, in his opinion, the wants and taste of the age may demand.

'As infidel opinions appear to me injurious to society, and easily to insinuate themselves into a man's dissertations on any subject, however remote from religion, no man ought to be appointed a lecturer, who is not willing to declare, and who does not previously declare, his belief in the divine revelation of the Old and New Testaments, leaving the interpretation thereof to his own conscience.'

He appointed his cousin executor of his will and sole trustee of the lecture foundation, providing further that each trustee should appoint his successor within a week after his accession to the office. He stipulated that the trustee should choose to follow him in preference to all others some male descendant of his grandfather, the Old Judge, 'provided there be one com- petent to hold the office and of the name of Lowell.' The study he had given to the most minute details of the bequest appears in the provision governing the fees that might be charged for the more abstruse courses for advanced students. In the event of inflation the charge for admission to a six-months course should be equal to the current price of two bushels of wheat. To keep the lecture hall from filling up with the floating population that even in those days was wont to *desipere in loco* on the Common, the trustee was directed to require of every person attending the lectures that he be neatly dressed and of orderly behavior.

It was a far-sighted benefaction shrewdly formulated in a majestic setting! The story of the success of the enterprise is part of the record of John Amory Lowell who as first trustee invested and multiplied the endowment, planned the courses, and selected the lecturers for more than forty years.

From Luxor, John, Jr., having joined forces with a young English explorer, penetrated Ethiopia on his Arab horse as far as the site of the ancient city of Meroe. But his dysentery had returned and he was attacked by a painful disease of the eyes. He felt it was time to push on to India. Following the advice of Mohammed Ali, he crossed the Nubian Desert, fourteen days by camel-back, to a small port on the western coast of the Red Sea, and chartered a schooner navigated by Arabs, to carry him with his attendants and impedimenta across to Mocha. They sailed on the sixteenth of December, 1835. Six days later he was shipwrecked. On the evening of the twenty-second, it came on to blow with blinding rain, they drifted among shoals — but let the traveller himself take up the tale:

'At the end of several hours, we struck on a coral reef. Then all hands jumped overboard to push the vessel off the rocks. My *sais* and cook joined the crew in this duty; but a fresh northwest wind, accompanied by rain and much mist, rendered their efforts unavailing. I retreated to my covered litter again, and put what gold was not already in my broad Turkish girdle, into my pocket. I did the same with my letters of credit. The water now entered fast through all the seams in the larboard side of the vessel. The men could not bail the schooner fast enough; and, as she continued to strike, it was evident that the leak would become worse. Yanni now called out, "They are throwing our cases overboard!" True enough; the hold of the little vessel had been crowded with my effects, and I now saw them floating alongside. There went my best tent, for its poles kept it from sinking, and the waves soon carried it out of sight. Here lay the box that contained my reflecting circle, and another with my Parisian rifle. These two boxes were large, and besides the above and various perishable articles, were filled with a variety of European luxuries and provisions. Macaroni, olives, tongues, the best of the biscuit, the best of the rice, sugar, and tea, were among the number.

'I kept nothing back, except my trunks of wearing apparel, my books, writing materials, a leather bag, into which I had thrust my journals, my pistols, certain gilt French Bagatelles for presents, and a few other articles.

'Presently the dragoman exclaimed, "The hands are going to quit the vessel, and I shall quit too." His threat did not disturb me, as I knew the poor fellow had not the wherewithal to buy a dinner without me; but I did not much relish being left alone on the deck by the seamen. I had always counted, if it came to the worst, on having their aid and the raft to put me on shore. As for swimming, I have not strength for that, especially in my clothes, and so thorough a ducking and exposure might of itself make an end of me. I entered my litter again to get a pistol, which I thrust into my girdle. Yanni exclaimed, "They are carrying away our raft!" I stepped again on deck and sure enough, the men were all in the water, foolishly attempting to put one of their packs of four great elephants' teeth upon a raft that could scarcely carry more than one. "That raft is mine," I exclaimed; "I made it, and it is tied with my cord, for the purpose of saving my effects." These people were accustomed to hear me speak with the tone of a master; they hesitated, and then slowly made off with the raft. "Quit that raft," said I; "I will shoot the first man who attempts to move it." I presented my pistol, and they all left the raft, much to my relief, for I should have fired had they persevered.'

In the end all the ship's company reached shore without loss of life, and returning in small boats rescued the more important baggage. The excitement and exposure following his previous illness had exhausted the traveller's strength. He took passage by steamer from Mocha to Bombay and arrived there on the tenth of February, gravely ill. Some Lowell cousins of the Bristol branch living there heard of his arrival and of his dangerous case. They did what they could for him, but he died on the fourth of March. One of them asked him if he wished to say anything to his friends in America, which he could convey to them, 'but he expressed nothing, and only directed his effects be sent with the simple notice of his death.' He died as he had long lived, in loneliness.

Of the three sons of Francis and Hannah, only Francis Cabot Lowell, Jr., was left. He lived and prospered until 1874. His life was stable, even static, like that of happy nations that have no history. Perhaps in his character as in his features there was more of Cabot in him than of Jackson. He married his second cousin, Mary Lowell Gardner, and divided his years between the ample country homestead in Waltham where Edward had lain in his last days and number 56 Beacon Street, one of the row of residences of which the English traveller, E. V. Lucas, wrote in 1826, 'The serene façades of the houses on Beacon Street overlooking the Common are as satisfying as anything in Georgian London.' After his death, his Harvard classmate, Ralph Waldo Emerson, wrote in his *Journal* a character of his friend which is an adequate brief biography:

'The death of Francis Cabot Lowell is a great loss to me. Now for fifty-seven years since we entered college together, we have been friends, meeting sometimes rarely, sometimes often; seldom living in the same town, we have always met gladly on the old simple terms. He was a conservative, I always of a speculative habit; and often in the wayward politics of former years, we had to compose our different opinions. He was a native gentleman, thoroughly true, and of decided opinions, always frank, considerate, and kind. On all questions his opinions were his own, and deliberately formed. One day he came to Concord to read to me some opinions he had written out in regard to the education now given at Cambridge. He did not leave the paper with me and I regret that I cannot recall its substance. However you might differ from him, he always inspired respect and love. I have never known a man of more simplicity and truth.

'I heard gladly, long since, from Dr. Hobbs, of Lowell's relation to the chemical mills in Waltham. His father, Mr. Frank Lowell, Senior, had founded them, and his son inherited in them an important interest. From whatever causes, the property had sadly depreciated. But Mr. Lowell undertook the charge of them himself, studied chemistry with direct reference to the work done in this mill, made himself master of all the processes required; corrected the mistakes; and against all advice stayed therein until its depreciated shares came up to par; then he sold his shares in the property and retired. A man of a quiet inward life, silent and grave, but with opinions and purposes which he quietly held and frankly stated, when his opinion was asked; — gently but with a strong will, and a perseverance which at last carried his point. Mr. Henry Lee Higginson told me how scrupulously honest he was, how slow to avail himself of the right to take up mortgages, the terms of which had not been kept. Mr. H. thought him romantically honest. And his truth was of the like strain. He said to me, at his house, that when his Club had lately met there, several gentlemen expressed to him their satisfaction at being his guests; and this led him to say that he did not believe he had ever expressed to any man more regard for the person than he really felt. Exact and literal in affairs and in intercourse, he was the most affectionate parent, and his children's children filled the house with their joy.

'His generosity was quiet, but sure and effective. Very strict in its direction, but ample in amount. He was the friend in need, silent but sure, and the character of the giver added rare value to the gift, as if an angel brought you gold. I may well say this, when I recall the fact that on the next day after my house was burned, he came to Concord to express his sympathy in my misfortune, and a few days afterward surprised me with a munificent donation from himself and his children which went far to rebuild it.[1]

'In college, I well remember the innocence of the youth when we first met; — and the perfect simplicity of his manners he never lost. Yet long years afterward I well remember that when we stood together to witness a marriage in the Stone Chapel, my wife inquired who was the gentleman who stood by me, and who looked so like a king; I was delighted by the perception.

'I dearly prize the photograph taken from Rowse's drawing of his head, which is an admirable likeness, my gift from his daughter, Georgina Lowell. His daughter tells me that he thought he did not interest his acquaintances. I believe he always had their entire respect, and a friendship akin to love.

'Fortunate in his birth and education, accustomed always to a connection of excellent society, he was never confounded with others by the facility of interests and neighbourhood, but remained as independent in his thought as if he had lived alone.'[2]

---

[1] On August 2, 1872, Emerson wrote to his friend in a hitherto unpublished letter: 'Your wonderful note bewilders me. I am accustomed to the kindness and nobility of my friends, but a gift like this I hardly dare to receive. Let me sit and think of it. It seems to imply a sacrifice somewhere which I ought not to permit. Let me think of it twice. . . . Meantime let me enjoy my wonder at the goodness of my friends.'

[2] The ever-quotable Colonel Henry Lee views him from a slightly different angle:
'He was a man of peculiarly even temper. He was a vegetarian. This led me to try a diet exclusively of vegetables. I could not find that it had any effect on my health or my temperament. The stomach was overloaded every day. Because Nature finding less nourishment in spinach than in beef called for much more food, so that after my meals I was heavy. Having satisfied my curiosity I gave it up without regret.'

One man's spinach is another man's poison!

Independence of thought persisted in his line. A son and a grandson as we shall see produced historical works based on original research that threw new light on two great confused periods and are still standard in their fields.

Independence of thought persisted in his line. A son and a grandson as we shall see produced historical works based on original research that threw new light on two great confused periods and are still standard in their fields.

3
CHAPTER

The Higginson-Amory Line
Mills, Money, and Lectures

THE SENIOR AND LONGER-LIVED BRANCH, in which the family's business and civic leadership usually rested, was carried on in the Rebel's only son. Their two lives covered a stretch of one hundred and fifty-three years. Even allowing for the boyhood of the father and the overlap, their combined period of continuous active public service was nearly a century.

John Amory Lowell, 'that little rogue,' after having been prepared at dame schools in Boston, M. Fontane's boarding-school in Paris, where it is recorded he refused to speak French until he had learned to speak it perfectly, Mr. Cumming's Latin School in Boston, and Mr. Wells's tutoring school in Cambridge, entered Harvard in 1811 at the customary family age of thirteen. His father took his pen in hand, if indeed it were not already

218

there, and produced sixteen folio pages not calculated to encourage roguishness:

'It is peculiarly your misfortune that a certain readiness in acquiring a superficial knowledge of subjects has given you a reputation with many of your friends of possessing talents, with which both you and I know you are not favoured. The necessity is therefore greater, to exert yourself to support an opinion which you are conscious is too flattering. The most prominent trait in your mind is the rapidity with which you comprehend a subject and acquire some plausible knowledge of it, unless this quality be equalled or exceeded by your feeble power of retaining what you have thus learned. . . . Let me, my son, now advert to a danger at the very thought of which I tremble because I consider it the greatest to which you are exposed. It is the most prolifick source of all other failings and even vices. You will already have anticipated that I allude to the habit of idleness. You have never been idle, and therefore can have no just conception of the degrading, powerful effects of this habit. But though you have not been idle, yet paradoxical as it may seem, you have not been studious. I have never been able to perceive in you till within the last three months, the smallest disposition to study for the sake of acquiring knowledge, or from a principle of duty.'

Perhaps the Rebel came to realize that he was not an infallible judge of juvenile character. He lived to see his son a successful merchant and banker, treasurer of four large cotton mills, trustee of the Athenaeum, member of the Harvard Corporation, sole trustee of the Lowell Institute, whose first lecture he heard two months before his own death, and the active head of the family. Or perhaps he was only the more firmly convinced of the value of good advice. He was hardly ironist enough to know that we learn nothing from precept and very little from experience. He had set a powerful example, the thing that really counts.

In his freshman year little John Amory lived, as his father had arranged, in the house of President Kirkland and under his eye. He was tutored by another housemate, Edward Everett, just seventeen and studying for the Unitarian ministry. In his sophomore and junior years he roomed in Massachusetts. He was rusticated for six months when, seeing a near-contemporary well known to him, but a tutor, passing in the Yard, animal spirits led him to protrude his head and shout, 'There goes Sammy Sewall.' During his senior year he shared rooms with John Gorham Palfrey, the future preacher, politician, post-master, and historian, in Holworthy. He applied himself seriously to his study from whatever motive, and secured, he says in his diary, 'at the minor exhibition a French oration, at the second major a mathematical part, at the third a forensic with Pickman, and at Commencement, August 30, 1815, a forensic with George Chandler.' The subject of the final disputation was 'Whether prosperity and the increase of wealth have a favorable effect on the manners and morals of the people.'

The decision was for the affirmative.

Two weeks later, he entered the store of Kirk Boott and Sons, importers of English merchandise. His diary of this period shows him working off his animal spirits in family reunions, theatre parties, cotillions, and juggling exhibitions in which he particularly delighted. He noted arrivals and departures of ships, the merchandise they carried and the proceeds of its sale. He read Adam Smith's *Wealth of Nations* and other stiff works in economics, and displayed the family's perennial fondness for leg-exercise by walking the four miles from Bromley Vale to the store at 30 State Street every day when weather made it possible. In 1819 he made a tour of the British Isles, following in the North, as his granddaughter, Amy, was to note, the pre-cise route taken the year before by two open-eyed young travel-lers of similar age, Charles Brown and John Keats.

On Saint Valentine's Day, 1822, he married his first cousin, Susan Cabot Lowell, daughter of Francis Cabot Lowell the first, and sister of his close friend and cousin, John, Jr. In their son, born in Bedford Place, another John — and a Federal Judge — Lowell, Higginson, Amory, Cabot, and Jackson blood were all commingled with delightful results. Two years after her death, in 1827, he married *her* cousin, Elizabeth Cabot Putnam. Augustus, their first son, was to follow his father in most of his treasurerships and trusteeships and beget the brilliant trio of our own time, Percival, Amy, and Lawrence.

The year of his first marriage, although only twenty-four, he became a director of the Suffolk Bank which he served for fifty-nine years, originating and establishing what was known as the Suffolk Bank System for stabilizing the value of the New England bank-note currency; and in the same year the prosperous firm of Boott and Sons changed its style to Boott and Lowell.

The elder Kirk Boott, originally from Derbyshire, had died in 1817, just after the second return from England of Kirk Boott, Jr. Born in Boston in 1791, the younger Kirk had been sent to England and prepared for Harvard at Rugby. At the beginning of his sophomore year in 1807, news of the Peninsular War and possibly the Rebel's eloquent denunciation of Anti-Christ, aroused his martial spirit. Despite the Embargo he was got over to England again, a commission was purchased for him, and after a brief indoctrination at Sandhurst he saw active service as an engineer officer attached to the staff of Lieutenant General Sir Arthur Wellesley, later the Iron Duke of Wellington. He took part in the capture of San Sebastian and the siege of Bayonne, both opportunities for engineers. A brilliant military career seemed open to him, but in 1812, at the outbreak of Mr. Madison's War, rather than bear arms against his mother country he resigned his commission and after the conclusion of hostilities came home. Handsome, efficient, of many capacities and talents, at once a martinet and an understanding gentleman, more a builder and administrator than a merchant, Confucius would have recognized him as The Superior Man. In 1822, he retired from the business of the Boott firm to become the agent in charge of the Merrimack Cotton Company's mill, and architect and builder of the city that was to bear the Lowell family name.

In 1824, the trading firm of John Wright Boott and John Amory Lowell was dissolved. From the time of his second marriage in 1827 and his removal from Bedford Place to the steep sunny hillside of Pemberton Square, John Amory Lowell's major business was the handling of the finances and the overhead management of cotton mills in Waltham, Lowell, and a little later, in Lawrence.

In December, 1821, a venturesome group consisting of the two Bootts, Nathan and William Appleton, Patrick Tracy Jackson, Paul Moody, the Lowell in-laws, Warren Dutton and Benjamin Gorham, together with Nathaniel Bowditch and Daniel Webster, given a few shares for mathematical and legal advice and window-dressing, organized the Merrimack Company, and within a decade turned a section o the peaceful village of Chelmsford with half a dozen houses into a mile of mills. To take full advantage of the power generated by the thirty-foot fall and distribute it effectively, they acquired and enlarged the Old Pawtucket Ditch around the falls and canalized the foaming waters of the Merrimack to the great inconvenience of the ale-wives and salmon.

At the second meeting of the founders, it was voted to sell twenty-five per cent of the stock to the Boston Company, which owned the mill at Waltham and also made cotton manufacturing machinery under the Lowell-Moody patents. John, Jr., Francis Cabot Lowell II, and John Amory Lowell were chief owners of the Boston Company, and thus came into the new and greater enterprise. Later the last named became a large holder of the shares of the Boott Mill, the Massachusetts Mill, the Locks and Canals Company, which was paid rent for the water power, and of the Boston and Lowell Railroad Company, which from 1830 carried the product to market. He was a director in all and at different times treasurer. In effect he drew a profit from all the process of cotton manufacture from the making of the machines to the financing of the sale of the finished cloth in the markets of the world. 'There is,' wrote Nathan Appleton in 1858, 'no man whose beneficial influence in establishing satisfactory regulations in relation to this manufacture exceeded that of Mr. John A. Lowell.'

We must try to answer for him and for New England the searching question William Blake put to Old England:

> 'And did the Countenance Divine
> Shine forth upon our clouded hills?
> And was Jerusalem builded here
> Among these dark Satanic mills?'

Jacksonian Democrats and contemporary proletarian writers answer with a resounding 'No!' Several young women who worked in the mills have replied with an eager starry-eyed 'Yes!' The truth lies somewhere between, and is largely a matter of dates.

It seems to have become fixed in the minds of many writers that from the beginning Lowell was the scene of starvation wages, sweatshop conditions of labor, and bad company-owned housing.

The first point is purely a question of what 'real wages' were, the relation of the pay received to its purchasing power, and the cost of living. The country girls, who, following Francis Cabot Lowell's philosophy of labor that he had put into effect at Waltham, ran the carding machines, spindles, and looms at Lowell, began as apprentices at $1.80 per week and worked up quickly to a peak that sometimes reached a dollar a day. In the eighteen-thirties and forties the average was $3.15 per week. In the competing mills of Lancashire it was four shillings. The weekly pay of domestic servants and workers in shoe factories in the United States ranged from seventy-five cents to two dollars, and school-teachers received 'paltry pittances' for a few months of the year and were destitute of employment for the balance of it. Herman Melville, for teaching the district school at Pittsfield and outfighting its bullies, was paid six dollars per quarter plus his board. The salary of Kirk Boott, who built for himself as agent a replica of the mansion in which Madame Jumel lived in marriage with Aaron Burr, was only $3000, though dividends on shares held by himself and his family averaged twelve and a half per cent on $90,000.

All the girls paid for board and lodging a standard rate of $1.25 per week, leaving them $1.90 over the cost of living. Out of this they accumulated dowries and put brothers through college. Two sisters working ten years supported themselves, their mother, built a house costing $600, $100 more than the boarding-house they lived in, bought a pew for $125, and had a balance of $400 in the bank. The total of mill girls' deposits in Lowell savings banks amounted, in 1845, to over $100,000.[1]

That the girls themselves were not unsatisfied is evident from the 'Song of the Spinners,' printed in their magazine, *The Lowell Offering:*

'Despite of toil we all agree,
Out of the mills or in,
Dependent on others we ne'er will be
So long as we're able to spin.'

The food and shelter they bought for their dollar and a quarter was good value for the money. According to Doctor Scoresby, an English traveller, they had three meals a day each with choice of tea or coffee, and hot meat at dinner, usually a roast of mutton or beef. The earliest boarding-houses Kirk Boott built were of frame, two and a half stories, on the golden section with an ell. Each had four chimneys, two at either end, to provide fireplaces for heat and ventilation in each of the six principal bedrooms. Later they were three and a half stories, of brick, in block-long units, bearing a singular resemblance to Massachusetts Hall at Harvard, the dormitory designed and built by President Leverett during John Amory Lowell's great-grandfather's time there, in 1720. Some present-day writers take a low view of their sanitation and ventilation. These,

[1] Coolidge, *op. cit.*

however, compared not too unfavorably with the conveniences and fresh air supplied in Colonnade Row. The girls slept four or six to a room in two or three double beds, but it was not long since the boys at Harvard had done the same. The English traveller, Captain Basil Hall, was sure in 1827 that the ventilation must be good, because the girls all looked so rosy and happy, and had such an abundance of energy for literary and musical pursuits in their off hours.

For an account of these we must turn to the idyllic pages of Lucy Larcom's *A New England Girlhood*. On the page facing her Preface she quotes Henry Vaughan's

'Bright shoots of everlastingness,'

and she found many such in the Lowell mills that would have surprised even the paternal management.

Lucy Larcom's father, a retired sea-captain who delighted in astronomical calculations and historical computations, described by a neighborhood poet as

'Philosophic Ben
Who, pointing to the stars, cries, land ahead!'

died in Beverly in 1834. A year later, his widow secured a position as housekeeper in one of the company boarding-houses in Lowell. After the first stage-coach journey of her life, little Lucy, aged eleven, with her mother, a sister, and a small brother, accompanied by a 'barrel of books,' were dumped in front of a house in one of the new brick rows just nearing completion. Then began what she always remembered as the happiest ten years of her successful and happy life, which was to include teaching literature in the eager West, writing for the *Atlantic* of Lowell, Howells, and Aldrich, and making anthologies with Whittier. 'I knew that I was glad to be alive and to be just where I was. A community where character alone commanded respect.' Harriet Robinson, who worked in the mills a little later and longer, and wrote about it in *Loom and Spindle*, felt the same way, though she expressed it less lyrically. Although the agent of the Appleton mill was reluctant to employ the two little Larcom girls of twelve and fourteen, he was finally persuaded to give them part-time work if they would go to school three months every summer as required by the Massachusetts law. The poet's industrial career began.

Passing to her work 'through a splendor of dahlias and hollyhocks,' she looked out from her spindle on 'the Merrimack that has blent its music with the onward song of many a lovely soul that clad in plain working clothes moved heavenwards beside its waters.' Though it was forbidden to bring books to work, she turned her own window and the seat under it into a muse's bower by pasting poetry cut from newspapers and magazines all around it. The next window was filled with geraniums in pots, 'the overseer's pets.' She made friends with bouncing bright-faced girls from the mountains and lakes to the north. In the evening they sang around the piano in the parlor of the boarding-house, and Lucy read Whittier, Longfellow, Holmes, Harriet Beecher, Irving, Poe, Cotton Mather, Shakespeare, Percy's *Reliques*, Chaucer, Spenser, Milton, Jeremy Taylor, Dryden, Pope (the last two with no enthusiasm), Wordsworth, Coleridge, Southey, Cowper, Burns, Johnson, Byron, Macaulay, Carlyle, Tennyson, *Blackwood's Magazine*, and the *Westminster* and *Edinburgh Reviews*. She studied German and made competent verse translations of lyrics by Goethe, Schiller, and Uhland. With the other girls, some of them great readers, too, she crowded into the Institute that had been set up by the management of the mills to provide cheap lectures, to hear John Quincy Adams, Emerson, or Whittier.

All this resulted in an urge for authorship in many an ardent girlish heart. The Larcom family began it with a periodical circulated in manuscript called *The Diving Bell*. A little later the Improvement Society of the Methodist Church started and printed *The Operatives' Magazine*, and a similar organization of the First Universalist, another which was soon merged with the first under the name of *The Lowell Offering and Magazine*, *Written and Edited by Female Operatives.* It was neatly printed at a local press and successfully published by William Schouler of Lowell who actually paid cash for contributions.

Each of the monthly numbers had as frontispiece a steel engraving of some famous painting (Turner's Bridge of Sighs was one) or woodcuts of local scenes, followed by forty-eight pages of stories, articles, poems, and editorials. A few of the stories were in the high-erected romantic vein of Mrs. Radcliffe, but most, including an amusing series of 'Incidents of Adventure' in stage-coaches and steam cars, were pictures of the New England life the girls had seen with their own eyes. Many, like the leader in the first number, 'Abby's Year in Lowell,' were autobiographic. The articles dealt chiefly with abstract subjects, such as 'Solitude,' 'Beauty,' 'History,' 'Twilight Musing,' and 'Kissing.' The poetry, save for thoughtful softly musical pieces signed 'L. L.,' was not notable. The editorials signed, during the later years of the *Offering's* life, 'H. F.' were very notable.

H. F. was Harriet Farley, whose 'great favorite book' as a child was *The Pilgrim's Progress.* She was the daughter of the Reverend Stephen Farley of Claremont, New Hampshire. In 1833, at the age of fourteen, the family being large, one sister an epileptic, her mother ill and deranged, and her father threatened with consumption, she went to the Lowell mills to aid in its support. At first this came only from the $1.90 a week left her after bare subsistence, but later from the profits of the magazine. In 1843, she and Harriot Curtis bought it back from Schouler, and both edited and published it until its demise in 1845. In 1852, her book, *Happy Nights at Hazel Wood,* was published in New York by Harpers, and two years later she married John Intaglio Donlevy, an inventor, and moved to that city. After his death she continued to live there, doing miscellaneous writing and lecturing on 'The Laws of Life, or Hints on the Determination of Sex.' She died in the New York Home for Incurables in 1907, at the age of ninety. In the correspondence of that fierce feminist, Caroline Healey Dall, preserved in the Massachusetts Historical Society, are three letters from Harriet Farley. Their acquaintance seems to have begun in their common friendship with Whittier. In one letter Harriet offers Caroline some sound remarks on the female character drawn from her observation of the mill girls:

'They are affectionate and fear that, to become self-protecting, self-sufficient, would render them less interesting to those they wish to please. They wish to be loved, and not until a woman has secured or relinquished affection can she willingly render herself more masculine.'

As time went on, the *Offering*, selling at six and a quarter cents a copy, won a substantial circulation throughout the Eastern States. The management of the mills welcomed the favorable publicity it gave them, and would have been glad to subsidize it, but except for occasionally buying up overstock of back numbers, wisely refrained from doing so, lest a shadow should be cast on its complete independence. In one vigorous editorial H. F. indignantly denied the charge that the editors and contributors were 'fools, dupes, decoys, etc.'

Abroad its *réclame* was tremendous. Harriet Martineau arranged to have a bound volume of the issues for one year reviewed in the *Athenaeum*, in the hope that young Queen Victoria would be inspired to suggest to her ministers that something should be done to raise the girls of the Lancashire mills to a similar level of well-being and mental alertness. A year later, *Mind among the Spindles*, an anthology of the best in prose and verse selected from the *Offering* by H. F., was published in London and had a wide sale. In France it was exhibited in the Chamber of Deputies as an argument in favor of industrialism. Professor, later President, Cornelius Felton of Harvard, in Paris during a sabbatical year abroad and sitting in on a course of lectures on English Literature by the eminent *littérateur* Philarète Chasles, was edified and surprised when he listened for an hour to an eloquent discourse on the merits of the *Lowell Offering*.

Charles Russell Lowell (1807–1870), eldest brother of the poet James Russell Lowell, merchant, cataloguer of the Athenaeum and Colonel of the Boston Cadets, with his son Charles Russell Lowell, Jr., future Beau Sabreur, who was to lose his life at the battle of Cedar Creek.

Robert Traill Spence Lowell (1816–1891), Episcopal clergyman, medical missionary in Newfoundland, teacher, hymn writer and novelist, was the first of the Lowell clan both to marry and to live away from New England.

These pictures of James Russell Lowell (1819–1891) and his first wife Maria White were made about 1848, the 'wonderful year' of married happiness before her health began to fail and in which his work first brought him international recognition and fame.

John Amory Lowell (1798–1881), only son of the Rebel, millowner, banker, Trustee of the Lowell Institute, Fellow of Harvard, where he was influential in strengthening the faculty and in the choice of six presidents, was the pillar of the family prosperity for three generations. With his close business associate, Abbott Lawrence, he founded the city which bears the latter's name.

From its founding the new city of Lowell and the social experiment that was going on there under the direction of the men of the family for which the city was named had been a Mecca for both French and English travellers.   None wrote of it more warmly than Charles Dickens in his *American Notes*, notes that were in most other cases a little sour.

One day in 1841 he was jolted up to Lowell over the new one-track railroad, and was 'met at the station by a gentleman occupying a position of authority in the mills.'   It could have been John Amory Lowell, whose trusteeship of the Lowell Institute was giving him experience in entertaining distinguished foreigners.   In reading the enthusiastic chapter on the mill girls one suspects that the guide, whoever he may have been, was a good showman.   Dickens is very éxact with figures about the savings-bank accounts and such, but the creator of *Oliver Twist* kept his own eyes open.   He noted that every girl had a sensible bonnet, and a good warm cloak or shawl, that all were extremely clean and remarkably healthy — how different from the girls one saw in Lancashire!

'They meet your gaze of sorrowful surprise
With a pale stare, half misery, half vice.'

He reaches his climax by recounting that when President Jackson or President Harrison, he is not quite sure which, was in Lowell some years since, he marched through three and a hálf miles of girls, seven thousand of them, all with parasols and in silk tockings!

Five years earlier, a better observer and more careful investigator from overseas had appeared in the person of Michael Chevalier, a young French economist, on a special mission from Louis Philippe, white hope of French radicalism, to investigate society, manners, and politics in the United States.   In his *Notes* he paints a vivid picture of the red and white city with its tasteful and comfortable houses, its fancy-goods shops and milliners' rooms without number; its canals, waterwheels, waterfalls, bridges, banks, churches, schools and libraries, 'for in Lowell reading is the only recreation.' As a good Frenchman he is puzzled by the manners and temperament of the daughters of the Americans of New England, 'double-distilled English.' He is worried about the dangers and temptations they will encounter crowded together in a strange town, a hundred miles and more from the parental *foyer*, but shrewdly concludes, 'they are under the safeguard of the public faith.' He supports his conclusion by a statement in a letter from an agent in one of the mills: 'There have been in our establishment only three cases of illicit connexions, and in all three instances the parties were married immediately several months before the birth of the child, so that in fact we have had no case of actual bastardy.' [1] 'Lowell,' he says, 'is not amusing, but it is neat, decent, peaceable and sage.'

In the life of Patrick Tracy Jackson, which he contributed in 1856 to Hunt's *Lives of American Merchants*, John Amory Lowell writes as if the social hopes of his Uncle Francis were still in process of fulfilment and everything was still for the best in the best of all possible industrial worlds. Fourteen years earlier Harriet Farley began to have her doubts.

In the *Offering* for January, 1843, she reviews Dickens's *Notes on America* and points out that his glowing picture of a feminine Utopia is slightly overdrawn:

'We trust that we feel grateful for his kindness, and proud of his approval; but we fear that we do not deserve all his commendation, that we are not worthy of such flattering compliments. He says "Firstly, there is a piano in a great many of the boarding-houses." That is true, but not in a great proportion of them. "Secondly, nearly all these young ladies subscribe to

---

[1] Forty years later, in a grimmer industrial era when the mill girls of the Periclean Age had married or gone West like Lucy Larcom to teach school, and given place to large immigrant families from Quebec or County Cork, sexual *mores* had deteriorated. In 1875, the Reverend Delmar Lowell, of Rutland, Vermont, projecting a genealogy of the family, wrote for advice to James Russell Lowell. J. R. L. replied, perhaps without consulting his cousin, J. A. L.: 'If you are making a pedigree you must be on your guard, for I have been told that all the foundlings in the city of Lowell (and there are a good many of them) are christened with the name.'

Circulating Libraries." We fear that *nearly all* do not thus subscribe, though very many are supporters of other libraries.
"Thirdly, they have got up, among themselves, a periodical
called THE LOWELL OFFERING." The *Offering* was got up by
individuals from *among themselves*, and they perhaps are worthy
of our author's applause, but the proportion of those factory
girls who interest themselves in its support is not more than one
in fifty. Still it is right that all should share the credit, if the
general rule is a just one, to judge of a body by their prominent
individuals. We are glad that Dickens saw so much to please
him in our "city of spindles," and regret for their sakes that so
broad a line of distinction must be drawn between us and our
sister operatives, across the Atlantic. Heaven speed the day
when sentiments, more worthy of enlightened Britain, shall
prevail among her rulers, and justice and generosity shall guide
their counsels.'

Having thus opened up the subject, she continues to discuss
it throughout the year; in April she has a leading article on
'Lowell,' its history, industry, and social condition, and makes
the attractive but impractical suggestion that this same amount
of capital, $10,700,000, invested in villages instead of a city
would have produced even more prosperity and happiness. Yet
she closes with a paragraph about the beauty of the teeming city
at night:

'One of the most beautiful sights, we have ever witnessed, was
these factories, from the bridge, which is seen in the engraving,
when all these factories were lighted up for the evening's labor.
The uniform and brilliant illumination, with the lights again
gleaming up from the calm Merrimack, the brightness of the
city beyond, the clear blue sky above, from which the sparkling
stars were sending down their glittering beams into the glassy
waters of the river, all combined to form a spectacle, which might
almost lead an observer to believe that our hard-working, matter-
of-fact city had been transformed to fairy land.'

In May she wrote at length about the health of the girls,

which was in general excellent, though she adjures them never to go out in threatening weather without an umbrella, and in italics to *drink nothing but cold water*, and urges that 'upon every corporation if not in every large boarding-house there should be a place for bathing, needed for cleanliness, health, and comfort. Let the Merrimack Company begin.' That company, John Amory Lowell's special responsibility, had already supplied a large common or reading room for its girls, and bathing facilities were eventually arranged.

In May she prints some correspondence with Harriet Martineau of not a little historic interest. After painting with strong words the shocking and shameful conditions of the working girls of 'Merry England,' Miss Martineau pleads for the abolition of the American import duty on cotton cloth:

'If your manufactures should be reduced you will be satisfied with a supply of your real wants, and forego the rest rather than that thousands of willing and industrious girls should have the sole alternative of a life of shame, and blindness, and death before the age of twenty-five. You will not give the weight of your influence, be it great or small, to the upholding of your Tariff, at such tremendous consequences to young creatures like yourselves.'

On this the twenty-six-year-old American Harriet comments with commendable caution. The tariff, she says, is too much connected with politics for her to say much about it. 'The tariff is supported by many, not on account of its protection, but as a source of revenue. We therefore have less belief that it will be repealed. But our influence is not given either to support or remove it.'

At the top of the Lowell industrial hierarchy, John Amory Lowell was doing everything he could to support it, not by a personal entry into politics, he was too busy and too averse to crowds and clamor for that, but as the *éminence grise* of the Cotton Whigs of Massachusetts, with his partner and close friend, Abbott Lawrence, out on the firing line beside Daniel Webster.

The old Federalist Party, long absolescent, had expired during Andrew Jackson's first administration. At the beginning of his second, the Whig Party was built upon its ruins by the coalition of those who hated and distrusted Jackson and all his ways and works. Henry Clay, just defeated by Jackson for the presidency, and Daniel Webster, were its prophets. In 1832, a new act had repealed the 'tariff of abominations' and while retaining the protective principle had lowered the duty on cotton cloth to, so the mill-owners thought, a dangerously low figure. In the panic year of 1837, most of the Lowell mills passed their dividends. But in 1842, the tariff was raised and four boom years followed. It was during these that John Amory Lowell and Abbott Lawrence projected and built the new city of Lawrence. The latter was prominently mentioned for the vice-presidential nomination in 1846, and again in 1850. From an unpublished letter of Edmund Quincy's we learn that in 1848, when a large thirsty congressional deputation came to Boston during a brief period of local prohibition to attend the funeral of John Quincy Adams, it was said that 'the acknowledged head of the cotton industry liquored the company at his own expense.'[1]

The demi-decade from 1837 to 1842 must have been anxious and overburdened for John Amory Lowell, yet it was precisely within these years that he launched the great undertaking of the Lowell Institute which had been entrusted to his sole charge by John, Jr., completing his last will and testament on the banks of the Nile.

On the evening of December 31, 1839, the Odeon Theatre and Concert Hall at the corner of Federal and Franklin Streets, seating two thousand, was packed to the doors with eager listeners to his excellency the Governor of Massachusetts, the trustee's old tutor, Edward Everett, discoursing for two hours on the life of John Lowell, so called Junior, and the aims of the foundation he had endowed. Three days later, the lecture was

[1] Communicated to the Massachusetts Historical Society by M. A. DeWolfe Howe.

repeated, again to capacity. Old John Lowell, the Rebel, was there the first night with his son, the trustee, *ci-devant* little rogue, and favored the orator, whom he had himself helped to appoint to the Eliot Professorship of Greek, with kind words on his performance. The formal season then opened with a series of twelve lectures on Geology by Professor Benjamin Silliman of Yale. To supply the demand and appease disappointed thousands who could not get in, the series was repeated. It was followed by eight on Evidences of Christianity by the trustee's old roommate, the Reverend Doctor John G. Palfrey, and by nine, also repeated, by the Lowells' academic protégé, Thomas Nutthall, on Botany. These were in no sense 'popular' lectures. The authorities discussed their subjects in high seriousness, often with considerable technical detail. It was adult education, university extension work of a high order. The demand for tickets was so great that the windows of the Old Corner Book Store where the tickets were given out were crushed by the crowd, and other arrangements had to be made for the distribution.

John Amory Lowell had done an extraordinarily good job. As executor of John, Jr.'s, will and trustee of the fund it created, he had managed matters so well that when the Institute opened the half of the estate devoted to it amounted to a round quarter of a million dollars, which, invested in mill stocks and short-term loans to merchants, would yield an annual income of not less than twenty-five thousand dollars. This permitted very generous remuneration of the lecturers. In the case of those holding professorial chairs their fee was often larger than their annual salaries, twice as large if the lectures were repeated.

In their selection the trustee had advice from specialists. But he was a wide reader himself in all the fields of knowledge covered by the courses, and was able to do the actual planning for himself. No such complicated trust was ever more scrupulously and faithfully carried out. During the forties in addition to the recurrent presentation of the Evidences of Christianity, usually by Doctor Palfrey, later supplemented by Mark Hopkins and others, avid audiences heard Jeffries Wyman on Comparative Anatomy, Charles Lyell on Geology, George Glidden on Ancient Egypt, Jared Sparks on American History, Asa Gray on Botany, O. M. Mitchell on Astronomy, George Hilliard on Milton, and, as a grand climax, Louis Agassiz, M.D., specially imported for that purpose, in three annual courses of twelve lectures each, always repeated, on the Plan of Creation as shown in the Animal Kingdom, Ichthyology, and Comparative Embryology. The Agassiz courses created nothing less than a *furore*, with reverberations throughout the world. To keep him in this country seemed the trustee's first duty. Abbott Lawrence, his close business associate, gave, in 1847, fifty thousand dollars to establish the Lawrence Scientific School at Harvard. The donor, the legislature, and the public expected a technical school of bridge and road building, but almost immediately the President and Fellows elected Agassiz Professor of Zoology and Geology to enjoy the income of the gift. This admirable arrangement was perhaps instigated, we know it was carried through, by John Amory Lowell, who in 1837, the hectic year in which he carried his mills and banks and a gas company through a major panic, settled John, Jr.'s, estate, and began the organization of the Institute, became, like his father and his grandfather before him, a member of the Harvard Corporation. The men he met at the fortnightly meetings, besides that very noble old Roman, President Josiah Quincy, and the treasurer, Baring's American agent, Thomas Ward, were the Reverend Professor, later President, James Walker, Supreme Court Justice Joseph Story, the Chief Justice of Massachusetts, Lemuel Shaw, and Nathaniel Bowditch, a practical navigator both ashore and afloat. He seems at first to have taken a modest yet useful part in the activities of the Corporation, including the not very happy election to the presidency of his old tutor, Edward Everett. But during the forty years of his service, he was to become in the judgment of Harvard's historian its dominating member.

With him began that prepotence of State Street in the University's affairs, as to which there have always been two schools of thought. In 1859, Emerson, *advocatus angelorum*, wrote in his *Journal*:

'Alcott said, that Cowley considered the use of a University to be for the cherishing of gifted persons.

'It is true that the University and the Church, which should be counterbalancing institutions and independent, do not express the sentiment of the popular politics, and the popular optimism, whatever it be. Harvard College has no voice in Harvard College, but State Street votes it down on every ballot. Everything will be permitted there which goes to adorn Boston Whiggism; it is geology, astronomy, poetry, antiquities, art, rhetoric; but that which it exists for, — to be a fountain of novelties out of heaven, a Delphi uttering warning and ravishing oracles to elevate and lead mankind, — *that* it shall not be permitted to do or to think of. On the contrary, every generosity of thought is *suspected*, and gets a bad name. And all the young men come out decrepit Bostonians; not a poet, not a prophet, not a daemon, but is gagged and stifled, or driven away. All that is sought in the instruction is drilling tutors, and not inspirers.'

This is appealing, but one wonders if it were not rather the expression of a passing mood than a considered judgment. Elsewhere Emerson expresses deep obligation to Channing and Everett as inspirers; and Professors Agassiz and Lowell, fellow members of the Saturday and Adirondack Clubs, stand high in his list of 'My Men.' There is much to be said for geology, astronomy, poetry, antiquities, art, and rhetoric in a well-rounded education. One shudders before the contemplation of a university where all the chairs would be occupied by poets, prophets, daemons, and Bronson Alcott. Perhaps ten years later, when he himself had become an overseer and was indebted to State Street for much of his own personal comfort and ease of mind, Emerson would have revised his judgment.

At the end of the forties, John Amory Lowell, on top of his other multifarious activities, produced the longest piece of writing on a single subject that had yet been printed and published by any of the family.

In 1845, Wright Boott, his old partner and friend, died by his own hand, leaving a will which named J. A. Lowell as executor. There were jealousies and dissensions of long standing in the Boott family, and one branch, headed by a daughter who had married Edward Brooks, set out to break the will. The case was in and out of court for many years. In 1847, a closely printed pamphlet appeared of 249 pages entitled, *A Correspondence between Edward Brooks and John A. Lowell, with Remarks by Edward Brooks referring to Documents attached*. This was followed the next year by one in larger type of 211 pages, *Reply to a pamphlet recently circulated by Mr. Edward Brooks*, by John A. Lowell. This was marked by notable firmness of character, concision of statement, inherited dialectical skill, and mastery of accounts. It carries conviction. In 1851 came a volume of 859 pages in exceedingly small type entitled *An Answer to the Pamphlet of Mr. John A. Lowell entitled Reply to a Pamphlet recently circulated by Mr. Edward Brooks with New Facts and further Proofs*, by Edward Brooks. This massive attack is rather against the will than against the executor. In it old psychic lesions and animosities rear their heads and prevent it from carrying conviction. When it appeared, John Amory Lowell had gone abroad for a year of very well-earned rest and the controversy was carried no further. During the decade in which he achieved the pinnacle of industrial power in Massachusetts, the third branch of the family, in the person of James Russell Lowell a grandson of the Old Judge, had reached national eminence, in lines not looked on sympathetically in State Street.

4
CHAPTER

The Russell-Spence Line
Animal Spirits Flower

ALL THE NUMEROUS LIVES of James Russell Lowell have a few pages concerning his forbears and family considered in relation to him. Here we must consider him in relation to his family, his life and work only as an episode in its long history. Perhaps the change in the angle of vision will give us a better view of both the poet and the clan.

In his *Study of British Genius*, under which he includes high talent, Havelock Ellis presents some interesting tables tending to show that in large families the talented one is usually either the oldest or youngest. All the six children of the Reverend Charles Lowell and Harriet Spence were of more than average mental ability, but the future poet, abolitionist, professor, editor, essayist, and diplomatist was the latest-born.

The first-born, Charles Russell Lowell, born in 1807, graduated from Harvard in 1826, was colonel of the Boston Cadets, and married Anna Cabot Jackson, daughter of Patrick Tracy Jackson, again 'practically a cousin' through the fraternal friendship of their fathers and grandfathers, and actually so in the third degree through the Cabot blood. He became a merchant and had a house in Winter Place, but during the panic of 1837 failed and lost together with his own a large part of his father's property which was in his hands to manage while both parents were abroad. Writing seven years later to C. F. Briggs in an unpublished paragraph of a letter printed by Norton, James Russell Lowell says that his father was 'tender to find excuses for him.' The clan in general seems to have considered it another piece of the Spence negligence. He went out of business and, after considering moving to Virginia or the West, settled in Cambridge and devoted the last years of his life to organizing and completing the first card catalogue of the books in the Athenaeum. Anna Jackson Lowell opened and conducted a successful girls' school. Emerson noted in his *Journal*, 'Mrs. Lowell said to me of her girls of fashion, "those who give themselves airs on no grounds whatever cannot be taught." ' Their eldest son, who all his youth regarded his father as the great authority on war, was the gallant and admirable leader of cavalry in the War Between the States.

The second child, Rebecca, who inherited more than her share of the excitable Orkney Island mentality, died unmarried in 1872. The third, Mary Traill Spence Lowell, married Samuel Putnam, and lived on to the year of the Spanish War. She was a scholar and traveller, a popular anonymous novelist, and a remarkable linguist. In his *Homes of American Authors* Charles F. Briggs, who knew her well, wrote, 'She converses readily in French, German, Italian, Polish, Swedish, and Hungarian, and is familiar with twenty modern dialects, besides Greek, Latin, Hebrew, Persic, and Arabic.' The fourth, William Keith Spence Lowell, born in 1813, was 'first scholar' in the Boston Latin School, when he died at ten.

The fifth child, Robert Traill Spence Lowell, born in 1816, was a man of talent approaching genius, and the first of the Old Judge's line to break completely with the Boston scene, and spend his days in regions from which the Dome of the State House is invisible. After his graduation from the family seminary with the class of '33, he finished the course in medicine, but withdrew before taking his second degree to go into business in Boston with his brother, Charles. In the aftermath of the panic of '37, he decided to enter the ministry of his mother's church. For two years he studied theology in Schenectady, with the Reverend Doctor Alonzo Potter, the former rector of Saint Paul's in Boston.

Ten miles from Schenectady, in the centre of the triangle of pleasantly rolling farm country that lies between the Mohawk and Schoharie Creek, was Duanesburg, the seat of his grandfather's old friend and fellow Continental Congressman, James Duane. Their political and legal careers were oddly parallel. Like the Old Judge, Duane, who had married the daughter of Robert Livingston, 'third Lord' of Livingston Manor, was for conciliation and slow to become a revolutionist. In 1775, however, he was for war, played a useful part in the Revolution and was rewarded with a federal judgeship. With his golden shoe and knee buckles, plump, rosy, and humorous, he was a congenial companion. He was an accumulator of real estate and his son inherited many thousands of acres of high farmland and forest. When the young theological student from Elmwood met and married Old Judge Duane's granddaughter, Mary Ann, later Marianna, and had seven children, no fault could be found by the marriage critics of the clan. She, too, was 'practically' a second cousin.

In 1841, he was ordained a deacon and spent a year in Bermuda as curate of the English Church. After his ordination as a priest he went to Newfoundland as a missionary, at once religious and medical, for the English Society for the Propagation of the Gospel.

In 1847, his health weakened by the distressing famine of

that year, he returned to take a slum parish in Newark. Later he held for ten years the family living of Duanesburg in the plain but richly furnished Christ Church Judge Duane had built in 1793. Then, wearying of the high pulpit, he was for three years headmaster of Saint Mark's School, almost but not quite within sight of the gilded Dome, and from 1872 until his death the admired and beloved Professor of the Latin Language and Literature at Union College in Schenectady, the market town of the country of the Duanes.

In 1858, he put his Newfoundland experience into a novel of six hundred pages, *The New Priest at Conception Bay*, that can still be read with pleasure and profit. Its publishers, Phillips, Sampson and Company, announced it in large type as the *best book ever written in this country*,[1] but failed the following year. It was favorably reviewed, though *sans* superlatives, in the *Atlantic Monthly*, of which his young brother, Jamie, had just become the first editor. In the same year in the same magazine appeared his well-known narrative poem, *The Relief of Lucknow*. He printed other work in both verse and prose that had a considerable popularity, but never quite of the quality of these.

He was a man of sensitive nature, abounding vitality, wide interests, and a practising humanitarian. Throughout his life he maintained a warm fraternal correspondence with Jamie, and died in the same year. The clan as a whole was inclined to look at him just a little askance as a *déraciné*.

The sixth child and fourth son of Charles and Harriet Spence Lowell was the problem child of his family and of American literature.

James Russell Lowell was born in Cambridge in the last house to the west on Tory Row, on Washington's Birthday, 1819. It was a year productive of poets and prosateurs, as well as Queen Victoria. In May, Walt Whitman, 'of mighty Manhattan, the son,' raised his 'barbaric yawp' in a frame dwelling at Hunting-

---

[1] Eight years after *The Scarlet Letter*, seven after *Moby Dick*!

ton, Long Island, and in September Herman Melville, grandson of old-time Boston's 'Last Leaf,' opened his eyes in a small brick house on Pearl Street in Manhattan itself. Lowell's more impressive birthplace that an earlier owner had named Elmwood, from its double row of leafy guardians, was frame to the eye, but with blind walls of brick to keep out the winter wind. As a 'Poet's Home' it was almost too good to be true. Save for a few scattered years abroad, he lived in it all his life, and died in it in 1891, a long stretch through three quarters of a century made migrant by two wars, four major panics, and the great movement westward into the noble country opened by the Louisiana Purchase.

It was the home of the poet that became a shrine, not that of any member of the two senior more plutocratic branches of the family. But it was the profits of law and commerce that bought it and dividends from cotton mills, Long Wharf, and the distillery that helped to maintain it. Of it the poet himself said: 'It was born a Tory and will die one.'

Elmwood was four miles or more from Boston Common where the cousins of the clan dwelt within the reflected radiance of the Dome, and its life was always a little aside from the family centre. Nevertheless, small Jamie was driven out not infrequently as far as Roxbury to be the particular pet, and later the affectionate friend, of his Cousin Amory, more indeed like a maiden aunt than a cousin, twenty-five years his senior. She was, he says, inextricably bound up with the primal associations of his life. After her death in 1873, he wrote:

'I can't tell how the thought of her kept Bromley Vale unchanged, and she brought my father and my Uncle John before me as they were in those old days. A great part of my Faery Land went to dust with her.'

How the busy gentlemen of Bromley Vale and Waltham, Beacon Street and Pemberton Square, looked at the auburn-haired, freckle-faced, bright-eyed little boy, the amiable Charles's youngest son, is not difficult to divine. Apart from Edward, his favorite nephew and recipient of advice, Uncle John was always more interested in the rose-lipped maidens of the clan than in its lightfoot lads, though not unconcerned with the principles and tastes of the latter. Of the soundness of the principles of Charles there could be no question. He was, says J. R. L., Doctor Primrose in the comparative degree, forever praising the old Federalist Party with George Washington at its head, or speaking of Jefferson as harshly as his kind heart would let him speak of anybody. Though he had met Wordsworth and Southey, his preferred poet was Pope. Jamie's early tastes seemed definitely in the groove. It is true that his elder sister, Mary, read him to sleep from the *Faery Queene*, but that was archaic enough to be safe. His early passion for Scott's novels was all right, and his intense interest in Gilbert White's *Selborne* very gratifying to lovers of trees and flowers like his uncle and cousins. He acquired during his freshman year at Harvard a volume containing the complete poetical works of Coleridge, Shelley, and Keats, but Collins, Cowper, Burns, Byron, Beattie, and even Young of *The Night Thoughts*, stood higher in his affections and were his more frequent models until a year or two after his graduation in 1838. There was no occasion for Uncle John to worry about his intellectual future.

His rustication for two months in his senior year to the custody of the Reverend Barzillai Frost of Concord was not unduly disturbing even to his cousin, John Amory Lowell, who had just become a member of the Corporation. There was good family precedent. John Amory himself had paid that penalty for his 'trifling insult' to Sammy Sewall and his revered Uncle Frank for a bonfire in the Yard. It was just another case of Animal Spirits. Jamie had celebrated his election as Class Poet well rather than wisely, and at evening chapel, rising in his front seat, had turned to the student body and bowed sweepingly to right and left, arousing inopportune applause. The piece itself, which is now a collector's item, could hardly have been more satisfactory or more allaying of any suspicions of his soundness that had been aroused when higher mathematics, the favorite indoor sport of the clan, proved to be his 'enemies.'

For a youth of nineteen the Class Poem, written on the spur of public occasion which was always to inspire his best efforts, was remarkable in vigor and variety. The couplet of Pope, the octave stanza of Ariosto and Byron, iambs, trochees, and tripping anapests, all are employed with fluent mastery. From Aristophanes down, the better satirists have been Tories, and this was Tory-Federalist satire on Emerson and Transcendentalism, Carlyle, Abolitionists, Temperance Agitators, Woman's Righters, and Vegetarians. The clan loved it, though the poet's cousin, Emerson's friend, Francis Cabot Lowell, Jr., may have shaken his handsome head at the passage where surprise is expressed that certain of the meat-eating men of history have reached an honored fourscore:

> 'In spite of all the meat and drink and mirth,
> That have been preying on them from their birth.'

In the years of mild storm and stress that followed the poet's graduation, he followed paths that diverged from the clan's straight and well-paved highway. Forty years ago his lifelong friend and literary executor, Charles Eliot Norton, in a letter to the present writer stated the case with characteristic precision: 'Lowell's family belonged to the Brahmin caste alike by inheritance and culture. But Lowell separated himself from this caste, to which by taste and culture he belonged, not only by his abolitionism, but by his choice of friends and by his marriage. Hence arose a division and conflict in his interior as well as his exterior life which were not happy for his natural development.' But like many precise statements, this lacked the ultimate precision of light and shade, of chiaroscuro and values.

Lowell was to become for a decade something of a rebel against the established *mores* of Boston, as his Uncle John, rebelling in the reverse direction, had been against those who would disestablish them. On the death of his inspiring wife, Maria

White, he began, as we shall see, to veer slowly to the right. After his return, a personage as well as a poet, from his ministry to the Court of Saint James's, with his brother Robert last surviving grandsons of the Old Judge, his well-brushed silk hat could be seen glistening on the hall table at the more important reunions of the clan.

In a prefatory note to Lowell's *Early Prose Writings*, Edward Everett Hale, who was two years behind him in college, says that at meetings of 'Alpha Delta' he heard him read papers on the old English dramatists which were the bases of those he afterwards published, and that they knew, when he graduated in 1838, that he was to be 'a distinguished poet widely esteemed and highly valued in the literature of the land.' But it was not until the influence of Cambridge had been overlaid by that of Watertown, several miles higher up the Charles River, that the correctness of the forecast began to appear.

His first two years after leaving college were a period of doubt and vacillation as to his future. The love of preaching was always in his blood, but he was unable to accept the dogmas of any church, even the liberal and humane one of Channing, his Uncle John, and his father. He began the study of the law at the Dane Law School, decided a month later to abandon it for business, but heard Daniel Webster make a speech in court and returned forthwith to Coke and Blackstone. Again a few months later he 'quitted the law forever,' but after receiving four dollars less expenses for a lecture in Concord, and substituting a few weeks for his brother, who had hurt his hand, as clerk in a coal-dealer's office, he drifted back to digests and commentaries. Since his junior year he had been tempestuously in love with a beautiful 'Miss B,' but without substantial progress in her affections. It was at this time that he put the cocked pistol to his forehead. His letters of the time are marked by a mystical melancholy with few explosions of parodies and puns. His mind was maturing. He buys and reads an anthology of Hesiod, Theocritus, and Moschus with a Latin translation. He reads the Greek dramatists, and their Elizabethan fellows, 'so nimble and so full of subtle flame.' His notebooks are full of the evils of slavery, and the Manchester riots caused by the American tariff on cotton bring tears to his eyes.

Early in December, 1839, he spent a week-end with his class-mate, W. A. White, at Watertown, and met his sister, Maria, a pleasant and pleasing young lady. 'She knows,' he says, 'more poetry than anyone I am acquainted with. I mean she is able to repeat more. She is more familiar, however, with modern poets than with the pure well-springs of English poetry.' After an exalted wooing at Watertown, Nantasket, and Cambridge, they became engaged in August, 1840, just as Lowell took his bachelor's degree in law. Maria was nineteen, Jamie twenty-one.

The ten years that followed, the decade in which John Amory and Francis Cabot Lowell consolidated their commanding positions in finance and industry, were for their literary cousin at Elmwood, in respect to both quantity and quality, the most productive of his life. It was nearly five years before the happy pair could marry. After the return of his parents from Europe in 1840, his mother's mind became definitely disordered, and Rebecca was subject to strange, tragic silences. During the four days each week his father had to be in town, Jamie never left the house. It was no place to bring a bride. But so close was the sympathetic bond between the promised lovers, the years of their long engagement and of their marriage may be considered as one period.

Maria White was a tall blonde girl of a delicate, pale beauty. Her elder sister, who lived on in Cambridge for ninety years to take a mild sweet interest in the book a young man from New York was trying to write about the husband of Maria, dead for half a century, had the appearance, manners, and tone of a more than commonly intelligent and amiable dowager duchess. One received from her the impression that Maria was the really bright girl of the family, and that the Whites were never quite sure whether Jamie, for all his talents, was really good enough for her.

Like most young persons of that eager Transcendental time, Maria White wrote poetry, but of a better fibre than the generality — better, indeed, than much of her young man's. Her verse that he brought together in a privately printed volume after her death has the unlabored accent that gives true distinction, as in the concluding lines of her poem 'Africa' in which the Dark Continent the slaves came from was symbolized as a colossal black figure of eternal sadness and mystery.

> 'Her great lips closed upon her moan;
> Silently sate she on her throne,
> Rigid and black as carved in stone.'

She was the leader of the celebrated 'Band,' a group of young men and women not otherwise now known to fame, at once earnest and gay, which led Lowell out of the shadows of his belated poetic adolescence, and provided an exciting and excitable audience for those ebullitions of animal spirits which for the rest of his life were to be at once his blessing and his bane.

Four months after the engagement, he writes to his classmate, her brother:

'I have just come from spending the evening at ——'s (where Maria is making sunshine just now), and have been exceedingly funny. I have in the course of the evening recited near upon five hundred extempore macaronic verses; composed and executed an oratorio and opera (entirely unassisted and, a la Beethoven, on a piano without any strings, to wit the centre table); besides drawing an entirely original view of Nantasket Beach with the different groups from Worrick's disporting themselves thereon, and a distant view of the shipping in the harbor, compiled from the shipping news of our indefatigable friend Ballard, of the "Daily," and making a temperance address; giving vent, moreover, to innumerable jests, jokes, puns, oddities, quiddities, and nothings, interrupted by my own laughter and that of my hearers; and eating an indefinite number of raisins, chesnuts (I advisedly omit the "t"), etc., etc., etc., etc., etc., etc., etc., etc., etc. . . .'

From the Band, Lowell learned a fuller appreciation of Tennyson and Keats. We hear no more of Beattie and Young, though echoes of the manner and metre of Pope are audible in his verse to the end of his life. And to the Band as well as to Miss White, Lowell owed the deepening and defining of his vague humanitarian impulses. A month before that exceedingly funny evening, slight and small with rosy cheeks and starry eyes and wavy hair parted in the middle, he had been a member of the Chardon Street Anti-Slavery Convention, and had written upon the cover of his Class Poem:

> 'Behold the baby arrows of that Wit
> Wherewith I dared assail the woundless Truth!
> Love hath refilled the quiver and with it
> The man shall win atonement for the youth.'

What that transcendental love was like in the sublunary flesh Colonel Higginson, always an interested observer of such matters, noted in his journal, following a call at Elmwood soon after their marriage:

'Ere long Maria came up and glided gently in at the door. James looked round with his face so radiant, put his arms around her and seated her in the big chair he had been in. Then he sat down close to her and gazed in her lovely face, and as we talked put his hand gently on hers and called her "dearest" and "darling," and seemed perfectly to idealize her, and I felt that their relation in poetry was cold and barren compared to that in their daily life and I was happy to be with such lovely beings. But alas! Maria has a sad cough. Oh, what a misfortune it would be for the world if she were to pass away.'

While still in the Law School, Lowell had contributed poems to *The Southern Literary Messenger*. During the two years he spent as an almost briefless barrister behind his own shingle or in the office of his distant cousin, Charles G. Loring, of the branch of the family that had not emigrated in 1776, he wrote for *Graham's Magazine*, corresponded familiarly, even fervidly, with Poe, published his first volume of verse, *A Year's Life*, and wrote for the *Boston Miscellany of Literature and Fashion*, founded and edited by his classmate, Nathan Hale, ten essays including one on 'Married Men,' chastely 'adapted' from, of all people, Paul de Kock. In 1841, he made four hundred dollars with his pen. The next year he was doing still better, and by the end of 1842, with board and very superior lodging assured him at Elmwood, he retired for the last time from the law forever. Lowells, however, were not wholly lost to the law. Six months after Jamie's retirement, a new John Lowell, later known as Judge John entered the Loring office. He was the son of John Amory Lowell and his first cousin, Susan Cabot Lowell. In him the bloods of the two senior branches of the Old Judge's line were blended to produce admirable and delightful human qualities.

James Russell Lowell's attempt to found the *Pioneer*, which was to be the Great American Magazine, cost him or his father fifteen hundred dollars, but his *Poems, First Series,* was a success in both this country and England. His *Conversations on the Old Poets* did even better. In a notebook of 1842 he pencilled, 'My heart beats like the trampling of a host.' He is full of large projects: a Cantabrigian *Sorrows of Werther*, an American tragedy on the trial of Ann Hutchinson, a biography of Keats. The first two were never written, and it remained for a fat little grand-cousin, with whom forty years later he used to shake hands at clan gatherings, to accomplish the last — definitively, in two volumes. The truth is that, for all the ten volumes of his Collected Works, James Russell Lowell never wrote a book. He only put newspaper and magazine contributions, poems, speeches, and lectures together. As in a moment of self-insight he confessed, his mind produced not thought but thoughts. His daily life at Elmwood during his formative period, ministering to two minds diseased, was not conducive to ordered research and constructive cogitation. Perhaps an excess of animal spirits doesn't beget major enterprises of the mind.

Following his marriage, the day after Christmas, 1844, the wedded poets went to Philadelphia, where the author of 'The Present Crisis,' that was at the moment being thundered from the lips of abolitionist orators, was to have a staff position on the *Pennsylvania Freeman* at the munificent salary of ten dollars per month. After five months of this, during which it is said the future author of the *Biglow Papers* gave his friends there a little more than enough of the Yankee dialect, he secured a better-paid post as leader writer for the *Anti-Slavery Standard*, published in New York.

They came back to Cambridge to make their home for the next eight years in the low-studded third story of Elmwood. His mother, with her darkened mind,

> 'Not so much of these is left among us
> As the hum outliving the hushed bell,'

had been taken elsewhere. Four children were born there, under the eaves.

Then began his most vigorous period of productivity. Maria's health was better and his own was superb. He struck out, so he says, three hundred times morning and evening with a pair of twenty-four-pound dumb bells, and acquired a 'whoreson appearance of health and good spirits' that infected men with a false opinion of his prosperity. There is, he says in his early essay, 'The First Client,' much mystery in whiskers. He had already acquired a beard, at first the Christlike Vandyke depicted in Page's portrait, then the more bardic type, worn by Longfellow, Melville, Whittier, Thoreau in later years, and Fields. Despite the smooth-shaven or only slightly side-whiskered countenances of Ticknor, Prescott, Holmes, and Emerson, the ambrosial beard was a symbol of the Flowering of New England. Horace Scudder carried his like an oriflamme into the Indian Summer.

Lowell's own full flowering came in 1848, when he was just
ten years out of college. In that year he published four volumes:
Poems, Second Series, *The Vision of Sir Launfal*, *A Fable for Critics*,
and the *Biglow Papers*. Regarded through the century-long
reversed telescope of time, the first two now appear of very modest
proportions. The *Fable* and the *Papers* are surely his best bids
for future fame, if not as one who has scaled the magic mountain
of poesy, at least as a most effective poet militant below, one
prompt like all men of his family at the seizure of occasions.

His kinsmen of the clan must have taken pleasure in the seldom
quoted lines on industrial and commercial Massachusetts em-
bodying what they themselves had thought but ne'er so well
expressed. The occasion was hot, for Leigh Hunt had recently
written, 'When I look towards America I seem to see a trades-
man's counter stretching along the entire Eastern coast.'

> 'Who is it that dares
> Call thee a pedlar, a soul wrapped in bank-books and shares?
> It is false! She's a poet! I see, as I write,
> Along the far railroad the steam snake glide white,
> The cataract throb of her mill hearts I hear,
> The swift strokes of trip hammers weary my ear,
> Sledges ring upon anvils, through logs the saw screams,
> Blocks swing to their place, beetles drive home the beams: —
> It is songs such as these that she croons to the din
> Of her fast-flying shuttles, year out and year in,
> While from earth's farthest corner there comes not a breeze
> But wafts her the buzz of her gold gleaning bees.'

The Rebel, had he been alive, would have liked this companion piece to Byron's *English Bards and Scotch Reviewers* as much
as he had the Class Poem ten years before. Francis, friend of
Emerson, even busy John Amory Lowell, banker, mill-owner,
lecture impresario, Fellow of Harvard, could not but have admired the warm, laughing characterizations making their hit
from their very first lines. Watch this parade of penmen when he
finally gets down to business after the thirteen rather rambling

pages that, as always in either verse or prose, were necessary to
warm him up:

'There comes Emerson first, whose rich words every one
Are like gold nails in temples to hang trophies on. . . .

Yonder calm as a cloud Alcott stalks in a dream
And fancies himself in thy groves Academe. . . .

There is Willis, all natty and jaunty and gay,
Who says his best things in so foppish a way. . . .

Here comes Parker, the Orson of Parsons, a man
Whom the church undertook to put under her ban
(The church of Socinius, I mean), his opinions
Being so (ultra)cinian, they shocked the Socinians. . . .

There is Bryant, as quiet as cool and as dignified
As a smooth silent iceberg that never is ignified. . . .
If I call him an iceberg I don't mean to say
There is nothing in that which is grand in its way.
He is almost the one of your poets that knows
How much grace, strength, and dignity lie in Repose. . . .

Here is Whittier, whose swelling and vehement heart
Strains the tight-breasted drab of the Quaker apart. . . .

Here comes Dana, abstractedly loitering along,
Involved in a paulo-post future of song. . . .

Here's Cooper, who's written six volumes to show
He's as good as a Lord.   Well, let's grant that he's so. . . .

There comes Poe, with his raven, like Barnaby Rudge,
Three fifths of him genius, and two fifths sheer fudge. . . .

What!   Irving? thrice welcome, warm heart and fine brain,
You bring back the happiest spirit from Spain,
And the gravest sweet humour that ever was there
Since Cervantes met death in his gentle despair. . . .

Here's Holmes, who is matchless among you for wit,
A leyden jar always full-charged from which flit
The electrical tingles of hit after hit. . . .'

And finally:

'Here is Lowell who's striving Parnassus to climb
With a whole bale of *isms* tied together with rhyme. . . .
His lyre has some chords that would ring pretty well,
But he'd rather by half make a drum of the shell
And rattle away till he's old as Methusalem,
At the head of a march to the last new Jerusalem.'

All are palpable hits. They are, after some book-reviews of
Poe's, the first fresh spontaneous unacademic literary criticism
of contemporaries produced in this country. They stand up
well in the light of the judgment of posterity.

After reading the *Fable*, Ruskin wrote Norton, 'He does me
more good in my dull fits than anybody, and makes me hopeful
again.'

But our poet militant was interested in graver matters than
the literary qualities of his contemporaries. At the Boston
Anti-Slavery Convention in May, 1844, at which a resolution
for disunion was carried 250 to 24, Lowell and Maria White
voted 'Nay.' He was never in the extreme left wing of the
abolitionists, but the leading articles that he wrote for the
Anti-Slavery Standard were an effective support to the eloquence
of Wendell Phillips and the transcendental thrusts of Emerson.
They did their author the service of checking, for a time at least,
the divagations of his natural prose style.

The annexation of Texas, with its extension of slavery, in 1845
and the ensuing war with Mexico, brought him an issue which
stirred him even more productively. His opposition to the conflict was, as he wrote Thomas Hughes, that essentially it was a
war of false pretenses:

'Believing that it is the *manifest destiny* of the English race to
occupy this whole continent, and to display there that practical
understanding in matters of government and colonization which

no other race has shown such proof of possessing since the Romans, I hated to see a noble hope evaporated into a lying phase to sweeten the foul breath of demagogues.'

This is quite an increase in the purview of the family's political vision since his Uncle John wrote that the Louisiana Purchase had 'no merit whatever.' He was right about the false pretenses, but the gods that shape the course of history work in very mysterious ways, and seldom disclose their intentions at the start. Perhaps our destiny in the Philippines, not so manifest to all in the beginning, was to set the colonial world a shining example of good will and ultimate justice.

The nine numbers of the first series of the *Biglow Papers* appeared in the *Boston Courier* and the *Anti-Slavery Standard* between June, 1846, and September, 1848, when, with the Parson Wilbur framework added, they were published in book form.

Here was a vehicle in which for the first time he could put all that he had, and all of the New England that he knew and loved, its common sense and canniness, its poetry and pedantry, its idealism, all minted into something as racy and of the soil as a pine-tree shilling. Read now after a century, the dialect seems just a little artificial, lacking the appealing authenticity of Burns's Scotch or William Barnes's Dorsetshire. The spelling, as Lowell came to feel himself, was overdone, but during two wars the phonetic singularity was the final element of success.

'An' you've gut to git up airly ef you want to take in God,'

and

'They didn't know everything down in Judee,'

were rolled savoringly on every tongue in the Northern States. They were widely savored in England, too, where Hughes wrote, in his Preface to the London edition:

'For real unmistakable genius, for that glorious fulness of power which knocks a man down at a blow for sheer admiration and then makes him rush into the arms of the knockerdown, and

swear eternal friendship with him for sheer delight — the
Biglow Papers stand alone.'

They were too much of the occasion to seem all that now.
They will stand as an historical document of the first consequence, and the affectionately humorous full-cadenced prose
of Parson Wilbur, in which Lowell let himself go after the con-
straints of leader writing, will continue to please and entertain
the sensitive ear.

In the twelve hundred pages of Richard Aldington's well-
selected *Book of Poetry of the English Speaking World* there are to be
found ten poems by Emerson, seven by Longfellow, eight by Poe,
five by Thoreau, eleven by Whitman, twelve by Herman Melville, and one by Lowell. When one, shocked by this, examines
the four volumes of Lowell's *Poetical Works* to find pieces that
should have been included, some old favorites are seen to be the
echoes of other and better poets, some, detached from the
warmth of their old occasion, seem mere poetic rhetoric, devoid
of the divine fire. Too many of them slip from the memory
five minutes after you have read them. You are driven reluctantly to the conclusion that the anthologist's taste was sound,
his judgment correct.

The one piece included was 'She Came and Went,' from the
Poems: Second Series, of that wonderful year of 1848.

It begins:

> 'As a twig trembles, which a bird
>   Lights on to sing, then leaves unbent,
> So is my memory thrilled and stirred: —
>   I only know she came and went.'

It ends:

> 'Oh when the room grows slowly dim,
>   And life's last oil is nearly spent
> One gush of light these eyes will brim,
>   Only to think she came and went.'

Blanche, his first child, born the last day of 1845, died in March, 1847. Mabel, who lived to be his stay and comfort when the room grew dim, was born in September. A third daughter lived only a few months. His only son, Walter, died in Rome in 1852, in his third year.

After the four volumes of 1848, he published no more books for sixteen years. His next was the collected series of *Fireside Travels*. He printed fugitive pieces in periodicals, and articles and reviews, an annual average of eight articles and four or five poems. The business and pleasure of his life was reading:

'Once snug in my attic, my fire in a roar, I leave the whole pack of them outside the door. With Hakluyt or Purchas I wander away to the black northern seas or barbaric Cathay; get *fou* with O'Shanter, and sober me then with that builder of brick-kilnish dramas, rare Ben; snuff Herbert as holy as a flower on a grave; with Fletcher wax tender, o'er Chapman grow brave; with Marlowe or Kyd take a fine poet-rave; in Very, most Hebrew of Saxons, find peace; with Lycidas welter on vext Irish seas; with Webster grow wild, and climb earthward again, down by mystical Browne's Jacob's-ladder-like brain, to that spiritual Pepys (Cotton's version) Montaigne; find a new depth in Wordsworth, undreamed of before, that marvel, a poet divine who can bore. Or, out of my study, the scholar thrown off, Nature holds up her shield 'gainst the sneer and the scoff; the landscape, forever consoling and kind, pours her wine and her oil on the smarts of the mind. The waterfall, scattering its vanishing gems; the tall grove of hemlocks, with moss on their stems, like plashes of sunlight; the pond in the woods, where no foot but mine and the bittern's intrudes, where pitcher-plants purple and gentians hard by recall to September the blue of June's sky; these are all my kind neighbors, and leave me no wish to say aught to you all, my poor critics, but — pish!'

In July, 1851, he sold some acres of the Elmwood land and for the sake of Maria's health, with their two children, their nurse, and a goat, they sailed from Boston for the Mediterranean.

During the eighteen months of their stay abroad, Lowell wrote few letters and made few notes in his journal. He was too busily occupied in seeing the sights and meeting poets and pundits in Rome, the Italian lakes, Switzerland, Germany, Provence, Paris, London, Oxford, and Cambridge, to carry on his customary copious correspondence other than letters to his father. His mother had died in an asylum the year before.

Maria was more active with her pen, and her letters to Mrs. Frank Shaw, mother of the future colonel of the colored regiment, give a pleasant picture of their *Wanderjahre*. As usual the clan was overseas in force and saw more of Maria than they had at home, and, so family tradition says, liked what they saw. She writes from Rome, 'There are fourteen Lowells here and their announcement at a party is quite formidable.' The poet-Lowells sailed for home in October, 1852, with Thackeray and Arthur Hugh Clough as shipmates.

During the year that followed, the last of Maria's life, her letters to her husband during his occasional absences in New York reveal the quality of their union. They are signed Molly, and though she used them to no other, her second-person pronouns for him are always 'thee,' 'thou,' and 'thine.' She tells him of plumbing troubles and tax bills as well as of poetic imaginings. She touches, not without humor, on disputes of long standing as to from which side Mabel derived her traits. The child, it seems, had an illusion that she couldn't use her right hand, but forgot it when playing with Spice, the dog. 'Remember, darling,' Maria writes, 'it comes from thy side of the house. Mr. John Lowell fancied himself dead once. I know of no such fancies in our family. It is delightful to be able to trace it directly to its source.'

In one of her last letters to him, she tells him that like Topsy she was born bad. 'But still bad as I am, I perhaps make thee happier than some better women. At any rate, I understand and appreciate thy intellect and nature, and do not thwart it very much, do I?'

She died, not unexpectedly, on October 27, 1853. Among the Lowell papers is a thin blue envelope addressed 'to Dr. Charles Lowell,' and endorsed by him in a quavering hand, 'From my sainted darling child.' It contains an unsigned holograph will or memorandum as to the disposal of her few effects. The first item reads, 'To my darling father I leave my cloak lined with fur to wrap round his knees and use in his sick room.'

Elmwood was a different house without her; Lowell was a different man, and was to become a very different writer.

BOOK V

Civil War

Colonel Charles Russell Lowell Jr. (1835–1864) of the Union cavalry sits for a photograph with Josephine Shaw, sister of Colonel Robert Gould Shaw of the colored regiment, just after their wartime marriage.

The Colonel's mother and 'best friend,' Anna Cabot Jackson, conducted a girls' school and compiled a well-selected and wide-ranging anthology entitled *Seedgrass*.

John Lowell (1824–1897), 'Judge John,' son of John Amory Lowell by his first marriage, with his cousin Susan Cabot Lowell, the last Federal Judge appointed by Lincoln, made decisions in maritime cases in which you 'smell the tar and hear the wind whistling in the rigging.' He forsook the streets bordering the Common within sight of the State House dome for the fields and woods of Chestnut Hill. He was equally celebrated for his wit and his roses.

Augustus Lowell (1830–1900) was son of John Amory Lowell by his second marriage with Elizabeth Cabot Putnam. During his reign as head of the senior branch, the family prosperity reached its peak. He married Katherine Lawrence, bought the estate in Brookline which he later christened Sevenels from the number of Lowells living there, and was the father of Percival the Astronomer, Amy the Poet, and Lawrence the Educator.

1
CHAPTER

Thunderheads

BY THE MID-NINETEENTH CENTURY the Periclean Age of Boston had been achieved and seemed secure. How the Athens of America looked to the eye from the summit of the State House is described by an anonymous 'Looker-On' in 'Local loiterings and visits in the vicinity of Boston' (1846):

'The Frog Pond glistens in the sunshine; and the "great elm" — a magnificent tree — stands conspicuously out from amongst its sylvan neighbors. Three sides of the common are bounded by brick and mortar, where merchant-princes reside, in homes to which commerce has invited genius and taste; but the fourth lies open to the country, and is washed by the bright waters of Charles River Bay, the cheerful villages of Roxbury, Brookline, Brighton and Cambridge, may be seen in the distance — their white houses sparkling from amidst groves of green — and here and there graceful spires taper up, their vanes glittering like burnished gold.'

Through the purple panes of their windows the merchant princes looked out on an amethystine world.

The Compromise of 1850 had for the time being decelerated the abolition movement, and though the Fugitive Slave Law was piling up incidents and suppressed feeling, steam pressure for swifter progress later, it was not until John Brown's soul first began to march for 'Bleeding Kansas' four years later that the distant thunderheads of civil war began to temper the sunshine on the Frog Pond. Let us review the positions, in the lull before that storm, of the three branches of the Lowells that sprang from the Old Judge's loins.

When John Amory Lowell, head of the senior line, came back from Europe in 1852, he could, like his father, write after his name the honorific letters LL.D. which had been bestowed upon him by his Alma Mater, but he was plunged at once into business and trouble. The long honeymoon of capital and labor in the Lowell mills was waning. The happy mill girls were marrying or going West to teach school. The booming business of weaving into saleable cloth the cotton picked by Southern slaves was taken over by large Irish families driven from their most distressful country by the famine of 1846–48, and by still larger French families from Quebec, where the birth rate stood second only to that of India. Successful mill management was becoming a superman's job.

In finance the addition to the world supply of a billion dollars' worth of gold and silver from the mines of California had started a tidal wave of overexpansion and frenzied speculation. John Amory Lowell saw coming, but could do little to avert, the great panic in the autumn of 1857.

On September 30 in that year, young Ben Crowninshield, a junior at Harvard, wrote in his engaging diary:

'Mother and Alice came out to see me. They brought the sorry news that Uncle Lowell had lost his property, as had several others of the most active business men in Boston.'

This, however, like the reports of an eminent death, was exaggerated. He pulled his mills and banks and the trust fund of the Lowell Institute safely through, at the cost of a slight cerebral hemorrhage that lost him the full use of his right hand. At the meeting of the Harvard Corporation on January 16, 1858, he resigned owing to 'pressure of private business.' The resignation was regretfully accepted, to take effect on the election of his successor. No successor was ever proposed and, though the resignation seems never to have been more than tacitly withdrawn, he continued to attend and eventually dominate [1] the meetings of the board in the election of six presidents, five treasurers, and ten fellows, until in 1877 he had completed a full forty years of service to the college. The annals of his family include, save one, no stouter fellow.

Meanwhile, his elder son, John, in his thirties, was rapidly rising at the bar, and in 1857 produced and printed a devastating criticism of the Dred Scott decision which may have been in Abraham Lincoln's mind when in March, 1865, he appointed him, his last judicial selection, to the Federal District Court. Augustus, the younger son, after preparing at the Boston Latin School, where from the Puritan revolt against Papist fast days even Christmas was still not a holiday, had graduated from Harvard in 1850. He took a degree 'void of invidious distinction,' but like all of his line did well in mathematics. Like his forerunners, too, he was fast on his legs and could leave the counting-room of Colonel Henry Lee, his cousin, where he was first employed, five minutes before the closing hour of the Exchange some hundreds of yards away, and arrive in time to do business. He married Katherine, daughter of Abbott Lawrence, his father's partner and friend, minister to the Court of Saint James's, where her wit and beauty, along with the culture and 'definite views' of her father, were duly noted. The Lawrences claimed Norman blood, too, from Robert Lawrence, who was made 'armiger' by Richard Coeur de Lion for bravery in scaling

[1] The resolutions passed by the corporation on his retirement say 'strongly influence.'

the walls of Acre in 1191. Percival, the first son of Augustus and Katherine Lowell, was born in 1854; Lawrence, their second, in 1855. Their seventh, Amy, the Postscript as she was called by the family, in 1874. These three lived on into our time, and exhibiting a diversity of Lowell qualities on their highest level, played notable parts in the troubled new world that began with the twentieth century.

In the middle branch, Francis Cabot Lowell II, of the vegetable diet and kingly countenance, pursued his even way. In his sons appears for the first time among male Lowells a disposition to take life less aggressively. George, the elder, a classmate of Augustus, never went seriously into any business or profession. He lived for half the year the life of a country gentleman at Cotuit, enjoying the sailing and the field sports of fishing and shooting. With his father he became a member, in the first year of its existence, of what a New York poet called 'one peerless club,' the Somerset. It occupied the mansion of Francis B. Crowninshield, which stood at the corner of Somerset and Beacon Streets on what had been the garden of the Old Judge's first house in Boston in 1776. His much younger brother, Edward Jackson Lowell, named for the young uncle who had died in his twenties, was, after a few years spent first in the glass business and then in the law, to devote his life to travel and historical scholarship. He wrote one book, *The Eve of the French Revolution*, which has become an authority in its field, and has been for more than half a century the best selling 'back list item' produced by any member of the family. In the mid-fifties he was at M. Sillig's celebrated school near Vevey on Lake Geneva, hearing lake water lapping with low sounds by the shore, filling his eyes with the grave beauty of mountains, and laying the foundation of the complete mastery of the French and German languages that was to serve him well. Through all this time the variety of surnames of the cousins of the clan was increasing. To the Higginsons, Cabots, Russells, Jacksons, Gardners, Gorhams, Putnams, and Duttons of the two earlier generations marriages of Lowell girls now added Lymans, Sohiers, Coolidges, and more Putnams. The clan was becoming less clannish.

While this young life was opening, that of the Reverend and amiable Charles, the Old Judge's last surviving son, was closing. By 1858, he had become feeble, totally deaf, and alarmingly excitable. He died at Elmwood in January, 1861. Of his three sons, Charles, the eldest, was living on Quincy Street in Cambridge, and by a wise plan of John Amory Lowell, the library's president, spending his days building the catalogue of the Athenaeum's one hundred thousand books, card by card. Robert Traill Spence Lowell, living with his wife's people at Duanesburg, was preaching in the family church, piling up the six hundred pages of his novel, and contributing poetry to the periodical press. His youngest brother, still 'Jamie' to him, was on the upward path of his prestige, but now less as a poet and reformer than as a scholar and man of letters.

In 1854, a few months after the desolating death of Maria, John Amory Lowell had invited him to give at the Lowell Institute a course of twelve lectures on Poetry with special reference to the great poets of England. He paid him the fee of twelve hundred dollars, a sum equal to the annual salary at that tim of a Harvard professor, in advance. The series began with great success on the evening of January 9, 1855. So great was the crowd that had to be turned away that each lecture was repeated and a supplement added to the fee.

But John Amory Lowell had more in his active mind for his brilliant cousin than a single course of public lectures. Just at that moment Longfellow, George Ticknor's successor in the Smith Professorship of Belles Lettres and Modern Languages, resigned to apply himself in his luxurious study at Craigie house wholly to poetry. There were six candidates for this distinguished and desirable chair. At the meeting of the Corporation on Saint Valentine's Day, James Russell Lowell, who had not been a candidate, but whose gifts as a lecturer were the talk of the town, was elected to fill it. John was tactfully absent from the meeting, one of the few times in forty years, but Charles G. Loring, Jamie's former legal mentor, was on hand to see that everything went through all right. So began the feeling that Barrett Wendell found at Harvard twenty years later. Longfellow was a poet who had been a professor. Lowell was a professor who had been a poet. He was given, as the custom was, a year's leave of absence, with full pay, for study abroad in preparation for his new work. After fifteen months spent mainly hard at work in Dresden, but with a summer's vacation in the South with his sister, Mrs. Putnam, and his friends, C. E. Norton and W. W. Story, he began the instruction of Harvard youth in the autumn of '56. A year later he, too, joined the Somerset Club, became the first editor of the *Atlantic Monthly*, and married his second wife, Miss Frances Dunlap of Portland, who had the care of his little daughter Mabel when he was abroad. The condition of Doctor Lowell and Rebecca made a return to Elmwood with a child not expedient, and they spent the first years of their life together in the home of Doctor Estes Howe on Kirkland Street.

The Russell-Lowell line, like the Higginson-Lowell and Cabot-Lowell lines, was producing bright and valiant boys in the third generation from the Old Judge. Charles Russell Lowell, Jr., born in 1835, graduated first scholar in his class in 1854. His valedictory oration, addressed to his classmates, the faculty, the distinguished alumni, the Governor of the Commonwealth, and the Sheriff of Suffolk County, was on 'The Reverence Due from Age to Youth.' It was an eloquent plea to Age to put the zeal and vigor of Youth to higher employment.

'When a young man is burning to do the world great service, it is falsehood to tell him that faithful labor is the best gift the world expects of him. If young men bring nothing but their strength and their spirit, the world may well spare them. But they do bring it something better: They bring it their fresher and purer ideals.'

A few weeks earlier, Anthony Burns, Negro preacher and slave escaping from his master in Virginia, had been arrested in Boston under the Fugitive Slave Law. Young Charles Lowell, with his classmate, 'retrospective cousin,' and best friend, Henry Higginson, tried in vain to see and plead with the Federal Judge who heard this case.

When Burns, guarded against a rescue that had already been attempted at the court house and given Thomas Wentworth Higginson a scar on his chin that he carried proudly to his grave fifty years later, was escorted down State Street to the wharves by eleven hundred militia reinforced by a mob of Boston merchants, the boys followed. As he was put on the ship that was to bear him back to bondage,[1] Henry said, 'Charlie, it will come to us to set this right!' It did, at the cost of the lives of Colonel Charles Russell Lowell, his younger brother, Captain James Jackson Lowell, and his first cousin, Lieutenant William Lowell Putnam.

· Throughout their boyhood the three boys were the favorite companions of their uncle, now known in the family as the Professor. He fought with them in their mimic battles when the snow was 'packing,' and Charlie was the 'young Telemachus' of *Moosehead Journal*.

Through the late fifties and the sixties the Professor took each summer a refreshing vacation from his books with the Adirondack Club which both he and Emerson celebrated in prose and verse. It began in 1857 when, accompanied by W. J. Stillman, journalist, painter, and seer, John Holmes, Estes Howe, and his own two nephews, Charlie and Jimmy, he explored the Adirondacks and found the perfect spot in the primeval forest on Tollansbee Pond, a watery *cul de sac* discharging into the Raquette River. Next year the boys stayed home and the personnel of the expedition consisted of a working majority of the Saturday Club. Longfellow was invited, but on hearing Emerson was taking a

---

[1] It is pleasant to note that a year later he was bought with money raised in Boston, liberated, and was being re-educated at Oberlin College when he died in 1862.

gun said, 'No, I'm staying home. Somebody will be shot.' Nobody was, and Stillman records of Emerson, 'He was the best listener I ever knew.' A distinction in that company.

Lowell himself was the Deerslayer of the party, more skilful with the rifle than the rod. Some years later Thomas Wentworth Higginson noted in his diary:

'Lecture at Medford. Stayed at Hallowell's; tea with Wasson. His guide in the Adirondacks said, "Do you know Jim Lowell?"

' "No; who is he?"

' "He's a fellow down your way; writes books and poems."

' "Yes; James Russell Lowell, I know him."

' "Well, he's a d——d ignorant cuss, ain't he!"

' (Then told of his wishing to be paddled on sunny side of brook, etc.)'

Indeed J. R. L. was hardly of a temperament for the contemplative man's recreation. The reader of his late and delightful essay on Izaak Walton would scarcely know that Piscator had ever gone fishing.

For hardy, even dangerous adventure he was always ready, and well prepared by his six hundred daily strokes with those twenty-four-pound dumb-bells. One of these was set down by Emerson in his *Journal*: [1]

'On the top of a large white pine in a bay was an osprey's nest around which the ospreys were screaming, five or six. We thought there were young birds in it, and sent Preston to the top. This looked like an adventure. The tree might be a hundred and fifty feet high, at least; sixty feet clean straight stem, without a single branch, and, as Lowell and I measured it by the tape as high as we could reach, fourteen feet, six inches in girth. Preston took advantage of a hemlock close by it and climbed till he got on the branches, then went to the top of the pine and found the nest empty, though the great birds wheeled and screamed about him. He said he could climb the bare stem of the pine, "though it would be awful hard work." When he came down,

[1] Printed by Edward Emerson in *The Early Years of the Saturday Club*.

I asked him to go up it a little way, which he did, clinging to the corrugations of the bark. Afterwards Lowell watched long for a chance to shoot the osprey, but he soared magnificently and would not alight. . . . Lowell, next morning, was missing at breakfast, and when he came to camp, told me he had climbed Preston's pine tree.'

Two years after the affair of Anthony Burns, John Brown, Puritan angel of wrath, 'at Pottawatomie in Kansas in person or through his agents,' in the well-chosen words of the standard historian, Edward Channing, 'murdered five defenceless and extremely objectionable men in somewhat cold blood.' A few months later came Judge Roger Taney's pro-Southern constitutional decision on the case of another slave, Dred Scott, who was denied his liberty after having been taken into a free-soil state. Combustible material to ignite Seward's 'irrepressible conflict' was piling up.

With the exception of young Charles and some coeval cousins, the Lowell clan seems at first not to have been greatly excited. They were Whigs; and Northerners of that persuasion, whether Cotton Whigs or Conscience Whigs, whether swayed by business and social connections with the great planters, or by old Federalist principles of sound government, were for conciliating the South, for appeasement.[1] John Amory Lowell and his son, Augustus, son and grandson of a fierce Federalist, and deeply involved in the management of banks and cotton mills, were a little of both. Remembering Emerson's account of Francis Cabot Lowell as a conservative in whom in the time of 'wayward politics' he had to adjust differences of opinion, there can be little doubt that he, too, was one of those referred to in a paragraph of his speech in New York on the Fugitive Slave Law in 1856:

[1] As late as April, 1861, Bishop William Lawrence's Appleton grandfather entered Charleston Harbor just in time to see the surrender of Fort Sumter. By the courtesy of General Beauregard he visited the captured fort, proceeded on his way to stay with friends farther South, and returned to Boston, still not convinced that the Confederacy was committed to rebellion.

'The plea on which freedom was resisted was Union. I went to certain serious men, who had a little more reason than the rest, and inquired why they took this part? They answered that they had no confidence in their strength to resist the Democratic party; that they saw plainly that all was going to the utmost verge of licence; each was vying with his neighbor to lead the party, by proposing the worst measures, and they threw themselves on the extreme conservatism, as a drag on the wheel; that they knew Cuba would be had, and Mexico would be had, and they stood stiffly on conservatism, or as near to monarchy as they could, only to moderate the velocity with which the car was running down the precipice.'

He returned to the subject with a clearer prophetic vision of what lay ahead in his speech on Kansas Relief in Cambridge six months later:

'I think the American Revolution bought its glory cheap. If the problem was new, it was simple. If there were few people, they were united, and the enemy three thousand miles off. But now, vast property, gigantic interests, family connections, webs of party, cover the land with a network that immensely multiplies the dangers of war.'

James Russell Lowell was a little behind his club mates of the Saturday and Adirondack clubs, in his political thinking in the new present crisis. Until the November election in 1860, his correspondence dealt chiefly with matters of scholarship and literature, arising out of his twin chairs as professor and editor. In October, 1859, just after the arrest of the Old Puritan at Harper's Ferry, he wrote to T. W. Higginson, who had proposed an article on the subject, 'I am a little afraid of John Brown.'

His abolitionist friends, however, were still counting on him. On his fortieth birthday, February 22, 1859, at a dinner of the Saturday Club, Emerson read a poem which does not appear in his collected works. In it the poet's old mistress, the Sibyl, is called on to tell Lowell's fortune. She announces, 'Strength for the hour,' and elaborates:

'Man of marrow, man of mark,
Virtue lodged in sinew stark. . . .
Most at home in mounting fun
Broadest joke and luckiest pun. . . .
But, if another temper come,
If on the sun shall creep a gloom,
A time and tide more exigent,
When the old mounds are torn and rent, . . .
Then the pleasant bard will know
To put the frolic masque behind him
Like an old familiar cloak,
And in sky-born mail to bind him,
And single-handed cope with Time,
And parry and deal the Thunder-stroke.'

This was perhaps a little rhetorical, but so were the parries and deals of the thunder-strokes when they came. So was most of the poetry and political writing of the period. It was reserved for a shy and retiring girl in her teens in Amherst, and for a stout young Lowell cousin not yet born, who was neither shy nor retiring, to choose words and put them together in a way to puncture the poetic rhetoric of the 'cosmic poets.'

In December, 1860, after the election of Lincoln by the new Republican Party, Lowell, though he would, he says, have preferred Seward, wrote to Charles Nordhoff, 'We have been running long enough by dead reckoning. It is time to take the height of the sun of righteousness.'

For five years his articles in the *Atlantic* and the *North American Review*, his Second Series of *Biglow Papers*, weightier and more moving than the first, his occasional poems, the 'Washers of the Shroud' and the 'Commemoration Ode,' were among the most effective writing done in the North. They were, perhaps still are, some of them, at least, familiar to every schoolboy. We will go to war, not with him, but with young Charles Russell Lowell, who essayed by direct action to set slavery right with the sabre.

2

CHAPTER

Beau Sabreur[1]

Charles Russell Lowell, Jr., scholar, mechanic, traveller, railroad treasurer, ironmaster, commander of a fighting brigade of cavalry — *beau sabreur* to the eye, but one with first-class brains and a gentle heart, all before he was thirty — was born in Boston in a house that stood a few doors from the Common in Winter Place. In him the *élan* of the Russell-Lowell-Spence line was mingled with the Jackson verve, and, at least so his cousin, Henry Higginson, thought, a touch of the Irish fighting spirit of his great-grandfather, Patrick Tracy. He prepared for college at both the Latin and English High Schools in Boston, as usual first

[1] The documentation of this chapter comes chiefly from Doctor Edward Emerson's *Life and Letters of Charles Russell Lowell*, with its more than one hundred pages of supplementary notes and references. *The Philanthropic Work of Josephine Shaw Lowell*, by W. R. Stewart, contains essential material. Also helpful have been the *Harvard Memorial Biographies*, and family letters in the possession of Mrs. Pierre (Louisa Barlow) Jay, daughter of Colonel Lowell's college friend and comrade in arms, 'the boy General,' Francis Barlow.

scholar, and entered Harvard at fifteen, the youngest member of the class of 1854. One classmate recalled his 'boyish beauty, his rosy-tinted complexion, his wavy hair, his bright eyes that could flash with merriment or glow with intense conviction.' Another wrote:

'He was unusually boyish in appearance, with a ruddy countenance overflowing with health and *animal spirits*, and a manner somewhat brusque. He did not win popularity at once; but as his powers and character developed, and toned down the rather boisterous life and manner of the body, he came to be proudly acknowledged, without a dissenting voice, as the foremost man of the Class.

'Plato was his constant study and his most valued authority; he also often referred to Lucretius, whose writings he read carefully in college; and he was familiar with the thought of the English and American transcendentalists. He loved mysticism.'

All his short life, 'By Plato' was his favorite oath, but his mysticism was the shrewd, practical, patriotic Yankee mysticism of Emerson. Notably in his Emerson-fed generation he made good his uncle's line

'And what they dare to dream of dare to do.'

After vowing sometime to set slavery right, and telling his audience at Harvard's Commencement of the Reverence due from Age to Youth, he spent six months in the counting-room of John Murray Forbes to learn business methods. His employer noted that 'he penetrated the mysteries rapidly' and became a warm and helpful friend. Later Mr. Forbes wrote to an Englishman who had offered his protégé a brilliant opening in the great international firm of Russell and Company in China:

'One of the strange things has been how he magnetized you and me at first sight. We are both practical, unsentimental, and perhaps hard, at least externally; yet he captivated me, just as he did you, and I came home and told my wife I had fallen in love.'

In the spring of '55, still in pursuit of practical knowledge, the twenty-year-old transcendentalist became a common workman in the Ames Company's mill at Chicopee, filing iron and cleaning old chains, studying every process and detail of ironmaking, particularly the kick of the gun, the reaction of the trade on the men in it, workmen, boss, and manager. No other member of his family so early developed so keen a social conscience. He believed in the discipline that makes character, but his interest and his sympathy lay rather with the hands than with the head office. As a present measure he started a singing class, and begged his friends to give him books which he could lend his fellow workmen to read in place of the wretched trash they had.

He himself was a hungry reader of solid books. His letters from his graduation to the time of the war record the reading of Matthew Arnold, Bacon, Buckle, Sir Thomas Browne, Byron, Bunyan, Carlyle, Cervantes, Chapman's Homer, Chaucer, Coleridge, Dante, Darwin, Fichte, Froude, Goethe, Hawthorne, Herbert, Humboldt, Kant, Henry James, Sr., Milton, Niebuhr, Novalis, Pascal, Benjamin Peirce, Raleigh, Richter, Ruskin, Schiller, Shakespeare, Spenser, Sydney Smith, Swedenborg, Thoreau, Whewell, Wordsworth, and others. But it is Emerson whom he most constantly quotes.

His admirable Jackson mother was a great reader, too. Sometimes they read the same books and corresponded about them. A year after he left college, she compiled and published a yeasty book in two fat little volumes called *Seed-Grass*, made up of high thoughts of ancient and modern writers. On the motto page one reads, 'The business of philosophy is to circumnavigate human nature.' The final quotation is a glimpse of Carlyle's into the clouded crystal ball: 'The merit of Albert the Courageous all lies safely funded in Saxon and German life to this hour.' Charlie wrote her that, though opposed to it on principle, as he detested selections, he enjoyed it extremely:

'How the great men do stand out among the merely able, or the merely earnest men: Bacon and Goethe by the side of Henry

Taylor and Carlyle, even Emerson and William Humboldt by the side of Helps, Kingsley, etc. Rather discouraging to us modern people.'

While at Chicopee, 'not a distant Grecian sky, but sons of Agamemnon may be nursed here,' he met Horatio Greenough's brother, Richard, also a sculptor and architect. From him and the Professor's friend, W. J. Stillman, he conceived an interest in bronze casting, and for some weeks was full of a plan for organizing to carry on that business, 'a concern which shall be permanent in the family, after the English and not the American mode.' Nothing came of it, however, and in the autumn of '55 he left Chicopee to take a promising head-office position in the rolling mills at Trenton, New Jersey. Here it seemed he had found his appointed work; but in the spring the endemic New England disease of tuberculosis, which at one time or another threatened all the members of his immediate family, laid its pale finger on him. Doctor James Jackson, his wise medical uncle, under whose care little John, Jr., a half-century before had surprisingly lived to grow up, diagnosed the case as curable. Ironically, as it turned out, he ordered him to avoid all strenuous action till after the age of thirty. Mr. Forbes, his ever-thoughtful patron, appeared promptly on the scene and took him South by ship to the West Indies and New Orleans. In that soft Southern climate his health improved, but it was evident that a longer time under sunny skies was needed to effect a permanent cure. Through the generosity of Mr. Forbes and his grandmother, Mrs. Patrick Tracy Jackson, it was made possible for him to embark on a fast sailing ship of eight hundred tons for Gibraltar. As always he made light of his intimate personal danger. To his anxious mother he wrote, 'As to fear about myself, why, as Emerson somewhere says, "I sail with God the seas!"'

During his two years abroad he sent home the most perceptive and enjoyable travel letters to be found among the hundreds of good *lettres de voyage* produced by five generations of touring Lowells.

He landed at Gibraltar and applied himself with force and originality to the task of restoring his health. He bought a horse and hardened himself to the saddle on the mountain roads of Spain, Switzerland, Austria, Italy, Germany, and Algiers, stopping in at M. Sillig's establishment in Vevey to see his young cousin, Ned, who must have been excited by the manner of his arrival. Even after he was joined by Henry Higginson and Stephen Perkins, who preferred to travel by chaise, he stuck to the saddle. Perforce he had to study the capacity and needs of the horse, and achieved a kinship with that noble animal that helped to make him the centaur that he became. He attended the manoeuvres of the Austrian and French armies, chiefly, as it seemed at the time, for their picturesqueness and intellectual interest. For exercise in Algiers he took lessons in swordsmanship from an eminent French *maître d'armes*. He made friends with English, French, Germans, and Italians, learned to speak their languages well, and so acquired understanding of men as well as horses. Few *beaux sabreurs* were ever as civilians better prepared for cavalry command. He arrived back home in July, 1858, brown, hard, and healthy, uncertain as to his future, though he had been corresponding with Henry Higginson about the possibility of the two of them settling in Bleeding Kansas and doing something to stop it.

For the time being *dis aliter visum*. He spent the month of August at Mr. Forbes's island principality of Naushon, riding, fishing, sailing, and coaching young William Forbes in algebra and history. There he was offered by his host and accepted the post of assistant treasurer of the Burlington and Missouri River Railroad. September found him established on the banks of the sullen Mississippi at Burlington, a town with 'an unfledged look, its pin feathers being still very apparent.'

He set up housekeeping in a small white brick house with an acre of land on the outskirts of the town, with as companions a young Bohemian, Leo Carker, who enjoyed the title of general freight and ticket agent, and later young Mr. Charles E. Perkins, who at a salary of thirty dollars a month had come from Ohio to assist the assistant treasurer as cashier, and was to rise to the presidency of the great C. B. & Q. In addition to his financial responsibility, the twenty-three-year-old treasurer had charge of the land grant of three hundred thousand acres given by the Government to assist in the construction of the road across the state. As the territory granted was far in advance of the point reached by the rails, the lands were proving unsaleable and a headache of a gigantic acreage. He was, Mr. Perkins records, a tireless worker, often staying in his office till midnight. Yet with a steady eye to his health he managed a daily ride on a little sorrel mare he had bought, and squeezed out somehow a half-hour a day for scholarly reading. Two months after settling in the unfledged town, he writes his mother:

'Put me in the first 200 pages of Peirce's book which was overlooked in the upper drawer of my bureau, also his Curves and Functions. Item, one pair of thin boots I left, as there may be gay doings among the Germans. If Uncle James has Child's Chaucer, perhaps he will lend me his Tyrwhitt's.

'I see Froude has launched a history of Henry VIII. He will never be able to manage him, the men are so unlike.

'. . . If Anna will lend me her little Pilgrim's Progress, I should like it, also your Pascal's Provincial Letters, — and my Amts German Grammar, if there is room, for I fancy even a box from home has limits of capacity. I should like my Spanish, English and my Greek Dicks.'

He concludes:

'You say you have a cough: if you don't get over it, I shall come home and take care of you; you must remember, when you are well I am well; you are the very root of my life now and will be perhaps forever.'

A year later, Mr. George Ashburner, of the house of Russell and Company of Hong Kong, turned up in Burlington, was entertained in the little white brick house at a supper including champagne, and a few days later wrote offering his young host a post in the Orient promising early position and wealth. It was declined in a letter that reveals the quality of the writer:

'A sound man feels that he has a right, himself, to dispose of himself, but a fellow who has been ill feels that his kindred have a new claim on him. My mother's hold upon me has increased tenfold within four years — and she *must* be included in my plans for the next ten years. She takes great comfort in my present position in Burlington, believes in the climate, and means to make her home with me a part of each year. I cannot disappoint her — and I know from my own feeling that, apart from the anxiety, the long separation would be very hard upon her.'

As the months passed and the thunderheads on the political horizon rolled up blacker and closer, the mood of his letters becomes graver. In May, '60, he wrote to his classmate and brother-in-law, George Putnam, 'How does the Chicago platform and nomination please the Puritans — it shows pluck, and that, in an American, generally argues strength. Deliberately I prefer Lincoln to Seward, especially since the latter's Capital and Labor speech which shivers a little in the wind's eye.'

Just before the November election he made an important change of base. He had never, he says, got over the 'iron-fever.' Though the pecuniary prospect was no better, he accepted an offer that came to him, again through the good offices of Mr. Forbes, to become an ironmaster at the works in Mount Savage, Maryland, a post of responsibility at the head of a small city of workmen.

There, in a border state, he became more acutely aware of the irrepressible conflict. In December, 1860, he made a business trip to New Orleans and saw the unfurling of the Pelican Flag when the news was received of South Carolina's secession. 'It was an instructive spectacle. I wonder whether the signers of the Declaration of Independence looked as silly as those fellows.' In February, he wrote to Mr. Forbes, who had gone to

Washington as a commissioner from Massachusetts to the so-called Peace Conference, that if the Commonwealth stood where Charles Francis Adams had put her she would look all right in history. 'We had,' he tells him, 'a Union meeting in this county some three weeks ago that was more anti-slavery than Faneuil Hall dares to be — but this is by no means the feeling throughout the state.'

Two months later, the real feeling of Maryland flamed into action. In Baltimore, where forty years before Federalist friends of his great-uncle, John, opposing Mr. Madison's War and held in protective custody, were murderously attacked by a mob, Massachusetts troops were fired on. Instantly resigning his place as ironmaster, all 'Charleynesses' as he called them forgotten, our *beau sabreur* made his way to Washington, arriving on foot, after communication with the North had been cut off. Foreseeing that the struggle to preserve the Union would be a long one, he saw in the army at once a call and a career. He wrote to his senator, Charles Sumner:

'I speak and write English, French, and Italian, and read German and Spanish; knew once enough of mathematics to put me at the head of my class in Harvard, though now I may need a little rubbing up; am a tolerable proficient with the small sword and single-stick; and can ride a horse as far and bring him in as fresh as any other man. I am twenty-six years of age, and believe that I possess more or less of that moral courage about taking responsibility which seems at present to be found only in Southern officers.'

Sumner passed the letter to Secretary Cameron, who had a look at the applicant and forthwith set steps in motion that gave him an unusual trust for a civilian, a captaincy in the Third United States Cavalry.

The young captain wrote his mother that he was too old to be tickled by a uniform. He felt the issues involved too gravely to be one of those of whom Melville wrote,

'In Bacchic glee they file towards Fate,
Moloch's uninitiate,'

but he was in high spirits throughout the summer and fall he spent recruiting for the cavalry in the Western Reserve, and it was in the true spirit of Boots and Saddles that in the early spring, in command of a thoroughly drilled squadron in a crack regiment of cavalry, he set sail with a motley transport fleet of tugs, barges, canal boats, three-storied river steamers, and clipper ships to the Federal beachheads at Newport News and Fortress Monroe for the capture of Richmond.

It was not long before the regiment knew that, in the captain of the squadron composed of Companies K and E, they had a real Leader of Horse. At the end of the war his orderly, Frank Robbins, wrote an account of his first important engagements at Hanover Court House and Slatersville:

'Our Regiment was advance-guard from Yorktown to Williamsburg;' at Fort Magruder 'Gen. Stoneman ordered us to draw in line and charge . . .' but 'the Rebs' cavalry charged us first. We fell back, and as we were crossing a swamp the Rebs overtook us. Capt. Lowell had charge of Companies K and E. The Rebs charged Company E first, and the Captain joined that Company with our Company K, and fought them with the sabre for about ten minutes — then we retreated out of the swamp. Our Captain ordered six men to go out as skirmishers from the right of the first platoon. I was one of the six that was sent out, and Sergeant R. was ordered to take charge of us. The Sergt. had been drinking too freely, and he said that *every one of us that didn't charge and kill twenty Rebs, he would put in the guard-house.* Our Capt. told R. he could go to the rear and consider himself under arrest; then he said he would lead us himself. When we got to the swamp, he ordered two of us to dismount and take saddles off the dead horses, while he and the other men skirmished. He laughed at us for dodging when we heard the shells whistle past; he said there was no use to dodge after we heard it whistle. . . .

'After the battle [of Williamsburg] we were advance-guard. . . . Major Williams ordered our Capt. to go through a path that led through a pine forest, with his two companies, and see what he could see. When we had got pretty near through, the rear guard came in and said that there was one hundred dismounted Rebs in our rear. Our Capt. said: "We are not going backwards, we are going forwards, — they will not trouble us." We went a piece farther, when our advance-guard came in and said that there was a thousand in advance of us. Our Capt. said: "We shall not turn back: I would rather fight one thousand fair than one hundred in ambush — we will go and see the thousand."

'When we came out of the woods, the Rebs were formed in line. One squadron of the Rebs fired on us and one squadron charged us with the sabre. Before they got down where we were our Capt. charged us on another squadron of theirs and charged five times until we made the big road. Our Captain was the first man through the rebel lines every time we charged through them that day. While we were fighting our Capt. rode after a retreating Reb with a shot-gun on his shoulder: our Capt. rode to his side and ordered him to surrender, — the Reb threw the gun across his arm and fired it at our Capt.; the shot lodged in his overcoat that he had on the saddle behind him. Our Capt. ordered Lt. W. to form the men in line on the road: he staid to see the men all off the field. Lt. X. was thrown from his horse in the first charge and when our Capt. was leaving the field to join his squadron he found him hid behind a stump, — he cried out, "Captain! Say Captain, have you seen my horse?" Our Capt. said, "I am not hunting your horse — you had better come and get on behind me, for you cannot stay there long." When they got to the squadron, the Rebs were making a charge on us, — then we could see our Regt. coming up behind us. Our Capt. charged the Rebs and we took a great many prisoners.'

His brother James wrote home a fuller account of the affair of the overcoat:

'I heard yesterday of a narrow escape which Charley had. He was charging, and came upon a man who aimed a double-barrelled carbine at him. C. called out to him, "Drop that!"

and he lowered it enough to blow to pieces C.'s coat which was strapped on his horse behind him.'

Charles never mentioned the matter, but, being asked by the girl who became his wife if it were true, replied, 'You can usually make a man obey you if you speak quickly enough and with authority.'

In the bitter slogging battles of the Seven Days with the army insecurely astride the flooded and bloodied Chickahominy, McClellan made his cautious change of base to a defensive position on Malvern Hill. On the thirtieth of June, Captain James Jackson Lowell was shot at Glendale, while re-forming his company's line. His friend, Captain Oliver Wendell Holmes, a hundred yards away, looked along the front and waved to him, looked again and he was down. Charles and his sister Anna, 'a good little girl' who was a nurse on a hospital steamer at Harrison's Bar, were both within a few miles, but neither could get to him before he died the following day. The officer of his regiment, who went to Nelson's Farm which had been converted into a hospital to bid him farewell, told of the warm firm grasp of his hand, and the composure of the smile on his pale scholar's face. Two surgeons who were left with the Northern wounded after the retreat from Glendale told the Confederate officers to talk with him if they wished to know how a Union soldier thought and felt.

After the Union army, stopped within sight of the steeples and sound of the bells of Richmond, had retreated back down the Peninsula or been transported by water to Washington, Captain Charles Lowell, 'for distinguished services at Williamsburg and Slatersville,' was brevetted major and chosen by McClellan the personal aide who, as it proved, was to serve him in the great battle of Antietam. Through the months of July and August, McClellan went into a temporary eclipse, but in September following Pope's disaster at the second battle of Bull Run and Lee's advance across the upper Potomac into Maryland threatening the Northern capital, McClellan in the hour of dire emergency was again given the command. His aide, though devoted to him personally, saw both his strength and his weakness with a clear eye. To Henry Higginson, who encountered him in the field during the march to the meeting of the armies, he said, as they lay in the grass during an idle hour:

'He is a great strategist, and the men have faith in him. He makes his plans admirably, makes all his preparations so as to be ready for any emergency, just as the Duke of Wellington did, but unlike the Duke of Wellington, when he comes to strike he doesn't strike in a determined fashion; that is, he prepares very well, and then doesn't do the best thing — strike hard.'

A neat preview of the judgment of history!

A week later, on the second day of the bloody struggle back and forth across the shallow fords and arched stone bridges of Antietam Creek, Charles, mounted and conspicuous, rode with orders from McClellan to his hard-pressed right flank. In the midst of a driving hail of lead which is still to be dug out from tree trunks and fences, he encountered a brigade of Sedgwick's division, broken and in full flight. Happy as a lover, he exerted his native power of command, checked the rout, re-formed the line, and rode back with it into the deadly woods by the Dunker Church. He escaped injury, but his favorite bright sorrel battle charger, Berold, that had carried him through the engagements of the Peninsula and the Seven Days, was less lucky. Let Frank Robbins his orderly tell the tale:

'The first I saw of Berold was at Fortress Monroe. There was where he was when the Colonel sent me to get him. I may be mistaken but I think he was seven years of age then. We went back to Washington, from there up into Maryland. The Colonel was on General McClellan's Staff. There was a fight the day before the battle of Antietam. I cannot remember the name of it. The Colonel rode Berold through it and at the Battle of Antietam he rode him, I think till about one o'clock when he went with some orders to General Hooker on the right. When we got over there the men was coming back in disorder. The

Colonel (or he was captain then) went in and helped rally them. There was a solid shot, or I always thought it was, struck the captain's scabbard and shivered it to pieces. He told me before we got back to Headquarters that he did not think Berold was worth much, that he thought he was soft and was giving out, he could only trot. When we got to Headquarters he told me to take the saddle off of Berold and saddle Bob, a colt that was sent to him. When I took the saddle off there was a great lump on each side of him as large as a hen's egg. I thought the Ball went in behind the Colonel's right leg and lodged just in front of his left leg just behind Berold's shoulder blade. It was a Minie Ball and was just under the hide. I took a knife, and cut through the hide and took the ball out and there was some splinters of the scabbard too, sticking in his side. If you examine the horse you will find the scars. At the same time his tongue was hurt. I do not know how it was done. He did not fall to hurt it, but when the colonel came into Headquarters Berold had his mouth wide open and I always thought he was shot in the mouth. You look at his tongue and it will show for its self that it was hurt terribly. He had his hoof split. It was always the opinion that it was a shell that struck it. The colonel told me to shoot him, that he would never be of use, but I could not. We moved camp and I went back four or five days to him. I put wet bags around him and the fourth or fifth day I took him to camp, led him twelve or fifteen miles. In about three weeks after, I turned him out in a field where General McClellan's horses was and he would run and lead them all around the field.'

Writing the following day to Mr. Forbes, the major soon to be colonel reported with characteristic understatement, 'We had a severe fight here Tuesday and a battle on Wednesday. . . . I have had my usual luck but shall have to buy a new sabre, and shall have one horse less to ride for a month or two.'

After the all but drawn battle — the Confederates had lost 14,000 men, the Federals 28,000, but Lee had retreated across the Potomac — he was chosen by General McClellan for the honor of carrying to Washington and presenting to President Lincoln the thirty-nine regimental standards captured at South Mountain and Antietam.

In the War Between the States it was still the custom, except on the sea and in the Deep South, to go into winter quarters when cold weather came, and delay offensive action until spring. It was suggested to Charles that he go home for the winter to raise in Boston a 'regiment of gentlemen.' 'Gentlemen?' he asked. 'What do you mean gentlemen, drivers of gigs?' But when the qualification was liberalized, he accepted the assignment and went North to organize the Second Massachusetts Cavalry, which he was to command. Its nucleus was a battalion of wild-riding young men from California, but the other two, recruited in Boston with some difficulty, were soon in camp at Readville, beaten into respectable form.

During this interlude in the fighting there were notable incidents. He went as a guest to a meeting of the Saturday Club, where he sat beside his philosopher and friend, Emerson, and listened with delight to the verbal sword play between the Professor and the Autocrat. He was a figure, too, in a memorable episode in the history of Boston clubdom. A group of gentlemen headed by Mr. Forbes, not liking the tone of the remarks about the war and Lincoln they heard at the Somerset Club, formed a new Union Club. The color of the affair is vividly conveyed in a speech by Colonel Charles R. Codman at an anniversary meeting of the younger club some years later:

'There was another club in Boston at that time, and there is now, known as the Somerset Club. Now, gentlemen, I was a member of the Somerset Club, — let that be understood, — and I remained a member of it for many years. I was not here at the time that this feeling broke out, but I was told that there were bitter divisions in the Somerset Club. We are all for the Union now, and those gentlemen in the Somerset Club were all for the Union then, but their views were different. Some supported Mr. Lincoln in his administration. Others did not, but found fault with everything that he did. But that is not so very strange. Everybody admires Lincoln today; everybody did from the moment that the shot was fired that killed him. There is no difference of opinion about Lincoln now. The very men, those of them who are still living, who criticised his administration, have long since come to admit that he was the greatest, or one of the greatest, of the American Presidents. But it was different at the time of which I am speaking. The Somerset Club was divided. A great many of its members found it uncomfortable to be there and hear the administration constantly abused, and they had much to do with the foundation of the Union Club.

'As a member of the Somerset Club, however, I was never unfairly treated, and they knew my opinions perfectly well. The first vote I ever gave was for Abraham Lincoln, and I was perfectly open about it. Being on that side, I was one of the minority in the club, but I was always treated with respect and consideration, and I never should have thought of leaving it because they did not agree with me on political questions. I well remember, gentlemen, at the time that these discussions in the Somerset Club were at the hottest, — I well remember, the cordial way in which I was saluted and greeted as I rode at the head of my regiment to the ship in the harbor which was to take us to North Carolina for the seat of war. (Applause.)'

On the ninth of April, 1863, the new club held its first meeting which concluded with a two-hour speech by Edward Everett that contained most of the material he delivered seven months later at Gettysburg. Perhaps some of his auditors felt, as Emerson did as he listened to a sermon by the same gentleman forty years earlier and scribbled,

'Let those now cough who never coughed before,
And those who always cough, cough now the more.'

Of the Lowells present and joining as charter members were the Colonel, his father, his Uncle James, who like Colonel Codman still retained his membership in the Somerset, and the future

Judge John Lowell. Francis Cabot Lowell and his son, George, early members of the Somerset, stayed put. The Union started life in 'rooms,' but within a few months moved into Abbott Lawrence's house at Number 8 Park Street. Thirty years later it annexed John Amory Lowell's house at Number 7. At meetings of the Saturday Club, Lawrence Lowell liked to say that the room in which they lunched had been the bedroom of both his maternal grandmothers.

Another incident of the winter was of a more distressful nature. His wife, who knew how the affair long preyed on his mind, wrote out a careful account:

'Stopping as usual, at eight o'clock one morning, at the recruiting station, he found the small squad of new recruits who were to be transferred that day to the camp at Readville, in a state of mutiny. Hearing the noise on his arrival, he descended at once to the basement, and the Sergeant in command explained that he had ordered a man to be handcuffed, that the others had said it was unjust and should not be done, and had resisted. Colonel Lowell at once said: "The order must be obeyed." "No! No!" shouted the men. He continued: "After it is obeyed, I will hear what you have to say, and will decide the case on its merits, but it *must* be obeyed *first*. God knows, my men, I don't want to kill any of you, but I shall shoot the first man who resists. Sergeant, iron your man." As the Sergeant stepped forward with the irons, the men made a rush, and Colonel Lowell shot the leader, who fell at once. The men succumbed immediately, some bursting into tears, such was their excitement.'

A few minutes later the Colonel reported to Governor Andrew. Entering his excellency's room at the State House, he saluted and said, 'I have to report to you, Sir, that in discharge of my duty, I have shot a man,' then saluted again and immediately withdrew. 'I need nothing more,' said the Governor to a bystander. 'Colonel Lowell is as humane as he is brave.'

While the Colonel was living in Burlington, his mother had

written him that all he wanted now was 'a wife.' He replied, 'A wife. I would as soon think of applying the indefinite article to *a* mother. If ever I meet *the* wife, the matter may have some interest for me.' It was early in this same winter that he met her.

Josephine Shaw was the younger daughter of Mr. and Mrs. Shaw, of New Brighton on Staten Island, close friends of the Colonel's Uncle James and Aunt Maria White Lowell. In 1863, she was nineteen years old. She had been well educated in modern languages, history, and literature during four years in Rome and Paris, with a final finishing in Boston at his mother's school. She was a slender, graceful girl, a fine horsewoman, with, as Richard Watson Gilder was to say in his memorial poem, not very poetically but truly, 'a thinking, inward-lighted countenance.' The resolute fine profile of her brother Bob, riding beside his colored troops that in Saint Gaudens's bronze march steadily forever down Beacon Street past the State House, was hers, too. Like him, she had the daily courage of humor.

As a young girl, Charles had known her casually as a friend of the family. Coming home from the bloody scenes of Antietam, he saw her with new eyes. She was beyond all doubt or question *the* wife. They seem to have become engaged almost at once. Adams Hill wrote him in March, 'I hear the arrow sped swiftly. In such matters haste is not waste.'

The 'roots' of Charles's relation to his mother, however, were never severed. His orderly, Frank Robbins, writes:

'After we went in camp at Readville and when the Colonel's Father and Mother came to live near the camp, one evening the colonel told me to come down and bring the horses about two o'clock. As we went back to camp I said to him his mother was quite a spry woman. He said, "Did you see her?" I said I did when she bade him goodnight. He laughed.'

We get lively pictures of Josephine Shaw in letters from two notably diverse observers. After her death in 1905, William James wrote to her daughter, Carlotta:

'She was surely one of our noblest and freest. I saw her first when she was eighteen years old, and had come with your Aunt Nellie to pay a visit at the Tweedys', in Kay Street, Newport. She seemed to me then superior to any young woman I had ever seen. A little later, as I was watching "dress parade" of the 54th regiment, she and your father, then just engaged I think, came whirling up on horseback, and drew up close behind where I was standing among the crowd of spectators. I looked back and saw their faces and figures against the evening sky, and they looked̄ so young and victorious, that I, much gnawed by questions as to my own duty of enlisting or not, shrank back — they had not seen me — from being recognized. I shall never forget the impression they made.'

Forty years after the war, one of the Colonel's troopers wrote to Mrs. Lowell herself:

'I remember you well, when you came to Camp at Vienna the bride of our gallant Colonel. I can see you today in my mind's eye, making your daily trip to the hospital, in wet weather equipped in a waterproof and little gum boots; the boys appreciated that and it was fully commented on in quarters.'

After Charles went back to the wars, leaving her Berold to ride as his parting gift, his letters to her became as constant and delightful as they had been in earlier years to his mother. He writes of Ruskin and Wordsworth, of amusing incidents of army life, of plans for travel together *après la guerre*, of the hazy beauty of the Blue Ridge, of the death of her brother in the assault on Fort Wagner: 'The manliness and patriotism and high courage of such a soldier never dies with him; they live in his comrades, — it should be the same with the gentleness and thoughtfulness which made him so loveable a son and brother and friend. . . . I am thankful they buried him "with his niggers." They were brave men and they were his men.'

To his deep regret Colonel Lowell, now protecting Washington in command of a brigade of cavalry, consisting of the Second Massachusetts and two New York regiments, missed the decisive battle of Gettysburg and saw nothing of the subsequent campaign, except in the protection of Meade's line of supplies in his advance into Virginia. From this it developed that for nearly a year after his marriage, October 31, 1863, he was occupied with operations against the elusive guerrilla leader, John Singleton Mosby, 'an old rat who has many holes,' who specialized in the capture, looting, and destruction of Federal wagon trains. Yet, despite the clamor in the North that Mosby's men when captured should be hanged, the Colonel wrote to Miss Shaw, 'Mosby is an honorable foe and should be treated as such.' After the war, the Old Rat said that Colonel Lowell's Second Massachusetts had given him more trouble and killed or captured more of his men than any other unit of the Northern army. These excursions and alarms, however, though frequent, were not of long duration, and had an agreeable sporting flavor of the chase that was not without its appeal to the Colonel. Perhaps they intensified rather than interrupted the half-year of happiness in the little house at Vienna.[1]

In the summer of '64, as the war's penultimate big push got under way in Virginia, Josephine went home to Staten Island, where her daughter, Carlotta, whom the Colonel was never to see, was born in November. What a soldier's wife she was is revealed by a note in her diary after she received a letter from her brother two years before:

'All the account of brave deeds, bayonet charges, calmly receiving the fire of the enemy and withholding their own, and

---

[1] Colonel Theodore Lyman, *en route* to Warrenton to assume a staff position at Meade's headquarters, wrote to his wife in August, 1863:

'The conductor (the dirtiest mortal I ever saw, but extremely energetic and capable) said we should have no trouble with guerrillas, as they had a very nice colonel in command near there, who had taken the wise precaution to seize the father and brother of the chief guerrilla and then to send a civil message to him stating that, if any trains were fired into, it would be his (the Colonel's) painful duty to tie said relations on the track and run an engine over them! This had an excellent effect.'

Colonel Charles was in command in that sector at that time, but the soiled conductor undoubtedly exaggerated the tale.

all the stirring accounts of courageous men, make one so long to be with them. I should of all things enjoy a forlorn hope (I think). Well put in, I suppose, but still I really do think so, for I'm not an atom afraid of death and the enthusiasm of the moment would be sublime.'

Meanwhile, the Colonel took the field with his brigade, now armed through his personal efforts with the new Spencer repeating carbine. In his first reconnaissance he led his command one hundred and ten miles in forty-eight hours. He himself, light, active, and tough, seemed incapable of fatigue. After seventy hours without sleep he was fresh and cheerful, and annoyed his officers by laughing at their woe-begone countenances. His boy bugler said, 'The only fault I ever could find with the Colonel was the places he led me into.' A sergeant stated, 'We always felt sure in however bad a place we were, that the Colonel could get us out all right.' When asked why, when scouting in a country of bushwhackers whose long hunting rifles were death to Federal officers, he always wore the crimson sash of an officer, he answered, 'It is good for the men to have me wear it.'

The end of July found him at Harper's Ferry looking for trouble, and ready either to take or make it.

Early in August, Grant, who was fighting it out all summer on the line of the Wilderness with a heavy loss of expendibles, decided that something must be done about the Valley. For three years that rich and lovely terrain, watered by the Shenandoah and commanded by the Massanuttens, had been a thorn in Federal flesh. It was the bread-basket of the Confederacy, and Grant's right flank and Washington in his rear were constantly threatened by divisions of infantry and brigades of cavalry in ragged grey pouring down out of it through the staggered mountain passes of the Blue Ridge, or across the Potomac into Maryland. He gave Sheridan command in the Valley with orders to turn its fruitful fields into scorched earth, and destroy it as a base of military action.

The Colonel at once took to his new C.O.

'I like Sheridan immensely,' he wrote his wife. 'Whether he succeeds or fails, he is the first general I have seen who puts as much heart and time and thought into his work as if he were doing it for his own exclusive profit. He works like a mill-owner or an iron-master; not like a soldier. Never sleeps, never worries, is never cross, but isn't afraid to come down on a man who deserves it.'

Four days after Sheridan took command, Lowell led the advance that met the enemy advancing north of Winchester, and after a sharp fight turned them about and drove them pell-mell through the town. Five weeks later, in the same terrain against a whole division he repeated the performance, and he did it yet again, a third time, in early October, in what was known in Union circles as the Woodstock races in which he was on the heels of the Confederates for twenty-six miles. During these weeks it was with difficulty that he was kept mounted. Thirteen horses, including his favorite, Ruksh, so named from Rustum's steed in Matthew Arnold's poem, were shot under him, and one, Atalanta, was stolen. Berold, who had come back to the war, proved uncontrollable under fire, and was sent back to grass at Staten Island, where he lived honored and petted to a great equine age.

In the first weeks of the Valley campaign, Jubal Early, not a military intellectual giant but a faithful fighter, had a considerable numerical superiority over Sheridan. Battles raged back and forth, up and down the Valley between Winchester and Harper's Ferry. Alternately the Colonel spearheaded attacks and fought bitter unfamiliar rear-guard actions. With his own eyes Sheridan saw him leaping rail fences to get at the foe, and once, when a stone wall proved too high for leaping, actually riding along it whacking their rifles with his sabre. He said, 'Colonel Lowell is a brave man,' and he knew of the administrative ability the Colonel had shown in the previous spring, when in four weeks he had completely reorganized the systems of supply for the great cavalry depot near Washington. He gave him a new command, the Reserve Brigade, composed of the First, Second, and Fifth United States Regular Cavalry with his own Second Massachusetts, and a battery of horse artillery.

In mid-September, Lee, under heavy pressure at Richmond and Petersburg, withdrew the veteran divisions of Anderson and Kershaw from Old Jubilee Early's command. Sheridan, learning from prisoners and his scouts that Early no longer had the advantage in numbers, took the offensive and the issue in the Valley was no longer in doubt.

This was in the third week of September, 1864. Within the fortnight the Colonel for the first time gave evidence of doubt as to his invulnerability to bullet, sabre, and solid shot. His cousin, William Putnam, had been killed at Ball's Bluff in 1861, his own brother, James, at Glendale, and his brother-in-law to be, Robert Shaw, at Fort Wagner in 1862. By 1864, few of his intimate friends had escaped death or grievous wounds, yet he had believed in his heart, or by constant reiteration to his men had made himself believe, that Death would not touch him. He had acted on his belief, in the front of the battle, yet with the valor that stops just short of foolhardiness. He felt, as he wrote to General Barlow, who was slowly recovering from dangerous wounds, in September in the heat of the Lincoln-McClellan election, 'There are better things to be done in this country than fighting, and you must save yourself for them too. . . . There are as many campaigns for a fellow as there are half years to his life.' [1]

---

[1] Two paragraphs in Colonel Lyman's letters to his wife, written some weeks apart, give a vivid picture of the 'Boy General,' who evidently had a liking for cherries:

'As we stood there under a big cherry tree, a strange figure approached; he looked like a highly independent mounted newsboy; he was attired in a flannel checked shirt, a threadbare pair of trousers, and an old blue *kepi*; from his waist hung a big cavalry sabre; his features wore a familiar sarcastic smile. It was General Barlow, commanding the first division of the Second Corps, a division that for fine fighting cannot be exceeded in the army. . . .

'The column marched so fast that I was sent forward to tell General Barlow to go more gently. I found that eccentric officer divested of his coat and seated in a cherry tree. "By Jove!" said a voice from the branches, "I knew I should not be here long before Meade's Staff would be up. How do you do, Theodore, won't you come up and take a few cherries?"'

Early in October, he wrote Josephine, Effy as he called her:
'I don't want to be shot till I've had a chance to come home.
I have no idea that I shall be hit, but I *want* so much not to now,
that sometimes it frightens me.'

On the seventeenth, he wrote her from his camp on Cedar
Creek, his last letter to her: 'Good Morning. Such a night's
sleep as I had — ten hours strong, only interrupted a few minutes
at *reveille*, waking up and reflecting cosily that it was not yet time
to turn out.' He wrote young Charles Perkins in Iowa: 'I hope,
trust, and believe you are doing all you can for Lincoln. I believe McClellan's election would send this country to where
Mexico and South America are.' He wrote to Mr. Forbes about
the death of Billy, a horse belonging to young William Forbes
that had been loaned him and killed under him in a charge a
day or two before: 'He was a dear little horse and was improving
to the last day of his life.' He wrote his mother: 'There is really
nothing to tell here. We are in a glorious country, with fine air
to breathe and fine views to enjoy; we are kept very active, and
have done a good deal of good work; I have done my share, I
think, — but there is nothing to make a letter of. I only write
this to make you write to me.' It was one of the good days, and
the eighteenth was another.

Meanwhile, Old Jubilee, encamped a few miles away to the
southeast under the shadow of Massanutten, had an idea for a
use of his depleted force that might more than fulfil the highest
hopes of Lee, his beloved leader — a surprise attack at dawn.
As he turned it over in his mind, the idea seemed better and
better. His heart and legs were not up to a mountain climb, but
he sent two of his corps commanders with spyglasses to the summit of Three Top to observe the Federal dispositions and report.
One corps of the Northern army, the Nineteenth, not held in
high esteem, was discovered to be in a key position of extreme

Barlow found plenty of campaigns to carry on after the war. As United States
Marshall at New York he captured and broke up a filibustering expedition to Cuba,
and as attorney-general of the state he initiated and carried through the first prose-
cutions of the nefarious Tweed Ring.

vulnerability, left of centre. Sheridan was known to be absent on a trip to Washington.

At two o'clock in the morning of the nineteenth, he called his generals together and ordered a concerted attack at five-thirty, before daybreak. The sun rose at six-fifteen in late October.

Providentially for the Northern army, the God, that the Colonel's twice great-grandfather told Colonel Titcomb's force, departing for the capture of Crown Point, is never neutral in battle, took a hand in affairs at Cedar Creek, got the Colonel out of bed at four-thirty and started him out on a reconnaissance in force in front of the right wing at five-fifteen. He encountered the enemy's advancing cavalry well out in no man's land, fought a sharp engagement with carbine and sabre, and set them back upon their heels. On the left flank three miles to the north the case was otherwise. The Nineteenth Corps, aroused from sleep by the shots of their pickets as they were driven in, were scarcely out of their blankets before their ears were affronted by the Rebel Yell and the company volleys of the foe. It was a foggy morning in the low land along the creek, and soon the mixture of fog and the smoke of gunpowder, what boys, fighting modern war in brigade strength in an element that in the Colonel's time was invaded only by observation balloons, call 'smog,' made a darkness lighted by the flashes of fire from the muzzles of muskets. It was a scene truly infernal. The left flank crumbled and fled, though the Sixth Corps contrived to hold briefly a series of backward positions. Stragglers so blocked the roads to Winchester that Sheridan, galloping towards the sound of firing, had to take to the fields. The Confederates, rank and file alike, collected rich booty from the Federal tents.

The Colonel's Reserve Brigade, still holding stoutly on the right, was ordered to the extreme left where the situation was now desperate. They rode for three miles along the front of the retiring battle, often under heavy fire. After the battle, General William Dwight, commanding the First Division of the Nineteenth Corps, wrote:

'They moved past me, that splendid cavalry; if they reached the Pike, I felt secure. Lowell got by me before I could speak, but I looked after him for a long distance. Exquisitely mounted, the picture of a soldier, erect, confident, defiant, he moved at the head of the finest body of cavalry that to-day scorns the earth it treads.'

Arriving at the village of Middletown, the Colonel dismounted part of his brigade, placed them with their repeating carbines behind a stone wall, and with the rest made two vicious charges that checked the advance of the lines of grey. When Sheridan cantered his foam-flecked horse in from Winchester, just before noon, he found Lowell's cavalry and part of the Sixth Corps the only troops actually engaged with the enemy. Sheridan sent an aide to ask the Colonel if he could hold the position. He sent back word that he could and would. The situation seemed in hand, though there was considerable annoyance from a Rebel battery near by and sharpshooters on the roofs of the houses in Middletown. Riding out to reconnoitre, a conspicuous and easy target, the bullet with his number at last found him, breaking his arm and striking him on the chest, without penetration but with such force as to collapse 'his poor lung' and cause faintness, bleeding, and loss of voice above a whisper.

He lay on the ground covered by his overcoat till mid-afternoon. Then Sheridan, his army re-formed and reinspired, ordered, 'Boys, turn back. I'm going to sleep in that camp to-night or in Hell.' In front of the Reserve Brigade was a destructive battery that must be captured. Against the urging, even the orders, of his division commander, the Colonel, by whispered commands to his aides, re-formed his brigade, had himself lifted into the saddle, drew his sabre, and charged, not as brigade commander in the rear of the line, but as colonel in front. Almost at once he was struck by a bullet and fell. The brigade rode on to the battery, was repulsed, but re-formed and took it on the second attempt. The Colonel was carried forward behind his charging cavalry into the village of Middletown and an old house that was serving as a hospital.

The surgeon of the Second Massachusetts Cavalry tells the story of his last hours:

'There were four or five that night in the room. Lowell lay on the table, shot through from shoulder to shoulder; the ball had cut the spinal cord on the way. Of course, below this he was completely paralyzed. Four others were lying desperately wounded on the floor. One young officer was in great pain. Lowell spent much of his ebbing strength helping him through the straits of death. "I have always been able to count on you, you were always brave. Now you must meet this as you have the other trials — be steady — I count on you." When he heard the groans of the Rebel wounded that were brought into the yard, he sent me away to look after them. As the night wore on and his strength failed, I said: "Colonel, you must write to your wife." He answered that he was not able, but I said it could be managed; so, putting a scrap of paper on a piece of board, I held his arm above him, putting a pencil between his fingers, and holding the hand against the paper, told him I thought he would find that he could use his fingers. And thus he wrote a word or two of farewell to her.'

He was twenty-nine years old when he died. He had done for a year the full work of a brigadier general. His commission to that rank was signed by Abraham Lincoln in Washington as he was making his last charge at Cedar Creek. When a day or two later, an aide arrived with this, and another for his immediate superior, General Merritt, as a major general, Merritt said, 'I would gladly give up this if he could only take that.' [1]

When Sheridan arrived on the scene of battle from Winchester, twenty miles away, the officer he first encountered was Captain William McKinley, of Ohio, worried but going strong. A few minutes later, he saw Colonel Rutherford B. Hayes of

[1] Just a month before at Winchester, Colonel George S. Patton, of the Twenty-Second Virginia, in command of a brigade, was promoted brigadier on the field of battle, only to receive a mortal wound before the day was done. His grandson, in command of a mechanized army drawn from every state of a reunited nation, was to leave a name more enduring than bronze in the annals of war.

the same state, bruised from a fall when his horse had been shot under him, but carrying on. Later in the day he met, embraced, and, so it is said, kissed Custer of the flaxen ringlets, picturesquely arrayed in hussar jacket and tight black velvet trousers, whose brigade of cavalry was making a good fight of it. Our *beau sabreur*, to whom he sent his first inquiry, he never saw alive. After the war he wrote to Josephine, sending her the originals of her husband's dispatches, whom he 'loved and appreciated,' and said, 'Had General Lowell lived, it is my firm belief that he would have commanded all my cavalry and would have done better with it than I could have done.'

One wonders if the course of our history might not have been different if on that fatal afternoon a half-ounce of lead had flown only an inch or two to the right or left.

John Buchan once delivered at the University of Cambridge a highly suggestive lecture on *The Causal and the Casual in History*. In the spirit of whimsey rather than of historical research, of Pascal's query what would have happened to the world if Cleopatra's nose had been a little shorter, he proposed a parlor game for historians, to work out how things would have been different if some small accident had been otherwise. He illustrates the object of the game by the death in 1920 from the bite of a pet monkey of young King Alexander of Greece, the protégé of the allies, of which Winston Churchill said, 'A quarter of a million persons died of that monkey's bite.' His most engaging speculation is what might have been the course of English history if Henry, the Prince of Wales, eldest son of James the First, had not at the age of eighteen on a visit to Sir Walter Raleigh, a prisoner in the Bloody Tower, to talk politics and admire the model ship, *The Prince*, that Raleigh had made for him, by chance breathed in the germ of the mysterious and malignant fever that caused his death.

He bore, the lecturer pointed out, no slightest resemblance to his brother, Charles, who became King and Royal Martyr. Inspired by Raleigh, he was a *revenant* from the Elizabethan

Age. He was an enthusiastic Protestant, to whom Protestantism was patriotism after the stalwart fashion of Old Noll himself thirty years later. When his father urged him to a French marriage, he replied, 'I am resolved two religions shall not lie in my bed.'

Had he lived, what might not have happened? Raleigh, a judge of men who had known some of the greatest of a great age, thought he possessed the brains and character of a military and political leader. He had personal magnetism, and what we now call social consciousness. He would have been, Buchan, a biographer of monarchs, felt sure, 'a people's king.' The change from the Tudor to the modern monarchy would have been of a very different kind. There would have been no civil war. Cromwell might have died the first general in Europe and Duke of Huntingdon, and Britain might have been guided into new constitutional paths by a great Scotsman, James Graham, first Duke of Montrose, who sometime about the year 1645, effected the Union of the Scottish and English Parliaments.

Well, just supposing the eye or trigger-finger of some unknown Southern soldier had been a little off on the afternoon of October 19, 1864. Brigadier General Charles Russell Lowell, soon to be promoted to Major General, and in command of all Sheridan's cavalry and doing better with it, would have come out of the war a popular hero. With his high social aims he would assuredly have applied himself to those better things than fighting of which he wrote Barlow. With his administrative ability he would have done them brilliantly well. With his personal magnetism and gift of leadership, what could have kept him from leadership? Ben Butler's drooping eye might never have looked out over the governor's desk beneath the Golden Dome at the top of Park Street. He had not the advantage of birth in Ohio, but he was born of the best stock in Massachusetts. There were no grocery kings or coal barons to be his political backers, but some of the solidest and ablest financial interests in Boston and New York would have been behind him. It is not impossible

that either Major McKinley or Colonel Hayes might never
have been a tenant of the White House and that Massachusetts
would have had a president midway between John Quincy
Adams and Calvin Coolidge.

What a Beau Sabreur of moral as well as physical courage
and prompt decision, inspired by the teachings of Emerson, and
practised in handling men individually and in the mass could
have made of the job! How different might have been the
course of history. Such speculation, as Buchan says, upsets any
mortal scheme of effects and causes. The President of the Im-
mortals has not chosen to take us into his confidence.

Five years after the war, Josephine Lowell visited England
recommended by Emerson to his friend, Thomas Carlyle. In
the course of their conversations, Carlyle gave vent to some of his
views about the War Between the States, against which he had
scolded and still grumbled. The 'Nigger Agony' he had called
it. Later she sent him a set of the *Harvard Memorial Biographies*,
with certain lives marked for him to read. He read the whole
and wrote her in words that serve well as a last valediction to the
Colonel and his unreturning comrades in arms:

'It would need a heart much harder than mine not to recognize
the high and noble spirit that dwelt in those young men, their
heroic readiness, complete devotedness, their patience, diligence,
shining valor and virtue in the cause they saw to be the highest,
while alas! any difference I may feel on that latter point, only
deepens to me the sorrowful and noble tragedy each of their
lives is. You may believe me, Madam, I would strew flowers on
their graves along with you, and piously bid them rest in Hope!
It is not doubtful to me that they also have added their mite to
what is the eternal cause of God and man; or that, in circuitous
but sure ways, all men, Black and White, will infallibly get their
profit of the same.'

BOOK VI

Victorian New England

1
CHAPTER

After the War

While the colonel in the saddle was fighting it out at the head of his brigade armed with carbine and sabre, the Professor in his easy-chair was doing his bit with the pen. In January, 1861, his father had died and he moved back from Kirkland Street to Elmwood. 'I am back,' he wrote, 'in the place I love best. I am sitting in my old garret, at my old desk, smoking my old pipe, and loving my old friends.' It was there, perhaps, with the wraith of Maria in her old chair, that Lowell the Poet had his second flowering.

In May he resigned the Trident of the *Atlantic* to Fields, who, as he forecast correctly, was to be a 'dining editor,' but he continued to print in its pages the poems that form the Second Series of the *Biglow Papers*.

In his 'L'Envoi: to the Muse,' written two years before, that somewhat preachy Lady had admonished him:

> 'The epic of a man rehearse,
> Be something better than thy verse.'

In losing himself in the mood of the war effort, he was, poetically, to find himself again. In the spring of 1863, the dark middle of the war, long-legged, mountain-climbing, free-thinking Leslie Stephen came over from the English Cambridge to see what the shooting was about, and visited Lowell at Elmwood:

'He showed me the photograph of a young man in the uniform of the United States Army, and asked me whether I thought that the lad looked like a "blackguard." On my giving the obvious reply, he told me that the portrait represented one of the nephews whom he had lost in the war. Not long afterwards I read his verses in the Second Series of *Biglow Papers*, the most pathetic, I think, that he ever wrote, in which he speaks of the "three likely lads,"

> "Whose comin' step ther' 's ears thet won't,
> No, not lifelong, leave off awaitin'." '

The Mexican War, subject of the First Series, involved no such great moral issue as slavery, and it started, not with a definite aggression by the enemy to heat the blood as at Fort Sumter. It was these factors and the experience of personal loss that gave the Second Series its superiority, and produced such stanzas as that on the death of the Colonel at Cedar Creek, where deep emotion floods and submerges all the tricky Yankee idioms save a few phonetic eccentricities like 'Wut' for 'what' or 'techstone' for 'touchstone.' Let us listen to it entirely without them:

> 'What's words to them whose faith and truth
> On War's red touchstone rang true metal,
> Who ventured life and love and youth
> For the great prize of death in battle?
> To him who, deadly hurt, again
> Flashed on before the charge's thunder,
> Tipping with fire the bolt of men
> That rived the Rebel line asunder?'

Even Parson Wilbur ceases to be a pedantic old figure of fun, and becomes a tenderly drawn distant portrait of the poet's father, and his own mouthpiece. It was the Civil War *Biglow* that led Emerson to write in his *Journal* in 1862, 'what a certificate of good elements in the soil, climate, and institutions, is Lowell whose admirable verses I have just read.'

At the end of 1863, Lowell accepted the editorship of the *North American Review*, with the proviso that Charles Eliot Norton should be the associate editor, and assume the not very laborious work of securing contributions for a quarterly magazine, and seeing it through the press. He himself became the chief contributor, writing, in addition to numerous extended book reviews, a leading political article in every issue for 1864, and in every other one for '65 and '66. The four for the first year all dealt with the coming election. Confessing disarmingly his early doubts of Lincoln's abilities and character, he goes all out for him with understanding and eloquence. 'His perilous task has been to carry a rather shaky raft through the rapids, making fast the unrulier logs as he could snatch opportunity. He did not think it his duty to run straight at all hazards, but cautiously to assure himself with the setting pole where the main current was, and keep steadily to that. He is still in wild water, but we have faith that his skill and sureness of eye will bring him out right at last.' In short, the 'brave foreseeing man, sagacious, patient,' of the 'Commemoration Ode.'

At the end of May, '65, a month after Lee's surrender at Appomattox, the President and Fellows of Harvard College, still dominated by John Amory Lowell, appointed July 21 a day of commemoration of the boys who had given their lives for the Union cause. The Professor of Rhetoric, Francis J. Child, was appointed to arrange the program. He asked his friend, the Professor of Belles Lettres, to prepare an ode for the occasion. Lowell accepted without misgiving, but for seven weeks found Minerva stubbornly *invita*. He struggled over the problem of form, trying first the mingled blank verse and rhyme of the choruses in Milton's 'Samson Agonistes,' but without satisfaction. In the end he turned to the loose-rhymed structure of his old master, Cowley: 'My ear was better pleased with the rhyme, that, coming at a longer interval as a far-off echo rather than an instant reverberation, produced the same effect almost, and yet was grateful by unexpectedly recalling an association and faint reminiscence of consonance.'

Despite his laborious experiments, the nineteenth of July, with the great occasion only two days off, found him with nothing but a few trial stanzas written out. He told Child it was impossible. On the evening of the twentieth he said to his wife, 'I must write this poem tonight. Go to bed and do not let me feel I am keeping you up, and I shall be more at ease.' [1]

He began it at ten o'clock. At four in the morning he came to her and said, 'It is done. I am going to sleep now.' He had written five hundred and twenty-three lines in six hours, a line and a half every sixty seconds.

After a brief rest he rose early and sought out Child, who took the manuscript 'and went a little apart with it under an elm tree in the Yard.' After reading a passage here and there, Child handed it back, saying, in reply to Lowell's question, 'Will it do?' 'Do? I should think so! Don't you be scared.' Later in the morning, the poet recited it to John Holmes and William Story, both of whom, he says, 'shed tears' and told him it was 'noble.' But the author of *The Fable for Critics* was still scared.

The day was fair but excessively warm. As the great hour approached, a long procession headed by our old friend, Colonel Henry Lee, closely followed by the President, the Governor, and the Senior Fellows, John Amory Lowell's spare form and bristly white beard visible among them, emerged from Gore Hall. It proceeded at a funeral pace not to overexert the many wounded youths in its ranks. Twice it circled the Yard as alumni and students fell in behind. By-passing the new Appleton Chapel,

---

[1] There is some conflict of evidence as to whether this was the actual night before or two nights before. The eleventh-hour aspect of the composition is not affected.

it poured slowly out through the gate and across to the old First Church, where all stood waiting while Bartlett, '62, a major general at twenty-five who had left an arm and a leg on a Southern battlefield, hobbled down the aisle. Charles G. Loring of the Corporation presided. After a matchless prayer of resignation and triumph by young Phillips Brooks of the class of '55, a hymn was sung, written by the Reverend Robert Traill Spence Lowell, 'Thy work, O God, goes on in Earth.' Then came an address by the Reverend George Putnam, John Amory Lowell's fellow Senior Fellow, and pastor in Roxbury, and the company with their ladies, thirteen hundred strong all told, adjourned for lunch to a pavilion that had been erected back of Harvard Hall. After this fortification there were addresses by Mr. Loring and General Meade, who had been hooded as Doctor of Laws two days before in a neat bit of Latinity: '*Qui periculosissima belli discrimine res publicae virtute et consilio restituit.*' Then there were shorter speeches by Governor Andrew, General Barlow, General Devens, Emerson, Admiral Davis, General Force, a poem by Oliver Wendell Holmes, and one by Mrs. Julia Ward Howe read by Mr. Eliot. At long last, after a salutation by a Doctor Thompson from their sister college in New Haven, the plump and bearded figure of Professor Lowell rose on the platform before the warm and weary audience to recite his ode. It was well keyed to the occasion, but not matchless like the prayer of Phillips Brooks in the forenoon. The odist was 'shaken' as he read it, but not many of the audience shared his emotion. Next morning the *Daily Advertiser* referred to it as a 'graceful poem which was received with the most decided demonstrations of satisfaction.' The long day was over and the commemoration came to an end with toasts and a search for speakers who had already gone home.

A day or two later, Lowell wrote to Miss Grace Norton with a rare flash of sound self-criticism: 'Like a boy I mistook my excitement for inspiration, and here I am in the mud. . . . I did not make the hit I expected, and am ashamed at having been tempted again to think I could write *poetry*, a delusion from which I have been tolerably free these dozen years.'

On the rebound, however, inspiration at last came to him, and he wrote and inserted in the poem before it was printed the sixty-six lines of the strophe in which all the thinking and feeling he had done about Lincoln the year before found voice in truly noble verse. If it were not for Whitman's throbbing valediction, 'O Captain, My Captain,' it would be indeed matchless. More than any other piece of contemporary writing it outlined the portrait of our greatest President, one of Plutarch's men, that has gone into history. The occasion had been seized, but retroactively.

Save in the deeply felt poem on the death of Agassiz, written in 1874 while he was abroad and after a long fallow period, Lowell the Poet was never again to reach this height.

In 1869, on reading Lowell's *Under the Willows and Other Poems*, Emerson wrote in his *Journal*:

'In poetry, tone. I have been reading some of Lowell's new poems, in which he shows unexpected advance on himself, but perhaps most in technical skill and courage. It is in talent rather than in poetic tone, and rather expresses his wish, his ambition, than the uncontrollable interior impulse which is the authentic mark of a new poem, and which is unanalysable, and makes the merit of an ode of Collins, or Gray, or Wordsworth, or Herbert, or Byron — and which is felt in the pervading tone, rather than in brilliant parts or lines; as if the sound of a bell, or a certain cadence expressed in a low whistle or booming, or humming, to which the poet first timed his step, as he looked at the sunset, or thought, was the incipient form of the piece, and was regnant through the whole.'

This is good criticism and sound aesthetics, but one wonders if in Emerson's subconscious mind there was not some faint irritated echo of the passage about his own poetry in the *Fable for Critics* eleven years before:

'In the worst of his poems are mines of rich matter,
But thrown in a heap with a crash and a clatter;
Now it is not one thing nor another alone
Makes a poem, but rather the general tone,

The something pervading, uniting the whole,
The before unconceived, unconceivable soul.'

Both critics were right. But as a master of 'pervading tone' the palm must go to the Concord, not to the Cambridge, poet. And in the worst of Lowell's, the thirty pages of 'The Unhappy Lot of Mr. Knott' for example, the mines of rich matter are missing.

As New England passed from its Periclean to its mid-Victorian phase, Lowell, until he emerged, through the *revanche* of letters, a late-Victorian diplomatist, was pretty exclusively the Professor. What he was like in that capacity is best described in the *Education of Henry Adams* in the chapter on Cambridge, 'a social desert that would have starved a polar bear,' but which Lowell held to be, 'taken altogether, the most inwardly civilized, most intimately humane among the haunts of men.'

Lowell, Adams says, brought back from Germany the only new and valuable part of its universities, its habit of allowing students to read with him privately in his study. There at Elmwood he convened his Dante classes, and the brighter boys of a score of classes read with him and listened to his wide-ranging talk and 'got good-humoured encouragement to do what amused them' — an early and competent application of the tutorial system.

It was the decade from 1867 to 1876 that saw the appearance of the long, learned, rambling, savory review articles that he brought together in *My Study Windows*, and the two series of *Among My Books*. Immensely admired in their day, they are not volumes to which the modern reader is irresistibly drawn to return. Their structure is shaky and their texture is loose. He seldom made the hard intellectual effort involved in critical comparison and analysis. The substance of the essays was pieced together from old lectures, and happy flashes of insight remembered from letters to sympathetic correspondents. Like the 'Ode,' they were written out at a great speed with the printer's devil at his elbow, and hurriedly, if at all, revised. Too often the style is marked, as he himself might have said, rather by logodaedaly than by verbal magic. Jack Chapman, puckish iconoclast, hit the nail on the head, though with unnecessary violence, when he wrote to his wife:

'In later life he got all barnacled with quotations and leisure. He pulls out pocketbooks and gold snuffboxes and carbuncled cigarette-cases, and emerald eye-glasses, and curls and pomatums himself and looks in pocket looking-glasses, and smooths his Vandyke beard and is a literary fop — f-o-p, fop. His prefaces — sometimes very nice, in spirit — but his later prefaces are so expressive — O my! so expressive of hems and haws and creased literary trousers.'

Yet at their best Lowell somehow gets into his bookish essays the quality of witty and learned extemporization that distinguished his talk and his correspondence. They seem, as he finely says of Dryden's prose, 'struck off at a heat, as by a superior man in the best mood of his talk.'

In the Lowell family it happened, as it does not infrequently in large superior families, that for two generations the fiery, public, outstanding men, the divines, poets, and soldiers, were in a single branch. It was the fruit of the loins of the amiable Charles that made literary and military history and was in the news. But the senior, the solid administrative branch, was not idle. After the strenuous two years of the great panic, John Amory Lowell in his sixties was taking it a little easier. He left more responsibility to his son, Augustus, and from the spring of 1860 to the autumn of 1862 was abroad with his family. After his return, just after Antietam, he found plenty to occupy him; particularly after 1864 when Augustus was abroad for two and a half years. Throughout the war years the business of securing raw material for cotton mills became more and more difficult, banks had to buy more government bonds than was always convenient, and the labor problem, both in respect to mill hands and white-collar workers, was becoming acute. Despite all this, his intellectual pursuits, remarkable for a financial tycoon, but not unique among Boston Brahmins, were not interrupted. His minister at King's Chapel, the Reverend H. W. Foote, says, 'it was his custom to rise long before the winter's dawn, and lighting his fire and lamp to secure uninterrupted quiet for the studies which task a robust mind.' Those studies included the higher mathematics, science, and later in the day history and literature, Latin, French, and contemporary English. It was thus that he acquired the knowledge to select wisely lecturers for the Lowell Institute and to meet them on grounds of a common understanding.

In 1860 he had entered the bloody arena of debate over the new doctrine of Evolution in a thoughtful and careful review in the *Christian Examiner* of Darwin's *Origin of Species*. His position was delicate. As early as '36, Emerson had written, addressing the caterpillar, 'How dost thou, brother: Please God, you shall yet be a philosopher.' The next year in the Jardin des Plantes in Paris he had 'a strange feeling of relationship' when he saw all forms of animal life graded from lowest to highest. The reviewer's friends and chosen lecturers, Asa Gray and Jeffries Wyman, were already evolutionists in 1859 when Darwin's book was published, and were immediately converted to natural selection. On the other hand, his personal importation and protégé, the great Agassiz, stood steadfastly for his master Cuvier's permanence of type. Throughout the review one feels the support, perhaps the advice, of Agassiz. It was the danger Darwin's doctrine threatened to revealed religion and the morals of Harvard College that chiefly disturbed the reviewer. He was a Rebel to evolution as his father was to revolution.

'Without intending to charge him,' he says of Darwin, 'with approaching the subject with any sceptical intention, we cannot but view his book as an arsenal in which the advocates of Pantheism will find their surest and deadliest weapons.' [1]

---

[1] It was just at the time J. A. L. was refuting Darwinism that the great Boston publishing house of Ticknor and Fields declined the opportunity to publish the

It may have been his views that inspired the President and Fellows two years later to admonish John Fiske, an avowed evolutionist, for reading Comte during divine service at Christ Church, and deprive him at his graduation of the tutorship in history to which his brilliant gifts seemed to entitle him. It was however, a new president, largely of Mr. Lowell's own making, that seven years later appointed John Fiske a university lecturer for advanced students and the public on Positivist Philosophy. *E pur si muove!*

In 1868, the Reverend Thomas Hill, who had guided the college not very brilliantly through six troublesome years, worn out by dissensions and bereavement, resigned in the expectation that he would be granted a year's leave of absence for rest and travel abroad. To his painful surprise, his resignation was promptly accepted by the corporation and the selection of a successor became the Fellows' chief business. For a decade John Amory Lowell had been keeping an eye on young Charles Eliot of the class of '53, grandson of his father's old friend and admirer, Samuel Eliot, who had founded the Greek professorship. This scion of the best Brahmin stock had not been popular as assistant professor of chemistry, but had been useful to the President and Fellows as one to whom could be confidently entrusted all sorts of minor administrative jobs. In '63 he was a candidate for the Rumford Professorship of Chemistry, but lost it to Wolcott Gibbs from New York, perhaps because his own friendly observer was in Europe and absent from the three meetings of the corporation at which the appointment was discussed. In 1865, when Eliot himself was spending two years abroad studying the educational systems of France and Germany, Mr. Lowell secured for him the offer of the position of superintendent of the Merrimack cotton mill. Young Eliot, however,

English *Scientific Series*, which included the works of Darwin, Buckle, Lecky, Huxley, and Tyndall. It was published in New York by Appleton, the first step, perhaps, in the transfer of intellectual leadership from the banks of the Charles to those of the Hudson.

was by that time too fully absorbed in education to think of going into a business, however profitable. He accepted instead the chair of Chemistry in the Massachusetts Institute of Technology, of which, significantly, the vice president was none other than John Amory Lowell. In 1868, he was elected an Overseer of Harvard, and two months later President Hill resigned. To Mr. Lowell it seemed a clear case of manifest destiny according to plan. He had no difficulty in convincing his associates of the Corporation that Eliot was the man of the hour, but the Overseers proved suspicious, vigilant, and recalcitrant. The classicists objected to him as a prejudiced scientist, and the scientists opposed him on the ground that he was an educational theorist. A group of the overseers started a boom for Charles Francis Adams, just back from his mission to England, but received no encouragement from that gentleman. The battle waxed hot, and John Amory Lowell was in the front of the fray very much as the Colonel had been in a grimmer warfare. When he reported to his candidate the objections that had been raised, Eliot with Olympian humor remarked, 'So far as I have heard the objections to me, I quite agree with them.'

In May the Overseers finally came round and the last and best of the six presidents whose election John Amory Lowell had controlled was inaugurated in October, 1869. He must have been a happy man as he heard that quiet but resonant voice proclaiming in precise and polished sentences his ideal of education:

'The worthy fruit of academic culture is an open mind, trained in careful thinking, instructed in the methods of philosophical investigation, acquainted in a general way with the accumulated thought of past generations, and penetrated with humility.' [1]

In the same year he moved his habitation in town. For forty

[1] There is a tradition that as far back as '63 Lowell had said to Eliot after the loss of the Rumford Professorship, 'Never mind, you will be President of Harvard someday.' Eliot's biographer, Henry James (3d), thinks this doesn't sound quite natural coming from a Fellow and a keeper of counsel like J. A. L. Whether he said it or not, he undoubtedly thought it, and did more than any other man to bring it about.

years he had lived at Number 7 Pemberton Square, three minutes' walk from his office on State Street, with a succession of summer residences at Nahant, Beverly, and Lynn Terrace. Now he bought and moved into Number 7 Park Street, next door to the Union Club at Number 8, where his brother-in-law, Abbott Lawrence, had lived for many years. Boston was edging out to the west. The Mill Dam to Brookline, along the route of the present Embankment, had been built some years before, and the Back Bay was now being bought by the bucket and sold by the yard. The Common had lost its tidal beach twenty years earlier to the Public Garden, and good houses faced it on both Beacon and Tremont Streets as far west as Arlington. But Park Street was still the umbilicus of the Brahmin world. It was, as Henry James remembered in his nostalgic *American Scene*, most melancholy, most musical of all his books, 'magnificently *honnête*.' It was 'founded on all the moral, material, social solidities instead of on some of them only — which made all the difference.' The solidities were enhanced by the residence there of the Lowells for more than a dozen years.

Nor was this calm acclivity without its amenities. Behind it, bounded in addition by Park Street Church, Tremont Street with its tide of carts, carriages, and herdics, the classic-porticoed Tremont House, and the dignified back of the Athenaeum, lay a quiet island of green and slate and granite, the old Granary Burying Ground. The abutting owners on Park Street all had keys to it. In the early morning the dogs were put out; later in the day the children, of whom there were many, played there; and on warm spring evenings, when it was too early in the season to move to Nahant, there were suppers *al fresco*. Strawberries and champagne were served, as one old resident remembered, on the convenient flat tops of the mossy marbles.[1]

[1] Doctor J. Collins Warren, 'Reminiscences of Park Street,' in *Old Park Street and Its Vicinity*, by Robert Means Lawrence. See also for a delightful and very intimate picture of the life of the Lowells at this period the three volumes, *Arthur Theodore Lyman and Ella Lyman: Letters and Journals, with an Account of those they Loved and were Descended from.* Prepared by their daughter Ella Lyman Cabot. Privately printed, 1932.

It was in these surroundings that John Amory Lowell spent a serene, bookish, and hospitable old age. His granddaughter, Ella Lowell Lyman, recalls his ample and well-furnished library:

'There was a library stepladder in the Park Street house, and whenever I had a chance alone, I would mount to the heights of the great mahogany bookcases (which my three brothers now have) and look inside the beautifully bound books. But many of them were in Latin and many more were French, which was discouraging to a child. There were French histories in eighteen volumes and a French Biographical Dictionary in fifty volumes. I liked far better the botany books, for they held gorgeous pictures of orchids and marvellous camellias.'

His men's dinners were large and notable. For the evening of November 11, 1872, he had invited the membership of the Massachusetts Historical Society to meet Mr. James Anthony Froude, who was in this country delivering very anti-Erin lectures on the English in Ireland. On the ninth, the great Boston fire, which destroyed seventy-five millions of property, broke out, and on the evening of the dinner it was still burning, though under control, only a block and a half away. Mr. Lowell was urged to call the party off, but he refused and carried it through with *éclat*. In a letter to his wife, Froude tells of the first night of the fire that he saw in the company of his host, George Peabody:

'We made our way into the principal street through the crowd, and then, looking down a cross street full of enormous warehouses, saw both sides of it in flames. The streets were full of steam fire-engines, all roaring and playing, but the houses were so high and large, and the volumes of fire so prodigious, that their water-jets looked like so many squirts. As we stood, we saw the fire grow. Block caught after block. I myself saw one magnificent store catch at the lower windows. In a few seconds the flame ran up storey after storey, spouting out at the different landings as it rose. It reached the roof with a spring, and the place was gone.'

His comment on the men he met in Boston is, like his later dealings with the lives of Thomas and Jane Carlyle, only half-truth, but with a core of insight:

'Their physical frames seem hung together rather than organically grown. . . . They are generous with their money, have much tenderness and quiet good feeling; but the Anglo-Saxon power is running to seed, and I don't think will revive. Puritanism is dead, and the collective sternness of temperament which belonged to it is dead also.' [1]

In 1877, the year in which his grandsons, John, son of Judge John and Lawrence, son of Augustus, graduated from Harvard, John Amory resigned from the Corporation after forty years of incomparable service. He continued to be the sole trustee of the Lowell Institute with no diminution of interest and activity, but taking his son, Augustus, whom he had named to succeed him, more and more into his counsels.

His life, as the years slipped by, became more and more centred and absorbed in his family. From the time of the birth of his first grandchild, he had at the birth of each established a trust in the Massachusetts Hospital Life Insurance Company that gave each on his or her twenty-first birthday a cash payment of ten thousand dollars, that they might 'never suffer want.' He took a minute interest in their growth and education, and the Park Street house echoed with the voices of growing boys and girls.

In 1881, in his eighty-third year, he became bedridden, and a Miss Williams, a 'cousin' through the Pickerings, was called in to be his practical nurse. Some of his conversations with her as reported by his granddaughter have a touch of that roguishness that his Aunt Nancy had noted fourscore years before:

Once, when she sneezed, he smiled and remarked: 'The regular Pickering sneeze.'

When she inquired, 'What Pickerings sneezed?' He replied, 'Every one of them from beginning to end.'

[1] Of Froude's own physical appearance Norton wrote to J. R. Lowell who was in Spain, 'His face exhibits the corporeal insincerity of his disposition.'

Again, when someone had spoken very highly of the Pickerings, she said: 'Why do they talk all the time about the Pickerings? Why do they not speak of the Lowells?'

'The Lowells can speak for themselves,' he answered.

Another time, very near the end, he said to his daughter, 'I am a poor miserable wretch.' 'We think you are the dearest treasure,' she said. Opening wide his china-blue eyes he answered, 'I take a queer way of showing it.'

He died November 13, 1881.

No Bostonian of his generation was the subject of more sincere and sorrowful obituaries and memoirs. In one of them is a sentence that cannot be bettered as a summary of his character:

'He seemed always to have a firm confidence in his own judgment, and that confidence seems not to have been misplaced.'

During the last twenty years of his life, John Amory Lowell saw his two sons, John and Augustus, whom as young men we have already met, rise to positions of responsibility and public esteem not incomparable with his own.

At first, after leaving the Loring office in 1845, John Lowell's practice was chiefly in the law of trust estates. Many of his cases were within the degrees of consanguinity which are prohibited in matrimonial but not in legal affairs. The panic of '57 led him perforce into the laws of bankruptcy, and by 1865, when he went on the federal bench, he was a recognized specialist in that rather dismal field.

As district judge he dealt largely, as his great-grandfather, the Old Judge, had before him, with maritime disputes, many of them prize cases arising out of the recent war. In his decisions 'you can,' as a seagoing legal admirer said, 'almost smell the tar and hear the wind whistling in the rigging.' After his promotion to the Circuit Court, the causes that came before him were for the most part highly technical matters of the law of patents. He published two volumes of *Decisions*. Young Oliver Wendell Holmes, just out of the Law School, in reviewing the first volume, criticised the Judge because he seemed always to try to find out first what was right between man and man, and then 'with almost superhuman ingenuity twist the decisions to fit his own ideas of justice.' When the second volume was issued some years later Mr. Holmes, whose legal views had enlarged in the meantime, found it 'refreshing to read decisions based on fundamental principles of law and justice, rather than decided upon the distinctions and differentiations of the numerous legal decisions.' The Judge himself was fond of saying that the best kind of law was that of the Cadi who decided each case in accordance with his own conviction of its inherent justice. He retired from the bench in 1884, and although he continued to give legal advice to important cases his life until his death in 1897 closely resembled that of his father and grandfather, given over to his garden, good works, and fireside satisfactions.

In 1853, he had married Lucy Buckminster Emerson, and in '58, the panic notwithstanding, or perhaps aiding, bought a large estate at Chestnut Hill, complete like Bromley Vale with woods, wild flowers, and a pond. Something of his life there is revealed in reminiscences by his nephew, Lawrence, written for the Saturday Club:

'He looked older than he was; and brought up by my father, his younger brother, with great admiration for my uncle, I cannot remember when I did not regard him as venerable. This was in fact a common sentiment. On one occasion when one of his children was ill during his absence from home, my father was at his house at Chestnut Hill early in the morning. Thinking the time short for taking the usual train at the station nearby he was in a hurry to go, but was told by the family that they never started until they heard the whistle of the approaching engine. On the way my father exclaimed that the train was starting, and ran to the station to find the train gone. Speaking to the station master about what he had been told he got the reply that the Judge was away; when at home they held the train for him. Meanwhile the people at Brookline had been complaining that the train was habitually a couple of minutes late; and the Judge every day walked calmly to the station quite unconscious that a train full of passengers was kept waiting for him. He would certainly have been shocked had he known it, and probably have wondered why he was the object of such consideration, for he did not treat himself as a public character. . . . He was gentle, peaceable and kindly toward others. Inside the low stone wall by the street that bordered his place there grew a row of lilacs, and one Decoration Day the flowering branches were ruthlessly torn away by passers-by. Instead of being exasperated, or trying to discover the offenders, he ordered sprays of the flowers to be cut the next year and laid upon the wall that people might take them as they walked.'

He was short and slightly stooped, with a graceful beard, black in the fifties, white in the eighties. His quaint and ready wit was appreciated in the courtroom as well as at the Saturday Club. No specimens of it have been preserved, but as Homer conveyed the beauty of Helen, whose face launched a thousand ships, not by description, but by a statement of the obstacles it overcame, we may gather the quality of Judge Lowell's wit from a note made by Henry Cabot Lodge after a dinner given for Edward Freeman, the English historian, who 'seemed to understand what was being said when he spoke and yet appeared utterly heavy and indifferent most of the time, not infrequently yawning. Seemed almost impossible that he should be a man of great historical reputation who had written some really good books. No snap, no quickness, no vivacity, no sympathy. Judge Lowell's dry and pleasant humor seemed to escape Mr. Freeman unless it was repeated.'

The panic of '57 marked a turning-point in the life of his half-brother, Augustus, too. In that year he retired from his association with Bullard and Lee to assist his father in carrying his banks and cotton mills through the big blow, and the strenuous war years that followed. In three decades thereafter he was president or treasurer of ten cotton companies, and director of as many more and of several banks. With him the family pocket-book reached its most distended proportions. In the years after the war the difficulty of labor management reached its limit, and the paternalistic attitude of the owners was worn away in a vicious circle of misunderstandings. Although a philanthropist in motive and practice, Augustus was a martinet in mill manage-ment. His son, Percival, records that his father was not wholly displeased when, passing through the North Station *en route* to the scene of action on the Merrimack, he overheard one of his em-ployees say to another, 'Sure, that Augustus Lowell is a hard man, but he's honest, he's honest!'

The age spirit, however, was at work in those miles of mills. In 1870, Wendell Phillips, 'Knight Errant of the Unfriended Truth,' was the leader of the labor reform party, which held that labor was the creator of wealth and entitled to all it created. That Marxian idea, however, was not popular with mill-owners and their agents. From 1876 to 1883, young William Lawrence had a cure of souls in the city that bears his family name. Through-out the seven years he tried hard to persuade the agent there to take the lead in stopping child labor completely, paying a weekly instead of a monthly wage, and in other humanitarian matters which that practical philosopher, Francis Cabot Lowell the first, had he been alive, would have thought good business. The progress made by the future bishop was inconspicuous, but before the end of the nineteenth century, after more than eighteen hundred major strikes, the principle of collective bargaining was established and the industrial air was clearing in Massachusetts, though the Commonwealth's primacy in the manufacturing world it was becoming more difficult to maintain.

When Augustus and his family returned from Europe in 1866, it was discovered that the line of the Old Colony Railroad was about to pierce the heart of Bromley Vale. It was, therefore, sold for development, except for the small house where the Rebel's two daughters, Anna and Amory, lived, and an estate, once that of Stephen Higginson, was bought on Heath Street in Brookline. The old colonial house had recently been pulled down and replaced by a large brownstone edifice, set amid well-planned terraces and luxuriant gardens. Augustus later christened the place Sevenels, from the mystic number of L's inhabiting it. There, with a succession of town houses for the winter, first on the Hill in Mount Vernon Street, then on the line of the Mill Dam at 99 Beacon Street, and finally on the new made land at 171 Commonwealth Avenue, he passed the rest of his life. How he spent his days when at home is told by his youngest daughter:

'He covered it with beautiful and exotic flowering shrubs brought from all parts of the world, and many rare and lovely flowers. The planning of the garden was entirely done by himself. He never allowed any one else to make any arrangements, or decide upon any matter of change or addition. Some idea of his fondness for flowers may be given when I say that he got up at six o'clock every morning and cut his favorites, the roses, with his own hands. I well remember one occasion when he cut a thousand roses in three days.'

Augustus Lowell, honest hard man and rose-lover, felt about Darwin as his father did, and as his grandfather had about Napoleon and Thomas Jefferson. He was a reader, but would not allow a volume of Shelley, the 'atheist,' in the house. It was not until his daughter, Amy, the Postscript and Poet, took over the premises in the new world of the twentieth century that Sevenels became one of the publicized and famous Lowell residences like Elmwood and Bromley Vale.

2

CHAPTER

Noblesse Oblige

Boston,' wrote E. L. Godkin in 1871, Irish-born editor of the militant *Nation*, 'is the one place in America where wealth and the knowledge of how to use it are apt to coincide.' The time has come when we must look a little more closely into the contents of the Lowell pocketbook and how it was spent.

After 1837, the Russell-Lowell line, though sometimes in easy circumstances, was never affluent. In the Higginson line the Rebel was more than comfortably well off. His son, John Amory Lowell, was definitely 'rich' for his time, and Augustus increased his inherited share of John Amory's fortune six or seven fold. In the Cabot line, Francis Cabot Lowell, though he died young, was longer engaged in commerce, industry, and real-estate operations than his brother, John, had been, and was still more comfortably off. Francis Cabot Lowell II, Emerson's friend, the only son to survive to old age, did nearly as well for his family pocketbook as Augustus had for his. In the two senior lines, between 1870 and the end of the century, the individual inheritance was usually either well up in six figures, or over the line in seven. The Lowell fathers that had the largest families seemed, providentially, to have the largest fortunes, and the unmarried daughters were well advised by their brothers, cousins, and men of business. The popular impression, that the words 'Lowell' and 'millionaire' were synonymous, was not wide of the mark.

How they spent it in the earlier generations that included John Lowell, the Rebel, Francis Cabot Lowell the first, his sons, John Lowell, the founder of the Institute, Francis Cabot Lowell II, and John Amory Lowell, we have already seen. With the single exception of the royal progress of John Lowell, so-called Junior, from Boston to Bombay, it went into dignified ease, comfortable family travel, gilt-edged bonds and shares, and good works. Harvard College, the Lowell Institute, the Massachusetts General Hospital, and the Athenaeum are still enjoying the usufruct of Lowell money; the Massachusetts Institute of Technology owes much to both the money and the management of Augustus Lowell. But beginning with the generation that came of age after the war, we meet a race of young men that did not find it either necessary or desirable to go into a business or profession for the sake of making more money. In his biography of Percival, Lawrence tells how his father, while driving the two little boys in to school, inculcated the idea that he had riches enough for all. They were to think of life as a field for the pursuit of knowledge. Five out of the seven of the group studied law, three reached eminence in that profession, but the primary aim of all, the thing that Henry Adams would have said 'amused' them, was the pursuit of difficult knowledge, legal, historical, ethnological, astronomical, architectural, or whatever, and the direction of the vehicles for its dissemination — in short, *noblesse oblige*.

First and not the least interesting of these was Edward Jackson

Lowell, youngest son of Francis Cabot Lowell II, whom we met and left at M. Sillig's school on Lake Geneva. He came home in 1857, and although delicate in health and obliged, as he says, 'to study with the aid of a reader as much Latin Grammar as was consistent with very little labor, and learned in four years about as little as was possible for a boy of that age,' entered Harvard with the class of '67, at the normal age of eighteen. In college he wrote poetry of good average undergraduate quality, was the 'Poet' of various clubs, and Odist on Commencement Day. He knew a vast amount of poetry by heart and repeated it to himself when alone. After graduation he spent the statutory six months abroad, married the daughter of Samuel G. Goodrich of Hartford, author of popular school histories under the pseudonym of Peter Parley, and at his father's advice spent a year in the business of importing glass. Not finding himself temperamentally suited for the operations of buying and selling, though he enjoyed two buying trips to Belgium, he took a year in the Harvard Law School, another in the office of Ropes and Gray, and in 1872 hung out his own shingle in Pemberton Square in association with Brooks Adams. His Cousin Lawrence in a memoir for the Historical Society says he lacked the *gaudium certaminis* that makes arguing in court so intensely attractive to many men; but it is not hard to imagine the arguments *in camera* that must have occupied the two historically minded almost briefless barristers. In 1874, left a widower with three small children, he abandoned the law to devote himself to his children and historical studies. Remarried in '77, to the daughter of George Jones, one of the founders of the *New York Times*, he went abroad in '79 to educate his two sons and a daughter, and himself undertook, in the archives of the little principality of Waldeck, formerly belonging to the Elector of Hesse, the monumental research which resulted in his first book, *The Hessians and other auxiliaries of Great Britain in the Revolutionary War*.

It was well received by historical scholars and is still the authority in its narrow field. He had found his work.

He began research for a full-length biography of Lafayette, as a vehicle for the comparative study of the American and French Revolutions. Soon his notes became so voluminous that he wisely decided to confine his subject to *The Eve of the French Revolution*. At this, during winters in Boston at 131 Mount Vernon Street and long summers at Cotuit with time off for sailing his cat-boat, the *Peep*, he worked steadily for seven years. It was published in 1892, and after more than half a century and running through thirty-three editions, it is still in demand. It is historical writing of the first class, the fruit of tireless research and philosophical reflection, set down in a brisk and vigorous style with a turn for epigram. In its imaginative use of significant detail to build up a picture of the life of a forgotten age, it is in the best modern manner.

He began his investigation with no preconceived ideas, no thesis; he arrived at a conclusion, very different from the over-dramatized opinions of Carlyle, which has been generally accepted by the writers who have followed him:

'The condition of the people of France, both in Paris and in the provinces, was far less bad than it is often represented to have been. The foregoing chapters should have given the impression of a great, prosperous, modern country. The face of Europe has changed since 1789 more through the enormous number and variety of mechanical inventions that have marked the nineteenth century than through a corresponding increase in mental or moral growth. . . . But while France was great, prosperous, and growing, and a model to her neighbors, she was deeply discontented. The condition of other countries was less good than hers, but the minds of the people of those countries had not risen above their condition. France had become conscious that her government did not correspond to her degree of civilization.'

As a competent historian should be, he is found in his letters to be a perceptive and forward-looking critic of contemporary life: To his cousin, Miss Frances R. Morse:

'Dresden, July 8, 1880

'. . . In your letter of June 16th you say of Mr. Ruskin, "He is a man of whom our indifferent and unenthusiastic generation may be proud." Now I am glad to be proud of Mr. Ruskin, with all his somewhat morbid nonsense, for he has keen eyes and a bold tongue, but I protest against saucing my generation. I am now about 34½ years old (just about a generation) and what has been done within my recollection? An indifferent and unenthusiastic generation has driven the Austrians out of Italy and abolished the temporal sovereignty of the pope. An indifferent and unenthusiastic generation has abolished African slavery in America, has conducted a great civil war merely by popular enthusiasm on both sides, and has restored material prosperity at least to the United States, while the political virtue of Americans is still so strong as to have stood the tremendous strain of four years ago.

'An indifferent and unenthusiastic generation has changed Germany from a collection of small half-despotisms to a great half-free state, fighting by the way two campaigns of which Napoleon would have been proud.

'An indifferent and unenthusiastic generation, after wild excesses, has set up in France a government which with all its faults would seem to be the best which that country has enjoyed since the seventeenth century at least.

'Even the nation whose youth play lawn-tennis on the beautiful Oxford turf, has advanced a little, a very little, out of Philistinism, but it's a hard drag. Much as I love and admire England, I cannot but confess that she is the stronghold of social bigotry. This makes a stay in England pleasant to people who have plenty of money and first rate acquaintances.

'I won't try to discuss the art of this indifferent and unenthusiastic generation. No one can criticize the art of his own time as compared to that of others, but I suppose the French landscape painters are believed to be very remarkable. In science it is universally acknowledged, I believe, that this generation is unrivalled, and has accomplished things that a century ago would have appeared almost too extraordinary for fairy tales.

'Finally, my beloved hearers, it is my belief that in future ages the nineteenth century will be pointed to as the age of Romance, when a young world awoke and looked about him, and first tried his young strength and broke some of his fetters and a good many of his playthings. The men of today are puzzled, and don't know where they are or where they are going. Some of them are discouraged, but I know very few that are indifferent, and those I look on as a survival, or as what they call now-a-days a *residuum*. No, this generation may be bad, subversive, violent, but it is neither indifferent nor unenthusiastic. . . .'

To the same:

'Paris, 20 Rue de Tilsit
'December 8, 1881

'. . . We are unfortunate in our generation in one respect, for undoubtedly fifty years hence it will be possible to drop Alice at school at Neuilly in the afternoon, and after dining behind the opera house in Vienna, drop in at Marlborough street in the evening. Now don't be perverse and say that that would not be a real benefit to us, for you know it would be delightful. Man could be just as heroic if space were, I do not say abolished, but diminished. Diogenes would still be free to sit in a tub, if it suited his humour, and it would require as much nerve to steer an electro-dynamic machine going six thousand miles an hour as to hold the tiller of an old oyster-boat. . . .'

As a critic of poetry he was not inferior to his cousin, the Professor of Belles Lettres. The sober judgment displayed in his paper, read just after the death of Tennyson before the Academy of Arts and Sciences, was unique in a month of unbridled eulogies, and close to the opinion of posterity. It concludes:

'The great poets come out with their literary baggage much reduced. From such a time of oblivion Dryden and Pope are just emerging. In its depths are Scott and Byron. To Wordsworth has fallen the singular fortune that his voice has been most clearly recognized by a generation subsequent, but not long subsequent, to his own. It may be that he will prove an exception, and that he will live and drop his Idiot Boys, and silly old men, and most of his Prelude and Excursion, keeping his noble sonnets and the best of his lyrics without a dormant time. But Tennyson seems likely to share the common fate, and its coming will probably not be long delayed; for he is a poet of the early part and the middle of this century, whose life was prolonged to extreme old age, but who learned nothing very new after fifty, any more than the rest of us do. What is likely to be his place when, in a future age, the lover of poetry collects on his shelves the best volumes of English verse? What will the "Abridged Works of Lord Tennyson" contain? A perfect answer to such a question cannot be given, but I think we may approach it. The volume will not be a small one. There will be in it many ballads and short pieces, some of them treating of classical subjects, like "Tithonus" and "The Lotos-Eaters," more with their scene laid on English ground. There will be a few exquisite lyrics. There will be several selections from "In Memoriam," and a passage or two from "Maud." There will be the "Idylls of the King," a good deal abridged. Of how many great poets of the old days is a larger proportion familiar to cultivated people?'

He had provocative ideas on education. An article by him in the *Atlantic* in 1888, 'A Liberal Education,' is a lively attack on the workings of Eliot's elective system:

'It is possible to graduate from Harvard College today without knowing whether the Spaniards discovered America or the Americans Spain. . . . The student must find his way through an ocean of knowledge with a chart but without a pilot.'

Who knows but this may have put into the head of his young Cousin Lawrence in his law office ideas that twenty-five years later he was to put into effect.

Besides his research and writing, Edward Jackson Lowell did much of that unseen, unrewarded work by which cultural education is maintained and advanced. He was for many years treasurer of the American School of Classical Studies at Athens, and for the last nine years of his life a hard-working trustee of the Athenaeum.

He died of a brain tumor at Cotuit in 1894, at the early age of forty-nine, leaving what might have been his true *magnum opus*, a work on the influence of the French Revolution in other countries, only just begun.

The life of his cousin, ten years younger, Francis Cabot Lowell III, much resembled his and ran true to family form. Son of George Gardner Lowell, he was born in a house at the top of Mount Vernon Street within a stone's throw of the Golden Dome, but spent seven or eight months of each of the years of his boyhood at Cotuit, where he prepared for his future work of a judge in admiralty by becoming an expert in swimming, fishing, and boat-sailing. Throughout his life he had a sailor's knowledge of wind and weather, and an instinct for channels and shoals that may have served him well on the bench, as an historical writer, and an effective member of the Harvard Corporation. Graduating from college in 1876, he had the scheduled *Wanderjahr* in Europe, two years in law school, and began the practice of that profession in the office of Charles P. Greenough. After a year he set up for himself, with his cousin and brother-in-law, Lawrence, as a partner. The firm of Lowell and Lowell enjoyed the comfortable warmth supplied by family and other trust business, but soon both the cousins took to the writing of literature and history.

Lawrence began the studies which resulted a decade later in the important work on *Governments and Parties in Continental Europe*, which brought him his appointment as a part-time lecturer at Harvard.

Francis, after the publication of an anonymous novel, *Simply a Love Story*, which his cousin thought had something of the quality of Jane Austen, but which nevertheless failed to set the Charles River on fire, turned to historical biography, and published in 1896, after ten years of research, a well-documented work on *Joan of Arc*, which has the fresh and vigorous qualities of Edward's *The Eve of the French Revolution*. It is a sound and useful work, but not quite so important as a contribution to historical literature.

While at work upon this, he found other active interests and occupations. From 1886 to 1893, he was a member of the Board of Overseers of Harvard, and from 1895 until his death in 1911, a member of the Corporation. Politics, the good citizen's service to the state, had a powerful attraction for him. He sat for three years in the Common Council of Boston, and for two in the lower House of the Legislature, a quiet but weighty member. In 1898, he was 'prominently mentioned' as a gubernatorial possibility, but accepted instead an appointment to the Federal District Court. In due course, following the exact steps of his great-great-grandfather the Old Judge, and his cousin Judge John, he was promoted to be a Circuit Judge, dealing as they did in the first instance with seagoing causes. He held his seat until his death in 1911.

The character of him, concluding a memoir in *The Later Years of the Saturday Club* by Lawrence Lowell, is as revelatory of the writer as of the subject:

'His serene and friendly nature made him think well of those with whom he worked, even when he had not previously esteemed them so highly. Affectionate to his friends, just to all, his temperament was, indeed, a happy one for himself, as well as for his family, his associates and the community he served. His philosophy of life was an unobtrusive optimism. He never fretted over what could not be helped, or worried about his own past actions. He had done what he believed to be right at the time, with the knowledge he then had, and that was enough. Full of information on many subjects, ready to express his views and not averse to argument, he was an agreeable companion on all occasions. Yet modern as were his knowledge, his attitude and his interests, he bore about him something of the spirit of the older worthies who made New England what it is. It might be said of him as he said of the grandfather for whom he was named, that he had the fortunate combination of a strong will and weak appetites.'

Two other Lowell lawyers of the fourth generation from the Old Judge, had distinguished careers at the bar and in the public service, Judge John Lowell's sons, another John, who did good service in the intricate legal work of the first World War, and James, the latter the family's fourth Federal Judge.

John, the elder of the two, graduated from Harvard with the class of '77, married Mary Emlen Hale of Philadelphia and became the father of a vigorous generation. By his fifteenth year out of college, he had become a leading figure as a trial lawyer in Boston courtrooms, and an ardent worker in raising the standards of the legal profession, as a member of the executive committee of the American Bar Association, and an editor of its *Journal*. During the First World War he was chairman of the War Service Association in Washington, which provided the Government with the most competent lawyers from every corner of the country to handle the intricate matters that constantly came in — Income Tax, Military Intelligence, Shipping Board, Housing Corporation, and a hundred more. Like all the men of his family, he was a lover of the outdoor life of his home at Chestnut Hill, with, it is recorded, a special passion for poultry. Indoor matters he left to the distaff side. In the American Bar Association *Journal* after his death appeared an appreciation by his cousin and law partner, Colonel William D. Sohier, which contains a picture of the domestic aspect of the Lowell men which is good for all branches of the family as far back as the Old Judge:

'No true living picture can be given of John Lowell, of his father or of his grandfather, if it is confined to attainments, intellectual capacity, occupations, be they public or private.

'It was their home in which they really lived, were their true selves. They never made their home, it was made for them by their wives. And what a home! Hospitable, comfortable, always homelike, always full of the children and grandchildren, nieces, nephews, relations, and hosts of others as well. Large informal lunches at which everyone dropped in. Family dinners once a week. Reunions never, because the intercourse was constant. Everyone knew everything about everyone else every day down to the latest baby's last rash or tooth. Sympathy, help, understanding, it was ever present, boundless, overflowing. This was the wife and mother part. Their part also to run the house, the household, the family, and oftentimes some other family as well, did trouble come.

'The Lowell men were never practical in home affairs, not even to the care of their own clothes, whether they should put on an overcoat, had their gloves, carfare.

'How they loved their home, their family! How they nestled into the armchair near the lamp and in front of the fire and read or conversed! Did they light that fire? Not a bit of it. Someone else did that. . . .

'For some unaccountable reason these Lowell men were shy, retiring, almost reclusive in private life, and yet each one of them came out on occasion publicly with an unexpected dynamic force, stated facts, reasons forcefully with convincing logic, coherence, and conciseness, always most effective and often entirely unlooked for, unexpected. They lived up to the motto on the Lowell coat of arms, "Occasionem cognosce."

'No doubt all the other Johns, James, Percivals, of former generations, had this same characteristic, but I can only write of the ones I knew.

'John, his father, his grandfather, were best in their homes, always gracious, interested, interesting, instructive, especially with the children. They all possessed that quiet, comforting manner that gave assurance of friendship, interest, sympathy, and made each one feel distinctly and personally at home.

'Personality, they all had it to excess, but all were different, very different, each from the other.

'As one met them, John, the tenth generation, was unique. He was emphatic always, talked right up, expounded his ideas, enthusiastically, earnestly always, with his head probably drawn down, a little on one side, with a smile a little awry, almost a grimace, with sparkling, glowing eyes, gritted his teeth and with emphatic gesture, one hand clenched beating his other palm to give more emphasis, if that hand wasn't on your shoulder or holding the lapel of your coat, and all in enthusiastic, earnest, yes, often extravagant, language which he poured into your ears.'

Animal spirits in permutation and combination!

In New York in the eighties and nineties, as well as in Boston, the name of Lowell was associated with good works, but more in the broad field of social and economic reform and public charities than with private philanthropy and the advance of scholarship and education. In 1894, just before his death, Edward Jackson Lowell, who said God had made him a Whig and he could not be changed, wrote to Miss Morse:

'30 West 37th Street
'New York, January 7, 1894

'. . . I saw Mrs. C. R. Lowell yesterday, and had a good deal of socialism and Henry George very pleasantly expounded to me. What nonsense it is! And yet I am enough in touch with my time to feel that it is not all nonsense. Not quite all. I confess that political economy, in its large sense, is a science in which I never get much beyond a feeling of bewilderment. The general propositions are so plausible, so true if you will take them in one sense, and so obviously untrue if you take them in another. The mode of argument generally seems to me to be as if a mathematician were first to prove that the three angles of a triangle equal two right angles, and then were to apply his reasonings to a triangle on a spherical surface.'

It is an engaging picture, the Colonel's vivid Effy, now become something of a warhorse herself, sitting at her desk in the library of her double house at 118 East 30th Street, with his sword hanging over the mantel, lecturing the clever sceptical cousin from Boston, treasurer of the School for Classical Studies at Athens, and trustee of the Athenaeum, on *Progress and Poverty*. More than he realized, she knew what she was talking about. In the forty years of her life after her *beau sabreur* fell at Cedar Creek she did, first yeoman's, and then high command work in the great movement to transform charity from private handouts to organized effort. She had a hand in the State departments that dealt with Reformatories for Women, the care of the insane, and of feeble minded women, dependent children, and almshouses. In the city of New York she was a leader in the Charity Organization Society, the establishment of the system of Police Matrons, and the Women's Municipal League. She was active in the Consumers' League, the emancipation of labor, civil service reform, and the improvement of the *mores* of tramps.

Though she met with disappointments and reverses, her work viewed in retrospect enlarged the area of the good life in the Empire State. What might she not have accomplished, as First Lady in the White House, with her fighting Colonel!

Before the end of the Victorian Period of New England, four other young Lowell men, Percival, Lawrence, Guy, and James, the future judge, were beginning to attract attention, but the story of their accomplishment and achievements, perhaps the culmination of the family talent, belongs in the book of the strange enlarged new world that came in with the twentieth century. Before entering that, we must take leave of James Russell Lowell in his final stage as active good citizen, public man and diplomatist.

While abroad for two years from 1872 to 1874, Lowell, with the clarifying perspective of overseas, had watched with deepening anxiety the political corruption of Grant's second administration. He had been shamed by the necessity of explaining and apologizing to French and English friends for Tweed and Fisk, and better-covered men in higher places; for

> 'Office a fund for ballot-brokers made,
> To pay the drudges of their gainful trade;
> Our cities taught what conquered cities feel
> By aediles chosen that they might safely steal.'

In his *Agassiz*, the two lines which now read,

> 'The land of Honest Abraham serves of late
> To teach the Old World how to wait,'

read in the original manuscript, 'The land of Broken Promise.' Friends persuaded him to soften the stinging phrase, but his bitterness persisted, and with it the impulse to action.

As the hotly contested election of 1876 approached, the independent wing of the Republican Party in Cambridge organized to defeat the nomination of Blaine, the 'Plumed Knight' from Maine, who was then at the height of his popularity, as well as of his notoriety for his dubious double connection with the franchise and securities of the Little Rock and Fort Smith Railroad. Lowell was invited to preside, did so, became permanent chairman of the committee formed for the organization of voters, and was urged to be himself a candidate for Congress. This he declined, but made at the caucus an able if somewhat academic speech for an honest independence in politics, and civil service reform. He was chosen as a delegate to the Republican Convention in Cincinnati, and on the seventh ballot had the satisfaction of seeing Hayes — not Blaine — more through the combinations of the Republican boss Roscoe Conkling than his own efforts, nominated as the Republican candidate for the office of President of the United States, and, with difficulty, elected.

A year before there had been talk of appointing him to a diplomatic post, London, St. Petersburg, Vienna, or Madrid. Hardly was Hayes in the White House before he sent his kinsman, Howells, to 'sound' Lowell about Vienna. The bookman of Elmwood took it calmly, and said he would think about it. Two days later he called on Howells and declined the Austrian mission, but as he rose to leave said, with a half-whimsical sigh, 'I *should* like to see a play of Calderon.' Six weeks later a Cunard liner, honorifically escorted by a coast guard cutter and a tug, carried him down the harbor accredited by the Government of the United States as its Minister Plenipotentiary to His Majesty the King of Spain.

'Jose Bighlow' was well received in Madrid and did good routine diplomatic work there. With the young King, his relations were intimate, even gay, to a degree not common between United States ministers and European monarchs. His dispatches to the State Department are of a literary quality not usually found in such productions, but he was far from happy. His 'suppressed gout' troubled him constantly, and during the last two years of the Spanish mission, his wife was desperately ill. It was with a feeling of home-coming that in March, 1880, he received his promotion to London, had his audience with Queen Victoria, and began what were to prove the richest and probably the second happiest five years of his life, surpassed only by his creative lustrum of 1845–50.

The story of the social, literary, and diplomatic success of Lowell's English mission is too familiar to need repetition in detail. He went to England, as Henry James had found him in Madrid, 'morbidly anglophobic,' sensitive to a certain condescension in foreigners, and still deeply resentful of England's choice of a horse to back in our War Between the States. He was on the defensive against British candid criticism of the orgiastic politics current in the Land of Broken Promise. This was all to the good at the start, in stiffening his hard Yankee core in his transaction of public business. A writer in *The Spectator*, who seems to have been privy to some of his conferences at the Foreign Office over the intricate and troublesome affair of certain Irish-American citizens who after a brief sojourn in the United States returned to

the Emerald Isle, incited Nationalist riots, and were put in jail
by the British authorities, reported that, while Lowell possessed
equally with Lord Granville the *suaviter in modo*, he was even
more capable of conveying the impression of *fortiter in re*. When
at the end of seven months of negotiation he had achieved the
release of the suspects, they refused to be liberated, and Justin
McCarthy told him cheerfully, 'Certainly, they are there to
make trouble.'

But the 'enchantments' and 'alluring arts,' by which, as
Holmes wrote, 'our truthful James led captive British hearts,'
were, quite simply, his gift for friendship, and his beguiling talent
for after-dinner oratory.

Two of his dearest friends of many years' standing, Tom
Hughes and Leslie Stephen,[1] were there to steer him about and
enlarge his circle of literary acquaintance. By his felicities of
speech, dukes, bishops, lord mayors, coal-barons, generals, ad-
mirals, cabinet ministers, judges, Queen's counsel, novelists,
poets, painters, critics, country gentlemen, Irish Nationalists —
these and their ladies were fascinated. No American ever saw
the inside of so many English country houses as Lowell, or was
more eagerly listened to across the dining-tables of Belgravia
and Mayfair. His animal spirits were more abundant than
those of Henry Adams and by their potency he penetrated
deeply into that 'Perfection of Society' which the latter had
somewhat ironically discovered twenty years before.

In the not far distant future electrical transcription and tele-
vision will record and preserve for posterity something of the
quality of the spoken word as it was actually spoken. It is an
alarming thought, but it need not intimidate us here. The

---

[1] Lowell stood godfather to Stephen's youngest child, and with the customary
token offered a poem entitled 'Verses which are to go with a Posset-dish to my dear
little God-daughter.' In the enumeration of the contents of the posset-dish was the
wish that she might have

> 'Her father's wit veined through
> With tenderness.'

The wish was fulfilled. The little girl was Virginia Woolf.

charm of Lowell's speech can best be gathered from some notes by Henry Cabot Lodge, who had listened to as much oratory as any man of his generation, and was suspicious of other men's eloquence:

'Of all that talk so enjoyed at the moment, one little anecdote which he told has always remained in my memory. He said that when he had just arrived in England, Lord Coleridge, who was reputed to be the best after-dinner speaker in London, said to him: "You will be asked very often to make an after-dinner speech and I wish to tell you how such a speech should be made. Select your anecdote before hand. When you are called upon, lead up to your anecdote, tell it, go gently away from it and your speech is made." It was excellent advice, as sound as it was witty, but I felt that the greatest humor in the story lay in Lord Coleridge telling Lowell how to make an after-dinner speech, for Lowell was a past-master in that art, and I have never heard anyone on such occasions who even approached him. He seemed to combine every quality that a speaker should possess. His voice was singularly fine and his enunciation, which is rare, was quite perfect, with an intonation that cannot be described, but which was singularly attractive. Many men make clever speeches, full of good points and very telling. Lowell not only had wit and humor in abounding measure, but he had also the imagination of the poet, the literary touch, a finished style, and a knowledge of all literature such as very few men, indeed, ever possess. I have heard him often in serious addresses as well as in the lighter moments of an after-dinner speech, and I always listened to him with envious delight. I can see him now on our Commencement Day, when he spoke of some of the early benefactors of the college of whom nothing was known and who have become mere names to a grateful posterity. I seem to hear again the beautiful voice as he said: "There is William Pennoyer of whom we know nothing, except that he comes down to us in that most graceful of attitudes with his hand in his pocket." '

At the unveiling of memorial tablets no man in England surpassed, perhaps had ever surpassed, him. But the best of his English speeches was his address on *Democracy*, his inaugural on assuming the presidency of the Birmingham and Midland Institute. It began a well-conceived statement, pertinent today, of the differentials of British and American democracy, 'England may be called a monarchy with democratic tendencies, the United States a democracy with conservative instincts.' It concluded in a peroration that is sufficient answer to the American critics who were accusing him of anglomania and an apostasy from democratic principles:

'Let us be of good cheer, however, remembering that the misfortunes hardest to bear are those which never come. The world has outlived much, and will outlive a great deal more, and men have contrived to be happy in it. It has shown the strength of its constitution in nothing more than in surviving the quack medicines it has tried. In the scales of the destinies, brawn will never weigh so much as brain. Our healing is not in the storm or in the whirlwind, it is not in monarchies, or aristocracies, or democracies, but will be revealed by the still, small voice that speaks to the conscience and the heart, prompting us to a wider and wiser humanity.'

In February, 1885, Mrs. Lowell, who had never recovered from her Spanish illness, died, and a few weeks later word arrived that his *pro forma* resignation on the inauguration of Grover Cleveland had been accepted, and that William Walter Phelps would succeed him. Efforts were made to keep him in England, and if he wished he could have had the University Professorship of English Language and Literature at Oxford. For some weeks he wavered between this and other attractive suggestions. In the end he realized that he was sick for home amid the alien corn, and sailed in June.

No American envoy abroad had ever received from the country to which he was accredited such a regretful farewell. The Queen said that during her busy reign no ambassador had 'created so much interest and won so much regard as Mr.

Lowell,' and from the other end of the social fabric, a deputation
of the Workman's Peace Society waited on him with some warm
resolutions embossed on vellum.   From *Punch* to the Thunderer,
the press was eloquent in his praise.   Perhaps the most dis-
criminating editorial, 'Ave Atque Vale,' was that by Theodore
Watts-Dunton in the *Athenaeum*.   'Fine as is the written work of
Lowell, his unwritten work is finer still,' and he points out the
curious and significant fact that not only did he establish a new
rapport between England and America, but also brought into
being a relation hitherto undreamed of between the literary and
official sets in England itself.

Back in America, first at Deerfoot Farm in Southborough
with his daughter, Mrs. Burnett, and later installed with her at
Elmwood, his health began to cause concern.   He walked out to
Beaver Brook, he told Howells, and found he could no longer
jump from one stone in the stream to another.   'It has come to
that with me!' he said.   He employed himself largely in letter-
writing, still using to favored correspondents the long 's' and
the repeated word at the turn of the page.   Sombre thoughts
creep into these later letters, but the old explosions of animal
spirits are there too.   The 'pervading tone' is still uncertain.
When a selection of them was published in two volumes after
his death, Henry Adams wrote to his English friend, Gaskell,
with the peculiarly candid eye the Adamses always cast on the
work of the Lowells: 'I agree with you about Lowell's letters.
They *are* deadly.   But what letters are not now?'   But surely
they were not, as Adams seems to have felt, mannered and
artificial.   They were the true expression of his mind, better,
as he well knew, at 'thoughts' than 'thought.'   Leslie Stephen,
who should have been a judge of letters, said of Lowell's letters,
'I don't think Cowper or Gray or anyone could write better.'
But he was writing this to Norton just after Lowell's death.

In addition to replies to 'the bushel of cold letters' he found
in his desk after every brief absence from home, he wrote a few
lectures, verses, and prefaces, and revised his later poems and
collected works for the press.

He appeared more regularly at the houses of his clan, and warmly welcomed any good listener to his study at Elmwood. He talked, it is recorded, in paragraphs. The broader social pleasures he had learned to love in England he found again in summer visits there. A month or two was always spent in lodgings at Whitby near the ruins of the old abbey by the North Sea where eleven hundred years before English Poetry had its birth, but he was much in demand during the London season. His favorite whist partner, John Holmes, who, unlike his brother Oliver, reserved his best goods for his friends, wrote to him in 1889, from 'Camb. Novanglorum,' 'Don't let them overwork you with their dinners, lunches and what not. Men have been lunched into eternity.'

That was his last summer in England. The next year his malady had increased to a point where it was presently diagnosed as cancer of the stomach. In the summer of 1890, Leslie Stephen, the most completely congenial of all his friends, came over for a visit of three weeks at Elmwood, and there were hours of wide-ranging talk, but the long tramps of earlier years were replaced by carriage exercise. The following spring the end was in sight. In the hot July of 1891, a delirium came upon him in which he fancied he was entertaining royal personages, and seemed continually imploring to be taken home to Elmwood. He died on the twelfth of August.

Henry James wrote Charles Eliot Norton two weeks later:

'Dear Lowell's death — the words are almost as difficult as they are odious to write — has made me think almost as much of you as of him. I imagine that you are the person in the world to whom it makes the most complete and constant difference that he is no longer here; just as you must have been the one most closely associated with the too vain watching of his last struggle with the monster. It is a dim satisfaction to me, therefore, to say to you how fond I was of him and how I shall miss him and miss him and miss him. During these last strange English years of his life (it would take me long to tell you why I call them strange,) I had seen a great deal of him, and all with the effect of confirming my affection for him. London is bestrewn, to my sense, with reminders of his happy career here, and his company and his talk. He was kind and delightful and gratifying to me, and all sorts of occasions in which he will ever be vivid swarm before me as I think of him. . . . Strange was his double existence — the American and the English sides of his medal, which had yet so much in common. That is, I don't know how English he was at home, but he was conspicuously American here.'

BOOK VII

New World Again

1
CHAPTER

Science: Percival

INTO THE MIND of Leonardo da Vinci, meditating one day on the swift flight of his years and the unresting march of history, flashed a visual image, Time, the River! He wrote down in the notebook that was always by his hand: 'In rivers the water that you touch is the last of what has passed and the first of that which comes: so with time present.' True, and handsomely expressed. But if you paddle down with the current for three centuries, the landscape along the banks changes as the river grows wider and deeper. Side streams have entered it from both the right and the left, some gin-clear, some roily with pollution. The very water itself has become something else again. The seventh world in which the Lowells exercised their hearts, minds, and imaginations, exhibited their animal spirits, opened their pocketbooks and seized their opportunities, was definitely a new one. For its *terminus ab quo* no better date can be selected than 1901, the first year of our own century.

If we look around us and compare what we see with the six worlds of Old Percival and John Lowell the Divine, the Old Judge, the Rebel, John Amory Lowell, the *Beau Sabreur*, the American Minister to the court of Queen Victoria, how vast the difference! We are living in a seventh world which of the family in the eighties only Edward Jackson even glimpsed.

Applied science has made man's life more full of new wonders than the thousand and one tales of Scheherezade. Electricity, once an amusing spark or an awe-inspiring bolt, has been discovered to be the wonder-working spirit of Aladdin's lamp. From the moment we wake up and turn on the radio till we turn it off with the bedside light at night, we owe to it directly or indirectly all our means of movement and communication. We push a button or turn a switch and everything happens from lighting a cigarette to moving a mountain. Pure science has penetrated almost to the last secrets of matter, and leaped some millions of light-years beyond the flaming ramparts of the world of Lucretius and Old Percival's contemporary, Galileo.[1]

On our own, to us important, planet two world wars are perhaps the birth-pangs of a great new age. Perhaps not. *Qui vivra verra*, and the average span of man's life is lengthening.

In the Western World at least, the standard of living, of education and intelligence, has risen to a level that partially submerges peaks of personality, modifies their prestige, and shortens the radius of their influence. Percival, Amy, Guy, and Lawrence Lowell loomed a little larger in the active life of their generation than they do in this or will in the next. It is the twilight of the gods. Yet all four of this mixed quartette, born and educated in the Victorian world, caught the pitch and rhythm of the new world that followed it. They marched in the van of the three-pronged advance in science, the arts, and education.

[1] An hour after this paragraph was polished off, August 6, 1945, word came through the ether that the energy within the atom had been drawn off, packed into a bomb and dropped on Japan, bringing to a sudden end the greatest of world wars.

Percival, save for a son of Robert Traill Spence Lowell, who died young and unmarried, first of the Boston family in two centuries to be named for Old Percival, was born in 1855 at 131 Tremont Street with a good view of the State House Dome across the Common.[1]

From his father's family he drew the qualities we have seen in four generations of three branches of a family remarkable for its unity in variety. From his Lawrence mother came, in the opinion of his brother, Lawrence, 'sociability, ease of companionship, and charm.'[2] His earliest letter to be preserved, written at the age of ten from M. Sillig's at Vevey to his mother, has his characteristic exuberance: 'For Papa, Lawrence and Katie, *1000 baisiers chacun, et gardez 10,000 pour vous même.*' He had been, he says, marked 99 in French, and forty years later, at one of his astronomical lectures in Paris, an auditor was overheard to exclaim, 'Why, he is clever, even in French!' A year later a little paper boat he was sailing in a pool left by melting snow in the garden at Sevenels came to grief. Retiring to the house, he celebrated the shipwreck in a hundred lines of Latin hexameters. At thirteen he became a watcher of the skies through a two-and-a-quarter-inch telescope installed in the cupola that crowned the family mansion. In college he did well both in mathematics and the humanities. Benjamin Peirce, the great mathematician, urged him to continue in that field, with a view to succeeding to his own chair, and his Commencement part was a disquisition on 'The Nebular Hypothesis.' A few months earlier he had won the Bowdoin Prize with an essay on 'The Rank of England as a European Power from the Death of Elizabeth to the Death of Anne.'

[1] *Biography of Percival Lowell*, by A. Lawrence Lowell, is an authoritative source of facts. The author believed that biography should concern itself, not with what the subject was, but with what he did.

[2] Perhaps this is a little unfair to his own stock. The Reverend John Lowell and the Old Judge were eminently sociable men. So was the Rebel in his unilateral way. But as to that, few of the family ever listened much. Amy Lowell confided to the present writer that one of the tragedies of her young life was that whenever she opened her mouth at table someone was sure to say, 'Amy, be quiet. Don't you hear Lawrence talking?'

After graduation in 1866, he made the Grand Tour from England to Syria with his cousin and freshman roommate, Harcourt Amory, tried without success to get into the war then being waged between Serbia and Turkey, and came home with his lifelong taste for travel and outdoor adventure thoroughly established. Not always enthusiastic about the promise of young kinsmen, his cousin the Professor referred to him in conversation as the most brilliant young man in Boston.

For six years he was employed in family business in the office of his grandfather, John Amory Lowell. He managed trust funds, was for a time treasurer of a cotton mill and a bleachery, and by shrewd investments acquired a portly pocketbook of his own. By 1883, he had had enough of this, and in the spring of that year, following his friend, Sturgis Bigelow, America's first cultural scout to Japan, he sailed to the Orient. His *Wanderlust* may have been heightened by the impulse to evade cousinly caps that were being set at him. In his second book, *The Soul of the Far East*, there is an ironic comparison of ancestor worship as practised by the Buddhists of Japan and the Brahmins of Boston who 'make themselves objectionable by preferring their immediate relatives to all less connected companions, and cling to their cousins so closely that affection often culminates in matrimony, nature's remonstrances notwithstanding.'

In Tokyo he hired a house, set up his own establishment with Japanese servants, and started with his customary thoroughness to learn the language. In August came a surprise. He was asked to accompany a special mission from Korea to the United States. The affair is described in a letter to Augustus from Sturgis Bigelow:

'After two days of unconditional refusal and one of doubt Percy has finally yielded to the wishes of the U.S. Legation here and accepted the position of Foreign Secretary and General Counsellor to the Embassy sent from Korea to the U.S.

'The position practically amounts to his having complete charge and control of the most important legation from a new country that has visited the U.S. since the opening of Japan. The U.S. authorities here are greatly pleased at having secured so good a man, as is natural. There were many applicants for the place. . . .

'He distrusts himself too much, he has great ability, he has learned Japanese faster than I ever saw any man learn a language — and he only needs to be assured that he is doing the right thing to make a success of anything he undertakes, whether science or diplomacy.

This was the last occasion in which there is any record of such distrust.

The mission of four, three poker-faced Koreans in silken robes and towering beach hats, with golden-haired Percival in the morning coat, striped trousers, and tile of diplomacy, were in Washington for six weeks. They accomplished their aim of establishing trade relations, and were back in Seoül before Chr stmas. There, as a diplomatic official, Percival was given a house forming part of the Foreign Office.

'From the street,' he writes, 'you enter a courtyard, then another, then a garden, and so on, wall after wall, until you have left the outside world far behind and are in a labyrinth of your own. Before you lies a garden; behind another surrounded by porticoes. Courtyards, gardens, porticoes, rooms, corridors in endless succession until you lose yourself in the delightful maze.' He speaks of the painting of landscapes on the walls, of a door cut out as a circle in the wall into which fit two sliding panels beautifully painted on both sides. 'Floor, ceiling, walls all are paper. But you would hardly imagine that what you tread upon, to all appearance square stone slabs, is oil paper so hard as even in sounds under your footfalls to resemble flags. . . . Through the thick sliding windows sifts the golden light into the room, and for the nonce you forget that outside is the dull grey of a cloudy sky and a snow-decked land of a December afternoon.'

The next ten years, save for occasional visits home to see four books through the press, were spent in Japan. The color of his

life there is depicted in an exuberant series of unpublished letters
to his friend and fellow Dedham polo player, Frederic J. Stimson, 'J. S. of Dale,' the future novelist and diplomatist:

'Behold me in imagination arrived in one of the loveliest cities
of the world — The means was unromantic enough, a railway
train. But in this age we should reach the happy valley of
Rasselas, if such existed, by the same means — The road lay
through a plain stretching from the hills on the one hand to the
bay of Ozaka on the other. On the other side of which twenty-
odd miles away rose range after range of hills all a uniform faint
blue in the distance. The sea sparkled and the land slept in the
calm of a beautiful autumn day. The only particularly note-
worthy feature of the landscape lay in the rivers which for some
unknown reason are raised several feet ten or fifteen, above the
surrounding plain and are protected by high embankments. This
turning of a wild god of nature into a tame one is amusing. One
is at once struck here in the south by the brilliant dress of the
women. Their taste is not up to that of their Tokio sisters but
they themselves are more beautiful. Another of the remarkable
equalizing effects of their dispassionate mother nature. . . .

'Yes, I must get a few lines off to you by this mail if only a few.
The one mistake of your life, my boy, is in not having been to
this morning land. Beg, borrow, steal, pack up, sell Atch short,
do anything that you get here, by hook and by crook if necessary
— but halt, it is too late this trip for I want you at Dedham
when I return. I'll send you photos instead, these children of
mine brought up by hand and partly by the bottle. Another
photo fiend named Samuel Luke, an Englishman, dines with
me this eve and joins me in mystic rites, red flame and potent
spells in a dark dark room. There was hatched the Hell I send
you, Miyanoshita no Ojigoku. . . .

'Why were you absent from a river expedition the other day.
Your humble servant, an amicus and two amicae gifted in the
musical line, not to mention boatmen and retainers all of whom
have to be remembered at least pecuniarily. After threading

our way through the innumerable canals which render the half of Tokio a mass of islands, we got into the river and gradually against the tide succeeded in gaining a suburban tea house. I carried my photographic apparatus but was balked of views. So the girls are lost to posterity. The Japanese are a deeply religious people. There was a more than usual fair at Asakusa, and as you know one of the main temples, to which one of the fair ones attempted to entice us. We did not entice much, but hauled up to a landing and allowed her to go. She departed to pray while we graciously waited for her The other amica, who was too lazy to move, amused herself by asking amicus to secure for her some cockle shells which attracted her infantile mind. Her childish delight, surprize and ignorant cruelty to these crustaceai were a striking index of the geisha mind. . .

'I have just been off for a short trip into the country with Sturgis Bigelow — to float down the rapids of the Fujikawa — lovely — Now I am on the eve of my polo party to which invitations go to you by this mail. I am afraid you will plead, not a previous but a past engagement. No matter off they go — I also send some prints of preliminary practice of the same — not instantaneous ones of motion but of statical celebrities. The young fellow, who reminded me of several young New Yorkers on the grounds at Newport, carries in his hand their mallet or bo-peep crook, which it more resembles and the numerous white dots in the other picture are the balls whose number is indeterminate, of which description you won't make much — but shall know eventually. Meanwhile keep up the good old game. . . .

'You don't deserve it, i.e. this epistle, for you write so uncommonly little. However Allah be praised for your line of the 12th April just this moment arrived from its long tossing about. Still of my clemency I will pour into thy receptive ear a trifling episode not without a certain local colouring — My friend Chamberlain says it ought to be entitled "Percival's priestess" or "Lowell's love." — I saw her first while I was walking in Nyeno (this may be translated "the very tip top") park. I instantly remarked upon her beauty to my companion, a damoiselle from across the water. She didn't think so. It is perhaps needless to remark this. But I do but chronicle history or his story as you please. I remember I said she was the most beautiful Japanese woman I had ever seen taking care of course to particularize the Japanese part of it. Well, the days rolled by and I found myself con amicos at Kameido admiring the wisteria. Wisteria indeed, mysteria; there she was again. I was with bold bad men, so I only murmured to myself Go to but I will know that fairy. Always be it remarked in a distant, quiet gentlemanly way. My well known antipathy to the sex fortunately renders this observation well nigh unnecessary. Still my resolve took no definite shape until, sometime later, I was again at Kameido on a picnic of the American legation. I had taken my camera along with me, having the wisteria in mind but with no ulterior object. However, all things work together for the good. There she was still and her image instantly suggested to my mind the advisability of rendering her immortal. Yes, but who was she, you naturally want to know. She was one of the sacred dancers or rather she was the sacred dancer for she performed alone. Flirtation's photograph or photographic flirtations; alliteration artful aid again. C. says he shouldn't think one's head under a black cloth would be exactly the attitude for the affair. But this only shows how no device however humble should ever be scorned. She stoops to conquer why may not he. Moral a dark cloth covers much wilyness. My boy was sent to ask if I might be granted the privilege of taking her picture. I might but would I wait a moment till she had donned some finer toggery. I then set to work to prospect for a better place than the platform from which she smote the hearts of men and discovered a nice little back alley among the trees. After an interview with the priest her father? she was persuaded so far to condescend. There the deed was done. I discovered subsequently that she was a virgin — to photography. It is confidently reported that the other kind existeth not in the island.

But we all know how difficult it is to prove a negative. The additional toggery consisted of an immense tiara, its apex a crescent moon. Instead of the hackneyed panegyrics customarily employed in describing loveliness, I will simply remark that she was most kissable. This otherwise commendable terseness is perhaps open to the objection of being egoistic rather than altruistic or better subjective rather than objective, the true philosophic standpoint. Thenceforth Pygmalion was but a shadow to me in intensity. I imagine to your dull eye of faith, the laboratory dark as Erebus, black as the crime perpetrated therein, save for the lurid glare of the patent lamp that threw its crimson dye of guilt upon the deed; the lovely image growing into life. In her bath too — of pyrogallic acid. Our friend Pyg. worked in the garish day. Such indecent exposure would have killed my little girl. She would have faded away for very shame — Our premières délices were passed before brutalizing man or even possibly objectionable nature had anything to say in the matter.

'Would it be indecent to add that I left her washing in her tub. Scientifically I had accomplished that most difficult of results, the establishment of a negative. — The end of the beginning — Armed with a part of herself, I dispatched my boy to the house of her fathers. No subtlety intended by the use of the plural. It is a pretty idea, that of the East, that in taking a photograph you take away a part of the soul. I invited the family to call. They did so — by a large majority. I asked them to come at seven. They came at six. Japanese are invariably previous. To make the matter worse I had to go a pleasuring in the country on that day, a dinner given me by a Jap friend some six ri out of town. N.B. a ri is 2½ miles. Of course it was impossible to get home in time by a slight gap of two hours and a half. Would she have left disgusted at my apparent faithlessness, tormenting doubt. I hired an extra man and bowled along right merrily my five miles from the railroad station. On reaching my door I saw jinrikishas standing outside. Ha, ha, the bird was still caged. When I entered there she was partaking familiaque of a Jap feast I had ordered — To etc etc etc was the work of a moment etc etc. I engaged what turned out to be the uncle in conversation while she whom I will call Miss Sweet Smile, sat by and listened. Then I showed them the house and its curiosities generally. I subsequently heard them remark to one another, "we have seen a lot of wonderful things today." The dear little thing touched the keys of the piano I thought rather cleverly for a novice. Her pretty cloven foot could touch the floor, as she sat in one of my low chairs and sipped her tea. And then she smiled so divinely. Here endeth this chap. For it is not written in the law of the Medes and Persians that a smile shall close the evening, whether it be male or female. In witness that deponent sayeth true, he encloseth of the same a print.

'I admire, my dear boy, your style and your ideas very much as you know and respect highly your literary criticism, but what do you mean by so decidedly preferring mine of the 29th Dec. to that of the 12th Jan. I have reread them both and for the life of me cannot discover the cause, though of course guesses are free. Pray cite chapter and verse in your next.'

As the reference to 'criticism' indicates, the two young hopefuls were seriously studying the technique of their trade. Percival was copying his communications in a letter book as literary material for the future, and in a final letter lays down his theory of composition:

'Somebody wrote me the other day apropos of what I may or may not write, that facts not reflections were the thing. Facts not reflections indeed! Why, that is what most pleases mankind from the philosopher to the fair, one's own reflections on or from things. Are we to forego the splendor of the French salon which returns us beauty from a score of different points of view from its mirrors more brilliant than their golden settings. The fact gives us but a flat image. It is our reflexions upon it that make it a solid truth. For every truth is many sided. It has many aspects. We know now what was long unknown, that true seeing is done with the mind from the comparatively meagre material supplied us by the eye. None of us ever knows what we ourselves look like except by the aid of two reflections. We perceive others directly. Is it owing to this, the difficulty and importance of the Γνῶθι σεαυτόν.

'I believe that all writing should be a collection of the precious stones of truth which is beauty. Only the arrangement differs with the character of the book.' You string them into a necklace for the world at large, you pigeon hole them in drawers for the scientist. In the necklace you have the cutting of your thought, i.e. the expressing of it and the arrangement of the thoughts among themselves.'

Chosen, the first of Percival Lowell's books, appeared in 1885. It was followed in 1888 by *The Soul of the Far East*, 'the colossal, splendid, godlike book' that started Lafcadio Hearn to the land of the Lotos. Then came *Noto*, his vivid travel tale in 1891, and finally *Occult Japan*, a careful study of the Shinto trances in 1894.

After the appearance of the first three, Hearn wrote to Basil Hall Chamberlain, his friend and Percival's, grandson of that Captain Basil Hall who had admired the rosy cheeks of the Lowell mill girls sixty years before:

'If I had Lowell's genius and Lowell's independence, how happy I should be. He can go where he likes, see what he likes, write what he likes and make beautiful books. I am heavily handicapped even in competing with writers as much below Lowell as he is above me.'

Occult Japan, published after he himself had been several years in Japan, pleased him less completely:

'It is a very clever book — though disfigured by absolutely shameless puns. It touches truths to the quick, — with a light sharp sting peculiar to Lowell's art. It is painfully unsympathetic, Mephistophelian in a way that chills me.'[1]

[1] Horace Scudder, who read and recommended the manuscript to Houghton Mifflin Company, took the same view. 'His work is occasionally marred by a little too obtrusive levity, but there can be no doubt he will get a good many readers, and more than he would if he had not been so jocose.'

For all that, no member of the family had ever written such prose as this. It is adorned with full-jewelled paragraphs:

'Just as we were turning the face of Screen cliff a sound of singing reached us, ricochetting over the water. It had a plaintive ring such as peasant songs are wont to have, and came, as we at length made out, from a boat homeward bound from the island, steering a course at right angles to our own. The voices were those of women, and as our courses swept us nearer to each other, we saw that women alone composed the crew. They had been faggot-cutting, and the bunches lay piled amidships, while fore and aft they plied their oars, and sang. The gloaming hid all but sound and sex, and threw its veil of romance over the trollers, who sent their hearts out thus across the twilight sea. The song, no doubt some common ditty, gathered a pathos over the water through the night. It swept from one side of us to the other, softened with distance, lingered in detached strains, and then was hushed, leaving us once more alone with the night.'

But color and cadence are used for the expression of accurate observation and wise reflection.

'Unless their newly imported ideas really take root, it is from this whole world that Japanese and Koreans, as well as Chinese, will inevitably be excluded. Their Nirvana is already being realized; already it has wrapped Far Eastern Asia in its winding-sheet, the shroud of those whose day was but a dawn, as if in prophetic keeping with the names they gave their homes, — the Land of the Day's Beginning, and the Land of the Morning Calm.'

Had he lived to the age of his brother, Lawrence, Percival might have seen that the bracketing of Chinese and Japanese was unfair. Even before Pearl Harbor it had become evident that the Superior Man, as defined by Confucius, was not dominant in Tokyo.

In the spring of '89 he was invited to deliver the annual Phi Beta Kappa Poem at Harvard Commencement. He made a flying trip home and arose before the society with, as he told

them, the aromatic odors of the East still lingering about him
and the salt spray of the ocean still moist upon his brow.

The odors of the East were pungent in the poem itself. Entitled 'Sakura no Saku,' it is *The Soul of the Far East* condensed
into three hundred lines in the pentameter couplet of Pope, a
favorite form of the family for four generations. The poet became personal only in the concluding lines celebrating two
brothers of the Phi Beta Kappa of 1829 sixty years before.
The first was his old instructor in mathematics.

> 'The one only our tear mist now can dim
> The brilliant image that is left of him.
> He was my master, though his spirit sped
> My mind refuses to believe him dead.
> Though but an echo find itself in verse,
> The Cosmos answers to the name of Peirce.'

The other was Oliver Wendell Holmes.

When he returned to Japan from this visit, Basil Hall Chamberlain arranged for him to lecture at a School of Languages in
order that as an employee of the Japanese Government he
might be excused from living in the English quarter. In his
first lecture he told his Nipponese listeners that they must become superior Japanese, not inferior Europeans. That unless
they did their destiny was destruction. Ten years before dis-
illusioned Lafcadio Hearn made the same discovery, he noted,
'Throughout the Orient truth is a thing unknown, lies of courtesy
being *de rigueur* and lies of convenience *de raison*; while with us,
fortunately, mendacity is generally discredited.'

And this he knew came, not from too much imagination, but
from too little: 'Imagination, the Japs lack it. Unless they acquire it, they will vanish off the face of the earth and leave our
planet the eventual possession of the dwellers where the day
declines.'

Both perception and prediction are at the level of genius.

Towards the close of a decade devoted to the study and ex-

position of Japanese life and thought, Percival Lowell was beginning to feel that it was time for a change. His early interest
in the starry heavens came back with a rush. On his last visit
to Japan in 1892, he carried with him a six-inch telescope, no
slight impediment for a world traveller. The direction of his
true life-work was determined.

> Chief of organic numbers,
> Old scholar of the spheres.

Cosmic speculation had always amused him. In his evenings
in the cupola peering through his two-and-a-quarter-inch glass
he had wondered whether space were indeed an uninhabited
desert, and in one of his Japanese books he had written:

'The actual is widening its field every day. Even in this little
world of our own we are daily discovering to be fact what we
should have thought fiction, like the Sailor's mother the tale of
the flying fish. Beyond it our ken is widening still more. Gul-
liver's travels may turn out truer than we think. Could we
traverse the inter-planetary ocean of ether, we might eventually
find in Jupiter the land of Lilliput or in Ceres some old-time
country of the Brobdingnagians. For men constituted mus-
cularly like ourselves would have to be proportionately small
in the big planet and big in the small one. Still stranger things
may exist around other suns. In those bright particular stars —
which the little girl thought pinholes in the dark canopy of the
sky to let the glory beyond shine through — we are finding conditions of existence like yet unlike those we already know. To our
groping speculations of the night they almost seem, as we gaze
on them in their twinkling, to be winking us a sort of compre-
hension. Conditions may exist there under which our wildest
fancies may be commonplace facts.'

Later he told George Agassiz, who had shared with him the
investigation of the Shinto trances and was to travel with him
through Space, that the transfer of his attention from Japan to
the Solar System came when the Italian astronomer, Schiaparelli,

who had observed fine lines on the planet Mars and called them
'canals,' had to cease his observations from failing eyesight. He
knew that his own was superb. Doctor Hasket Derby, the leading ophthalmologist of his day, had told him it was the keenest
he had ever examined. Since leaving college he had continued
to exercise his mind with problems in both differential and in-
tegral calculus. He felt it his manifest destiny to take over Mars
from Schiaparelli.

With him to decide was to act. 'When you have made up
your mind that a thing must be done, and done quickly, do it
yesterday.' In the present case there was not a moment to be
lost. It was late in 1893 when he came home for good from
Japan, and the point of closest opposition of Mars and the earth
for some years would be reached the coming summer. An observatory must be established at once, but where? The thing
that makes the little star twinkle is the atmosphere. The light
rays from distant star or reflecting planet come straight as arrows for their millions of light-years till they strike the air of
earth. Then they are bent and bent again as they pierce a denser
or less stratum. The strata are continually shifting and mingling
with the currents of warm or cold air rising or descending above
the surface of the earth. The light rays are diverted a little from
side to side, and the star or the planet twinkles. As Lawrence
picturesquely puts it, perhaps thinking of his grandfather John
Amory Lowell's infirmity, it would in the case of a planet be like
trying to make out the detail on an elaborately decorated plate
held up by a man with a palsied hand.

The spot must be found within the limits of the United States
with the most nearly static atmosphere. Preliminary studies and
staff work pointed to Arizona. Thither in March, 1894, an
assistant was sent with the much-travelled six-inch telescope.
Observations were taken at Tucson, Phoenix, and Tombstone.
After receiving the telegraphic reports from there, Percival, who
had remained in the East to secure equipment, wired 'Flagstaff,'
and there early in April work began. The spot chosen was in the

centre of the great plateau of northern Arizona, a pine oasis, rising three thousand feet above the desert, or two thousand above
sea level, culminating ten miles away in the San Francisco
Peaks towering in the air 12,872 feet above the sea.

'To see into the beyond,' Percival wrote, 'requires purity; in
the medium now as formerly in the man. As little air as may be
and that only of the best is obligatory to his enterprise, and the
securing it makes him perforce a hermit from his kind. He must
abandon cities and forego plains. Only in places raised above
and aloof from men can he profitably pursue his search, places
where nature never meant him to dwell and admonishes him
of the fact by sundry hints of a more or less distressing character.
To stand a mile and a half nearer the stars is not to stand immune.'

On the first of June, ten weeks after the selection of the site on
Mars Hill, two telescopes, one of twelve and another of eighteen
inches, were fully installed, complete with pier, bed-plate, clock-
work, and dome. Observations were begun.

The results of the first year's work surpassed expectations. As
summarized by Percival in the first volume of the *Annals* of the
Lowell Observatory there were:

'1st, the detection of the physical characteristics of the planet
Mars to a degree of completeness sufficient to permit of the
forming of a general theory of its condition, revealing beyond
reasonable doubt first its general habitability, and second its
particular habitation at the present moment by some form of
local intelligence;

'2d, corroboration and extension by Professor Pickering of his
discoveries at Arequipa with regard to the forms of Jupiter's
Satellites; *

'3d, the discovery and study by Mr. Douglass of the atmos-
pheric causes upon which good seeing depends.

For twenty-two years Mars Hill was the centre of Percival
Lowell's life. He travelled about, making many trips to Europe,
lecturing in numerous colleges and before learned societies, but

---

* These discoveries have since been doubted.

always in the spring coming back to the station of departure for Mars. Three commodious bungalows were built surrounded by masses of flowers, and so placed as to obtain in view the full value of the peaks and shoulders of the San Francisco Range. His life was not all star-gazing. Friends from the East were continually visiting him, along with scholars of the spheres from Oxford, Paris, and Rome. He cultivated the flowers by day as he did the stars by night, and took long tramps with his friend, Judge Doe, for geological and botanical purposes, and observation of the habits of butterflies, birds, squirrels, rabbits, rattlesnakes, coyotes, bears, and deer. He took a hand in local party politics on the anti-union-labor Whig side, and had a flair for finding small adventures. 'Rode twelve miles into the forest on the front of the cow catcher and saw a terrific bull fight in a pretty little valley where Greek met Greek for the possession of the herd. The two champions toed the line with great effect. . . . An' you love me, send me the best Chaucer ———'

In 1895, he published *Mars*, his first book in his new field, and journeyed to Paris to lecture and to consult Edouard Mantois, who had cast for him a twenty-four-inch lens for a new telescope. He dined at the house of Flammarion. 'There were fourteen of us, and all that could sat on chairs of the Zodiac under a ceiling of pale blue sky, appropriately dotted with fleecy clouds, and indeed most prettily painted.'

Mars aroused wide interest in astronomical circles and spheres. It was a sensational success with press and public. Little attention was paid, however, to the book's literary art. The prose is even more richly jewelled than the best of the Japanese work:

'To sally forth into the untrod wilderness in the cold and dark of a winter's small hours of the morning, with the snow feet deep upon the ground and the frosty stars for mute companionship, is almost to forget one's self a man for the solemn awe of one's surroundings. Fitting portal to communion with another world, it is through such avenue one enters on his quest where the common and familiar no longer jostle the unknown and the strange. Nor is the stillness of the stars invaded when some long unearthly howl, like the wail of a lost soul, breaks the slumber of the mesa forest, marking the prowling presence of a stray coyote. Gone as it came, it dies in the distance on the air that gave it birth; and the gloom of the pines swallows up one's vain peering after something palpable, their tops alone decipherable in dark silhouette against the sky. From amid surroundings that for their height and their intenancy fringe the absolute silence of space the observer must set forth who purposes to cross it to another planetary world. . . .

'As I was watching the planet, I saw suddenly two points like stars flash out in the midst of the polar cap. Dazzlingly bright upon the duller white background of the snow, these stars shone for a few moments and then slowly disappeared. The seeing at the time was very good. It is at once evident what the other-world apparitions were — not the fabled signal-lights or Martian folk, but the glint of ice-slopes flashing for a moment earthward as the rotation of the planet turned the slope to the proper angle; just as, in sailing by some glass-windowed house near set of sun, you shall for a moment or two catch a dazzling glint of glory from its panes, which then vanishes as it came. But though no intelligence lay behind the action of these lights, they were none the less startling for being Nature's own flashlights across one hundred millions of miles of space. It had taken them nine minutes to make the journey; nine minutes before they reached the Earth they had ceased to be on Mars, and after their travel of one hundred millions of miles, found to note them but one watcher, alone on a hilltop with the dawn.'

His final conclusion is cautious, and carefully and logically stated:

'To review, now, the chain of reasoning by which we have been led to regard it probable that upon the surface of Mars we see the effects of local intelligence. We find, in the first place, that the broad physical conditions of the planet are not antagonistic to some form of life; secondly, that there is an apparent dearth of water upon the planet's surface, and therefore, if beings of sufficient intelligence inhabited it, they would have to resort to irrigation to support life; thirdly, that there turns out to be a network of markings covering the disk precisely counterpartising what a system or irrigation would look like; and, lastly, that there is a set of spots placed where we should expect to find the lands thus artificially fertilized, and behaving as such constructed oases should. All this, of course, may be a set of coincidences signifying nothing; but the probability points the other way.

'. . . If astronomy teaches anything, it teaches that man is but a detail in the evolution of the universe, and that resemblant though diverse details are inevitably to be expected in the host of orbs around him. He learns that, though he will probably never find his double anywhere, he is destined to discover any number of cousins scattered through space.'

His later books, *The Solar System, Mars and Its Canals, Mars as the Ab de of Life, The Evolution of Worlds,* and *The Genesis of the Planet,* go little further than this expression of a logical probability. They were better documented from observed phenomena, and more elaborately reasoned. Patches of purple prose are less frequent, but there are paragraphs memorable for style as well as content. Take this scientific restatement and corroboration of Lucretius' poetic forecast of the end of his world:

Here is Lucretius, in W. H. Mallock's free translation:

'Globed from the atoms, falling slow or swift,
I see the suns, I see the systems lift
Their forms; and even the systems and their suns
Shall go back slowly to the eternal drift.

'Thou too, O Earth — thine empires, lands and seas —
Least, with thy stars, of all the galaxies,
Globed from the drift like these, like these thou too
Shalt go. Thou art going, hour by hour, like these.

'Nothing abides. Thy seas in delicate haze
Go off; those mooned sands forsake their place;
And where they are shall other seas in turn
Mow with their scythes of whiteness other bays.'

Here is Percival Lowell:

'But though we cannot as yet review with the mind's eye our past, we can, to an extent, foresee our future. We can with scientific confidence look forward to a time when each of the bodies composing the solar system shall turn an unchanging face in perpetuity to the Sun. Each will then have reached the end of its evolution, set in the unchanging stare of death.

'Then the Sun itself will go out, becoming a cold and lifeless mass; and the solar system will circle, unseen, ghostlike, in space, awaiting only the resurrection of another cosmic catastrophe.'

His last, perhaps his greatest, astronomical achievement was his discovery of the planet Pluto that he never lived to see. Back in the middle of the eighteenth century, certain watchers of the skies discovered that Uranus, hitherto catalogued as a fixed star, was really a planet. For a century astronomers were worried by perturbations in its orbit that seemed to be caused by the pull of another planet, swinging around the sun in a great ellipse and twice as far away. In 1846, such a planet was discovered, twice within a month, by Leverrier in Paris and a Doctor Galle in Berlin, working together, and a young Mr. J. C. Adams of Cambridge University entirely on his own. It was christened Neptune.

In 1908, Percival observed a certain small perturbation in the orbit of Neptune. After six years of observation and calculation of distance, density, mass, and velocity, he worked it out. It was a divagation of one hundred and thirty-three inches in the orbit of a planet 2,792,000,000 miles away, and taking one hundred and sixty-four years for its swing around our common sun!

Instructions were given to turn the big refractor on the indicated spot in the inverted bowl we call the sky and search for Planet X. This was in 1914. It was not until 1930, fourteen years after Percival Lowell was himself with the stars, that Clyde Tombaugh, a young man brought up as a farmer, but with a natural love of astronomy, who was working at Flagstaff in the pursuit of Planet X, found on two photographic plates taken some days apart a body that moved in a way to suggest, not an asteroid, but something vastly farther off. For seven weeks it was seen to follow the path plotted by Percival. It could be none other than his long-sought X. The discovery was announced to the world on his birthday, March 13. Following the precedent that the discoverers of celestial bodies are entitled to christen them, the observers at Flagstaff selected the happy appellation of Pluto with ♇ as its symbol. Astronomers of the future will be forever reminded of Percival Lowell by the planet he discovered but never saw.

In 1897, abstruse mathematical calculations at high speed, nightly observations and loss of sleep, a general burning of the candle at both ends, had left him in his forty-second year in a state of nervous collapse such as were recurrent with his great-grandfather, the Rebel. For four years he was absent from Mars Hill. Part of the time he was at a farmhouse he had taken at Chocorua, loafing, studying trees and shrubs, and sending to Professor Charles Sargent, of the Arnold Arboretum, rare specimens that won the sender both gratitude and admiration. But the greater part of the four years were spent in rest and foreign travel in Bermuda or on the Riviera, where he joined forces with William James, in similar neurasthenic case, and agreed with his discovery that 'ethics is a tardy compensation for the sins one has neglected to commit.'

By 1900, he had recovered sufficiently to forsake his *dolce far niente*, of which he was very weary, and take the twenty-four-inch lens with a new light tube in four parts to Tripoli to observe a total eclipse of the sun. It had a device for photographing the corona, through this, the largest lens that had ever been used for that purpose. On the day of the eclipse, the weather was clear and the results excellent. In his private journal, under the heading 'An Eclipse Trip to Tripoli, being the sequel to the Valet and the Valetudinarian,' he recorded, 'The Arabs, the

common folk, told their friends beforehand that the Christians
lied, and when the affair came off, that they had no business to
know being infidel.'

He was called that in Boston, too. He was seldom if ever seen
either in King's Chapel where Lawrence was treasurer, or Saint
Paul's Episcopal Church in Brookline where Amy for some years
joined loudly in the responses. From these conspicuous absences, and a cosmology that ill accorded with the Pentateuch, he
was reported an atheist, but fortunately not until after his father's death. When asked if it were true, he answered obliquely,
'I believe in keeping the laws. What chaos would happen if
they were not kept!'

Before his illness he had bought for his life *en garçon* a small
high house on the upper side of West Cedar Street. There during the winter season a young editor and publisher from New
York, passing with a bag of manuscripts to his own modest
establishment in the next block, used to observe him every
weekday at five-thirty. His handsome head was to be seen
vis-à-vis the *Boston Evening Transcript* beneath a life-sized plaster
Venus similar to those that infest the Athenaeum. Visibility
was perfect, for the shade was always raised to the very top of the
window as if to admit no impediment to a message from Mars.

Usually two or three times each winter he would look in at
the publishing offices on Park Street occupying one of the old
family mansions there to inquire into the continuing sale of his
Japanese books or discuss the possibility of a new edition. This
reporter has met many of the so-called great men of his time, but
none with a more potent personal quality than Percival Lowell.
He agrees with another witness that one felt it even before, or
almost before, he entered the room. It was as if one had been
suddenly deposited in a powerful magnetic field. No one could
see much of him without feeling the truth of the fervent words of
one of his associates at Flagstaff, 'He was buoyant with strength,
ambition, love, sincerity, nobleness of purpose, in fact all that
was highest in life.' An unimpeachable witness once saw him

personally eject his butler down the steps of his house on West Cedar Street and hurl a steamer trunk after him, but such violent exceptions do not disprove the truth of the concluding sentence of the characterization just quoted: 'He was a dynamic force, yet gentle as a child.'

In 1908, at fifty-three, he married Miss Constance Savage Keith, his nextdoor neighbor. On their honeymoon trip to Europe the happy pair, to the edification of the British public, made a balloon ascension in London to photograph the paths in Hyde Park to see how measurable lines would appear in aerial pictures. He had found an admirable and sympathetic helpmate, and in the last years of his life developed, rather surprisingly, some of the characteristic domestic qualities of Lowell men that have been described in a previous chapter.

In the autumn he lectured before six colleges in the Northwest on Mars and other planets, going so far as to say explicitly for the first time, 'That Mars is inhabited we have absolute proof.'

He came back to Flagstaff tired and overstrained from much speaking and entertainment, and spent several consecutive nights with little sleep in the effort to ascertain the exact distance of Jupiter's innermost satellite from the parent planet. On November 12, 1916, a cerebral hemorrhage ended his life. Before he lapsed into unconsciousness he said, 'I have always known it would come like this, but not so soon.'

His substantial estate shrunk in settlement owing to the large number of shares it contained in futuristic enterprises, aeronautics, radio, and motion picture, but it was amply sufficient to carry out the principal provision of his careful will. He had established a trust not unlike that established sixty years before by John Lowell, Jr., to carry on the Lowell Institute, to provide for the permanent work of the Lowell Observatory at Flagstaff. Like its model it stipulated that the trust should be administered by a single trustee, and named his cousin, with whom he had much in common, Guy Lowell.

2
CHAPTER

The Arts: Guy, Amy

IN THE PURSUIT OF FAME, that last infirmity of noble minds, the food that dead men eat, architects suffer both advantages and handicaps. The products of their creative genius and business management are not hung away from the crowd, to be sought out in quiet galleries, or squeezed into corners of dusty shelves in libraries. For better or for worse, they stand out in the open air in prominent positions for all men to admire or dislike. *Litera scripta manet*, but it does not hit daily and nightly thousands willy-nilly in the eye. The architect does not advertise. There is no Building of the Month Club to boom his work. Except for his fellow architects and a few enlightened amateurs of their art, how many admirers of a fine building can recall, even if they have ever heard, the name of its creator? When a man rebuilds a city like Sir Christopher Wren, or in brick and mortar expresses the spirit and culture of an age like Bulfinch, his name lives as long as his work stands. But in ninety-nine out of a hundred cases the architect must solace himself with the knowledge that, though his name may fade from memory, his work if sound and good will gladden the eye and color the subconscious minds of succeeding generations.

Guy Lowell could have found satisfaction in this reassuring thought. Large happy families are still living in his admirable country houses on Long Island, the North Shore of Massachusetts Bay, and the islands off the coast of Maine, or taking their ease in his large Dutch Colonial farmhouse that is the Piping Rock Club. In the Yard of Harvard, the family 'seminary,' are Emerson Hall, the new Harvard Hall, the new Lecture Hall, and the President's House he built for his cousin Lawrence, with its nostalgic reminiscences in detail of the 'Palace' the Old Judge built on High Street in Newburyport in 1772. The beautiful Fenway façade of the Boston Art Museum, Simmons College that confronts it, the delightful *ensemble* of Andover Academy, where so many of his forbears went to school and led their classes, all are his work. At the lower end of the island of Manhattan rises the imposing and convenient mass of the hexagonal Court House that cost twenty million dollars and took the better part of two decades to build. At the opposite end of the size scale is the small but perfect jewel of a village library at Boscawen, New Hampshire. All this in less than thirty years of active professional practice with time out for the First World War.

He was the son of historically minded but forward-looking Edward Jackson Lowell, and was born in Boston at his grandfather's house, 56 Beacon Street, August 6, 1870.[1] Like his father he received his early education abroad, at Dresden and Paris, and entered Harvard with the class of 1892. He was a tall slim boy, not strong, and with the family predisposition to digestive infelicities, but he had the stout Lowell legs and heart

[1] For an excellent account of the character and life-work of Guy Lowell see 'A Memoir,' by his fellow Taverner and friend, Arthur Stanwood Pier, in the *Harvard Graduates Magazine* for June, 1927.

and made the track team in his junior year. In the dual meet with Yale he came in third in the gruelling mile run. In his senior year he was first in the Intercollegiates, with the excellent time of 4 minutes 33⅔ seconds, a Harvard record that lasted for several years. All his life he followed the family habit of running upstairs, the more flights the better. He was one of the early members of Chapter Zeta of Delta Phi, later known as 'The Gas House,' which included such delightfully disparate young men as 'Jack' Morgan, Winthrop Ames, and George Santayana. After Harvard he spent two years at the Massachusetts Institute of Technology studying architecture under the inspiring Frenchman, Despradelles, and five more at the Ecole des Beaux-Arts in Paris. There he was indoctrinated with the French belief in sound and logical basic planning, admirable ballast for the exuberance that a large share of the family's animal spirits had given to his natural style. The result was an easy and light-hearted classicism.

In 1898, his last year at the Ecole, he married Henrietta Sargent, daughter of Charles Sargent, of the Arboretum, and in 1899 settled down happily at home to the business of expressing his taste to meet the needs of his clients in houses and college halls. Within a very few years his ability and useful connections had brought him enough important commissions to have contented the ordinary architect. It was with characteristic Lowell audacity that, in 1912, he seized the large occasion of an announced competition for a great new Court House for the city of New York, to cost twenty millions, one of the plumpest professional plums that had ever been offered American architects.

The story of the award cannot be more compactly told than it is by Arthur Pier.[1]

'In the competition for the Court House seventy architects entered the preliminary contest, as a result of which ten were selected to enter the final competition against twelve others who were among the best known architects in the country. Thus, in

[1] *Op. cit.*

winning the competition, Lowell surmounted a double hazard. His plan for a circular court house illustrated his ingenuity; it introduced a new idea into the architecture of public building, that of bringing the visitors and occupants to the hub of a wheel and then distributing them along the corridors as spokes to the periphery. The design insured the utmost economy of space, as well as ease of distribution, and it provided for court-rooms that would be light and free from noise. Another advantage that it presented was in the arrangement of the domestic engineering; all pipes and conduits were carried in alternate layers, above the spokes of the wheel, or corridors, by means of mezzanine stories, and thus were accessible at any time without interference with the normal activities of any of the occupants of the building.'

Work was started in 1913, and the completed building was dedicated in 1927, a week after its architect's death. For fourteen years, with two offices, one in Boston, one in New York, dividing his time equally between them, he struggled against jealousy, petty city politics, and parsimony. In the end his high-spirited persistence and grasp of a myriad details conquered all obstacles and opposition. The building came out a hexagon instead of the full circle, the amphitheatre of his first conception. The greater part of his fee of one million dollars had vanished in expense.

In sport as in architecture competition was the breath of life to him. A few years before the First World War his early catboat sailing at Cotuit suddenly developed into an interest in the international Sonder Class racing that William the Second was promoting, along with the Germanic Museum at Harvard, to cement ties of friendship between the Vaterland and the United States. The means were sound, whatever may be thought of the ultimate end. Guy Lowell acquired a summer home at Marblehead and developed such skill in the handling of the able little boats [1] that he skippered one of the American entries three times. After his final victory at the Kiel races, the Sabre Rattler gave a party complete with champagne for the presentation of cups and

[1] Built to the formula length + beam + draft not over 32 feet.

scrolls and pennants. Guy Lowell reported the ceremony in a letter home.

'The aide de camp brought a small table — we stood the whole two hours, — and the aide pulled the string that tied the portfolio on the end away from us and the Emperor with his one hand pulled the string on our side, and only pulled out the loop and made a hard knot. "Oh, I have made a Gordian knot!" he said. I started to untie it. "Please cut it, Mr. Lowell," he said. "Only Emperors cut knots," I said. "Republicans untie them." He roared, and as I picked the knot apart said, "That's the devil of it; you Americans are so clever at untying knots." '

When a few years later the sabre flashed evilly from its scabbard and the Old War came on, and Guy Lowell went overseas as chief of the Department of Military Affairs of the American Red Cross in Italy, the racing flag of the *Cima* that had shown her graceful stern to the German Sonder fleet fluttered over the radiator of his Packard command car.[1]

During the period of his war service in 1917 and 1918, his ambulances carried 150,000 sick and wounded men, his rolling canteens served 750,000 a month, his rest-houses established at fifteen large railway stations offered comfort to 4,200,000. He disbursed over a million dollars, wisely and well. He received the first military medal for valor that was pinned on an American coat in Italy. In the language of the Duke of Aosta, who read the citation: 'During an intense aerial bombardment, Padua, December 28, 1917, he manoeuvred and directed with exemplary calm the services for rapid rescue, directing other volunteers and carrying of the wounded to the hospital.'

He wrote home of the climax of the fireworks, 'I have a suspicion I swallowed the burning butt of my cigar.'

Three other medals and eloquent citations came to him the following year. His reports home show an artist's appreciation of the 'drab, misty color of war,' and a soldier's grasp of the problems of strategy, tactics, and logistics.

[1] This statement of a friend is denied by his wife, who was on the ground. Perhaps it was in his mind's eye.

In the annals of his family not even Percival showed such talent in so many and such different fields. No astronomer himself, his management of the Flagstaff Observatory for over a decade and his personal polishing and repolishing of the twenty-four-inch lens were factors in the final annexation of Pluto. He painted pictures, composed both words and music of a light opera, wrote and illustrated with his own photographs workmanlike books on *American Gardens, Smaller Italian Villas and Farm Houses*, and *More Smaller Italian Villas and Farm Houses*, was an accomplished collector of Dresden china, and an eager and learned gastronome. His last piece of writing, read at the Thursday Club after his death, was entitled 'Man's First Great Passion, or Dining from Fig-leaf to Tuxedo.'

In January, 1927, the Court House at last completed and ready for dedication, he sailed with his wife for his beloved Italy in the spirit of a boy out of school. During the ship's call at Madeira, the Nemesis that pursues superactive men of restless energy overtook him as it had the Rebel and Percival. He died of a cerebral hemorrhage on February 4. His body was cremated in Italy and his ashes brought home for burial.

As in the case of Percival, the characterizations at once the most touching and the most convincing come from members of his office staff, daily fellow workers. One of them affirms:

'For many years we here had the privilege of being in almost daily contact with as gentle and great a man as we shall ever know. He was never too busy to listen to our little personal problems, and though his world was so different from ours, he grasped so quickly the details of our particular difficulties and as quickly helped us to a definite solution. His mind was always thinking way ahead, while we dwelt on the immediate necessity of a solution, so that his advice aided us not only for the present but for the future as well. I cannot remember his once saying an unkind word. He was the best influence in my life.'

Up to this point in the long chronicle play of the Lowells in

New England, the protagonists have been men. There have been charming daughters, delightful maiden aunts, attractive nubile cousins, passing by the slightest of changes into the rôle of admirable wives. But the occasions they seized were of the fireside and boudoir. Now in the thirteen yeasty years that included in their middle the First World War, one of the distaff side assumes the centre of the stage. She possessed the virile qualities and talents of the family to a singular degree, attracted the limelight irresistibly, and all but stole the show.

Amy Lowell was born at the family place on Heath Street in Brookline, February 9, 1874. Her father was forty-four, her invalid mother forty-two. Her brother Percival was nineteen, Lawrence eighteen. Her nearest sister, Elizabeth, later Mrs. William Lowell Putnam, was twelve. She was an important Postscript.[1]

She was first named Rebecca Amory Lowell after the cherished great-aunt, Amory, the Rebel's daughter, who had died two months before, but at her christening her given name was trimmed to Amy, to its bearer's subsequent annoyance and regret. She first appears in characteristic action at the age of two, when, with the family coachman, Burns, an ex-jockey, holding the reins behind her, she drove a spanking pair to and from church one Sunday morning. Burns taught her to ride as well as drive, and on some occasions to behave. It was a common observation in Boston of the gay nineties that 'Amy Lowell was brought up by the coachman.' A little later she gave the evidence of her grief that she had not been born a boy. An early friend reports, 'She always tried to walk exactly like her brothers

---

[1] *Amy Lowell: A Chronicle with Extracts from her Correspondence*, by S. Foster Damon, is a narrative of seven hundred and fifty pages, at once intimate and accurate. For a perspective view of the Imagist movement that she organized and led, see *Convention and Revolt in Poetry*, by John Livingston Lowes. Originally a series of lectures delivered before the Lowell Institute. The present writer was not unacquainted with his present subject. For a dozen years, as he has stated in another place, he 'dealt with her, disagreed with her, fought, capitulated, made up and smoked the cigar of peace without victory, to fight again, but with never a break in confident friendship.'

Percy and Lawrence, striding along with her head down and her hat crammed over her ears.'

At six she began book collecting; *The Rollo Books,* authentic tales of New England childhood, her first acquisitions. At eight she made the first of her many trips abroad, touring with her family in Scotland, England, France, Belgium, Holland, Italy, Germany, Norway, Denmark, and Sweden 'at a fearful rate of speed.'

Not long after her return from this gigantic *giro* came an ominous event of which the true gravity was to appear only as the years went by. At a party she had eaten a large plate of rice. Her brother dared her to eat another. She did, but when it was time to go home it was found that her coat would not button across her stomach. 'And,' she said, 'it never buttoned again,' evidence of a physical maladjustment that grew worse as she grew older. She was never to be easy and happy with her body.

At nine on the way home from California she composed her first poem, a rather Imagistic piece on Chicago. It is decidedly free verse, but it concluded in the best family tradition:

> 'The folks go
> On the lake
> in sailboat
> and barge.
> But for all
> of its beauty
> I'd rather go home,
> To Boston,
> Charles River,
> and the
> State House's
> dome.'

Late in the same year Percival came home briefly from Japan with the Korean Mission, bringing along as his own secretary an accomplished youth of seventeen, Tsumejiro Miyaoka. Amy sat in his lap, pulled his raven hair, listened to his legendary tales of old Japan, and made her first acquaintance with things Japanese. For ten years Percival sent her frequent letters on Japanese-decorated notepaper. As she wrote later in reply to an enthusiastic fan letter from a Japanese admirer, 'every mail brought letters and a constant stream of picture prints, kaki-monos flowed in upon me, and I suppose affected my imagination, for in childhood the imagination is plastic. . . . Japan seems entwined with my earliest memory.' At twelve she read *Alice in Wonderland* and Charles Carryl's *Davy and the Goblin*, and began to write goblin stories herself. She was at that time best described, a childhood contemporary says, as 'obstreperous.'

At fourteen in fancy-dress costume, at a bazaar held to secure funds for the Perkins Institution for the Blind, she personally sold a privately printed edition of some of her goblin tales, entitled *Dream Drops* and took in the sum of fifty-six dollars. Percival, Lawrence, and Elizabeth were all writing and the two young men publishing. The Postscript was not going to be left behind.

A few months later she had a meeting with her cousin James, in which he seems to have been unaware of her as a budding author:

'I remember so well that last time I saw him, standing in front of the fire at my Aunt Mary Putnam's [who was also his sister]. I was a young girl then, very young, and most impressed to be en route to a college boat race. Our party convened at Aunt Mary's, and I was hauled into the library to say how do you do to Mr. Lowell. I was frightened to death and he was obviously bored; had we but known it, it was the old and the new meeting in furious conjunction, but we did not know it. I was afraid of his grandeur and his reticence, and he considered me a poor little girl whom he had to speak to. I went on to my boat race, where my side lost (I shall never forget that), he went on his slow and stately way to the grave, and the stars went on their courses, — to what end, I wonder, alas! I wonder.'

In a letter to another correspondent she wrote:

'I am grateful to you for comparing me with James Russell

Lowell to the detriment of the latter. This may sound unkind, but if you had had that elderly gentleman held in front of you as a model and a shining goal all your life, you would realize the delight I take in reading such words as yours.'

At the age of fifteen, on January 1, 1889, she started a diary, noting near the beginning that she is 'a great rough masculine strong thing.' Yet in October she is 'struck all of a heap' to find herself in love, hopeless love. With admirable candor she sets down that she is 'ugly, fat, conspicuous and dull, — to say nothing of a very bad temper.' In 1890, when she was sixteen, she first sprained an ankle. In the thirty five years of life remaining to her she was to sprain it again eight times and the other one, ten. In the same year she was confirmed, first met Mr. Bernard Quaritch, the London bookseller, was cast as Tony Lumpkin in *She Stoops to Conquer*, but was made to give it up, discovered the poetry of John Keats in Leigh Hunt's book on *Fancy and Imagination*, and first made herself at home in the ancestral alcoves of the Athenaeum:

> 'Long peaceful hours seated on the floor
> Of some retired nook all lined with books. . . .
> Every nook and cranny is our very own.
> The dear old sleepy place is full of spells.'

It was there that she acquired, more by the light of nature and inheritance than by instruction, the spirit and methods of a scholar.

In 1891, at the age of seventeen, she learned to ride a bicycle and was presented to society. Sixty dinners were given in her honor. Well instructed in the Terpsichorean art by Mr. Papanti, and like many stout persons light on her feet, full of animal spirits and free of social inhibitions, she was a popular partner with the youth of Harvard, and at dances always had a good and rather noisy time.

The next nine years in which Amy Lowell passed from girlhood to womanhood were full and varied. She became en-

amoured of the stage, saw all the great actors of the time and
acted herself in numerous amateur performances. She travelled
abroad with girl friends suitably chaperoned, and came to know
England, Italy, and Egypt well. In the land of the Sphinx,
where she had been sent in the hope that the warm desert air
and a vegetarian diet would benefit both her health and her
figure, she had an adventure curiously parallelling that of John
Lowell, Jr., with his mutinous crew sixty years before, though
with a different weapon in her hand. She had observed that
the Arab crew of her dahabeah stood in awe of her fountain pen
from which, though no ink-pot was visible, ink flowed as if by
magic. When therefore she was being hauled up the mild rapids
of the First Cataract and the crew approached her in a body, as
if terrified, to demand a special bonus of baksheesh for completing the ascent, she advanced on them with the ink-dealing,
perhaps death-dealing pen, threatening them like a javelin.
Pen proved as mighty as pistol. They fled in real terror and
eagerly hauled the boat up and over the great lip of the Nile at
the rapids top. The gift of command was always to be hers.

Her travel letters home are in the best family manner, as vivid
and copious as those of the Rebel, John Lowell, Jr., either of
the two Edward Jackson Lowells, the Colonel, or the Professor,
and with a certain unction of their own, a special gusto of adventure. One about the over-advertised dangers of the descent
of the Cataract concluded: 'I am glad I am an American and
was brought up like a boy, and I am glad for every single time
that I have been spilt out of a carriage. There! . . .'

One of her spills behind a runaway horse might have resulted
in serious injury or worse had it not been for an exhibition of
daring, agility, and strength on the part of Lawrence.

After her return from Egypt, not perceptibly benefited in
either health or figure, she had a prolonged attack of neuras-
thenia, 'the real thing where you live with a perpetual headache, and the slightest sound jars you all over.' It lasted nearly
seven years. In the midst of it, in 1900, her father died. In the

settlement of his ample estate it was arranged that Amy should take over Sevenels. *Incipit vita nuova.*

At twenty-six, mistress of the Mansion, with no one to talk back to her, and in enjoyment of an income that, until she had converted nearly half her capital into rare and useful books and manuscripts, ran close to six figures, her health improved and she became an even more commanding figure in her world.

Her first move was to interest herself in the schools of Brookline. At a town meeting called for the purpose of removing an official glaringly incapacitated by old age, no one wished to hurt his feelings, and so much laudation of his past performance was uttered that it began to look as if nothing constructive would be done. Fearful lest the need of the children should be sacrificed to sentiment, Amy, always the realist, climbed on the platform and told the meeting in a voice of resonance and authority exactly what was what. Hisses mingled with applause, but the difficult deed was done, and a new official was appointed. When she descended from the platform, horrified Lowell women informed her that it was the first time any of the distaff side had spoken in public. Even some of the Lowell men, strong individualists as they were, seemed, if not like the women, shocked, at least seriously startled.

As a result of this crusade she was elected a member of the executive committee of the Brookline Education Society, and chairman of the library committee of the same organization. She made a speech to open a public conference on the question, 'Is the Present System of High School Education Prejudicial to Individual Development.' For a young woman in her twenties who had never been exposed to the advantages of a college education, it was a remarkable effort:

'Perhaps the two qualities which more than any others go to the making of a strong personality are character and imagination. Character means courage, and there is a great difference between the collective courage of a mass of people all thinking the same way, and the courage of one man who cares not at all for public opinion, but goes on his way unswervingly. Our national ideal as to the moral attitude is high. What the people understand, and what they all agree about, that they will do; but it is not so easy to find men who are willing to think and act at variance with the opinions of their neighbors.

'The difficulty with American civilization is that it is essentially vulgar in tone, not so much in manner as in essence. The theatres, the newspapers, the popular amusements, all show this. The few people with refined ideas and cultivated tastes can make no impression against this mass of Vulgarism. The tendency is not so much directly vicious as it is undermining and deteriorating. The cheap and tawdry exert their fatal influence throughout the whole national life.

'No national trait strikes such horror into our European neighbors, and none does us so much harm, as our constant sense of hurry. "Evolution, not revolution, is the order of development," says Mr. Hughes in his book on comparative education, and evolution is a process requiring much time. Nature cannot be hurried, there is no such thing as cramming. What is not digested is simply forgotten. A congested curriculum results in the proper assimilation of no one subject. And what can we think of a primary school taught by one teacher, in which the children were taught seventeen subjects, with fifteen minutes given to each subject, as was the case in one school in Brookline!'

Here speaks the Lowell mind, as we have seen it in the Rebel, and John Amory Lowell, and shall presently see it in the educational policies of Lawrence.

In 1902 and 1903 came her first successful foray as a propagandist. There was trouble at the Athenaeum. A majority of the proprietors had been sold the idea that the old place, haunted by Lowell ghosts, was congested and inconveniently located; that it should be cashed in as a valuable plot for commercial development and that the library, severed from its companion the Old Granary Burying Ground, should be re-erected on the new-made land across the Public Garden. Two valiant women,

Amy Lowell and Katherine Loring, took the contrary view.
Amy wrote and printed her effective poem, 'The Boston Athenaeum,' and they enlisted the aid of Percival's pungent pen
from Flagstaff. They secured attractive plans and feasible
estimates for enlarging the old Beacon Hill premises. Appreciation of the value of association and historical sentiment prevailed by a narrow margin over the restless American lust for
change.

But just before that Athenaeum propaganda piece, Amy had
written at the age of twenty-eight another poem on an impulse
that may be taken as the fountain and origin of her poetic career.
On the evening of October 21, 1902, she saw Eleanora Duse play
La Giaconda and *La Citta Morta* by the Italian Rapagnetta, who
had taken as his *nom de théâtre* Gabriel of the Annunciation.[1]

Amy tells the story thus:

'I had always felt that I could write, and I longed to write. I
tried my hand at novels, short stories, and plays, but it did not
dawn upon me that I could write poetry. Then Eleanora Duse
came to America on one of her periodical trips; that was the year
she was acting in the d'Annunzio plays. I went to see her, as I
always went to see everything that was good in the theatre. The
effect on me was something tremendous. What really happened
was that it revealed me to myself, but I hardly knew at that time.
I just knew that I had got to express the sensations that Duse's
acting gave me, somehow. I knew nothing whatever about the
technique of poetry, I had never heard of *vers libre*, I had never
analyzed blank verse — I was as ignorant as anyone could be.
I sat down, and with infinite agitation wrote this poem. It has,
I think, every *cliché* and every technical error which a poem can
have, but it loosed a bolt in my brain and I found out where my
true function lay.'

The poem itself, some seventy lines of indifferent blank verse,
though not anything to write home to other Lowells about, was

---

[1] There are two schools of thought about this; some authorities, particularly those
who most admire him, insist he was born d'Annunzio. The evidence is conflicting.

something to have written. 'I began to write,' she says, 'not specifically about Madame Duse, but simply out of the fullness of the vision of poetry she had given me.' The concluding lines are straight to the point:

> 'We feel the throbbing of a woman's soul,
> A woman's heart that cries to God and fears!'

The newborn poet saw Duse every night of her engagement in Boston, followed her to Philadelphia, was introduced to her while she was resting in bed, had a brief but inspiring talk, and came away 'almost on air.'

The next seven years, though they saw the building-over of Sevenels, the swift growth of her important book collection, lively adventures as a producer on the amateur stage, and a European tour, chiefly by motor, that took her as far as Greece, were spent in the secret service of the Muse. In 1910, she sent four sonnets to Ellery Sedgwick, editor of the *Atlantic*, who had married her distant cousin and constant friend, Mabel Cabot. He accepted all four forthwith and printed one, 'Fixed Idea,' in his August number. She was on her way! And the Gods sent her the perfect companion for the course.

On March 12, 1912, at a reunion of a club henceforth to be called The Purple Lunch Club, with the manuscript of her first book, *A Dome of Many Coloured Glass*, almost ready for the press, she met the deservedly popular actress, Ada (Mrs. Harold) Russell. They recognized each other at once. In 1914, Mrs. Russell became her travelling companion and a little later her housemate, called by the 'little name' of Peter. All that Charles Brown and Joseph Severn together did for John Keats, Ada did for Amy, plus eleven solid years of that woman's work that according to the ancient proverb is never done.

It was not for nothing that in *John Keats*, published three months before its author's death, the dedication page, the first to be found in any of her works reads 'To A. D. R. This and all My Books.'

A Dome of Many Coloured Glass from Shelley's lines, 'Life . . . stains the white radiance of eternity' — was published in October, 1912. It contained the Athenaeum poem, 'The Fairy Tale,' a memory of her own troubled and troubling childhood, versified recollections of Bromley Vale and incidents of her foreign travels, pictures of Mount Monadnock in spring and other scenes in the Dublin country where she had acquired a summer place, two pieces inspired by the art of Japan, and most significant of all a sonnet on a first edition of Keats. The format of the book, which was to be preserved for all her works except the bivoluminous *John Keats,* its handy size, paper label, and striking color contrasts, was adapted from Keats' own design for his. Like Keats and like his Endymion, the author of the *Dome* was revealed as a moon worshipper. Its pale radiance colors all her works. But though she was already an omnivorous reader of poetry, there was little imitation in her book. She had, as Sir Philip Sidney advised, looked in her heart and written.

Its success was modest. Less than three hundred copies were sold in the first year, and the reviewers seemed chiefly interested in the fact that she was the sister of the president of Harvard, and wondered what he would think of it. Stimulated by the taste of print and publicity, she soon got into her stride. In the next thirteen years, in addition to the monumental life of Keats, she printed more than six hundred poems in magazines and newspapers which were collected in ten individual volumes. She wrote eighty-four reviews and articles which made up three volumes of prose, and she carried on a vast correspondence. The carbons fill a large filing cabinet, and run well into the thousands. She gave a century of lectures and readings. During these same years she had four major operations for a progressive umbilical hernia, suffered from gastric neuralgia and acute eye-strain, and had a constant high blood pressure, sometimes running up to the terrifying figure of two hundred and forty. Yet the shelf of her published works was steadily lengthening. She was an even stouter fellow than her grandfather, John Amory Lowell.

The urge that kept her going was what she felt to be her mission, to lead a militant movement in poetry, to march at the head of its drums and trampling.

It was a new world again in Poetry as in Science and in Society. Even before the far from futuristic *Dome* was published, E. A. Robinson, Edgar Lee Masters, Vachel Lindsay, Sara Teasdale, and Ezra Pound were writing a new kind of verse. It all fitted in with the harnessing of electricity, the new conception of astronomical space, skyscrapers, jazz music, the Russian ballet, the presidency of Theodore Roosevelt, and the Ford car. There were distant echoes of the fanfare in the *Dome*. But it was not until 1913, the year after its publication, that Amy overseas became fully aware of what was going on in the poetry bookshops of London and Paris, met Ezra Pound, grasped the basic idea with great force, and, to use the imagistic word, ate it alive. She had a poem in Pound and Aldington's first anthology, *Des Imagistes*, published in February, 1914, and a group of imagistic pieces and experiments in polyphonic prose in *Poetry* for April. In May she corrected the proofs for her first completely characteristic book, *Sword Blades and Poppy Seeds*. On June 23, Amy and Ada, complete with her mulberry-colored Pierce Arrow and two chauffeurs in livery to match, sailed on the *Laconia* for Liverpool. She reached her customary quarters at the Berkeley Hotel on July 3, five days after the assassination of the Archduke Francis Ferdinand at Sarajevo.

In the hectic month that followed, Amy, despite a painfully sprained ankle, seized one of the most striking occasions in the family history. Ezra Pound had rather lost interest in Imagism, and had organized a new group of 'Vorticists,' specimens of whose work had been published in a volume called *Blast* just before she landed. On July 17, she gave an Imagist dinner-party. Pound and his wife were there *honoris causa* and the other guests were Richard Aldington with H. D., his wife, John Gould Fletcher, F. S. Flint, who was eating his heart out in the Post Office, the Hueffers, Allen Upward, and the anti-Hellenic sculptor, Gaudier-Brzeska. These, with the elimination of Pound and subsequently Hueffer, and the notable addition of D. H. Lawrence, formed the squad of Imagists of which Amy was to become at once angel and top sergeant.

On Sunday, the third of August, resting in Bath after a visit to Thomas Hardy in Dorchester, rumors of war made the mulberry-colored car turn its polished brass radiator back toward London. The next day Sir Edward Grey made his great simple speech in the House of Commons. That night war was declared.

Amy joined the Hoover committee that was trying to help Americans home, cabled for ten thousand dollars to swell its funds, and, her ankle being better, met trains at Victoria with a placard across her imposing chest to aid and direct bewildered refugees from the Continent. Despite this activity, she went ahead with the poetic war, wrote her poem, 'Astigmatism,' dedicated to Pound, and planned the first volume of the *Imagist Anthology*. On the first of September she sailed for home, where awaiting her on arrival she found the first copy of *Sword Blades and Poppy Seeds*.

> 'I have whetted my brain until it is like a Damascus blade,
> So keen it nicks off the floating fringes of passers by. . . .
> My brain is curved like a cimitar
> And sighs at its cutting like a sickle mowing grass.'

The book was published by Macmillan in September, the first volume of *Some Imagist Poets* by Houghton Mifflin in the following spring, and a second collection in 1916.

The two great offensives in the Poetic War came in the winter of 1914–15, and again in 1917–18. By the end of 1918, the guns were stilled in the poetry magazines and newspapers as on the torn and trampled fields of Europe. An uneasy peace had been established in the United Nations of Parnassus. The bloody details of the campaigns are available in a score of books and need not be retold here. The literary creed of the Imagists was stated, and restated with variations, in prefaces and manifestoes without number. In his *Convention and Revolt in Poetry*, John

Lowes caught the two battle cries of the New Poetry, and stated them simply:

1st.   War on the eloquent.
2nd.   Death to the *cliché*.

The aim was to achieve the exact just word and unblurred image. It was, in short, an attack on what the new poets liked to call the Cosmic School of Poetry, exemplified by Tennyson in England, and by James Russell Lowell as much as anyone in America. And it was to a large degree achieved. A fresh note, a new reality, came into the poetry of the English-speaking world, and the elder poets since Keats have never looked quite the same to us again.

The publisher of the *Imagist Anthologies* cannot in the least recall it, but he must accept Amy's statement in a printed letter that once in the joy of battle he exclaimed to her, with more force than elegance, 'We are putting Cosmic Poetry on the blink.'

In retrospect there is seen to be a certain impermanency in the poetry of the Imagists. Lacking the mnemonic aid of rhyme and regular metre, it eludes the memory. Like the work of the 'Georgian Poets' that it ran with in time, too much of it is open to the attack of the South African singer who wrote:

'They use the snaffle and the curb all right,
But where's the bloody horse?'

Of all the Imagists, Amy, it is now clear, had most of the potency of life in her. Her organizing ability stepped up the influence of the school and prolonged its existence, but if we may judge by representation in anthologies and sales of individual volumes, it is by Amy Lowell's own writing that Imagism will be most long remembered. Of her books of poetry some seventy-five thousand copies have been sold, and in both English and American anthologies of modern verse selections from her work usually outnumber any other of the group. It takes two to make a poem, a good writer and a good reader. Amy's vivid story-telling, *Pictures of the Floating World*, *Legends*, her *Men, Women and Ghosts,* her polyphonic prose historical pieces in *Can Grande's Castle,* have a way of finding out their predestinate readers. The *Selected Poems,* sensitively edited by John Lowes, fulfils at least a publisher's definition of a classic. It continues to sell.

Towards the end of her comparatively short life, she was turning back to regular verse forms and rhythms more in harmony with the native genius of English poetry, writing less objectively and with a warmer feeling. Had she lived longer, her position as a standard minor poet might have been more secure. Four stanzas from her poem entitled 'On Looking at a Copy of Alice Meynell's Poems, Given Me, Years ago, by a Friend,' show her final mood and direction:

'And you are dead these drifted years,
How many I forget. And she
Who wrote the book, her tragedy
Long since dried up its scalding tears.

'I read of her death yesterday,
Frail lady whom I never knew,
And knew so well. Would I could strew
Her grave with pansies, blue and grey.

'Would I could stand a little space
Under a blowing, brightening sky,
And watch the sad leaves fall and lie
Gently upon that lonely place.

'So cried her heart, a feverish thing.
But clay is still, and clay is cold,
And I was young, and I am old,
And in December what birds sing!'

The years from 1920 to 1925 mainly devoted to the slow accumulation of material and the writing of the life of Keats, included several periods of serious illness, extensive travel, and lecturing at home and abroad. The prodigal hospitality at Sevenels continued, but her appearances at her own dinner-parties became later and later. Once or twice she never came down at all from the third-story quarters where she turned night into working day. The seven large bouncing bundles of long hair that climbed over you after dinner, and were discovered on closer contact to contain affectionate sheep dogs, were no more, but the vast table in the rich and stately library was still piled solid with travel books and murder stories to the height of two feet, and eighteenth century memoirs by her bedside. The ten thousand long light Manila cigars she had bought during the Old War to secure her future were still under consumption. Cigarettes had proved inadequate, and a pipe she discovered burned small holes in the meticulously stretched bedclothes beneath which she wrote. Like the men in her family, save Cousin James, his father and his great-grandfather, she had found that a good cigar was a smoke. She liked to tell of an occasion when the mulberry motor had ceased suddenly to function and the proprietor of the village garage hesitated about charging the cost of repairs.

'I'm Amy Lowell,' she told him, 'the sister of the President of Harvard. Call him up and he'll tell you I'm good for the bill.'

The proprietor called Kirkland 7600, and did so, stating the case in some detail.

'What's she doing now?' asked Lawrence.

'She's sitting across the road on a stone wall smoking a cigar!'

'All right, that's my sister.'

In the summer of 1921, while bedridden after an operation, she worked off her energies in the rapid composition of her *Critical Fable* which was published anonymously the following year. The secret of the authorship was well kept. The inquiring reader was thrown off the scent by the unknown poet's exceedingly candid portrait of Amy Lowell:

> 'Conceive, if you can, an electrical storm
> Of a swiftness and fury surpassing the norm;
> Conceive that this cyclone has caught up the rainbow
> And dashed dizzily on with it streaming in tow.

Percival Lowell observes Venus by daylight through the twenty-four-inch telescope at Flagstaff with which by night he studied the canals of Mars. Through it after his death was observed the planet Pluto which he discovered and located but never saw.

Although his Uncle George of Cotuit had gone in for sailing and field sports, and his Cousin Percival had been a very dashing polo player, Guy Lowell with his Sonder class boat *Cima* was first of his clan to make his mark in international sportsmanship. Distinguished architect and admirable writer, he was a notable example of the family's varied talents.

This, the last photograph of Amy Lowell, was taken by her child-hood's friend Florence Wheelock, who as Florence Ayscough collabo-rated in her translations of ancient Chinese poems. Certain of her ear-lier pictures seem almost those of an identic twin of her twice great-grandfather, the Old Judge. Even here, worn with illness and over-work, the resemblance can still be traced. She inherited his optimism, and his gift for seizing the occasion, and getting things done.

Lawrence Lowell was in his eightieth year when this photograph was made for the use of a sculptor who was working on his bust. It is an admirable likeness and a striking illustration of the persistence of type through five generations from the Reverend John Lowell of Newbury.

Imagine a sky all split open and scissored
By lightnings, and then you can picture this blizzard.
That is, if you'll also imagine the clashes
Of tropical thunder, the incessant crashes
Which shiver the hearing and leave it in ashes.
Remember, meanwhile, that the sky is prismatic
And outrageous with colour. The effect is erratic
And jarring to some, but to others ecstatic,
Depending, of course, on the idiosyncratic
Response of beholders. When you come to think of it,
A good deal is demanded by those on the brink of it.'

No sooner was the book out than she started an enthusiastic boom for Leonard Bacon, whose 'Banquet of the Poets' had amused her, as the brilliant author of the *Fable*. It was so announced by Henry Canby in the *Saturday Review*. Leonard was flattered but indignant. Guess the author of the *Critical Fable* became a popular literary game. Among those featured were Amy Lowell and Leonard Bacon, Gamaliel Bradford, Conrad Aiken, Louis Untermeyer, Masters, Don Marquis, Nathan Haskell Dole, Christopher Morley, Wallace Irwin, and, to his mingled consternation and delight, Ferris Greenslet. Of course no one of them save Amy Lowell, nor all of them together, could conceivably have written it. It was not until the English *Who's Who* of 1923 came out that the authorship was disclosed.

When we consider the low physical state in which it was composed and compare the facility, force, and justice of her appraisal of her contemporaries and herself, with the same qualities of Cousin James's *Fable for Critics* written by its author at a period of 'whoreson health,' it is evident that Amy and not James was the supreme literary exponent of Lowell animal spirits.

Meanwhile, the eleven hundred and sixty pages of *John Keats*, the book that, as Amy liked to remember, James Russell Lowell had planned to write but never did, were steadily piling up. Few biographies of its time have involved more energetic and far-ranging research. Applied to so short and limited a life as Keats', the effect of the multiplicity of intimate detail was tremendous. Perhaps just a little too tremendous.

Late in 1924, a chauffeur in mulberry uniform delivered the completed manuscript to the publisher who was to have a fortnight to read it and say what he thought about it. An appointment on Park Street was made for five one afternoon. The hour came, five-thirty, six, no Amy! Finally at six-thirty she arrived with something of the aspect of Turner's 'Old Temeraire,' apologetic and as always completely disarming. Perhaps at this date the interview may be reported in its *ipsissima verba*:

'Well, Ferris, what about it?'

'Amy, it's a great book, but you have given the reader the whole process of your research and your thought, not just the results, which are what he wants. I have put faint pencilled brackets about some sentences and paragraphs which would be better out. The more the marble wastes, the more the statue grows.'

'Ferris, you are a dear good boy, but you don't know a thing about biography, not a damned Thing!'

The interview was prolonged until after seven. In the end the publisher was embraced by the biographer, patted on the shoulder and reassured that he was a good boy, but no deletions were made. As Carl Sandburg once told Florence Ayscough, 'arguing with Amy was like arguing with a big blue wave.'

The book was published in two stout red volumes in February, 1925. It was enormously successful in America, four editions ordered in five days, less so in England. Lawrence, though he cared little for poetry, read it through carefully and found it better than he expected. He said that had he known Keats in the flesh he did not think he would have liked him. It was not the biography to end biographies of John Keats who thought his name was writ in water, but it will stand as an authoritative source book for future biographies, a monument to its author's sympathetic understanding and intellectual energy.

Through February and March she had a flood of gratulatory mail, and planned a trip to England to accept invitations to lecture in sixteen appropriate and distinguished places, including the Keats House, the Poetry Bookshop, Eton College, and the

Universities of Oxford and Cambridge. She was to sail on the *Berengaria* on April 26. On April 9, a 'complimentary Dinner in Honour of Miss Amy Lowell' was given in the ballroom of the Hotel Somerset. Some hundreds of distinguished persons were on the whole rather pleased when the guest of honor arrived an hour late, and distinctly gratified when with the coffee she produced her capacious cigar-case. There were laudatory speeches covering every phase of her work by men and women who knew what they were talking about. Glenn Frank, editor of the *Century*, speaking out of turn to catch the midnight train for New York, nominated her for President of the United States. At 1:00 A.M. Amy arose, saying that in the speeches of the evening she hadn't recognized herself, but she hoped her cat 'Winky' would when she got home, read 'Lilacs' and 'A Tulip Garden' in her best style, acquired, she said, from a family of orators, received congratulations and a silver bowl, and went home — perhaps to work.

On the eleventh, the day she was to leave for New York to lecture before sailing, a fierce pain struck through her. Absolute quiet was ordered, and her sailing was cancelled. On May 2, she wrote her publisher, her last letter, enclosing a list of corrections for *Keats*. 'I have two nurses now and I am no good at all for anything. The sooner we get through these corrections the better.'

An operation was decided upon for the thirteenth. On the morning of the twelfth she said to Mrs. Russell, 'Peter, I am done! Why can't they leave me alone.' Later in the day she suddenly found her hand numb. Looking in a mirror she saw the right side of her face drop.

'Pete,' she said, 'a stroke.'

She became unconscious immediately and died an hour and a half later. To those who had worked with her it was as if a force of nature had been turned off.

As one broods over her life and work, one is less conscious of the 'electrical storm' and 'tropical thunder' than of the warm stout heart of a quintessential Lowell.

3
CHAPTER

Education — Lawrence [1]

Abbott Lawrence Lowell, twenty-one months younger
than Percival, eighteen years older than Amy, was born in
Boston, December 13, 1856. In him as in them, the fateful
chemistry of the chromosomes from ancestral inbreedings,
identic inheritance of acquired characteristics, and similar en-
vironment in early life, produced typical family character and
ability at its highest level. Some subtle influence beyond the
calculation of genetic science was the cause of certain nuances
of temperament in him. But no Lowell was ever more family
conscious.

Lawrence in 1864 was too young to be placed with Percival
chez Sillig. Instead he travelled with his parents along the

---

[1] Pending the publication of the official life of Lawrence Lowell, now in preparation by his friend and literary executor, Henry A. Yeomans, it would be neither
desirable nor discreet to present much biographic detail here. The present chapter
offers a few highlights relating him to the history of his family. It is drawn from current sources and personal acquaintance.

Mediterranean littoral and in France, and was brought back to Heath Street, Brookline, and Beacon Street, Boston, in 1866, to be prepared by Mr. Noble for Harvard, which he entered in 1873. In college he showed the habitual Lowell proficiency in both history and mathematics. In the former field Assistant Professor Henry Adams gave him a final grade of 93, surpassed only by his classmates, Lindsay Swift with a 95, and George Woodberry with 97. In Mathematics, of course, he took the highest honors. He had the family legs as well as the brains. In his sophomore year he won both the half-mile and the mile runs on the same day in two minutes, nine seconds, and five minutes, two and a half seconds respectively — creditable but not brilliant. In the spring of his senior year in the three-mile race, where sound cardiac arrangements and a stalwart character are even more important than speedy legs, he breasted the tape in sixteen minutes, fifty-six seconds, very good going for that heart-breaking distance. Endurance for the course was to be a lifelong characteristic.

After graduation from college in 1877, the same year that his grandfather, John Amory Lowell, retired from the corporation, and two years in the Law School, he began to practise the law, as we have seen, in association with his Cousin Francis. They filled in their time, which was not consumed by any spate of clients, in collaborating on a law book, *The Transfer of Stock in Corporations*, a subject in which both had a personal as well as a professional interest.

Lawrence married his cousin-partner's sister, Anna Parker Lowell, in 1879, and buying a suitable house at 171 Marlborough Street, settled down, in a childless but singularly happy marriage, to a busy and agreeable life of mingled law and letters. He became a contributor of solid articles on serious subjects to Thomas Bailey Aldrich's *Atlantic Monthly*, and in 1889 published his first work in the field that he was to make his own, *Essays on Government*, to be followed seven years later by *Governments and Parties of Continental Europe*.

The *Essays on Government* dealt with such topics as 'Cabinet Responsibility,' 'Democracy and the Constitution,' 'The Responsibilities of American Lawyers,' 'The Theory of the Social Compact,' and 'The Limits of Sovereignty.' They are learned, logical, and lucidly expressed, notable work for a young man of thirty-three, but they seem in a queer way just a little labored. The family animal spirits lacked in him, the effervescence which gave spontaneity, vivacity, and punch to the writing of Percival and Amy. The same ability and the same sense of something missing are found in his broader and more important work on the *Governments and Parties of Continental Europe*. Lawrence for a time was polo player too, but never with quite the hard-riding brilliance of Percival, who nearly finished both himself and George von L. Meyer in a collision of ponies at Myopia. He took his exercise by-passing the elevator and running twice a day up six flights of stairs to his office at 53 State Street.

Meanwhile, he was playing a vigorous part in the work of the Boston School Committee to which he had been elected after a sharply contested election and he was maintaining a close interest in the 'Seminary.' Francis Cabot Lowell became an Overseer in 1886, and a member of the Corporation in 1895. There were many discussions of Harvard affairs and policies between the two. What more natural than that in 1897, Lawrence, whose book on *Governments and Parties* had been published and well received the year before, should become a part-time lecturer on Government in the new department that had just been subdivided from History. From the beginning the lectures went well. His teaching was marked by clarity and precision of statement. They were, one of his old students says, an inspiring interpretation of the significance of experiments in governmental methods. His course, Government 10, a study of modern government, soon became one of the most popular in the college and reached an average registration of four hundred students. In 1900, at the instance of President Eliot, not unmindful perhaps of what a Lowell had done for him thirty years before, he was appointed Professor of the Science of Government and closed his law office, after twenty years of it, forever.

For eight years he gave Government 1, on the history and science of government, in alternate years continued his lectures in Government 10, and went on with the slow preparation of his own most important book, *The Government of England*, which finally appeared in 1908. At its publication it was hailed as on the level of its opposite number, Lord Bryce's *American Commonwealth*. With its more limited scope and less lively style, it is hardly that. Yet, considering that England has no written constitution, that there is a paucity of printed material, that he had to deal with a series of precedents, traditions, and habits from Magna Carta down, each liable to change and diverse interpretation, it was a magnificent piece of intellectual analysis and well-rounded presentation. Its material came mostly *viva voce* from such men as James Bryce, Joseph Chamberlain, Lord Fitzmaurice, Frederic Harrison, Sir Frederick Pollock, Sidney Webb, and Graham Wallas. It is the unbookish nature of the source that gives the book its feel of prime reality.

His interest in all phases of education was deepening. In 1900, Augustus, his father, died, and Lawrence succeeded him as the third sole trustee of the Lowell Institute. One of his first steps was to add to it, to be administered through Massachusetts Institute of Technology, a school for the training of industrial engineers. Later, in connection with Harvard, he provided courses for teachers of science, for the first time employing the current price of wheat, as stipulated in John Jr.'s will, to determine the fee, $2.50 per semester.

At Harvard in the spring of 1902, he was appointed a member of a 'Committee on Improving Instruction.' After a year spent in analyzing nearly two thousand academic case histories secured from students, it issued a yeasty report. Two sentences in the section, known to have been written by Professor Lowell, state convictions that were to shape his future policy. 'There is in the College today too much teaching and too little studying,' and 'Every serious man with health and ability should be encouraged to take honors in some subject.' [1] Five years later, he was chairman of a committee 'to consider how tests for rank in college may be made a more generally recognized measure of intellectual power.'

For once it was not that a Lowell seized an occasion, but rather that an occasion seized him. In November, 1908, just as this committee was completing its deliberation, Charles Eliot in his seventy-fifth year, after forty strongly contested constructive years in the president's chair, tendered his resignation to take effect in May, and offer for seventeen more the inspiring spectacle of a majestically serene old age. The selection of his successor was practically automatic. The retiring President, the Corporation, and the Overseers for once saw eye to eye. On January 13, 1909, Lawrence Lowell, another Brahmin and Unitarian, but an educational theorist of a different school, more a Greek than a Roman, was elected by the Corporation, meeting on State Street, and confirmed forthwith by the Overseers.

At his inauguration in October, standing on a temporary stage erected on the west front of University Hall, with no aid of amplifier, he began by very audibly informing a gathering of several thousands that Aristotle had said man was by nature a

---

[1] Among his papers was found the following record of an ancestral suggestion to the same end:

Extract from a letter of John Lowell, 1821

'He begins by urging that exhibitions should be given for excellence in special subjects, and that they should be of a more scholarly character.

' "I would then declare when he was called up to receive his degree in what and in how many branches he did excel. Those thus distinguished shall hereafter be so marked in the Catalogue.

' "Thus Edward Everett optimus Ling. Graec., Lat., Heb., et Math et Med. etc., etc.

' "In this detail I do not mean to express any precise ideas as to the project, but only to exemplify it. Defects no doubt will be seen in it; the principle however I think is supportable and I expect wonderful effects from it.

' "I infer this from the extreme interest excited by the College honors as they now are distributed and from the effects of that very imperfect and I may almost say ridiculous institution the Phi Beta Kappa which if it has any merit it is only that of an excitment to application." '

social animal, and that the business of an American college is to develop his powers as a social being. Education is not knowledge. It is an attitude of mind, 'an ability to use information rather than a memory stocked with facts.' He sketched his plan of 'concentration and distribution,' an integrated curriculum like that of the Oxford Honors School, six out of sixteen elective courses in some one chosen field, the balance to be general courses in wholly unrelated fields. He broached his ideas for a tutorial system and Freshman Halls, and expressed his hope that at Harvard as at Oxford and Cambridge there might be a marriage of learning to the fine art of living.

Bishop Lawrence has recorded in his autobiography that, as he and the new president were taking off their gowns in cousinly intimacy, he said:

'Lawrence, your address is a pretty radical break with the past.'

'No,' was the reply. 'The same old ship on the same old course, only on another tack.'

In his eulogy on President Eliot, delivered before the Massachusetts Historical Society in 1927, Lawrence Lowell pointed out that a university was a strange kind of industry in that its output is knowledge and men. The success of its management can be judged only after a generation. Seen now in that perspective it is evident that he himself, both materially and intellectually, was an able builder. With the aid of the Harkness donation the new Houses gave the tutorial system a habitation and a name, an enlarged physical plant of appropriate dignity, and the beauty of perfect utility. During his incumbency more new construction was completed than in all the three preceding centuries and the total population of Harvard's city of learning, including both students and faculty of the college and graduate schools but excluding the new School of Business Administration, rose, the First World War and the Great Depression notwithstanding, from 3909 to 7884, or one hundred per cent. But 'his greatest achievement,' says the University's historian, 'was that he sold education to Harvard College.'

To the outside observer it would seem that hardly less great was his unfaltering support, throughout the Old War and the uneasy peace, of the freedom of professorial speech, of what before the days of the Nazis was known to an admiring world as *Lernfreiheit*.   The most celebrated and significant case was that of Harold Laski and the Boston police strike.   Laski, an outstandingly brilliant graduate and Exhibitioner of New College Oxford, had landed in Boston via McGill University in 1916 at the age of twenty-three.   A youth of advanced ideas and copious speech, he seemed in conversation to fulfil the Lowell ideal of concentration and distribution, to know everything about something and something about everything, even, on occasion, everything about everything.   He came well recommended, and though, it appears, he was never notably *persona grata* to Mr. Lowell, he received three annual appointments as Instructor and Tutor in Political Science, and in 1918, was promoted to Lecturer and Tutor in the same department.   In the autumn of 1919, the Boston police voted to join the American Federation of Labor and struck for higher pay, shorter hours, and better conditions of work.   To the general public this action of public servants seemed pure Bolshevism, the bugaboo that was currently terrifying the Western World.   Lawrence Lowell, lawyer and descendant of lawyers and federal judges, shared this view, and at his suggestion several hundred Harvard boys joined the temporary police force to preserve order and enforce the law.

At this juncture Mr. Laski, perceiving that his favorite principle of 'pluralistic liberty' was being invaded, addressed a public meeting of the wives and girls of the striking officers, praising the conduct of their men as a step in the forward march of Liberty. The speech was widely reported and heavily headlined in the metropolitan press.   Laski was denounced in State Street and Wall Street as a traitor and a Bolshevik.   His dismissal was demanded in a flood of letters, including some from Harvard's most generous benefactors.   It was a searching test of the principle that President Lowell had enunciated in his Annual Report two years before:

'In spite, however, of the risk of injury to the institution, the objections to restraint upon what professors may say as citizens seem to me far greater than the harm done by leaving them free. In the first place, to impose upon the teacher in a university restrictions to which the members of other professions, lawyers, physicians, engineers, and so forth, are not subjected, would produce a sense of irritation and humiliation. In accepting a chair under such conditions a man would surrender a part of his liberty; what he might say would be submitted to the censorship of a board of trustees, and he would cease to be a free citizen. The lawyer, physician, or engineer may express his views as he likes on the subject of the protective tariff; shall the professor of astronomy not be free to do the same? Such a policy would seriously tend to discourage some of the best men from taking up the scholar's life. It is not a question of academic freedom, but of personal liberty from constraint, yet it touches the dignity of the academic career.'

Despite the clamor and his own personal views, the president stood firmly for his principle. He told the governing boards that if they exercised their undoubted legal right to dismiss Mr. Laski, who held no permanent appointment, his own resignation would be immediately and irrevocably in their hands. Neither action took place. Some months later, Mr. Laski received a call to a full professorship in the University of London, and returned to England, where he was to play a leading part in the greatest peaceful revolution in English history.

President Lowell's extra-curricular activities were no less notable. As early as 1915, he was active in the organization of the League to Enforce Peace, and chairman of its executive committee. When the foundations were laid in England for the League of Nations, he led in the fusion of the two movements. When in March, 1919, the ratification of the covenant was before the Senate, it was his suggestion, the result of a conversation with ex-President Taft in a Pullman, that led to his memorable debate with Henry Cabot Lodge in Symphony Hall. There were 72,000 applications for tickets, 3200 got in.

The Senator's remarks throughout were an appeal to the emotions. 'Let us not go through a dark tunnel of umbrageous words with nothing to see at the end but the dim red light of Internationalism.'

President Lowell addressed himself only to the reason of his auditors. He read the first draft of the covenant paragraph by paragraph, explaining and interpreting it. He admitted its infelicities and shortcomings, but with impressive earnestness insisted that its ratification was the world's only hope of permanent unity and peace. Who can doubt today which had the better of the argument?

Of another extra-mural episode there is less unanimity of endorsement. In the spring of 1927, Niccola Sacco and Bartolomeo Vanzetti, after six years of imprisonment and the law's delay, had been convicted of the murder and robbery of a payroll messenger in South Braintree, largely, as half the world believed, through mass hysteria and the closed mind in Massachusetts, and prejudice on the part of a judge, who, while the case was still *sub judice*, boasted on the first tee of a golf course of what he had done to those 'anarchist bastards.'

Sentence of death had been pronounced in April, and Vanzetti, the Emerson-reading fish peddler, had made his statement:

'If it had not been for these thing, I might have live out my life talking at street corners to scorning men. I might have die, unmarked, unknown, a failure. Now we are not a failure. This is our career and our triumph. Never in our full life could we hope to do such work for tolerance, for joostice, for man's onderstanding of man as now we do by accident. Our words — our lives — our pains — nothing! The taking of our lives — lives of a good shoe-maker and a poor fish-peddler — all! That last moment belongs to us — that agony is our triumph.'

The case had now finally come up to Governor Alvan Fuller,

with the same half of the world urging executive clemency, at least to the extent of commutation of the sentence to life imprisonment.

The Governor was an honorable man trying desperately to see his duty and do it. That was the opinion of Vanzetti, who ought to have known. From the Charlestown Prison he wrote to Mrs. Glendower Evans:

'As you know, I spoke with the Governor for about 90 minutes at both his interviews with me. . . . We are his opposite all at all and all in all, while our enemies are officers to him in all most everything. Consciously, subconsciously and unconsciously he cannot escape to be tremendously influenced and predisposed against us. But he gave me the impression to be sincere; had made great efforts to know the truth as was not settled, at least deliberately, against us, before to begin his inquiry.

'Of course I may be wrong, but this seems to be the truth to me.'

In April many leaders of opinion in the Commonwealth, fully aware of the danger lurking in the prevalent mass hysteria, were greatly disturbed. Bishop William Lawrence, that wise and open-minded statesman of the Church, initiated and organized a committee to consider what should be done. On the eleventh they sent the following letter to the Governor:

'Two men, having been tried by the Courts of Massachusetts for murder, have now been sentenced to death. Confidence in the Courts of Massachusetts, which has justified itself for generations, leads its citizens to assume that the sentence given is just and should be carried out.

'There are, however, we believe, thousands of citizens of the Commonwealth who, having read or studied such parts of the proceedings in the Superior Court as have appeared in the public press, have serious doubts as to whether these two men have had a fair trial.

'They were, as the law requires, tried by a judge and jury and found guilty. Motions for a new trial on grounds of newly discovered evidence were heard by the same judge and denied. Exceptions on points of law were taken to the Supreme Court and unanimously overruled. But the Supreme Court could not under our law reconsider and revise the findings of fact of the trial court or the exercise of the trial judge's discretion. Hence have arisen the doubts of the citizens for whom we venture to speak.

'Knowing well your sense of justice, your integrity of purpose, and your courage when assured of the rightness of your position, we ask with great earnestness that you call to your aid several citizens of well-known character, experience, ability, and sense of justice to make a study of the trial and advise you. We believe that it is due to the exceptional conditions of the case, to yourself, and to the State that these doubts be allayed and that it be made evident to all citizens that the Commonwealth has done full justice to herself as well as to these men, and also that you may have strong and intelligent support in whatever decision you may make.'

The Governor was very glad to accept the suggestion. He referred the case for review to a commission of three leading citizens of the Commonwealth, now on the defensive in the Court of World Opinion, and named Judge Robert Grant of the Probate Court of Suffolk County, President Lowell of Harvard, and President Stratton of the Massachusetts Institute of Technology.

The friends of the two condemned men, who now included most of the writers, teachers, and journalists of the country, were hopeful, but Vanzetti had his doubts. He wrote on July 21: 'From the commission interview I got the impression that President Lowell and President Stratton are honestly-intentioned men, and not hostile to us by predetermination, yet it seemed to me that despite their great scholarship they had not understood certain most vicious actions of the prosecution and the iniquity of Thayer's conduct.'

His forebodings were correct. The commission reported that

the two men had enjoyed a fair trial, made no recommendation for clemency, and they were executed on the night of August 22.

Of the three commissioners only Judge Grant ever made any written comment on their proceedings. In the chapter devoted to the subject in his autobiography, *Fourscore*, he complains that while he having been named first in the appointment had expected to act as chairman, Lowell had casually taken the chair at the first meeting and continued to occupy it. He also notes that on the occasions when the commissioners called on the Governor to discuss the case he himself and Doctor Stratton took the elevator up from the basement, whereas Lawrence Lowell at seventy-one 'would nimbly ascend like an antelope' the forty-one granite steps, with ten-inch risers, leading to the main entrance and the Executive Chamber. Whether self appointed chairman or not President Lowell was the ablest member of the commission and largely influential in its unanimous report. All his life he had shown an open and flexible mind. It was perhaps closed at one point only, against any action or consideration tending to show a flaw in the administration of justice in the Commonwealth of Massachusetts.

Disappointing as the report was to millions, it never raised the slightest question of Mr. Lowell's devotion to duty as he saw it, though, like Cotton Mather's error of judgment in the matter of Salem witchcraft, it may impair his fame. His decision has seemed more tragic with the years that have brought new evidence and a fuller reconsideration of the old. For himself he was totally free of any *arrière pensée*. In a letter dated February 17, 1932, Lawrence Henderson, who was the president's principal adviser in the founding of the Society of Fellows, reports a significant conversation:

'About ten days ago I went to see President Lowell in order to discuss the work of the Society of Fellows. After our business was completed, Mr. Lowell began to talk about the choice of his successor and the importance of scholarship as a qualification. Presently I said to him that I thought his opinion, that it is easy to find a suitable person among the Faculty, in one respect very unintelligent because he fails to recognize the importance and the rareness of one or two of his own qualities. In particular I mentioned the fact that he has always been able to make decisions promptly even when he had less information than he would have desired, not to worry about the decisions before or after making them and even when they turned out to be wrong, and not to lie awake nights thinking about such questions.

'He then paused, and, as nearly as I can remember, said, "I have lain awake just two nights. One was about the Technology affair — and I have forgotten what the other was about." '

One wonders if he ever knew or, if he knew, would have been greatly disturbed, that in the reading room of the Athenaeum, inner shrine of the Brahmin temple, in the words of the inscription by its doorway, 'A retreat for those who would enjoy the humanity of books,' on the morning of August 23, 1927, a slip was found in every magazine reading in part as follows:

'On this day Nicola Sacco and Bartolomeo Vanzetti, dreamers of the brotherhood of man, who hoped it might be found in America, were done to a cruel death by the children of those who fled long ago to this land for Freedom.'

It was in the next year, 1928, that a happy surprise gave Lawrence Lowell the greatest interest of the last lustrum of his presidency. One autumn day Mr. Edward S. Harkness, Yale '97, was ushered into his office unheralded but not unannounced, for he had been kept waiting, and before he was seated offered three million dollars to build and endow an 'honor college' with a master and resident tutors. The gift was accepted, it is recorded, in less than ten seconds. What is not recorded are the emotions experienced in New Haven, where the authorities of Yale had received the same proposal, but had hemmed and hawed. Mr. Lowell and Mr. Harkness found themselves seeing so perfectly eye to eye that in less than a month the benefaction was increased to ten million to provide a total of seven Houses, three to be built from the ground up, and four from existing Halls with alterations.

Lawrence Lowell's dream of restoring to Harvard the ancient collegiate art of fine living was at last to become solid in steel and brick and stone. Always interested in the details of the building process, a competent amateur architect himself, he watched the erection of the Houses, making almost daily inspections from cellar to roof. He ascended unfinished staircases and ladders to the confusion of Phantom, his fat and faithful golden cocker, who, as Henry Shattuck, frequently of the party, noted with a treasurer's eye, would stop behind to finish the remains of some workman's lunch. No detail of plumbing or closet space was too minute for his critical attention, and in matters causing delay in construction he was masterful. Despite the depression that descended on the country soon after work was begun, the first House was finished in 1930, and all were ready by the autumn of '32.

He chose that season to announce his retirement the following year at the age of seventy-seven. In the interval he quietly applied some millions of dollars from his own investments and the estate of his wife who had died two years before to the founding and endowment of the final feature of his academic dream, the Society of Fellows. The Society was to consist of twenty-four Junior Fellows, brilliant young men under twenty-five, who in two stretches of three years each were to do research or write, but not take courses or study for a degree, and seven Senior Fellows, not to be confused with the members of the Corporation, selected from the faculty and governing boards. All were to dine, and dine well, together and exchange ideas not less than once a week. As *primus inter pares* of the Senior Fellows, Mr. Lowell wrote and for the rest of his life gravely spoke to each new Fellow these words:

'You have been selected as a member of this Society for your personal prospect of serious achievement in your chosen field, and your promise of notable contribution to knowledge and thought. That promise you must redeem with your whole intellectual and moral force.

'You will practice the virtues, and avoid the snares, of the scholar. You will be courteous to your elders who have explored to the point from which you may advance; and helpful to your juniors who will progress farther by reason of your labors. Your aim will be knowledge and wisdom, not the reflected glamour of fame. You will not accept credit that is due to another, or harbor jealousy of an explorer who is more fortunate.

'You will seek not a near but a distant objective, and you will not be satisfied with what you may have done. All that you may achieve or discover you will regard as a fragment of a larger pattern of the truth which from his separate approach every true scholar is striving to descry.

'To these things, in joining the Society of Fellows, you dedicate yourself.'

On the evening of the day in September, 1933, when Lawrence Lowell handed the sceptre of Harvard to James B. Conant, and moved out of the house on Quincy Street, Cambridge, that a Lowell had built for a Lowell, and back to Marlborough Street, Boston, the present writer had the instructive experience of dining with him tête-à-tête in a club denuded of convives by a national holiday. The ex-president was in the mood of a boy out of school. He talked of the past, anecdotally of eminent men he had hooded with doctoral plumage and citation, or consulted about the government of England, at some length of his great-grandfather the Rebel, whom he thought the most brilliant bearer of the Lowell name. But he talked more of the future. Had he not already a few years before bought himself a motor, had an accident, been arrested for speeding, and lost his license, he undoubtedly would have done that now. As it was, he told of writing and, *occasionem cognosce*, publishing plans, and of the war he saw darkening both the eastern and western horizons of our continent.

Some time before his retirement, he had been sounded by

Henry L. Stimson, President Hoover's Secretary of State, to see if he would accept the ambassadorship to England. It did not appeal to him. He wanted to finish at Harvard, and then to write.

His first order of business was to give some months to the study of astronomy in preparation for the biography of Percival that was published in 1935. It would have been a better book if he had spent a few weeks with Plutarch and Boswell. In 1936, in collaboration with George Grafton Wilson, retiring Professor of International Law at Harvard, he wrote a fantasie entitled *A History of Recent Wars*, supposed to be published by Badger, Weasel and Company of New York in 1950. It tells of the outbreak of war between England, Germany, and Italy, and the United States and Japan ten years previously, i.e., in 1940 — not a bad piece of soothsaying. Its aim was to show the wilful blindness of the British Foreign Office and our own State Department to the gravitation of events. It was never published, but he spoke publicly and wrote earnestly to the press in favor of a boycott on scrap iron and oil to Japan. He offered his Boston publishers a series of *Letters from Advent Island*, the short satirical pieces he had read from year to year at the dinners of the Signet. The letters were from the dictator of an imaginary island where our social institutions are carried to their logical limit. Charities are organized at the point of a gun, college courses are based on athletics, though there is a huge stadium for scholastic contests — an early and super Information Please. The government, he says, is neither Hippocratic, Hypocratic, Hypocritic, but Hypercritic — government by fault-finding. It was clever and amusing, but the publisher's reader, who chanced to be a member of the Signet, found that when read, instead of being presented by the author 'in serious fashion, but with the well-known twinkle in his eye,' it lost something essential for publication.

The best and ripest work of his retirement is to be found in his *What a University President has Learned*, published in 1939.

Take this bit of Baconian practical wisdom with more than a touch of intellectual autobiography:

'Much of the success of the administrator in carrying out a program depends upon how far it is his sole object overshadowing everything else, or how far he is thinking of himself; for this last is an obstruction that has caused many a good man to stumble and a good cause to fall. The two aims are inconsistent, often enough for us to state as a general rule that one cannot both do things and get the credit for them.'

In one eloquent passage we find his final thought about education, his feeling for the endless generations of young men that march through college halls:

'The great need of the present day is wisdom, the calm unimpassioned search for enduring truth, not so much concerned with immediate action as with the slow adjustment of human relations. During the World War one thought of the moon shining upon the pale faces of the dead on the battlefield — faces of young men who would have been the thinkers and statesmen of the future, killed by conditions which neither they, nor perhaps anyone else, could have controlled. They are gone, and how much may have been lost to the world with them we shall never know, for they were among the choicest of their kind.

'Where shall wisdom be found and where is the place of understanding? Surely it should be where the pressure of interests is lowest, where passions should be least inflamed, where men are most free to think and write their own thoughts, where the anxieties of the present do not exclude the contemplation of the past and drawing therefrom a horoscope of the possibilities of the future. These conditions ought to be most nearly fulfilled in our universities, colleges, and other seats of higher learning, so far as they are free from political and financial pressure; and in the experience of the writer they are in this country far more free than is sometimes supposed. The cases of interference with the expression of opinion have been rare, and have been met with the kind of protest that shows how rare they are. Such an institution lives not for its day alone, but to train future pilots, and for the light it may give to those who must navigate shoals where others have been wrecked.'

He lived through the first three years of the Second World War. The sound of human voices faded from his ear, and his erect figure became bent and strangely foreshortened. Yet one saw him striding across the Common at better than four miles an hour, overcoatless in the coldest weather unless snow was in the air. You held your breath as the swift bent figure plunged across the stream of traffic on Charles Street, royally regardless of stop signs; only to be reassured by the broad, satisfied grin with which he greeted you on the other side. To one not unacquainted with New England history and the part his family had played in it, he came to seem something of a *revenant*. As a last leaf he was an utter misfit, and would have been even if there had not still been green and fruit-bearing branches on the family tree.

On the sixth of January, 1943, three-hundred and seventy-two years after the birth of Old Percival when our story began, at the age of eighty-seven he joined ten generations of his clan in the silence of the *Ewigkeit*.

EPILOGUE

Trial Balance

EPILOGUE

Trial Balance

O<small>F THE FAMILIES</small> that came overseas in the first half of the seventeenth century to found a new England, and are still here, perhaps a half-dozen can be called *leading* in the full sense of the word. Two have stood a little out in front, the single presidential, quasi-royal line of the Adamses, and the triple line of the multifarious Lowells. A Plutarchian comparison of the Quincy family and the Boston clan is not free of pitfalls, but an application of the method of trial and error may give a better appreciation of both.

In 1636, a middle-aged Henry Adams, a farmer who lived with eight sons and one daughter in Somerset at Barton St. Davids, twenty miles from Old Percival Lowell's Bristol, preceded him by three years to the Bay Colony and settled at Mount Wollaston, now Braintree. He was less of a figure at Braintree than Percival was to be at Newbury, but on past performance the odds in the family steeplechase were fairly even. For three quarters of a century neither family revealed its true form.

Early in the eighteenth century, during the reign of the first of the Georges, both began to show. When in 1726, young John Lowell, M.A., took over the new Third Church in the thriving seaport of Newbury, a Reverend Joseph Adams had already been for twelve years pastor of the church in the tiny village of Newington, the Bloody Point of Indian Massacre, in New Hampshire eighteen miles away. Joseph, born in 1688, had graduated from Harvard at the age of twenty-two. The college steward and the faculty had agreed in ranking him in the antepenult position of a class of fourteen.[1] His 'powerful voice,' noted by an eminent nephew in his diary, echoed from his pulpit for sixty-eight years. 'His conversation,' says the diarist, 'was vain and loquacious, but somewhat learned and entertaining.' A widower at sixty-nine, he remarried at seventy and took his bride to the commodious parsonage built in 1694, which still stands. In 1783, at the patriarchal age of ninety-five he ceased to be Harvard's oldest living graduate, and was buried under the meeting house.

The 'Bishop of Bloody Point' was a stout character, but a less attractive one than the tolerant pipe-smoking Reverend John Lowell.

The union of Joseph's brother, a John Adams, a solid man and a brewmaster, with Susanna Boylston had as its first fruits *the* John Adams, diarist, publicist, signer of the Declaration of Independence, diplomatist, second President of the United States; for half a century an international figure of distinction in the Revolutionary world. Eight years older than John Lowell, the Old Judge, he graduated from Harvard five years earlier. From the seventeen-sixties onward as co-executors of wills and joint counsel in murder trials down to the first year of the new century, when the retiring President made his midnight appoint-

[1] Shipton, *op. cit.*

ment of John Lowell as Chief Justice of the Circuit Court of Massachusetts, the two were in close, if not always admiring, association. Both were potent men genetically, and indelibly stamped their descendants with their own features and traits. To compare them is to contrast the chief characteristics of the family and the clan for four succeeding generations.

Physically the Adamses, though not abounding in animal spirits, were of a stouter stock than the Lowells. With them longevity was the rule, not the exception. Of the six outstanding Adamses, John, John Quincy, Charles Francis, and his three sons, Charles Francis Jr., Henry, and Brooks, the average span of life was eighty-one years, of twelve leading Lowells it was only fifty-eight. Their *élan vital* frequently ended in a cerebral hemorrhage.

Of John Adams, Sir John Temple said in Paris in 1782, 'He is the most ungracious man I ever saw.' He was gruff as well as ungracious, but from his copious and introspective *Diary* in which the above trade-last was noted, not without a certain complacency, one divines that his prickly manner was protective armor for a morbidly sensitive nature, a mind pathologically apprehensive of trouble ahead. A hundred years later, John Hay, best friend of John Adams's great-grandson, Henry, most sensitive and apprehensive of his race, liked to address him as Porcupinus Angelicus. John Adams was a pessimist who always feared the worst, but a stoic who toiled to achieve the best. He was a lonely uxorious soul, a poor mixer. The merit of his quality was that he never hesitated to make grave decisions and initiate momentous action on his sole responsibility; its defect was his lack of the human touch. His conviction that the slightest compromise was a flaw in his own integrity, too frequently made action end in political and personal disaster.

His contemporary, John Lowell, was a born charmer, of men as well as women, with the gift of personal popularity and success. His career if set down in parallel columns with that of John Adams might have a slight flavor of opportunism, of oc-

casionem cognosce. Where Adams was a pessimist and a stoic, the Old Judge was an optimist and an epicurean. Despite his gout, he believed instinctively that everything was going to turn out all right, and busied himself to expedite that happy consummation. John Adams was a man of generalizations, impatient of the concrete, but with a noble strength of character that could implement general ideas towards ultimate fulfilment. The Old Judge had a sharp eye and a ready hand to seize the concrete materials of his daily occasions and carry them swiftly through to admirable ends. These characteristics persisted in their descendants.

As for accomplishment, that of John Adams indisputably was on a higher level than that of John Lowell. He determined the choice of George Washington as commander in chief of the Continental Armies. Though he seems not to have contributed greatly to either the substance or the form of the Declaration of Independence, his ability in debate accomplished its prompt passage. On his own initiative and single-handed he put through the timely Dutch loan and received the recognition by Holland of the independence of the fighting colonies. He was the dominant member of the peace commission that made the Treaty of Paris, and an effective first minister to an inhospitable England after it was signed. As President he averted a foolish and perhaps disastrous war with France, at the cost of his own political future. The twenty-five years of his retirement at Quincy, the last fifteen largely occupied in friendly philosophic correspondence with his old foe, Thomas Jefferson, were the next most inspiring spectacle *de senectute* our annals have to offer, surpassed only by the precisely opposite old age of his son.

The accomplishment of John Lowell was in a more local field. It is hard to think of any man of the Revolutionary period who did more to promote the progress of New England in so many lines. He helped make state law in its legislature and interpreted the federal law in its courts. He assisted in establishing its financial structure, in making its commerce profitable, and in providing canals and better roads, new means of domestic transportation. As a member of the Harvard Corporation he strengthened the practical base for the advance of education. A man of true good will and a notable mixer, he helped heal old sores, draw partisans together, and improve the morale and *esprit de corps* of his community. Although he never quite reached a position of national eminence and power, he did more than his share of the mental world's work of his time and place.

John Quincy Adams, ablest of his family, and John Lowell, the Rebel, most brilliant of his clan, both devoted admirers of their respective fathers, continued on paternal lines. They were within two years of being exact coevals, and within one of being classmates at Harvard. Lowell, the younger, was the first to finish his course. But Adams, before entering as a junior, had been for a year at the age of fourteen private secretary to Francis Dana, United States Minister to Russia, and for another had occupied the same position with his father in Paris. Their paths were continually crossing, and at each contact heat was generated and sparks flew, usually to scorch the pages of Adams's *Diary*.

The ardent, excitable Lowell lacked the stalwart strength of the Potomac-swimming Adams and his inherited gift of implementing lofty generalizations. When they differed in politics, Adams, in the light of history, is seen to have been right, Lowell wrong. We must weigh the public services of a Rebel, that have been catalogued in a long chapter, against the Treaty of Ghent and the subsequent English mission, the conception and first formulation of the Monroe Doctrine, the four years of a free-for-all fight in the White House to 'improve the conditions of the people,' the defeat for re-election perhaps more honorable than victory, and the final seventeen years in Congress battling for the abolition of slavery.

How shall we strike a balance between the inspiring championship of great ideas for a country, whose full realization was

deferred, and effective participation in the accomplishment of
plans to extend the good life in a city and a commonwealth?
And in the contra-account on the Lowell side we must not forget the vision, courage, and practical ability of Francis Cabot
Lowell which gave New England its leading position in the new
industrial age, which, for better or worse, like it or not, was inevitably upon us.

Again, in the period of the Civil War and its aftermath, the
unique service of one must be offset against the more common
but little less valuable work of many: On the one hand, we have
Charles Francis Adams, who by his Brooks marriage first brought
some measure of financial ease into the life of his family, toughest
and best-balanced of American diplomatists, who represented
the Union in London during the dark days of the Rebellion, and
won battles hardly less decisive than Gettysburg. On the other
hand, we have James Russell Lowell with his able editorials, his
second series of *Biglow Papers*, and his later ministries to Spain
and England, dealing with issues less fundamental indeed than
those C. F. Adams faced, but more than adequate to the occasions presented; John Amory, Augustus and Francis Cabot Lowell
II, carrying on the industry of the North which supplied the
sinews of war; and Colonel Charles Russell Lowell, the Happy
Warrior, who but for that fatal second bullet at Cedar Creek
might have risen to the highest office.

In the half-century following the Civil War, the accomplishment of both families became more varied, but their basic
characteristics were not visibly modified. Plutarch would have
one generation of the longer-lived Adamses to compare with
two of the faster-burning Lowells. We may pair John Quincy
Adams II and Edward Jackson Lowell II, who died with their
promised achievement in politics in the one case, in the writing
of history in the other, uncompleted. That leaves four Adamses
that did notable work over the turn of two very different centuries, Charles Francis II, Henry, Brooks, and Charles Francis
Adams III, ex-secretary of the Navy his great grandfather

founded. These we must balance against eight Lowells, Judge
John, his son, John, Francis Cabot III, Judge James, Percival,
Guy, Amy, and Lawrence.

The Lowell fortunes derived from industry and finance,
abundant source of wise philanthropies and educational endow-
ments, can be noted and set aside for the final grand balance.
The valuation of the law made by the three Federal Judges
is a subject too technical for analysis by a layman. In the sum of
things those hundreds of cautiously made and precisely phrased
judicial decisions were surely a substantial contribution to the
Justice that is at once cornerstone and cupola of a Free
Society.

In science, Henry Adams's half-ironic formulation of a bio-
logical law governing the dynamics of the history of this battered
caravanserai, in which save for one dark blow he lived so agree-
ably for more than eighty years, which owed much to the more
masculine and even more pessimistic mind of Brooks,[1] was
balanced, perhaps outweighed, by Percival Lowell's prodigious
mathematical feat that put the finger on a new planet previously
unknown and unsuspected, where the outer edge of our solar
system drops off into space. In the field of art the delightful and
provocative generalizations that grew out of Henry Adams's
minute and brooding study of the Catholic cathedrals of Mont
Saint Michel and Chartres, find their opposite numbers in the
architectural productions of Guy Lowell in the thinner New
England tradition. As usual the palm for the big idea must go
to the Adams; to the Lowell, the practical award for handsome
concrete and brick structures, perfectly adapted to their purpose,
serving generations of men.

In literature, the thoughtful writing of Lawrence, the brilliant
beautiful prose of Percival, the effective work of Amy in both
prose and free verse, all on balance add up to less than the sum

[1] It was exactly half a century ago that Brooks foresaw and foretold a time when,
in a world weakened by war, by exhaustion, or by both combined, 'disintegration
may set in, the civilized population may perish, and reversion take place to a primi-
tive form of organism.'

of the stimulating intellectual forays of Brooks with their season-
ing of bitter humor, the candid historic and biographic appraisals
of Charles Francis II, the monumental nine volumes of Henry's
*History of the United States in the Administrations of Jefferson and
Madison*, plus *Mont Saint Michel and Chartres*, and, *par excellence*,
his *Education*, in which the Adams habit, unbroken in four generations of keeping an intimate journal, suffered a sea-change
through the family gift for generalization into an ironic, mock-
modest, third-person masterpiece which holds a secure position as
one of the significant works of the modern world.

In education the scales are weighted on the Lowell side. John
Quincy Adams and Henry had brief but brilliant careers as professors at Harvard. In three different generations the Harvard
Board of Overseers has had the benefit of caustic Adams criticism,
for three decades an Adams, still living, Charles Francis III, had
charge of Harvard's vast and swiftly growing investments, but
all this fails to balance the two hundred and ten man-years of
service and leadership and millions of dollars of endowment
given by the Lowells, to say nothing of the vision and practical
management contributed to the Lowell Institute and the Institute of Technology. A Lowell today carries on as an overseer of the 'Seminary,' and sole trustee of the Institute.

Adding up the two long pages of history's ledger, the totals,
like the odds and the honors, are fairly even. The credit entries
on the Adams side are larger, but those on the Lowell page are
longer. And the moving finger of the Recording Angel has surely
noted innumerable acts of human kindness and good will unknown to the minutes kept by Clio. New England is proud of
both. It is not easy to think of another American family that has
done more for its country through a longer period on a higher
level.

Flood tides of immigration from overseas and the rise of new
and vigorous stocks have partially submerged the old Boston
clans. Names unknown to the mossy marbles in the Old Granary
Burying Ground have flooded over those of the Lowells and the

Adamses and their cousins and trustees, as the sky-filling architecture of the Federal Building and the United Shoe Machinery Building has dwarfed, if not diminished, King's Chapel and Park Street Church. Yet the old churches and the older families still stand, symbols and examples we shall be ill advised to ignore, the enduring core of the living and fruitful past.

THE END

THE BOSTON LOWELLS IN DIRECT DESCENT FOR ELEVEN GENERATIONS FROM PERCIVAL LOWLE
WHO SETTLED IN NEW ENGLAND IN 1639

This skeletonized genealogy gives only the members of the family who are discussed in the present volume

Generations
from
Percival Lowle

1

Percival Lowle
b. in England, 1571; d. in Newbury, Massachusetts, 1664
settled in Newbury, Massachusetts, 1639
m. in England, Rebecca ——; d. in Newbury, 1645

2

John Lowell
b. in England, 1595; d. in Newbury, 1647
m. (1) in England, Margaret ——   m. (2), 1639, in Newbury, Elizabeth Goodale, b. in Yarmouth, Eng.; d. 1657

3

John Lowell
b. in England, 1629; d. in Boston, 1694
m. (1), 1653, Hannah Proctor   m. (2), 1658, Elizabeth Sylvester,   m. (3), 1666, Naomi Sylvester

4

Ebenezer Lowell
b. in Boston, 1675; d. in Boston, 1711
m. 1694, Elizabeth Shailer, of Hingham

5

Rev. John Lowell
b. in Boston, 1704; d. in Newburyport, 1767
m. (1), 1725, Sarah Champney, d. 1756   m. (2), 1758, Elizabeth Cutts Whipple, d. 1805

6

John Lowell — 'The Old Judge'
b. in Newburyport, 1743; d. in Roxbury, Massachusetts, 1802

m. (1), 1767, Sarah Higginson, d. 1772   m. (2), 1774, Susan Cabot, d. 1777   m. (3), 1778, Rebecca Russell Tyng, d. 1816
(Higginson-Amory Line)   (Cabot-Jackson Line)   (Russell-Spence Line)

7

John Lowell — 'The Rebel'   Francis Cabot Lowell   Rev. Charles Lowell
b. 1769; d. 1840   b. 1775; d. 1817   b. 1782; d. 1861
m. 1793, Rebecca Amory, d. 1842   m. 1798, Hannah Jackson, d. 1815   m. 1806, Harriet B. Spence, d. 1850

8

John Amory Lowell	John Lowell — 'John Junior'	Francis Cabot Lowell, Jr.	Edward Jackson Lowell	Charles Russell	Mary Traill Spence	Rev. Robert S.	James Russell
b. 1798; d. 1881	b. 1799; d. 1836	b. 1803; d. 1874	b. 1807 d. 1830	b. 1807; d. 1870	b. 1810; d. 1898	b. 1816; d. 1891	b. 1819; d. 1891
m. (1), 1822, Susanna C. Lowell m. (2) 1829, Elizabeth C. Putnam	m. 1825, Georgina M. Amory	m. 1826, Mary L. Gardner		m. 1832, Anna Cabot Jackson	m. 1832, Samuel R. Putnam	m. 1845, Marianna Duane	m. (1) 1844, Maria White m. (2) 1 Frances Du

9

John Lowell — 'Judge John'	Augustus Lowell	George Gardner	Edward Jackson II	Col. Charles Russell 'Beau Sabreur'	Lt. James Jackson	Lt. Wm. L. Putnam	Mabel
b. 1824; d. 1897	b. 1830; d. 1900	b. 1830; d. 1885	b. 1845; d. 1894	b. 1835; d. 1864	b. 1837; d. 1862	b. 1840; d. 1861	b. 1847; d. 1872
m. 1853, Lucy B. Emerson	m. 1854, Katharine B. Lawrence	m. 1854, Mary E. Parker	m. 1868, Mary W. Goodrich				m. Edward Burnett

10

John Lowell	Percival	Abbott Lawrence	Amy	Francis Cabot III	Guy Lowell
b. 1856; d. 1922	b. 1855; d. 1916	b. 1856; d. 1943	b. 1874; d. 1925	b. 1856; d. 1911	b. 1870; d. 1927
m. 1883, Mary Emlen Hale	m. 1908, Constance Keith	m. 1879, Anna Parker Lowell		m. 1882, Cornelia P. Baylies	m. 1898, Henrietta Sargent

11 Ralph Lowell, b. 1890
m. 1917, Charlotte Loring

Index

Index